Historicizing the French Revolution

Historicizing the French Revolution

The Two Hundred Years' War

Antonino De Francesco
Translated by Stuart Wilson

BLOOMSBURY ACADEMIC
LONDON • NEW YORK • OXFORD • NEW DELHI • SYDNEY

BLOOMSBURY ACADEMIC
Bloomsbury Publishing Plc
50 Bedford Square, London, WC1B 3DP, UK
1385 Broadway, New York, NY 10018, USA
29 Earlsfort Terrace, Dublin 2, Ireland

BLOOMSBURY, BLOOMSBURY ACADEMIC and the Diana logo are trademarks of
Bloomsbury Publishing Plc

First published in Great Britain 2022
Paperback edition first published 2024

Copyright © Antonino De Francesco, 2022

Antonino De Francesco has asserted their right under the Copyright, Designs and
Patents Act, 1988, to be identified as Author of this work.

Cover image: Robespierre, Maximilien de, 6.5.1758 - 28.7.1794, French politician,
execution, contemporary copper engraving. (© INTERFOTO / Alamy Stock Photo)

All rights reserved. No part of this publication may be reproduced or transmitted
in any form or by any means, electronic or mechanical, including photocopying,
recording, or any information storage or retrieval system, without prior
permission in writing from the publishers.

Bloomsbury Publishing Plc does not have any control over, or responsibility for, any
third-party websites referred to or in this book. All internet addresses given in this
book were correct at the time of going to press. The author and publisher regret any
inconvenience caused if addresses have changed or sites have ceased to exist,
but can accept no responsibility for any such changes.

Every effort has been made to trace copyright holders and to obtain their permissions for
the use of copyright material. The publisher apologizes for any errors or omissions and
would be grateful if notified of any corrections that should be incorporated in future reprints
or editions of this book.

A catalogue record for this book is available from the British Library.

A catalog record for this book is available from the Library of Congress.

ISBN: HB: 978-1-3501-8691-0
PB: 978-1-3501-8690-3
ePDF: 978-1-3501-8692-7
eBook: 978-1-3501-8693-4

Typeset by Deanta Global Publishing Services, Chennai, India

To find out more about our authors and books visit www.bloomsbury.com and
sign up for our newsletters.

Contents

Acknowledgements		vii
Introduction		1
1	The rules of all revolutionary history, 1789–1815	7
2	Confronting France's revolutionary past, 1815–47	45
3	From national myth to the myth of nations, 1848–75	93
4	A republican history?, 1875–1914	139
5	The revolutionary use of history, 1914–45	181
6	Revolutionary orthodoxy and historians' heresies, 1946–89	219
Conclusion: The ashes of the revolution?		257
Notes		271
Index		306

Acknowledgements

This book was originally published by Perrin in France in 2018. Compared to the original French edition, the current version presents a few additional bibliographic references in the footnotes citing the main reference works. I have, on the other hand, erased the bibliography of the selected writings which were originally in chronological order, choosing instead to quote the works throughout the text. It goes without saying that I have incurred many a debt with friends and colleagues alike. I would like to thank Patrice Gueniffey once again, to whose intellectual generosity I owe the suggestion, back in 2011, to write an essay on the historiography of the French Revolution, and Benoit Yvert, from Perrin, who not only accepted the project but also encouraged me to expand the chronological framework back to 1789. A huge thank you also to Pierre Serna, a friend of long-standing, for the passion he puts into his work on the history of the French Revolution: his enthusiasm is always contagious. Thanks, too, to Stuart Wilson, who had the difficult task of translating my Italian. It is evident that many persons have aided me in revising this book for the English edition. I am especially grateful to Fabio Dimartino, whose perfect knowledge of English proved so useful in the necessarily tedious details of revision. Francesco Dei, Francesco Dendena and Amanda Maffei have patiently helped me in order to complete this edition.

This book is dedicated to my wife Alessandra and my children, Cecilia and Carlo.

Introduction

Towards the end of 2015, an academic controversy briefly found its way into the headlines: the *Institut d'histoire de la Révolution française*, the cornerstone of studies relating to the revolution, established in 1937 at the Sorbonne thanks to the encouragement of eminent historian Georges Lefebvre, risked closure, its members invited to join another research body, the *Institut d'histoire moderne et contemporaine*. It was a decision dictated by the financial crisis: research support had to be rationalized and therefore spending centres cut. The protests of those who had directed the institute, including Michel Vovelle and Jean-Clément Martin, as well as Pierre Serna, at the time still running the glorious establishment, went for little. Needless to say, the *Institut* had made a decisive contribution to revolutionary studies and still constituted a point of reference for those abroad who addressed the topic. Attention was drawn to the fact that the institution decree was signed by Jean Zay, minister and Resistance martyr, whose ashes had just been transferred to the Panthéon. It seemed all in vain to point out that the institute was a concrete and functioning symbol of Republican France, called upon to reaffirm its values of democracy and secularism in the context of a brutal threat to their existence. In short, balance sheet outweighed sensibility; and the protests served only to confirm the institution's right to exist in the framework of an accounting and administrative management assigned to the other entity. So, thanks to a mere question of callous bureaucratic calculation, the annexation was carried out and Pierre Serna was the last director of a body that, not long before, on the occasion of the 1989 bicentenary of the revolution, had been the driving force behind the celebrations.

The episode may simply seem one of many to which we should all have become accustomed, thanks to the constraints placed on research support in the context of an unprecedented economic crisis after the Second World War. The repercussions should not, after all, even be irreparable: those who study the revolution will continue to do so, there is no lack of associations – starting with the *Société des études robespierristes* – that make the theme the very reason for their particular existence on the public scene, and there are still many teachers in French universities who will continue to carry out their investigations into the subject.

However, the extinction of the institute founded by Lefebvre has a worrying significance, given that it certifies the divorce between the revolution and the national political tradition, which had founded France's own specific identity on 1789 and at the same time legitimized its presence on the international scene. After all, if the revolution is absorbed into the general stream of modern and contemporary history, it goes without saying that it no longer constitutes a defining moment in itself and is placed on the same level as other events that, in a like way, have contributed to making France what it is today. But which events?

The revolutionary tradition, in other words, seems to be undergoing an apparently irreversible decline. It is a difficult puzzle to solve without starting from the consideration that it was the French elites themselves who were the first to distance themselves from a political and cultural model which appeared to them obsolete and therefore useless as an identifier in the globalized world of the twenty-first century. Of the many reasons that led to a rediscussion of the traditional cornerstone of French citizenship, two in particular seem worth remembering here: on the one hand, the destiny of the idea of Europe following the collapse of communism, which, in France, too, fostered public discourse on the subject of supranationality. Reproposed at European Union level, this ended up leaving the defence of a love of homeland – something that by then the establishment itself thought had a suspicious ring to it – to the extremist wings, both right and left, of the political spectrum. And, on the other hand, there were the triumphs of globalization, revealing to policy, increasingly subordinate to economy, that the paths of nationalism were now far too narrow for those who wanted to experience the age of new markets.

These two elements soon combined, greatly contributing to the loss of the republican identity on which modern France had built its image in Europe. Patriotism thus became the banner of those who found in it a solution to the unravelling of social protections that the new economic order seems to impose and there is no doubt that in this operation – a predatory one, to a large extent – its constitutive link – the principle, that is, of elective nationality – ended up, thanks to the economic crisis, dwindling in consistency. The return to fashion, in today's France, of a nationalism that does not derive directly from the republican identity, seems to confirm this fear.

However, the challenges of Europeanism and globalization, while appearing side by side, did not intermesh at all – indeed, they entered on a collision course, so much so that the latter soon prevailed over the former. European identity – in France, as elsewhere – has thus gone into crisis, precisely because the triumphs of globalization have confirmed the unrealistic nature of the old continent's role on the international stage, no longer perceived as a bulwark with respect to the threat of emerging countries. However, the economic crisis has only exacerbated a sense of rejection towards the EU, thought to be a much less reassuring possibility than the nation state. There was no shortage of signs of this, and it officially came to light in 2005, when the popular referendum in France rejected the proposal for a European constitution.

It is not by chance that this date also constitutes a sort of watershed in studies of the French Revolution. In the early years of the century, following the collapse of the Soviet Union and the return of freedom throughout Europe, with the ancient belief in communist revolution buried forever, the triumphs of a political interpretation of 1789 suggested the development of a perspective inspired by Western values. No coincidence, then, that a transnational dimension thus took shape, which saw as its keystone both a return to the juxtaposition between 1789 and the American 1776 and a new interest in mutual exchange, in the field of political practices, between France and her sister republics of Holland, Switzerland and Italy. After 2005, something seemed to come to a halt – the effects of the many challenges thrown down to the central significance of the French Revolution having in the meantime made themselves visible. British historiography's (re)discovery of the empire and a renewed history of the Atlantic, both already intent on clashing with every proposal of centrality from the old continent, were joined by global history, which openly contested 1789, treating it as only one event among many that had accompanied the difficult birth of the contemporary world.

The French Revolution has thus lost the centrality that it held on to for so long. The old adage that its developments would give rise to modernity has the sound today of a suspect paean in honour of a European world, the inequities of which not even its own vanishing would absolve. A British historian of the revolution, Charles Walton was, with some subtlety, able to note that the very idea of coupling revolution and modernity involves a brutal process of exclusion between an *us*, being those who were responsible for 1789 or shared its values, and a *them*, collecting together those who rejected or did not experience its effects. Beware therefore – concludes Walton – of an equivalence between modernity and 1789: it would drag with itself the stigma of the inevitably racist and colonialist origins of European supremacy and end up doing harm to the revolutionary process.[1]

In this way, in any case, the significance of the French Revolution, as it was for so long understood, seems to be undergoing a worrying decline. Today, very few would be willing to subscribe to what an unassuming Italian historian of the immediate post-war period, Virgilio Titone, stated in 1960, in the lecture halls of Palermo University:

> Whenever, wishing to consider our present, we turn to the past, we cannot fail to take into account the great revolution as the very origin and ideal source, not only of the events that were to come, or of many aspects of them, but of the same problems whose solutions we are still wearing ourselves out in search of today.[2]

These words sum up what was in the minds of, first the revolutionaries themselves, and then their followers – especially those historians who dedicated their greatest efforts to the event – and what they never missed an opportunity to reiterate: 1789 was the dawn of a new era, nothing after it was the same as it was before and, in order to proceed further down the path of progress, it had always to be taken into account.

All this appears today as a lingering and naive trust in the future, marked by blatant historical determinism, which is not worth laying too much blame on. I do not know – I don't think anyone knows – if the refusal to make 1789 the example through which to interpret the present moment is the end of the line for an antiquated story, or if it merely represents a setback that the future might at some point get round to reversing. All in all, a number of indications do suggest that a specific historiographical journey, one that originated hand in hand with the formation process, and then the power politics, of nation states, has indeed run its course, with no visible means of support to aid its recovery, at least in the short term.

Its fate is heavily burdened by the condemnation of the modernity that 1789 had created, with its claim to build something completely original in the history of humanity. Skewed to the advantage of the white population and the old continent; nourisher of racisms, imperialisms and colonialisms; promoter of unjust hierarchies around the world – modernity seems to enclose the original sin of the West: it constitutes, therefore, a category to be set aside, proclaiming the gospel of repentance or shrouding itself in shameful silence.

And yet, there is an obligation here to reiterate that it would be ungenerous to forget that modernity was much, much more. We are reminded of this – again from Palermo, but now at the beginning of the twenty-first century – by a historian who died before his time, Paolo Viola: while it did indeed symbolize the triumph of Europe and its spread throughout the world, it was a period, accompanied by violence, injustice and abuse of power, that has left not only nationalism, racism and totalitarianism as a legacy but also – in addition to capitalism – cultural and political pluralism, inclusive institutional rules embodied in democratic practices and a civilization of work and reformism.[3] And all this – which I do not think can be forgotten – has been accompanied by the memory of 1789 and by reflection on its developments: contributions that legitimize it on the one hand and contest it on the other.

When writing about the revolution, after all, this was what was at stake: on the one hand, it meant accepting the modernization process that followed to indicate what other steps should be taken; on the other, rejecting it, underlining how any further concessions in the field of the democratization of social life involved the disappearance of an order that the revolution had profoundly damaged but had not yet utterly destroyed. This was the point that would, from the very beginning, animate every reconstruction of the revolutionary story:[4] on one side there was concern for the new world that seemed to be taking shape and the attempt, through denunciation, to check its growth; on the other, the hope that modernity, despite dramatic difficulties and a serious lack of preparation, was truly on the march and that the social and political presuppositions of the revolution would not only find shape, but could even be continued, perfected, completed. It was a clash that would never come to an end, given that the counter-revolutionary element would be very busy in the field of historical writing, imbuing large sectors of French society with its own rejection of revolutionary values. At the same time, in the revolutionary years, the threat of an anti-revolutionary ideological universe did not prevent furious quarrels in the opposing field, where the division would soon be, not between (constitutional) monarchists and republicans, as much as, once the Crown had been crushed in 1792, between those who hoped for a social interpretation of the revolutionary process and those who supported the democratic identity of the new order. After the revolution, those divisions, long sidelined thanks to the will of Bonaparte, would all duly reappear in the individual historical works dealing with 1789.

A liberal reading, however, would not erase either the democratic or republican version, while the latter – as early as the 1830s – was not able to silence the socialist voice; all together, meanwhile, they would never be capable of damming the stream of counter-revolutionary writings. These are divisions that are found scattered throughout the whole history of modern France: from the impossible Restoration to the 1830 reappearance of the tricolour fla; from the revolution of 1848 to the years of the Second Empire; from the birth of the Third Republic after the defeat of Sedan to the difficult years of the Dreyfus affair; from the secular, democratic and social shift in the early twentieth century to the Great War; from the crisis of the parliamentary Republic in the 1930s until the collapse of 1940, and, beyond 1945, many, many more.

Over this long period of time, the revolution was a constant point of reference in terms of dialoguing with the politics of the present moment and offering opportunities for comparison that could be useful in indicating eventualities and dangers. In contrast, counter-revolutionary discourse continued along the path that went back to the revolutionary years, drawing on the roots of religious traditionalism to give visibility to a *France profonde*, forever unwilling to renounce its identity in the name of the political modernity prefigured by the values of 1789. This was a pastism endowed with great political flexibility, the result, like the revolutionary spirit itself, of the meeting of cultural sensibilities and social groups that were also very different one from the other, and its attempt at government in Vichy would be a baleful one.

However, the role of 1789 as an instrument of confrontation, provocation and dissent did not concern only France. It soon spread to other national states, to Great Britain, Russia, Germany, Italy and the United States (a Europe outside of Europe par excellence), where all reference to the revolutionary events became intertwined with their own historical tradition, constituting a sort of compass in the search for their own path to modernity. Then, for a good part of the twentieth century, October 1917 would restore the easy game of comparison between one revolution and another. Praise from the communist camp was lavished on the precedent of the Year II revolutionary government – so much so that the passing of the political baton between 1917 and 1793, even though occurring in the field of the European left, would not invalidate, but rather in some ways even revive, the myth of the French Revolution.

There is a somewhat predictable tone to this argument, especially today, in the wake of François Furet's work, when the ideological nature of revolutionary historiography is no longer a matter of dispute. However, it does not seem to me that the opportunity has, to date, ever been taken, to read the construction of the political culture of the principal states of Europe and America through the historiographical developments of the revolution. There are, of course, countless works on individual authors – and how many classics the history of the revolution can boast! – but I still feel the lack of an attempt to place the individual works that came out of France in close dialogue with one another and then intertwine them with those published in other countries. In this way, it might be possible to verify how, concretely, an idea of revolution (and at the same time of counter-revolution) has contributed to the definition of a European identity capable of attracting other worlds to itself – beginning, appropriately, with the United States. This choice seems an important one to me also in terms of accompanying, from yet another angle, the consideration of how the historical discipline has played a decisive role in the birth of the political category of modernity. At this particular moment in time, with the revolution taking more than one broadside for having long been the ideological support of European dominance, I do not think it wholly useless to try to sum up how writings on the revolution have made a decisive contribution to the birth and affirmation of those national historiographies, which, between the nineteenth and twentieth centuries, went hand in hand together with the rise of the old continent.

By widening the discussion to take in the United States, I felt it was important to remember that, while it is true to note the Eurocentric character of the readings of the revolution that took place up to almost the end of the twentieth century, this was a perspective that did not prevent the best histories of the revolution from accompanying the democratization process around the world. They emphasized impetus and resistance, but also extraordinary accelerations and terrifying deviations. In other words, nobody would deny that the inattention shown towards the colonial world – starting with the problem of slavery and the revolt of the black population of Saint-Domingue, which interacted so greatly with the political mechanics of the Hexagon – has weighed, and weighed heavily, on a broader approach to the significance of 1789. Nonetheless, it seems to me unjustifiable to raise considerations of either sufficiency or worthlessness in relation to a tradition that has itself largely constructed the discipline of historiography, only because it did not offer, in the times in which it came to be, what it was impossible to provide. After all, I have no wish to be regarded as an epigonic late-comer from last century's historiography: this is demonstrated by the fact that the pages that follow are transnational in nature, since the centrality of the revolutionary histories written in France does not detract (at least in my opinion) from the particular historiographic processes of other countries. The fact remains, and it is something I do not intend to hide, that this is a work that, in more than one direction, moves against the current. Its promise is to draw interest back towards a history – that of the tormented path of political modernity – which many today would have us believe is definitively exhausted. It is difficult to say if time will end up proving them right.

1

The rules of all revolutionary history, 1789–1815

Historiographical accounts of the French Revolution were already being written as it was still taking place, in an attempt to rein in an event that had completely overturned the political and social frames of the centuries-old kingdom of France. Where were the origins of such a wide-ranging and violent movement to be found? Where to place it within the frame of a philosophy of progress which had shaped the cultural universe of the eighteenth century? One of the earliest answers came from the very last of the *philosophes*, Condorcet, and it would later influence the whole historiographical debate for centuries to come: in spite of its contradictions, the revolution was the outcome of a path towards progress that had begun centuries earlier.

Such a thesis was refuted at once and opposed by the enemies of the revolution, also thanks to Edmund Burke's forceful remarks, venturing forth along the meanders of history to reveal the imposture of a Revolution built on the abstraction of universal principles. And yet, how were they to explain the power of the revolution? De Maistre thought it divine punishment, Barruel a freemasons' plot that had long been in the making by the enemies of Church and Crown.

Caught in the crossfire of pamphlets, a history of 1789 written there and then came into its own which Bonaparte, now emperor, lay aside for a time by forcing through a memorial truce of which Toulongeon and Lacretelle became the most zealous mouthpieces. However, after the fall of Napoleon, there was once again room for a historiographical debate, to which new fuel was added, in particular, by the posthumous work of Madame de Staël, who first introduced the idea of a two-pronged revolution: in opposition to 1789 and to its ideals of liberty, the origins and legitimacy of which ran through the history of France, starting from 1792 another revolution had arisen, the poisoned fruit of contingency and violence. Condemnation of the latter soon went hand in hand with celebration of the former, turning into the manifesto of an entire generation of liberal youth that refused the policy of oblivion fostered by the Bourbon Restoration.

1. The death of Condorcet

Paris, summer 1793: the French Republic, which had come into being a year earlier following the insurrection of 10 August 1792, was already hanging in the balance. The demonstrations of 31 May and 2 June 1793 in front of the National Convention, elected to give France a new democratic constitution, had forced the assembly to expel twenty-nine deputies, all belonging to the so-called Girondin faction. The triumph of the other party, *la Montagne*, 'the Mountain', which had taken advantage of popular protests to settle accounts with opponents, however, provoked the outrage of those who saw in that decision an attack on popular sovereignty. With the news of the event, many provincial cities tried to offer resistance, including armed dissent, to the political changes in Paris: the war on the frontiers, which broke out in April 1792, and the uprising in the Vendée, which exploded in March 1793, were now joined by a federalist revolt – so called because the Convention saw in the protests an attempt to break up the unity of France itself. To put an end to the resistance, the Convention swiftly finished drawing up the constitution and put it to the vote of the country's leading assemblies. Popular consensus was, apparently at least, complete: even the rebellious cities voted in favour, in the naive belief that, once the constitution had been ratified, the Parisian assembly would remit the mandate, call new legislative elections and give a second chance to those who had been expelled. Instead, as is known, the Convention postponed making use of the constitution until peace was reached and remained exactly as it was, justifying the decision with the dramatic circumstances France was living through at that time.

At the beginning of October, the dream of building a democratic republic based on open parliamentary confrontation was now in pieces: the evolving procedures towards freedom, which had accompanied the revolutionary process since 1789 and which were certified by the establishment of opposing political sides, appeared to be an attack on revolutionary unity and provoked a sharp, downward spiral towards authoritarianism. Repression once again rocked the parliamentary hall: after crushing provincial protest through force of arms, the Convention officially indicted the Girondins deprived of their liberty in June, arrested another seventy-three deputies who had protested against the coup and voted to outlaw nineteen others who had meanwhile fled.

This last group included Caritat, *ci-devant* Marquis of Condorcet: there was a warrant out for his arrest for protesting against the days of May 31 and June 2 in a message to his Aisne voters and for then expressing public criticism of the constitutional text submitted to popular approval. One of the most brilliant intellectuals of the time, at the outbreak of the revolution he was already known as an upholder of freedom: an enemy of slavery and trafficking, in favour of the rights of religious minorities and women, and against the death penalty. In 1789, he had followed the revolution with enthusiasm, even though he only became a public figure in 1791 on the occasion of the king's flight to Varennes, when he was one of the first to declare himself republican.

Elected shortly thereafter to the Legislative Assembly, he proposed there a plan for public education that would inspire the creators of the republican school a century later. In favour of a war of freedom in the spring of 1792, he supported the swing towards republicanism of August 10; re-elected to the National Convention, he refused, in accordance with his principles, to vote for the death sentence of Louis XVI. Author of a constitutional project – by far the most democratic ever proposed throughout the revolutionary decade – Condorcet was for a long time on the side of the Girondins, only to distance himself from the group on the eve of the days of 31 May and 2 June 1793. This did not prevent him from protesting against the violence perpetrated on that occasion: hence the arrest warrant, which forced him to hide in the apartment of the widow Vernet, between the convent of Saint-Sulpice and the Luxembourg gardens, where he remained from July 1793 until March 1794, when, no longer feeling safe in the city, he was about to leave Paris. Instead, he was arrested, to be found dead in prison the next day.[1]

In the long months spent in hiding, despite the dramatic nature of his situation, he held firm to the belief that knowledge of the past made it possible to draw a positive picture of historical events. In the widow Vernet's home, in the midst of the Terror, he found a way to draft his *Esquisse*, a work that suggests that the triumph of the work of civilization, duly verifiable in humanity's millenary history, would have been accomplished thanks to 1789: revolutionary developments would put an end to the still-prevailing systems of political tyranny and economic and commercial monopoly.[2] Condorcet's dramatic death was lost in the turbulence of the Terror, but it would later constitute a point of reference, when Thermidor ended the Robespierre dictatorship and the newfound freedom of the press made it possible to reflect upon the mistakes that had been made and to reiterate – despite the dramatic evidence put forward – the defence of the decision in favour of revolution.[3]

This is the case of the many pages produced by the eclectic writer Pierre-Louis Prudhomme, the founder of the well-known democratic newspaper *Révolutions de Paris*: in the aftermath of the Terror, in order to lay claim to the democratic character of his political commitment, he offered a picture of the many cases where the revolutionary process had gone astray. In his hallucinatory account, published in 1797, conspiracy plots and increasing violence stained the republican path with a thousand crimes and as much suffering, casting a sinister light on the very origins of democracy. As the long title states,[4] the denunciation of crimes was accompanied by that of the inadequacies of the patriots, who, unprepared as they were, had facilitated the criminal intentions of those who only intended to take advantage of the new republican order for their own particular purposes.[5]

Prudhomme's writings – which endeavoured to link the eruption of violence on the political scene to the criminal affairs of a few – were in line with the political culture of post-Robespierrist France, which, since Thermidor, had tried to play down the period of the Terror as a mere parenthesis in the development of the republican process. In the months after the fall of the Incorruptible, the assembly denied nothing with regard to the crimes committed, but everyone ascribed them to the Robespierre faction, while also trying to salve the guilt of having proscribed the Girondins by re-admitting those who survived the repression. There was, in this context, no lack of public demonstration of esteem for those whom the Mountain had immolated: in April 1795, the Convention decided to promote the posthumous printing of Condorcet's *Esquisse*, ordering the purchase of 3,000 copies.

Shortly thereafter, with the Year III constitution coming into service, the period of the Directorial Republic (1795–99) began and the work benefitted greatly from the stabilization of the republican order: six different editions appeared, proving that the *Esquisse* was a sort of reference text to define the profound significance of the revolution. It was very well suited, moreover, to the cultural policy of post-Robespierrist France, which claimed to have brought the revolution to an end, and proposed to delineate its history in terms of a precise line of continuity from 1789 to the Year III constitution. This was indicated by the Convention, which, in October 1795, just a few days away from dissolution, decided that the Republic would fund the reprinting of the works of the Protestant pastor Jacques Pierre Rabaut, a member first of the Constituent Assembly and then of the Convention, guillotined during the Terror. These works included, above all, a concise history of the French Revolution, which appeared in April 1792 as a revised and enlarged edition of an *Almanach historique de la Révolution française* which came out at the end of 1791. The work was a great success at the time, with two editions immediately circulating in English and a third in French in 1793.[6]

The Italian translation, in Nice, also appeared in 1796, which speaks volumes about how Directory France saw the *Précis* as a fixed point around which to retether a reading in the context of the continuity of the events following 1789.[7] Indeed, those pages constitute a eulogy to the historical necessity of the French Revolution: Rabaut, a Protestant pastor from the Midi, who had already made a name for himself before the convocation of the Estates General with some writings in favour of religious freedom, launched therein the myth – destined for great things in the years of the Restoration – of an inevitable and necessary revolution. In the work, Rabaut sets himself the task of linking the events in France to their American precedent, while at the same time being careful to defend all the Constituent Assembly's most important decisions. The work clearly shows a need to describe the revolution as a sort of reaction against abuses, which, nonetheless, spread everywhere as they were throughout the country, forced the assembly to make a clean slate of the *ancien régime*. It was the very unacceptability of a myriad of privileges, transformed into as many abuses, to the advantage of a very small part of society, that became the basis for revolutionary radicalism in France. The country was forced to distinguish itself from the American model, given that there was no aristocracy in the new world, no state religion, no feudalism that had been able to extend its oppressive influence throughout social relationships. This explained why the Constituent Assembly had departed from the American model on constitutional terrain, too, and had raised the level of confrontation: Rabaut denied, for example, that the days of October 1789 – when the people of Paris went to Versailles to force the royal family to follow them back – were the wise strategy of the Duke of Orleans and Mirabeau, as reactionary circles liked to insinuate. He complained of the risk that the American colonies would ally themselves with the British in order to prevent the revolution from putting down roots overseas, and he had harsh words for Prime Minister Pitt, who he thought took advantage of British public opinion in favour of France's revolutionary cause. Above all, in the aftermath of Varennes, he was not slow to use the term 'counter-revolution' when pointing his finger at the enemies of change.

Rabaut, writing between 1791 and 1792, also went further to the left than the Assembly, complaining that after Varennes it had not wanted to run the risk of taking stock of the consequences of Louis XVI's gesture and had somehow ordered 'that the Revolution was over'. In the notes that he added to the second edition – most likely written in the very first months of 1792 – this dissent was reinforced by his refusal to support the war, which he referred to as the 'last blow of kings', by his reiterated confidence in the progressive results of a revolution that was the 'cause of all mankind' and which he described as a clear 'product of Enlightenment'.[8]

All this explains why there was reawakened interest in Rabaut in Year III: he described a heroic and humanitarian period of the evolution before everything was engulfed in a wave of violence and made it possible to draw a precise line of continuity between the revolution of 1789, the Republic of 1792 and the constitutional decision of 1795 to renounce the Terror.

In the Directory years, when it was intended that the developments of 1789 were to be brought to an end, his *Précis* proved useful to the first histories of the revolution, which set themselves the task of dealing with it as an event, now concluded, that could be written about with a certain sense of detachment. Rabaut's pages were a handy starting point to begin to explain what followed the dissolution of the Constituent Assembly, to demonstrate that the Terror was an excrescence on the healthy tissue of the revolution and that the constitutional Republic had rounded off a history that Year II had risked leading astray from the path of justice and freedom.

In this regard, the most popular works were those by Antoine Fantin Desodoards – a man of letters who had frequented Girondin circles, had links to Louis Sébastien Mercier and who would spend a lifetime waiting in vain for a call from the *Institut national* – and by François Pagès, who was, at the time of the constitutional monarchy, already engaged in composing historical sketches of recent events.[9] Both works, published in 1797, made clear reference to Rabaut's writings in their descriptions of the operations of the Constituent Assembly and then jointly proposed the image of the revolution in terms of a process initiated by the widespread need to break society free from the shackles of the *ancien régime*. It was a process, however, that factional struggles had plunged into the violence of the Terror, with first Thermidor, and then the constitutional experiment of Year III, helping to draw it back to its original course.

The similarities between the two works – which caused Fantin to denounce Pagès as a plagiarist – are explained by once more referencing post-Robespierrist political culture, which on the one hand attempted to re-establish links back to 1789, but on the other, in order to legitimize itself in the eyes of a public opinion that had been severely disoriented by the ferocity of the political struggle, repeatedly denounced the spirit of faction as the main culprit responsible for the uncertainties in republican strategy. This aporia between the desire for continuity and the need, on the other hand, to explain away a blatant discontinuity, was the basis for the somewhat ambiguous deployment of Rabaut's work, which came in useful to illustrate the origins of the revolutionary movement but was openly criticized for drawing up a wholly positive balance sheet for the Constituent Assembly.

François Pagès, especially, whose political background lay further to the right than that of Fantin Desodoards, was careful to point out that factional poison had been poured into the political body of France from the time of the first revolutionary assembly. He also insisted on the serious responsibilities of the Constituent Assembly for the dramatic developments of the revolution that followed its dissolution. Fantin Desodoards had been writing along the same lines – hence the accusations of plagiarism

– since the articles he had published in Mercier's *Annales patriottiques*, whose many pages set themselves the task of inspiriting a history of the revolution that renounced discoursing on the usual events to give instead ample space to the author's reflections regarding the unexpected outcomes of the political clash.

His *Histoire philosophique* was very much indebted to Prudhomme's work, mentioned above, insisting as it did on the break represented by the eruption of violence onto the political scene. It was, according to Fantin Desodoards, an unleashing of forces deliberately triggered by mediocre figures who were otherwise unable to occupy the political limelight – who had, in that particular area, played out their only game for achieving power. The triumph of Jacobinism was therefore the consequence of a sudden acceleration in the clash between factions, and this latter had to assume responsibility for the dramatic events that followed the birth of the Republic. From this angle, Fantin Desodoards's work – which also intended to refer to the criteria of analysis and observation prescribed by the *Institut* – took on a clear political form: it sounded like a heartfelt plea to recompose that unity of the republican world which, in the aftermath of August 10, had soon ended up in fragments.

Needless to say, this recomposition of the parties was destined to find a conclusion in the elaboration of cultural models that accompanied the reproposal of traditional social balances. According to Fantin Desodoards, the dissolution of the factions – even of those Girondins who still called for vendetta and who he himself had sympathized with – constituted the first, necessary step in an operation to bring peace to the revolutionary society. The latter would then have to piece together the will to stabilize this new order by means of a new philosophy, which, among other things, would have to be able to re-establish the regulatory role of a consolatory religion.

In this context, history came in useful for the drawing up of precise conclusions regarding the present moment: on the one hand, it suggested that the claim to greatly reduce economic inequalities, perhaps even abolish them altogether, was an operation that would subvert social equilibrium, leading to the spirit of faction returning stronger than ever; social distinctions, on the other hand, destined to establish a new intellectual elite, would serve as a bulwark against the tidal wave of violence that had swept the Republic away. History thus became the confirmation of a political process that slowly, thanks to the acknowledgement of the impossibility of putting a new social order in place, returned to identifying its own point of balance. This search for a place to anchor the revolutionary process explains why the *Histoire philosophique* – despite the criticism it was subjected to – became such a success, rapidly gaining a name for itself even beyond the narrow confines of the Hexagon. With factionalism laid to rest, aspiring to indicate the correct means through which the new order's point of equilibrium might be fixed, Fantin Desodoards perfectly interpreted the expectations of the most conservative part of Directory society. He thus provided the latter with a historical response, confirming the prospect of stabilization around a centre that was both political and social.

There is no doubt that from this point of view he was far more effective than Pagès, who also made use of some of Prudhomme's ideas, especially when he emphasized the various plots that had marked the developments of the revolutionary events. He was not, however, able to transform his work into the complete reflection of a political project. This result – making history into a tool to shore up a political framework – was instead the principal intention of Fantin Desodoards in his writings and this explains why he went back repeatedly to his work. The first edition of 1796 was immediately followed by another in 1797, and then another four in 1801, 1807, 1817 and 1820, accompanying the changing phases of French politics, from the triumphs of the Consular period, to the Empire, and even up to the Restoration.

Unsurprisingly, from time to time the different editions offer different versions and readings of the same historical events. While this led to Fantin Desodoards being denounced – depending on where the criticisms originated – as a dangerous Jacobin, or a crypto-monarchist, one accusation he always had to suffer, perhaps especially in the aftermath of the return of the Bourbons, was that of barefaced political opportunism. In reality, he held steady to the original thrust of his work, simply adapting his pages to a changing political climate, which, each time, seemed to him to bring the revolution to an end – concluding, in other words, that period of violent factional clash which had shipwrecked the far-reaching results of 1789. The various editions are the perfect demonstration of this, from time to time shifting the moment that a positive outcome arrives for the revolution – first to the Consulate, then to the Empire and, finally, to the restoration of (constitutional) monarchy. In all these stages, he glimpsed an increasing assimilation between parties that had previously opposed one another, and all of them, in a similar way, seemed to indicate the closure of a period of internal dissension which had prevented France from ever being been able to find a balanced stability.

In this long trajectory, the founding date of change would soon shift from the Directory period to the Napoleonic years, since, as is well known, General Bonaparte's coup d'état was launched in order to fight against the parties that had torn French unity apart. Finally, it would be possible to silence the spirit of faction that had continued to pollute political life in the Directory era.

Brumaire, in other words, seemed to signal a return to the profound values of the revolution with the ending of the first, dramatic phase of the life of the Republic and to hold out the possibility of returning to a revolutionary path that had so abruptly gone astray. Not surprisingly, all First Consul Bonaparte's initial moves were in the direction of bringing a peaceful solution to the situation in the country. His policy was to stretch out the hand of friendship towards political groups that were very different from each other and previously highly confrontational – a policy of *ralliement*, a 'rallying together', designed to reconcile democratic and conservative republicans, constitutional monarchists and even the Catholic Church. It found a way to suggest a return to the history of recent times, with the aim of promoting a narrative of the revolutionary years where 1789 found its natural conclusion in Bonaparte's new order. Needless to say, the Directory's historiographical fortunes were soon destined to run aground, never able to recover from the pernicious way in which the Year III constitutional regime had met its fate.

However, the descent into hell of the Directory – quickly identified as the cesspool for all the evils of revolutionary politics – did not prevent the historiographic blueprint developed while it was in power from brilliantly surviving it, suitably adapted to the politics of *ralliement*. So, as mentioned above, Fantin Desodoards returned in the Consulate years with another revised and adapted edition of his work, while the publishers Treuttel and Wurtz decided to bring out a follow-up to Rabaut's *Précis*, proposing an addition to it that brought the work up to more recent times by the journalist of clear monarchical sympathies Charles Lacretelle.[10] At the same time, the publishers also printed the work of another Constituent Assembly member, François-Emmanuel Toulongeon, who, after the Terror, had been a supporter of the Directory.[11] Guiguet and Michaud, meanwhile, also started publishing the work of one of Louis XVI's ministers, Antoine-François Bertrand de Molleville, forced, after August 10, to find refuge in England for many years.[12]

While respect for the new Napoleonic order seemed uppermost, these works nevertheless contained profound differences and offered a reading of revolutionary development where, notwithstanding the politics of *ralliement*, deep-rooted political divergences were revealed between parties that had once fought each other bitterly and were now pacified only forcibly. Fantin Desodoards, long accused of having been close to the Girondins, in the 1801 edition, which also retained the initial structure of the work, was the only one to make Brumaire a revolutionary conclusion to the first Republican period, assigning to First Consul Bonaparte the task of finally healing the wounds of a France that had already suffered too greatly from the torments of violence. Taking a similar line, François-Emmanuel Toulongeon concluded his own narrative with Napoleon's return from Egypt; his discussion of French history dating back to 1789, however, was very different.[13] A member of the Constituent Assembly, forced to leave Republican France and returning in the aftermath of Thermidor, he had joined the *Institut* in 1797. His opinions were close to those of the elderly Minister Jacques Necker, who, during the Directory years had, from his exile in Switzerland, published certain considerations regarding the revolution, which will soon be touched upon here. Toulongeon made his feelings clear about the deficiencies of the Year III constitution and his work as a whole was concerned to obscure in Brumaire – deliberately excluded from the discussion – the conclusion of a regeneration process that 1789 had commendably begun and 1793 had brutally plunged into a tumult of partisan violence, with the Directory having done little to offer a solution.

Alongside these works, which certainly responded to the First Consul's call for collective pacification, others, taking advantage of a freedom of the press that Bonaparte believed could work to his advantage, instead reproposed the old line of disapproval of 1789. Charles Lacretelle, called to take over and develop Rabaut's work, moved cautiously in this regard, publishing five volumes between 1801 and 1806 where he dealt with the events from the Legislative Assembly to the Directory.[14] The official purpose remained that which Bonapartist power was hoping for – a history that paid little attention to factions, where historical balance overcame the spirit of the cabal. Yet, beyond the declarations of principle, which also run through Lacretelle's pages and make his writings a pedagogically ambitious summary of what has just occurred, it is clear that the nightmare of the Terror continues to play a decisive role in his reconstruction and lends weight to his criticism of Rabaut's work. While the latter, as already mentioned, ended with the Constituent Assembly and the extraordinary work that it had done, Lacretelle sees the period of the Legislative as mere preparation for the Republican Terror and is keen to point out that the basis of the drift into ferocious violence had been put in place by France's first revolutionary assembly. Moreover, in the volumes that follow, Lacretelle's monarchical sympathies are anything but hidden and at the end of a discussion that editorial commitments oblige him to keep on the edge of balance, it is not difficult to perceive his resounding lack of faith in 1789 itself. Proof is provided by his perplexities with regard to the unfolding of events and, above all, the attention he gives to those episodes that seemed to lead the revolution towards the spiral of violence. He also refers complacently to the shortcomings of the Directory, whose anti-religious policy and repression of monarchist dissent are repeatedly evoked as examples of the illiberal aspects that were its distinguishing characteristic. Lacretelle's work indicated clearly monarchical leanings ready to coexist, for want of anything better, with the Bonapartist proposal of a coming together of all the French. It was, however, destined only to be fully understood in the aftermath of 1815, when the author would return to his work, this time accompanying it with his own notes on the Constituent Assembly. Here, in open opposition to Rabaut, he wrote that it was the Assembly itself that had sown the evil seed of violent, terrorist revolution.

However, if, during the Bonaparte years, Lacretelle was forced into adopting a position of precarious balance, the same cannot be said for the publisher Michaud. Also in 1801, publishing the writings of the elderly minister Bertrand de Molleville, he wholly adopted the executive line, recalling that 'the more a government needs to consolidate, the more it intends to restore calm, the more it must encourage the zeal of writers who uncover in people the misfortunes of revolutions and who reveal the hidden motivations that are used to overthrow societies.' In Michaud's opinion, Bertrand de Molleville excelled here in this pedagogical work, being able to show how the first two revolutionary phases – interpreted first by the action of the Constituent Assembly and then the Legislative – thereafter linked hands in the context of the spirit of faction: the difference between the two political phases lying in the fact that, in the aftermath of 1789, 'the nation found itself at first divided into several parties, each of which manifested their demands but did not yet dare to support them by violence'. When the Legislative Assembly appeared on the scene, 'the horrors of a democratic revolution', launched in the aftermath of the taking of the Bastille, gave way to a 'spirit of anarchy' and the 'populace, become sovereign, exaggerated all demagogic ideas, denatured all social principles'.

This was enough to render the Napoleonic period anxious with regard to the results of the *ralliement* policy, given that, beyond a certain surface consensus, it did not seem be having much success at a more profound level. And in fact, until the defeat at Waterloo, there persisted the two different readings originating from the trauma of the Terror, 'each armed against the other'. On the one hand, there were those who had immediately fallen in with the republican idea, and who thought it fundamental to find a balance between the preceding and successive periods of the revolutionary government: for them, Brumaire appeared a positive solution to the dilemma of a political process that could not seem to find a point of equilibrium. On the other hand, there were those who looked back from the trauma of the Terror to the days of the Constituent Assembly, pinpointing the original sin of the monarchy, from which the horror arose, in the convocation of the Estates General.

In the aftermath of Brumaire, the young Corsican general's assumption of power seemed to make a third way useless, although this was something that, in the years of the Year III constitution, a number of Republicans, both right and left, had believed in. Denunciation of the Directory political system – whether criticized for the political fragility of the Legislative Assembly or for the authoritarian attitudes of the first Convention – therefore ended up silencing those who had in mind a historical precedent that saw the new Republic finding stability in terms of a parliamentary structure. Silence became complete in the years of the Empire, a sort of *tertium genus* between Republic and monarchy, when it was forbidden to regard the revolutionary decade as a period not necessarily destined to end with Napoleonic triumph.

One figure made sorely aware of this was Pierre Paganel, a member of the Legislative Assembly and then of the National Convention, who in 1810 made the mistake of presenting to the emperor his just published work on the revolution.[15] Here, he praised the work of the Constituent Assembly, exalted the turn towards republicanism and refused to demonize Year II. Instead, he preferred to underline the inadequacies of revolutionary politics and to see Brumaire as a traumatic phase of transition that was decisive in terms of putting an end to the anarchy that had long prevented the stabilization of a new order. Paganel probably believed his homeland would do well by him, linking as he did Brumaire to the salient phases of the revolution and contrasting it with the Directory, treated as exemplifying a pusillanimous and unjust regime.

However, the work must have sounded like a testament to unacceptable republicanism, and was promptly sequestered and, in 1813, even destroyed. In 1810, presenting one of the few remaining copies to the former president of the United States, Thomas Jefferson, Paganel admitted being guilty of having 'written with the intention of maintaining pure a tradition that every day took pleasure in disguising itself as an absurd novel': precisely for this reason, he said, he was certain that it could not fail to interest 'the first magistrate of a people that has happily ended its revolution'. Jefferson replied by thanking him for a work that revealed 'the fatal errors that have lost to nations the present hope of liberty' and entrusting the development of freedom on American soil with the task of cancelling 'the impressions left by the abortive experiment of France'.[16] It was the acknowledgement, from the other side of the Atlantic, too, that French politics still prevented the writing of a history of the French Revolution that maintained its distance from the political moment. More deeply, however, it was also the apparently irreversible crisis of the republican model, which in the Year II, as in the Year III, version seemed, albeit for opposite reasons, now erased from France's political memory.

2. Prophets of the past?

The histories of the revolution in the Napoleonic era illustrate how the *ralliement* policy had found its proper balance in the decision to nominate Brumaire as the end of the revolution. It then depended on what was meant by the conclusion of 1789: for those who had believed in the revolution, it meant that Bonaparte had finally brought it to completion – even though one imposed from above. For those who had opposed it, the coup was instead the long-awaited repudiation of ten years of dissolution. The image of Brumaire as the final act of the revolution, still an established commonplace even today, arose, in short, from the combination of different expectations, where the contribution of the monarchists, co-opted in the meantime by Napoleon's *ralliement* policy, was of substantial consequence. It was a world that only the birth of the Republic, in 1792, could have brought together, since previously Crown supporters had had very little in common with each other. It was a fault line that did not pass only between supporters of the constitutional monarchy – such as Lafayette, Mirabeau and the Duke of Orleans – and the supporters of the *ancien régime*: even among the latter, there were a variety of very different positions. Some nourished poignant nostalgia for the old order, others instead had considered some form of change inevitable, others were full of admiration for the English model, few believed that the *ancien régime* could really survive the crisis of the late eighteenth century.

All these positions, aligned after Brumaire in the name of obeisance to the new order, had benefitted from the brilliant counter-revolutionary literature that had accompanied the events following 1789 from the beginning. One of the first to take a stand against the new developments in France was the former Controller-General of Finances Charles Alexandre Calonne, who, after the failure to convene the Assembly of Notables in 1787, had found refuge in London. His letter of February 1789 caused a sensation, when – referring to the French monarchist tradition – he pointed out that the sovereign had made a serious mistake when he had decided to convene the Estates General. A year later, with the face of France already changed, Calonne, now able to say he was justified in predicting the disaster the monarchy was facing, went on to compose a long article, meticulously contesting all the Constituent Assembly's deliberations.[17]

His arguments were only a mixture of pastism and traditionalism, which limited themselves to proposing a thaumaturgical return to the past. Indicating that France was equipped with a constitution, he even suggested harking back to the rulings of Philip the Fair to recompose – always based around the aristocracy alone – a new government order. This ideological universe, anchored to the example of an *ancien régime*, won over the first wave of émigré nobility on the one hand, but, on the other, exposed him to the derision of those who remained in France and witnessed events there: despite having words of disapproval for the move towards revolution, they admitted the crisis of the *ancien régime* which had precipitated the disaster. These included Antoine de Rivarol, a man of letters who went into politics in the summer of 1789, who accused Calonne of having released the revolutionary genie from the bottle. Convening the Assembly of Notables, he had

> revealed to the eyes of the people what should never be shown to them, the lack of wisdom, even more than the lack of money. The nation could not find a single statesman in this assembly; and the government lost our confidence forever. This is what will happen every time that the ministers consult the people.[18]

In this controversy, which indicated the unpreparedness of the *ancien régime*'s ruling class as the real reason for the disaster, a new counter-revolutionary generation joined the fray. Their position was different compared to that of the original wave of monarchists: while they maintained the precondition regarding the sacredness of the monarchy, they also believed that the Estates General had been an unavoidable step to escape from the crisis into which Court policy itself had plunged the entire nation. These were opinions that Rivarol was sustaining from the columns of his *Journal politique-national*, which appeared on the very eve of the taking of the Bastille and lasted until November 1790. Despite his profound knowledge of Montesquieu and Rousseau, he launched an attack on the philosophers, holding them responsible for the overthrow of the natural order of things. He denounced the elimination of the founding values of society and repeatedly demonized the revolutionaries' rejection of the civilizing heritage of previous centuries.

However, these were considerations that he developed gradually, only after seeing the failure of the attempts to make 1789 an opportunity for the monarchy's revival. The reactionary shift occurred with the taking of the Bastille, to become fully formed in September, when the Constituent Assembly rejected the proposal of a parliamentary monarchy along English lines. It became incontrovertible in the aftermath of the days of October, when Rivarol made it clear that, with the march of the women on Versailles to bring the royal family back to the city, the handover from the sovereign to the people had taken place. At the end of 1789, Rivarol knew, in short, that the monarchy no longer existed in France and that the sacredness of the king's person was destined to be overwhelmed by the sovereignty of the people. However, he postponed going into exile for a long time, deciding only on the eve of 10 August 1792, and for this reason becoming a champion of the counter-revolutionary cause only for the stylistic motifs his brilliant writing had introduced.[19]

Rivarol's journal, which repeatedly emphasized the barbarity of the Parisian populace – 'always cannibals, always flesh-eaters' – and the greed of speculators and financiers, and which never failed to denounce the responsibilities of the aristocrats who crossed over into the revolutionary camp, became required reading in pastist circles. The same could not be said, however, when it came to his political ideas. His proposal to build a new relationship between sovereign and aristocracy, making use of the English example to fill the void left by 1789, was soon dismissed as mere illusion.

His failure was that of the entire *monarchien* group, hopelessly occupied in the early days of the Constituent Assembly in trying to turn Louis XVI into an English king.[20] He reflected the political struggle within the monarchist camp, where the first group of émigrés regarded later arrivals with great suspicion, often saddling them with serious responsibility in relation to the birth of the Republic. It was a disagreement that suggested to many a pragmatic (and unscrupulous) use of the past, which allowed them to argue not only with the constitutional monarchists who supported 1789 but also with those who, while devoted to the figure of the sovereign, refused to praise the *ancien régime* in each and every situation. History became, in other words, the instrument for recovering the value of a national political tradition – a tradition equally damaged on the one hand by the rationalism and metaphysical certainties of the revolutionaries and on the other by the pernicious illusion of being able, through the Estates General, to rebuild the relationship between the sovereign and the privileged classes on new grounds.

This perspective makes it possible to evaluate the success of Edmund Burke's *Reflections* in counter-revolutionary circles.[21] Appearing for the first time in London in November 1790, there were already eleven English and three French editions by the beginning of 1791, while countless works all over Europe made reference to it, whether in terms of support or rejection.[22] The author was an Irish Whig politician, who had until then upheld the opinions of the American colonists: faced with events in France, however, he had taken up his pen to ensure that the ideas of 1789 did not cross the Channel.[23] His work is, in fact, an indictment of the very idea of revolution, its lucidity establishing it as a classic of conservative political philosophy. Unsurprisingly, the book is still read today as a moral work within which the very foundations of all revolutions are rejected through severe and perspicuous argument: they are depicted as destructive upheavals, deniers of freedom, destined to plunge every political society into popular violence.

This traditional reading of Burke's work should not, however, conceal the fact that, at the time, he had set himself a much more limited task. His main aim was to reiterate that there was nothing at all in common between the glorious English Revolution of 1688, thanks to which the English constitutional model was formed, and what occurred in France in 1789. In his eyes, the events of the latter were the exact opposite of what had taken place a century earlier on English soil. Then, the flight of the Catholic James II, which had allowed parliament to assume a central role in the institutional structure, had only re-established an ancient and traditional system of government, around which English freedoms had over time found their form and their shield. Now, the decisions of the French Assembly and the actions of the Parisian people signalled only a terrifying headlong rush, the end of which could only be the collapse of all established order beneath the blows of plebeian violence.

Burke bolstered his negative reading of 1789 by making use of two principal arguments: one concerned financial conspiracy, which had led some speculators to make use of assignats as a tool to demolish the socio-economic power of religious and aristocratic ownership; the other, the cultural action of a political circle, the product of cosmopolitan, radical and anti-religious Illuminism, which had for a long time been determined to take power over the whole of Europe. The coming together of these two interests had led to a frontal attack on the Church, envisaged as the true bulwark of *ancien régime* France's socio-economic order. Burke went further, prophesying that this particular commingling of interests had led to the founding of a sect fated to drag France, and, with time, all of Europe, into a maelstrom of destructive violence, at the end of which the only solution seemingly available would be a vague and general despotism.

It was a militant intervention, in other words, though this was often obscured by the ability of his pen to transform the denunciation of the events in Paris into a manual of political theory. In constructing his work, however, Burke drew heavily on many criticisms regarding 1789 that counter-revolutionary figures in France had already dismissed: while he had read the writings of Calonne, he read those of Rivarol only at a later date – though he was prompt to state that he heartily agreed with every word of them. He was, in any case, able to work everything into a prose where events and reflection accompanied theoretical analysis and political perspective for the present moment: for this reason, his *Reflections* was an inspiration to many and soon set the tone for the literature on the revolution that would shortly thereafter come crowding into the monarchist camp.[24]

And yet, although there is no doubt that Burkian pragmatism inspired the empirical reaction of those who, throughout history, refuted the triumphs of reason, it is worth pointing out how different – depending on sensibility and cultural profile – were the perspectives (and the results) of this raising of the shields. In most cases, in fact, the recourse to history, in the sense of a past to be sacrizilized, constituted an antidote to the horror of the present times and ended up spreading the frailest of veils over the desperate yearning for a period in the distant past that had, after all, never actually been truly experienced. Others, however, resorted to history in a different manner, refusing to make it a refuge from present storms in order to transform it into a tool that would make it possible to provide an explanation for recent events. In the context of overt historicism, the poignant nostalgia for an old order, deemed immutable, was thus destined to give way to the claim that the laws of political and social life might be deduced from the past.

The discovery of the positivity of history was, however, made by men who crossed over into the counter-revolutionary camp only after having been undecided in their attitude towards 1789.[25]

This is the case of René de Chatreaubriand, who started his philosophical considerations on the revolutions in London exile in 1793, but only after travelling to the United States and then returning to France in 1791, when the king's failed flight convinced him to leave.[26] Similarly, Geneva-born Jacques Mallet du Pan, also in 1793, composed his notes on the revolution after having tried in vain, from 1789 until the fall of Louis XVI, in the pages of the *Mercure*, to keep alive a *monarchienne* hypothesis involving the stabilization of the Crown.[27] The Savoyard count Joseph de Maistre, meanwhile, began working on his *Considérations* in 1793.[28] He had withdrawn from the revolution after the taking of the Bastille, but in 1792 had tried to adapt to life in the Republic, even serving, albeit briefly, in the ranks of the national guard. Louis de Bonald, who later followed his cultural line to the letter, had instead been a supporter of the 1789 watershed, so much so that in 1790 he was again elected to the departmental administration of Aveyron.

In line with what has already been said regarding Rivarol, all these men belonged to a political universe very different and irremediably distant from that of those who gazed back with nostalgia to the *ancien régime* – the former had taken their distance from 1789 through reflection on the concrete significance of the events that followed on from the birth of the National Assembly. It is no surprise, therefore, that their considerations – where history constituted the filter through which to purify the profound meaning of recent events – were much broader in scope than those of the others. For all of them, in fact, popular violence and the wickedness of individual protagonists garnered meaning only in the context of naturalistic sociology, where the anthropomorphic element gave way to reflection on the destinies of the collectivity.

Hence the apparent contradiction of a cultural world dominated by history, which, however, never wrote directly about history. The main counter-revolutionary writers allowed themselves to be guided by the past but they preferred to rewrite it to provide support of their philosophical assumptions and their political purposes. This is what the reading of Mallet du Pan's *Considérations sur la nature de la Révolution de France*, published in August 1793, suggests: the work is a violent moralistic polemic against the revolutionary disasters, with the author setting himself the task of drawing conclusions from the death of Louis XVI to suggest that the leadership of the revolution went to those who, in 1789, had attempted to overthrow the *ancien régime* while still holding fast to the monarchical identity of France.[29]

The main stylistic motifs circulating in counter-revolutionary circles return to its pages, but these are now more than merely a cry out against the horrors of popular violence and the intrigues of the revolutionaries, becoming the supporting framework for a reflection on the reasons that led to the collapse of the traditional alliance between king and people. Going far beyond invective and controversy, Mallet du Pan proceeded to dissect the revolutionary years, the uniformity of which fragmented in the face of certain stages indicated as decisive for the development of the subversive process: the convocation of the Estates General, the assembly of the orders, the days of 5–6 October, more so even than the taking of the Bastille, the collapse of the monarchy and the Feuillants on the day of insurrection of 10 August 1792, the defeat of the Girondins, too, at the hands of the Montagnards – all these were seen as the significant stages in a fatal process, marked by the progressive transfer of power from the sovereign to the multitudes.

When dealing with the question of how all this could have happened, Mallet du Pan passed lightly over irreligiosity and the spirit of the time, the intrigue of some and the responsibilities of many, to point to the fragility of the monarchy: through the convocation of the Estates General, it had lit the fuse that would bring about the conflagration of August 10. In this way, his pages yoked 1789, through an inexorable acceleration, to 1792, political process intertwining with social upheaval, with the result that the hendiadys of liberty and equality translated into a democracy that was actually dispossessing people of their property.

This conclusion, which indicates the presence of a social issue within the revolution, ended up further confirming the line of continuity with regard to revolutionary developments. The belief that 1789 was a foreshadowing of the Republic and then the Terror represented, however, a point that soon became central to the counter-revolutionary imagination, It was destined to raise questions about the previous political experience of Mallet du Pan himself and to legitimize the reactionary opinion that the monarchy's initial error was the foundation of all subsequent steps. In this way, the revolution became a homogeneous whole – something to be rejected entirely, of course – where it was not possible to introduce distinctions or even glimpse in its course any other destiny than that of popular violence.

One writer who would take Mallet du Pan's idea of an indivisible history of the revolution to extremes was abbot Augustin Barruel. Since 1788, he had been a spirited contributor to the columns of the *Journal ecclésiastique*, a widely read newssheet in the French religious world, and he had made a careful investigation of the events of 1789. Until the collapse of the monarchy, he had indeed believed that the revolution could help Catholicism greatly in the work of the spiritual reconquest of France, supporting the Church's submission to the new order as long as it did not attempt to interfere with the religious sphere. Up to the moment of the Civil Constitution of the Clergy (July 1790), which induced him to break with the new authorities, Barruel, too, saw the fragility of the monarchy as the profound cause of the revolution and attributed the radicalization of the new order to the weakness of Louis XVI. His considerations were silenced by the collapse of the monarchy, when the September Massacres – which Barruel escaped purely by chance – forced him to seek refuge in England. On the other side of Channel, in the climate of an increasingly intense struggle against a regicidal republic, his opinions regarding the revolution changed. After the Terror, in the Directory years, between 1796 and 1798, he published in London a history of the Jacobin faction.[30] Here, summarizing a thriving journalism that went back to the mid-eighteenth century, Barruel denounced the revolution as the outcome of a cunning conspiracy. The way had been prepared by philosophers dispensing unbelief and atheism throughout Europe: the Freemasons – soon becoming followers of Illuminati Communism – carried out the first steps and the Jacobins, heirs to both these groups, completed the strategy through the Terror.[31]

The success of the work lay in its skilful mixture of motivation and responsibility: the rejection of modernity made it an easy thing to tar everyone with the same brush and identify 1789 as the point of convergence of a subversive, multifaceted conspiracy. The compliments that Burke sent to Barruel – even going so far as to predict that the work 'would be epoch-making in the history of humanity' – all go to show that, throughout the whole revolutionary process, the counter-revolutionary world had now come to reject any sort of responsibility for the collapse of the *ancien régime*, laying the blame squarely on a demonic plot hatched by enemies of the monarchy and the church. The unscrupulous deployment of that particular polemical issue, the idea of a conspiracy theory, was something that the revolutionaries themselves had previously built their success on. It was now transferred to the other side of the argument, which turned its meaning on its head to explain, and, by now in this way only, the reasons for the old order's collapse. It was a reconstruction that was contested from within the counter-revolutionary camp itself, with those who had at first attempted to come to terms with the events of 1789 – like Mounier, once leader of the *monarchiens* in the Constituent Assembly – protesting against any conjoining of the first revolutionary phase with what followed.

However, they were soon isolated: Joseph de Maistre, forced to find refuge from Savoy in nearby Geneva, in turn confirmed the unity of the revolutionary process in his *Considérations sur la France*, published anonymously in Basel in 1797.[32] His work appeared at the most difficult moment for the supporters of the monarchy, because the Republic, having overcome the crisis of Year II, had resumed the offensive in Europe. However, the author showed great confidence in the fact that, in the future, the Republic would fall, and the monarchy would once again rise from the ruins its barbarities had brought about. His writings, which sound like a mere act of faith in the values of the old constitution, took their place in turn alongside those criticisms of the abstractionism of 1789 to which Burke's work had given great visibility. However, the originality of his arguments lay not so much in the prophetic tone but in his decision to read the events following 1789 in very different terms. If, for the other writers on the counter-revolutionary side, the violence and barbarism of the revolution were the proof of the deep evil generated by eighteenth-century rationalism, and the Terror was the poisoned fruit of the sick Jacobin tree, for Maistre those same dramatic events seemed to reveal the divine presence in the French nightmare.[33]

This appearance was evident to him in the apparent invincibility of French society which, despite being torn apart by the Terror, was still able to successfully deal with the coalition armies of the European powers. And the presence of a divine will that stirred up the wind of destruction was also visible in the human mediocrity of the revolutionaries – surely only God could have wanted such miserable individuals to replace the legitimate sovereign. The violence that embroiled France, viewed by other counter-revolutionaries as an unnatural monstrosity, for Maistre was instead the clear sign of divine justice in action: through such atonement, it intended to allow France to regain its place within Christianity. From this point of view, following the lesson of Bossuet, who stated that an excess of evil tended towards good, he was able to establish a profound alterity between violence and malediction: the horrors that the French were experiencing were not the result of madness, but rather the proof of a divine plan of redemption – with the whole population called upon to lose itself in agonizing expectation. In this context, even the Terror found a sort of rehabilitation. Maistre attributed to the Robespierre dictatorship the merit of having forged, through the threat of indiscriminate violence, a national spirit that had helped save France from foreign invasion. In this way, by allowing the revolutionary events to be seen as an example of a divine work of purification, Maistre could paradoxically come to a conclusion in favour of the Republican armies, identifying in armed counter-revolutionaries a serious danger for the unity of the country, given that the victory of foreign powers would have meant the end of its centuries-old unity. With the Terror, in other words, God had punished the French for their terrible sins – but, at the same time, he had wanted to save France from the abyss in order to allow it to resume, even stronger than before, the path assigned to it by Providence. Thus Maistre distanced himself from the counter-revolutionary forces: while they were apparently right to take the fight to the atheist Republic, they were, at the same time, wrong to do so – their triumph, through the steel of foreign bayonets, would have signalled the end of France's civilizing mission.

It is difficult to say what, at that specific moment, Maistre's brilliant pages would have conveyed to the emotional universe of his contemporary readers: some would have found there a reactionary's confident words regarding the return of the monarchy, just when such a thing seemed impossible; others would have felt a sense of comfort in the face of the turmoil of the recently concluded Terror.[34] For others, however, the dramatic schism brought about by 1789 became the means by which one story ended and another would begin. With the Terror once again subsumed within the history of France, the way was open for it to be possible to grasp the meaning of recent events and as a consequence derive lessons for the future. Brumaire benefitted greatly from this particular perspective: the Concordat of 1801, above all, which allowed First Consul Bonaparte to bring to an end the dispute with the Church begun ten years before and which some regarded as merely a shrewd trick, while others saw in it the end of the wretched parenthesis indicated by Maistre. The counter-revolutionary arsenal that had developed, in the wake of Burke and in parallel with the revolutionary process, remained to bolster a dynastic revival. But the politics of *ralliement* could take advantage of the cultural debate that the revolution's significance had stirred up on the right and Bonaparte seemed to appear – to many monarchists, too, and not only constitutional monarchists – the man who, on behalf of Providence, had brought the period of persecution to a close.

3. A world amazed

The revolutionary events were at once a reason for expectation and concern far beyond the borders of France. People were astonished by what occurred in 1789: men chosen from territorially based assemblies, representatives of the interests and claims of a circumscribed local class, had instead taken it upon themselves to represent a nation that existed only in their own heads and had given birth to a Constituent Assembly. The goal was a new order: liberty for all, rather than the liberties of a few, and equality in place of privilege, were the objectives of legislative activity that, through a constitution, would put an end to absolutism. The dramatic moments of the revolution – from the Tennis Court Oath to the taking of the Bastille, from the night of August 4 to the days of October – demonstrated to international public opinion the profound depth of the changes that were taking place in France. Reactions were various, whether of anguish or exhilaration, to the tempest that struck the Bourbon dynasty. While subsequent developments only confirmed the enormity of the events, the real turning point was the war: the decision of the Legislative Assembly to launch a crusade for freedom, which would liberate the peoples of the entire continent from the old order, was the start of an era destined to continue up to Waterloo – an era that would also foster an even broader approach to 1789.

The study of the revolution took on a truly European dimension, significantly conditioning ideas regarding the destinies of the various nations called upon to deal with the challenge. It was a perspective that found particular momentum after the fall of Robespierre, when first the Directory period and then the Consulate government – accompanying the progress of the French armies – forced countries to consider the impact that the political discourse originating with 1789 might have beyond French frontiers. Until the declaration of war, debate in continental Europe on the subject of revolutionary events kept pace with the dispute between revolutionaries and counter-revolutionaries: then, the success of the French armies, especially in the Directory years, dictated a change of viewpoint. Ideas regarding 1789 became even more closely connected to the futures of the countries that had to come to terms with the political modernity of France.

In Germany, the first reconstructions already date from 1790, but the point of view remains internal to France, oscillating between interest in epochal change and perplexity when faced with the extremism of the Constituent Assembly.[35] Friedrich Schulz, a man of letters who had been a direct witness of Parisian events from June to October 1789, immediately published his own version of the events.[36] The writings grew out of his travel impressions but were set forth as a real selection of political reflections. The claimed impartiality of his words, swinging between admiration for the members of the Constituent Assembly and fear with regard to the scenes of violence, does not absolve the royal couple. But while he contemplates the worrying weakness of the latter, he does not hold back from lavishing praise upon the *monarchiens* in the Assembly. His conclusion was pitched in tones of cautious openness to the spirit of the times, suggesting that the revolution was not without a certain legitimacy. Schulz's optimistic hope was that the people's movement, despite the excesses it had been guilty of, would soon, thanks to the guidance of the Enlightenment, be steered back to follow a line of measured progress.

A work by Ernst Brandes also appeared in 1790 and was soon translated into French.[37] Its bias towards the monarchy was this time openly declared, delivered through a voluble paean to the British system, which he reputed to be a point of reference which the French revolutionaries themselves would do well to keep uppermost in their minds. Brandes had no doubts regarding the origins of 1789: the responsibility of the aristocracy, portrayed as incapable and rapacious, was extremely serious; however, in accordance with the precepts of the British model, he believed that it should still be reserved a privileged role in conducting affairs of state.

Shortly thereafter, however, the developments of the revolution swept the *monarchiens* from the scene and, as in the French-speaking world, Burke's writings were once again very much in favour. In Germany, Justus Möser, one of the leading figures of the German Enlightenment, played a decisive role. Since 1789, he had protested that the developments of the revolution could soon affect the life of the small German states. He went on to attack the revolution and to energetically defend the system of privileges: between 1791 and 1792, alongside the growth of revolutionary fever in France, his denunciation of equality under the law and popular sovereignty inspired a philosophical novel, *Der Arme Freie*. In the book, on the lines of Voltaire's *Candide*, Möser narrates the deeds of a free peasant who refuses an advantageously profitable return to conditions of servility, only to see that his great love for the new principles does not lead to a better life – indeed, his devotion to the principles of his new state brings his own existence to a sad end.[38]

Circulating at the same time as Möser's work were the writings of August Wilhelm Rehberg, a high-ranking official in Hanover.[39] Published during the Terror, his book summarizes the response of the conservative German intellectual world to the revolutionary challenge of France: in Rehberg's view, the revolution was only a futile attempt to found, through reason, a new world opposed to that of the old order. The error lay in the demand to eradicate the centuries-old rule of privilege from the European social body: Rehberg believed that in fact the opposite was necessary – namely that a small elite of mature people could make use of it, applying it to the improvement of a social order that could not in any case be challenged.[40] This was terrain where the use of tradition, in the sense of an instrument of government, found strength: the insistence on the class identity of each established order was a clear reference to the pages of Edmund Burke, who in Germany had, among other things, the advantage of being translated by Friedrich von Gentz. Gentz had made his debut in the world of politics praising the American revolution and had at first been fascinated by the events of 1789, but the rapid development of democracy had brought him back with great admiration to the words of the Whig politician.[41] As we have seen, Gentz was not alone in his path – passing from revolution to counter-revolution as a response to the Constituent Assembly's action in government and to the handover from this to the Legislative Assembly. It was also a course followed by Wilhelm von Humboldt, who was in Paris in 1789, where he looked on the revolution with admiration – only the events of 1792, destined to lead to the collapse of the monarchy, led him, perhaps thanks to Gentz's ideas, to align himself with Burke's proposals.[42]

In any case, Gentz was a brilliant interpreter (and promoter) of the counter-revolution in Germany: after translating Burke in 1793,[43] he produced the German version of Mallet du Pan the following year.[44] His stance in these matters proved so decisive that, in the Napoleonic years, he was a trusted adviser to the Prince of Metternich. In his opinion – and this was the main legacy of Burke and Mallet to his ideological universe – the revolution would be conclusively regarded as a crime against God and against humanity: through abject fanatics dominated by a false concept of the Enlightenment and of reason, it had dared to attack the laws of nature.

Conservative criticism of the revolution, going hand in hand with that of a more particularly religious nature, met with great success in southern Europe, too. This was exemplified in Italy, where it is no coincidence that Burke's ideas were equally popular. There as well, resistance to the new order in France grew out of criticism from conservative spheres, which previously had shown interest in the experiment of the Enlightenment, before, in the aftermath of the Parisian events of 1791, shifting to strictly religious terrain.

It is a trajectory encapsulated in the vicissitudes of a curious pamphlet printed in Italy after the Varennes affair by a Sicilian adventurer, Saverio Scrofani, who had lived in Paris until 1790.[45] Back in Italy, he gave his own interpretation of the events with *Tutti han torto* (Everybody is wrong), a short treatise on 1789 and its developments, which went through an astonishing seven editions in just two years.[46] Scrofani argues with 'those who claim that Montesquieu, Rousseau, Voltaire, Raynal and the Encyclopédie were the cause of the revolution', reminding his readers that revolution and philosophy never shared the same era. With these words, he wished to remove all traits of extremism from the period of Enlightenment, restoring it to a position of prudent reformism. It was an objective, however, that led Scrofani to broaden his field of investigation, thereby introducing an original examination of the condition of France: in his view, in 1789, the revolutionary uprising had been a necessity, given that the oppressiveness of the enormous public debt was too unequally shared in such a rich and prosperous country. It was a very pragmatic view of the French situation, which clashed fiercely with the reconstructions of a moralistic or judicial kind so prevalent in the writings of the time. Great economic interests, said Scrofani, lay behind the conflict, ensuring that little purity of intent informed the movements of all the political parties. The aristocracy and the clergy bore serious responsibilities for the surfeit of privileges and unacceptable immunities that they had long benefitted from, but the Third Estate, too – which, Scrofani emphasized, was dominated by proprietors, a very different thing from the common people – was not without its negative aspects, too quick in offloading the tax burden onto consumers alone. This perspective, which denounced error and egoism across the board, but also, in addition to the universalistic proclamations of revolutionary rhetoric, illustrated France's renewed policy of aggression, was developed in a second expanded edition, published in 1792. Here, Scrofani described the radicalization of the political process following the failed flight to Varennes in the context of a tense confrontation between positions that were extreme (and therefore equally wrong). The vehement defence of the period of reform (in Italy as in all of Europe) was not, however, a stance that could stand up to the developments of the revolutionary war and outraged reaction to the work was not long in arriving. In 1793, another anonymous pamphlet – penned, however, by the Swedish Jesuit Lars Birger Thiulen – came out, with the contrasting title of *Tutti han ragione* (Everybody is right): it reiterated the link between the Enlightenment and the violence in order to insinuate that Scrofani himself was a revolutionary. The Sicilian, fearing how things might go for him, decided it would be a good idea to publish a follow-up to his work in 1794, the *Continuazione del Tutti han torto* (Continuation of Everybody is wrong), wholly expunging the memory of his previous effort, with the protest against liberticidal revolution absolutely clear. It would be easy to conclude that Scrofani's seesawing reflects the opportunism of an adventurer – one who, not surprisingly, would be swift to return to a democratic and republican position as soon as Bonaparte's troops invaded the peninsula – if it did not more generally indicate the interpretative contortions which all the supporters of 1789 were forced to adopt as soon as the revolution jettisoned the reassuring semblance of constitutional legality in order to lose itself in the twists and turns of popular violence.

For this reason, those who still believed in the revolution liked to compare it to a natural catastrophe or an illness: it was a way to escape the arid debate regarding the legality or otherwise of recent events in order to more or less legitimize the violent and subversive traits as well. In Germany, all this began to take form in 1792, when the poet Christoph Martin Wieland – the strongest supporter of the French in the intellectual elite at that time – stated that questioning the legal validity of the revolutionary surge was equivalent to arguing about the legality of 'an earthquake in Calabria or a hurricane in Jamaica'.[47] His words echoed those of another great German poet, Friedrich Gottlieb Klopstock – whose revolutionary fervour the events of 1792 had cooled, but not yet completely extinguished[48] – as well as Immanuel Kant's remarks concerning the 'cry of nature' that resounded beyond the Rhine and those of Georg Forster, still ready to extol the French Revolution as 'a work of nature's justice' and in 1793 actively involved in organizing the Mainz Republic. Johann Gottlieb Fichte replied to those who – like Rehberg and Humboldt – denounced the destructive nature of volcanic eruptions, recalling that revolutions were placed 'under the laws of nature' and concluding that to support them was so generous in the order of things as to restore greater fertility to lands previously devastated by torrents of lava.[49]

With these words, we are now a long way from the evolutionistic ideas that dominated Condorcet's work: here there arises the theme of a course of events faced with a sudden forward plunge, with revolution as an abrupt and unpredictable acceleration. The consequences of this reading of the birth of the Republic and then of Terror in the guise of a beneficial tsunami became clear in 1794, when revolutionary troops permanently entered part of Germany and overturned the traditional framework of the *ancien régime*. Support for the post-Robespierrist period and the advance of the troops of Directory France was almost unanimous among the younger generations: in the theological seminary of Tübingen, Hegel and Schelling are said (with little clear evidence) to have planted a tree of freedom;[50] Fichte applauded the Year III constitution and also attempted to improve it through a project that reconciled popular sovereignty and representation; Hölderlin, another student at the Tübingen seminary, published the tragedy *Der Tod des Empedokles* (The Death of Empedocles) and the epistolary novel *Hyperion*, both metaphors for the revolutionary process within social realities to a large extent unprepared for the experience of modernity.

Even Brumaire did not interrupt the triumph of the revolutionary model in its universalistic dimension, which all supporters of France – from Hölderlin himself to

Fichte to Hegel – looked upon with interest, if not with open satisfaction, given that it seemed to them to set the Republic once again on an even keel. Then, in the years to follow, there came the time of disillusionment as Bonaparte swiftly claimed the imperial Crown, thereby appearing to reduce the huge expectations raised by the republican message to mere French national interest. However, it would be a slow process, the – always painful – act of distancing destined to take place only with the birth of the French Empire, when it seemed that the proclaimed federative aspect of the new order served only to veil Paris's dominion over the rest of continental Europe. In the meantime, First Consul Bonaparte was seen as the figure that had resolved the Directory's excessive fragility and given force to a statehood that was both constitutional and respectful towards popular sovereignty (even in the transfigured context of plebiscitary logic). For this reason – and the discourse spread all over Europe under the direct control of French armies – he still continued to enjoy a broad consensus for a long period of time. This was destined to translate, in the properly historical sense, into a recovery (and in an adaptation to new territorial contexts) of the perspectives suggested by the post-Thermidor period.

The most significant example in this regard is provided by the publication in 1801 – in Milan, capital, thanks to Bonaparte's second military intervention, of the newly restored Cisalpine Republic – of the work *Saggio storico sulla rivoluzione di Napoli* (Historical essay on the Neapolitcan revolution). This historical essay was written by a southern exile, Vincenzo Cuoco, during his brief exile in France, where he had fled to escape the repression initiated by the return of the Bourbon king to Naples in 1799.[51] Cuoco offered an original response to the many problems circulating in a Europe under the control of French armies: taking as an example the brief and dramatic story of the Neapolitan Republic (January–June 1799), soon overwhelmed by Cardinal Ruffo's forces, he not only introduced his thoughts on the overall meaning of the French Revolution, pairing 1789 together with Brumaire, but also started a parallel comparison with what, through the bayonets of the Republican armies, had taken place in Italy.[52]

The work, as its author explicitly admitted, was therefore an operation designed to take stock of the significance of the revolutionary process and the parallels it had revealed as soon as its universalistic message was transformed into the armed excursion of the Republicans into Europe. From this point of view, the similarities were evident with the current debate in Germany – but the discourse could certainly be extended to the Batavian and Helvetic Republics: everything Cuoco wrote here followed the thread of a constant comparison between the example of the original revolution and its concrete manifestation in the neighbouring states of the *ancien régime*.

According to Cuoco, in fact, the revolution in France had been a revolution within the bounds of legality until the beheading of Louis XVI – the gradualness of the events had allowed it to maintain a broad consensus that excluded the need to resort to the metaphor of an earthquake-style event to explain the radicalization of the political process. Robespierre also enjoyed an initial consensus, putting an end to the factions that were tearing apart the life of the Republic and saving it from assault by foreign forces. It was a legacy soon squandered, however, because the authoritarianism of the revolutionary government quickly became intolerable. The lack of freedom – the only real engine of any revolution – required all the parties to stand together against the tyrant and return to a government program in line with what the nation wanted. This, in Cuoco's eyes, was the happy period of moderation, where the revolution was once again in harmony with collective sentiment. The Directory ran swiftly through all its popular credit with its execrable policies, facilitating the return of factions and leading to serious cases of embezzlement in France's Sisters republics: only Bonaparte, with Brumaire, was able to cut through the entanglement in order to let the revolution resume its proper course. Cuoco's approval for the French watershed of 1799 was also useful to him, however, in terms of underlining the contradiction of the extent to which the degradation of political life in post-Robespierrist France had gone hand in hand with the triumphs of its armies abroad. This meant that the Sisters republics – especially those that had sprung up on the Italian peninsula – were exposed to (but were also guiltily hurrying to emulate) a revolutionary model that was soon in crisis in France itself. There thus evolved in his pages the consideration – one destined for great success in the political culture of modern Italy – that the republicanization of the peninsula had been a passive revolution, carried through by the French at bayonet point, without the Paris government having a clear political line in this regard and – above all – without the existence of a broad consensus in Italian society. Denunciation of the Italian patriots' subordination to the French example, which wanted them to renounce their specific political-cultural traditions in the name of a misinterpreted cosmopolitanism, was given a more profoundly constitutional cast in the appendix to the work. Here, Cuoco criticized the constitutional project of Mario Pagano – with the return of the ephorate that Sieyès had been so keen on – because, regardless of that novelty, it seemed to him based entirely on the example of the French document of Year III.

In this way, Cuoco's work, although it arose from the same concerns as those of the German patriots, came to opposite conclusions: while Hölderlin extolled the spirit of sacrifice of the Republicans forced to act in a backward social world, Cuoco, indicating the presence of two peoples separated by an enormous distance, denounced the abstractness of the patriots and of an order based on a foreign example that was totally inadequate in terms of encapsulating Italian specificity. These bitter thoughts did not mean, however, that he wished to distance himself from France: in his eyes, the revolutionary years seemed to have founded a political modernity that alone could have allowed the peninsula to make up the gap that separated it from Europe's most advanced countries and for this reason he held firm to the importance of the new Bonapartist order. Unsurprisingly, then, in his historical essay, subordination to France, which he did not try to hide, became a painful and yet necessary period of transition. In this way, all of Italy could rise from the condition of decadence into which it had been dragged by the *ancien régime*: hence the eulogy of Bonaparte. This became even more pronounced in 1806, when, in the extensively revised second edition of the work, Cuoco toned down his republican enthusiasm, without his belief in the imperial order entailing the renunciation of the construction of a national political model. Rather, he continued to see the French instruments of government as of great value that – once, however, rendered compatible with the peninsula's social framework – would carry on being of enormous use in assisting in the reorganization of Italian society.

We are not, then, so far from the evolution of political thought in Germany, where the most significant case is that of Fichte, who would remain faithful to the republican movement until the end of 1799, when he even wished for a French military triumph to prevent the stagnant waters of conservatism from submerging Germany once more. Shortly thereafter, he would salute Bonaparte as the revolutionary star, returning to illuminate the skies of Europe. Later, in the new political framework formed by the Napoleonic Empire, his ideas in a truly national context were clearly set out, in 1808, in his *Reden an die deutsche Nation*. And it was precisely in such a context that the analogies with the Italian case described by Cuoco show their undoubted force: Fichte in turn fought against constitutions founded on 'labile and empty abstractions', despised the reigning dynasties, placed the political future of Germany in a setting of profound national cultural renewal and insisted on the new patriotism of the Germans as the real handhold to overthrow Napoleon's expansionist despotism through the ancient revolutionary values derived from France. In other words, Fichte's move towards nationalism was inspired by the values of a Germanic sentiment that, while harking backwards in time, and to the Reformation in particular, to find its origin, remained firmly anchored in the framework of values established in the previous years through republican virtue.

In other words, as with Cuoco, the rejection of Napoleonic imperialism did not exclude deferential admiration for the revolutionary model and the decision to backdate through time the origins of a national identity alternative to their neighbour's across the Rhine was a largely instrumental operation, aimed at escaping an otherwise suffocating French embrace. The road lay open: in Germany, as in Italy, a national history had come into being, its contradiction being that, while it originated directly from the French example, it arrived on the scene disdaining any link of parentage with the outside world.

4. Over the Ocean and across the Channel

In 1789, the most enthusiastic comments on the news from Paris came from afar. The young United States of America, who owed their birth to the alliance with France during the war of independence against the British, were thrilled to see their blossoming freedom bear fruit in the most important country in Europe. Until then, it had always been said that American liberty was an exception, the unrepeatable political product of a new world, where the cultural models of Europe had achieved a marvellous cross-fertilization with the particularity of the new world's social structures and geography. America's 1776 seemed to be a unique fact that old Europe – dominated by aristocracy, feudalism and guild rules – would never be able to imitate. Now, however, and with great suddenness, everything seemed to change: the American Revolution was not a circumscribed event, but an epochal transformation with an impact destined to be felt in the old continent. The *Boston Gazette* of early September 1789 testifies to this sentiment, when, commenting on the events in France, it sets out a clear chronological order for freedom's course:

Liberty will have another feather in her cap. The seraphic contagion was caught from Britain; it crossed the Atlantic to North America, from whence the flame has been communicated to France.[53]

The newspaper – very close to the Hamilton Federalists, who had taken the lead in the country after the ratification of the 1787 Philadelphia constitution – reflected the opinion of those who, while applauding the new events in France, continued to believe that liberty was in nature an essentially British affair. It had made its appearance in England with the Glorious Revolution of 1688, had almost naturally found its way over to the new continent, where it had been greatly invigorated, and from there, redefined, had made the journey in reverse, to land on the shores of absolutist France.

It was a plausible reading in some ways, which in turn foreshadowed two different, and soon opposing, developments: on the one hand it hinted that the root of each new political model lay in Britain, in the example that the Americans, in choosing a written constitution, had refused, but at the same time had always had in mind. On the other hand, there was nothing to exclude the fact that the American centrality in this game of political ricochet might also foster the return – and a vehement one – of the idea of liberty in the United Kingdom, where there was no lack of dissent towards a conservative policy that the loss of the colonies had made even more rigid.

The forecasts soon seemed to come true: in London, the Reverend Richard Price, who at the time of the war of independence had supported the colonists' cause from England, greeted the taking of the Bastille with enthusiasm and in a speech given on 4 November 1789 to the Revolution Society in memory of 1688, remarked upon the close connection between the three revolutions.[54] In his opinion, modern freedom in Europe and America had begun with the flight of James II, when the victorious resistance of the English had made it possible to establish a government that the people wanted. The changes that followed on from 1688 had allowed the founding of a model of liberty that eighteenth-century English politics had soon directed towards the benefit of certain elites only: its universal value, however, had returned to flower first in America and then in France. In other words, the fall of the Bastille was the culmination of a political perspective that had arisen a long time before in England itself, and to England full restitution was now deserved.[55]

These were words that said everything with regard to how the century of British freedom had been largely debased by a very reductive interpretation of the revolution against the last Stuart and, not surprisingly, provoked the prompt reaction of Edmund Burke. His *Reflections*, which, as has been seen, swiftly brought inspiration to the counter-revolutionary ideological universe, began with the more limited intention of contesting Price and addressed British public opinion in order to reaffirm the primacy (completely inimitable, because incomparable) of the English model. The work's great success in continental Europe should not, however, obscure the fact that, while his work at first met with approval in England, it soon also aroused a great deal of dissent. Mary Wollstonecraft[56] and Catherine Macaulay[57] provided him with an almost immediate answer: the former suggested that Burke's obsession with noble and chivalrous attitudes was an allegory of a false and court-besotted ruling class, not very distant from France's own crumbling aristocracy. Macaulay, meanwhile, looked again at the interpretation of 1688 to suggest that France – transforming itself into a parliamentary and constitutional monarchy – had simply imitated England at the end of the seventeenth century.[58]

This perspective, which reflected an entirely internal disagreement within English politics, benefitted from many contributions that were all close to Price's positions: George Rous, reading Burke's desperate yearning for ancient constitutional models, compared him to a 1688 Tory;[59] Brooke Boothby saluted France as 'a great and generous nation animated with one soul, rising up as one man to demand the restitution of their natural rights';[60] while Charles Pigott stressed Burke's condescension towards France's religious fanaticism and aristocratic *fainéantise*.[61] Joseph Priestley, however, enjoyed the greatest success, underlining in turn the popular nature of the French Revolution and its similarities with America and also praising – again against Burke – the new religious policy.[62]

In all these cases, the French Revolution was actually an opportunity to speak about England and its difficult political equilibrium in a period shaken by the demands for wide-ranging parliamentary reform. A good example of this was Scottish historian James Mackintosh's *Vindiciae Gallicae*, published in May 1791, when the political situation in France seemed to have stabilized. The text summarized the wishes of a Whig political class that refused the political involution of the group supported by Burke and sustained the need for a prompt liberal reform of the British parliamentary system. The structure of the work suggested that Mackintosh intended to praise the right thinking of those in Britain who endorsed the revolution in France: 1789 was proposed as inevitable and necessary, the work of the French National Assembly was meritorious and popular violence was convincingly justified by the despotism of the old order. There was a need, therefore, for agreement between France and Great Britain on the issue of political modernity, where the differences between 1688 and 1789 were recognized but were brought together around the common paradigm of liberty.[63]

A fascinating and immediate proposal, it was destined to prevail over Burke's gloomy predictions. The myth of a France reconjoined with England in a perspective of freedom had also benefitted from the decision of Tom Paine – the English writer who had contributed most to the American Revolution – not to insist on the transmissibility of the republican model in the old continent. Publishing the first part of his *Rights of Man* in London in February 1791, Paine had in fact accepted the monarchical and liberal nature of revolutionary France and had implicitly excluded the possibility that the republican model could take root.[64]

It was a decision that, in an attempt to undermine the conservative resistance of British politics, forced him into the strident contradiction of denying his own origins. However, the risk seemed one worth taking: as early as 1791, he believed that the example of the French Revolution was more useful than that of 1776 in terms of conducting a political struggle within England itself. As is well known, politics moved quickly to reject the idea. In July 1791, the shots fired on the Field of Mars against the protesters demanding the removal of the king revealed the progress of republicanism and dealt a serious blow to the popularity of Lafayette, responsible for giving the orders to open fire on the crowd. Paine thus decided to abandon him, publishing the second part of the *Rights of Man* in February 1792, again in London.[65] Here, the democratic model of American origin, founded on universal suffrage and legislation attentive to social issues, once more occupied the foreground. It was a sensational turnaround, dictated, once again, however, by the intention to shake things up in the British political framework. If, previously, Paine had thought that the example of France's constitutional monarchy was a useful means of doing this, now, faced with the new political structure, he returned to the old belief in a universal republicanism that could, on two sides, from America and France, exert pressure on Britain's conservative bastion. It was a choice that, in the short term, would further radicalize positions in the English political world, but that, for this same reason, would draw Burke's hitherto dwindling stance back into the limelight. In this way, it became clear that in Britain it was by then increasingly difficult to maintain an attitude towards the French Revolution that was not either one of wholehearted consensus or wholehearted rejection. In the next few months, the developments of international politics did the rest: first, hostilities broke out between France and the Austro-Prussians; then, the August 10 insurrection which brought the monarchy to an end; and, finally, the birth of the Republic, preceded by the horrible echo of the September Massacres, had the effect of stirring up the democratic spirit, while at the same time also helping to revive the loyalist cause. Britain was invaded by a horde of pamphlets, most prominent being those that denounced the French Revolution and intended to oppose the growing success of Paine's work along the lines of the stylistic motifs that Burke had long made available. The loyalist cause was praised through noting the quality of the British political system, where the foresight of virtual representation shone out, together with the decisive role of property as an instrument of political selection. Complete identification was established between the legislative moment and the general will. Ultimately, in this war of pens, the polemical spirit was directed against Paine in order to demonstrate that it was inequality itself that formed the basis of British wealth, since only subordination could ensure freedom. Any imitation of the French model was thus condemned accordingly. It was a perspective with swift repercussions in the world of political struggle: Burke himself, having built up close relationships with some of the most important French émigrés, called for military intervention against France in alliance with the Austro-Prussians. Faced with this strategy, the Whig party soon found itself in difficulty, accused of suspected sympathies towards Paris. The dispute reached its climax in the early months of 1793, when the beheading of Louis XVI allowed conservative circles to assert that 1789 had turned into another 1640 rather than a revolution similar to that of 1688. In February, the circle was closed by Britain's entry into the war. The debate on the reform of the British political system came to a halt: from that moment on, any proposal to that effect was branded as a mere ploy to bring revolution to the island – and, therefore, republicanism, equality and, as a result, civil war.

However, it would be simplistic to conclude that the hostilities interrupted the bond of solidarity that had been established between France and Great Britain in relation to ideas concerning liberty: this is shown by *An Impartial History of the Late Revolution in France*, which provoked great interest in London.[66] The anonymous work, published in 1794 in two volumes, put forward a Whig reading of 1789: the occurrences in France were described as necessary and meritorious, and only the sudden, destructive acceleration of events prevented a conclusion with the constitutional ruling of 1791. For some, indeed, not even the fall of the monarchy and the birth of the Republic had completely extinguished the shift towards liberty inherent in 1789. Only the fall of the

Girondins, following the intervention of the Parisian populace against parliamentary representation, had plunged French politics into the horror of ochlocracy.

The work was an attempt to energetically defend 1789 in contrast to 1793, the dawn of freedom compared with the drama of mob violence, an idea that would continue for a long time in British public opinion. In 1797, for example, another anonymous work came out in London, *Biographical Anecdotes of the Founders of the French Republic*,[67] consisting of short essays about France's main revolutionary figures. It was a great success with the public, so much so as to induce the printer to present a second volume in a blaze of publicity, where the meaning of the operation was promptly clarified: without hiding anything of the violence that raged through France, only the Terror itself, portrayed as a meteorite that crashed down into a society in search of liberation, had essentially impeded 'the progress of general freedom'.

These editorial initiatives, where the political line and the curiosity of public opinion regarding the dramatic evolution of French events blent together, showed that British interest in the developments of 1789 never faded. Radical circles contributed to this, since the English political class had, for a long time, to face up to the challenge of those who reminded the public that the war on France, the disastrous effects of which the population soon became aware of, had served to silence every voice in favour of political reform. In short, although news of the Terror and dictatorship continued to arrive from Paris, although Paine had even been imprisoned by the Montagnards as a counter-revolutionary agent, and although love of country was appealed to against the old enemy across the Channel, the British radical circles maintained a freedom of action that was destined to cause the government a great deal of anxiety. It is no coincidence that, at the end of 1795, when Republican France, after abandoning Robespierrism, had already approved the new Year III constitution, Prime Minister Pitt had to resort to an alleged attack on the person of the king to bring an end, through specific legislative provisions, to the freedom of action of democratic societies, sending their organizers for trial and forcing many of their members into exile.[68]

There is, however, dating from that same period, *An Historical Sketch of the French Revolution*, a voluminous essay by Sampson Perry, a doctor with ideas similar to Paine's, where the revolutionary events are reconstructed in strict agreement with the political line of Directory France.[69] In its many pages, Perry openly declared that he wrote to refute the superficial and erroneous things that had been written about the French Revolution in England. He thus composed a eulogy to the insurrection of 10 August 1792; distanced himself from Robespierrism; re-evaluated, albeit with different emphases, the many victims of the Terror in the Republican camp; and, above all, adopted the line of the Thermidorian left. He denounced the factiousness of the Club of the Jacobins, while at the same time condemning the two-thirds decree that ended up making it possible for the will of the few to prevail over that of the majority, and contested the restrictions on voting rights in the Year III constitution. Needless to say, through the French example – which, according to Perry, also remained the polar star for navigating towards democracy in Britain – his target was actually English politics and, through an easy game of analogy and allusion, it was the policies of George III's ministers that came under accusation.

Perry's implications, after all, reflected the dramatic British political situation, where Pitt's decisions seemed not only to decree the destiny of democracy in England but also to annul even the most limited political reform. Playing to a large extent on patriotic sentiment, underlining the subversive logic that inspired the supporters of France, the prime minister's actions had helped political debate swing round to follow the line of Burke's ideas. Unsurprisingly, as early as 1796, the latter went hand in hand with the government's own political direction and obliged those who supported Pitt to adopt them as their own. One example is offered by William Playfair's *History of Jacobinism*, an enormous work attacking the Jacobins,[70] where, while counter-revolutionary discourse is angled in support of violent disagreement with democratic circles, it is not difficult to see within this how radicalized positions on the right had also become. Playfair in fact launched a robust assault on John Moore, who had authored a history of the revolution that, despite prudently breaking off at the beginning of the Republican period, nevertheless made an attempt to firmly uphold the importance of 1789.[71] It was a sign that it was no longer possible to maintain an attitude of comprehension in relation to the first phase of the revolution at least: it could only be considered as the vile source from which all the crimes of the Jacobin faction had thereafter poured forth.

One striking case in this regard was that of James Mackintosh, who, in 1791, had defended the liberal values of the French Revolution and had accused Burke of adopting a counter-revolutionary stance. He now admitted all his mistakes and confessed how completely wrong he had been: subsequent events had shown that the French Revolution was not a moment of freedom, but a pernicious, violent and blasphemous event – one to be very careful of indeed, since it threatened to expand, through sectarian proselytism, all over Europe.[72]

It was the triumph of Burke's ideas, their success transferring buoyantly to the other side of the Atlantic.[73] Hamilton Federalists, who had looked on dismayed at the birth of a French republic driven by mob violence, insisted vociferously on the profound difference between the two republics – even to the point of advocating a rebalancing in political relations with Great Britain in order to prevent a shift away from democracy: the rebellion of the Black slaves in Saint-Domingue towards the end of 1791 confirmed to them that such a thing brought with it not only violence and anarchy but racial levelling, too. Their concern found brutal confirmation in the diplomatic action of the French minister Genet, who arrived in America in 1793 with the task of negotiating an alliance against Britain. In a move that constituted astonishing interference in the internal affairs of the United States, he even made a direct appeal to American public opinion to convince President Washington to abandon neutrality. Faced with the predictable resistance of the Hamilton-dominated executive, Genet even went to the lengths of threatening an uprising similar to the Parisian August 10 – one that would sweep away the Federalist-Feuillants and a George Washington accused of being a king-president.

The repercussions were not long in coming: conservative circles found it easy to denounce the democratic societies of America as gathering places for dangerous extremism and repeatedly insinuated that the French Revolution was a political monster destined to devour American freedom. It was the starting date of a new path for US politics, always proposing itself as an alternative – when not openly hostile – to revolutionary France, which not even the fall of Robespierre and the concomitant arrival in Paris of the US ambassador James Monroe, the politician at the time most sympathetic to the cause of the French republic, was able to hold back.

The United States became terrain for relentless propaganda against the atheistic and violent aspects of the revolution – stereotypes of which were imported directly from Great Britain. This took place through the work of an English journalist who had come to America, William Cobbett: he first opened a print shop and immediately published Burke's text and then proceeded on his own to start a frenzied campaign against the American Jacobins,[74] one that ran along the reactionary and pastist lines that in Great Britain, thanks to Playfair's work, were doing so well. It was an operation with a wide-ranging impact, which would soon lead a variety of religious figures to turn their backs on an initial stance that, in accordance with the logic of millennialism, had seen them applaud a revolution that finally seemed to punish Catholicism's excess of faults.

American democratic circles responded to this profoundly conservative movement, which shored itself up with the horrors of the Terror to distinguish the American Revolution from its French counterpart, by asking President Washington and his successor Adams for American politics to return to their revolutionary origins. In this context, it is worth having a look at what Tom Paine was doing: from a France that had left the Terror behind, he went back to insisting on the need for an Atlantic revolution – one involving the two republics in a plan to crush, thanks to popular participation, the reactionary coalition that seemed to bind the French and Anglo-American counter-revolutionaries together in a sort of international pastism.[75] In the years of the Adams presidency (1796–1800), this bitter confrontation was resolved to the advantage of the conservative faction: neutrality, although officially declared, translated into siding with Great Britain and, almost to the limits of war, had a damaging effect on relations with Directory France. The Republicans of Jefferson and Madison suffered greatly, so much so that they were forced to fall back on a more prudent position, which, while not demonizing France, nevertheless suggested that the unrepeatability of American equality be placed at the centre of political action.

It was, after all, an almost obligatory move if they wanted to relaunch the fight against the Federalists with any chance of success: Jefferson's extraordinary victory during the presidential elections of 1800 confirmed that insistence on the political originality of the United States was the only discourse that won a broad consensus, while the need for prompt reconciliation with the Federalists suggested prudence in relation to France. In the aftermath of electoral triumph, Jefferson had spoken of a second revolution that followed on from that of 1776 – thus plucking from Jacobin political discourse a stereotype that had been in circulation since 10 August 1792. Bonaparte had done exactly the same thing only a few weeks earlier, on the occasion of the Brumaire watershed. Despite this, there was nothing in the air to suggest that an alliance with France was more likely. In fact, Bonaparte's policy soon ended up worrying those who should have been his most valuable allies in the international panorama: in 1802, the Treaty of Amiens with Britain and the parallel decision to settle accounts in Saint-Domingue with Toussaint Louverture convinced Jefferson that France, although a republic, intended to make a powerful return to the American scene.

Not even the cession of Louisiana in 1803 and military defeat in Saint-Domingue were enough to make the US president change his mind, and over the following years he was always ready to express a harsh judgement on Napoleon, who had now become Emperor of the French. The authoritarian drift of revolutionary France convinced Jefferson that America was indeed the only land of liberty and it is no coincidence that under his rule the foundations were laid for the isolationist policy that his successor Madison would transform into the resumption of hostilities with Great Britain. The subsequent president, meanwhile, the former Jacobin Monroe, in 1823 would transform the policy into a doctrine which, over time, US foreign policy was constrained to follow.

It was a difference that would also influence the image of the French Revolution in America – the image of an extraordinary occasion that was, however, dramatically lost. Proof of this is the editorial success, again in 1810, of *An Impartial and Concise History of the French Revolution*, a deft synthesis of revolutionary events in which warmth of feeling towards men who sacrificed everything for the cause of freedom is accompanied by indignation towards 'an ambitious usurper, whose sole object appears to be universal dominion and personal agrandissement'.[76] There were strong echoes of the old Whig reading of 1789 in this perspective, angled, however, to the advantage of an audience proud of having conquered what in France, despite the enormity of the events, had only proved to be a mirage.

From this point of view, although radicalism's moment had now passed, the political-cultural model of the United States thus continued to remain distinct from that of the mother country. There, instead, the brief interlude of the Treaty of Amiens in 1802 had allowed a breathing space to take stock of the ten-year political-military confrontation with France through the repeated denunciation of revolutionary violence. It is no coincidence, therefore, that the first historiographic intervention on the French Revolution was produced precisely at that juncture: in 1803, John Adolphus published a *History of the French Revolution*, which constitutes the first attempt to take a step back from the immediacy of the political clash in order to establish, along the lines laid out by Burke, the characteristics of the French events.[77] The latter were thus presented as the product of a pernicious, subversive spirit that had made its appearance in France in the aftermath of the American war, fuelled by a revolutionary nobility that looked to the example of Lafayette and Mirabeau. Its main reference point, however, was the Duke of Orleans, whose overweening ambition was responsible for the dramatic misfortunes of the Bourbon monarchy.

And yet, in this reconstruction, in which liberal readings of 1789 were savaged and the main authors who, on both sides of the Channel, had given them credence, were criticized, what stood out was the uniformity given to the political process in France: there was nothing to separate 1789 from 1792, the Terror from Thermidor, the Directory from Brumaire. The history of the revolutionary decade in France had been dominated by authoritarian and liberticidal elements, which had accompanied the political process all the way from the Constituent Assembly to Bonaparte. And yet, although the author made it a point of honour to come out resolutely against the revolution, he did not abandon himself to invective: his description of events is a measured one, allowing the reader to infer the consequences of being in the presence of such a deplorable series of circumstances. In this way, British historiography on the revolution came into being, where misgivings with regard to 1789 did not stray from a desire to remain true to the facts, distinguishing itself from the specifically ideological dimension which – according to British writers – was destined to run riot across continental Europe. It was a purity of intent both made much of and largely surreptitious: over and above the frail protestations of interest in the dispassionate study of the events, there projected the cumbersome portrait of the unrepeatable diversity of British political culture – something that would soon, as a result of the exhausting armed confrontation with Napoleonic France, consolidate around the exceptional nature of Glorious Revolution of 1688.

5. The last revolutionary dispute

In 1818, on the initiative of her son Auguste and son-in-law, Duke Victor de Broglie, the Baroness Germaine de Staël's posthumous work *Considérations sur les principaux événements de la Révolution française* was published.[78] It immediately gained wide acceptance: it seemed to be more than simply an anthology of memories of life lived, wholly claiming the epochal experience of 1789 for French history and tradition. The *Considérations* have become a sort of foundational work, around which, it is customary to agree, the historiography of the French Revolution took shape. This circumstance was favoured by the fact that the work, coming out in the early years of a Restoration established in the context of a constitutional structure, set itself the task, after a quarter of a century and with enthusiasm still at a messianic level, of reproposing the idea of liberty inherent in the long-before revolutionary watershed.[79] For this reason, Staël would soon become the high priestess of studies on 1789: hers seemed the first attempt – compared with the many controversies that circulated during the events themselves – to cleanse the reading of the revolution of any critical intimation and to insist instead on its progressive nature. This was the context in which the contrast that she introduced between 1789 and 1793 was to be interpreted, where the former was the dawn of the new era of liberty and the latter signified only the descent into hell of the great expectations that followed on from the collapse of the *ancien régime*. However, should a reader go back to the *Considérations*, taking care to correlate the work to Staël's political life as a whole, it is clear that her last effort was not the result of a disillusioned look back at a revolution now faded into the past, but rather a summary of her beliefs in the aftermath of 1815, when painful rethinking was required with regard to her previous participation in French political life. In other words, Staël's unfinished pages retained a direct line with her previous writings and had a far more pronounced militant aspect than – with so much praise lavished on the historical aspect of her work – has often been credited.

It could hardly, after all, be otherwise: since the events of 1789 and thereafter, and then throughout the Napoleonic years, Staël had always been keen to dictate a sort of political line to the new France and in that regard, albeit with little success to show for it, she would never, not even in the years of the Restoration, have wanted to change her ways. She had, anyway, been an excellent witness and an ambitious interpreter of the whole story from the very beginning: daughter of Jacques Necker, the minister of Louis XVI who had summoned the Estates General, she had shared in the battle to restore the monarchy, following her father in both success and misfortune. At the Swedish embassy, where her husband was ambassador, she presided over a political-cultural salon where she attempted in vain to dictate the policy of a political transformation along English lines. The defeat suffered by the *monarchienne* group – a patron of their cause, Staël had looked on the faction with great sympathy – did not prevent her from maintaining a role in the political debate of the moment. Enthusiastic about the prospect of a new, monarchical and constitutional France, Staël continued to follow the revolution from close at hand and remained true to her own convictions even after the flight to Varennes. At the end of 1791, in the aftermath of the birth of the Legislative Assembly, she assisted in the rise of her lover of the moment, the Duke of Narbonne, who, at her suggestion, becoming Minister of War, wanted to declare war on Austria in order to relaunch the image, by then too politically tarnished, of Louis XVI.

In 1792, Staël obviously opposed the fall of the monarchy, and only swift flight to Switzerland allowed her to escape the September Massacres. But she never lost faith in the values of 1789, and in the period of the Terror itself, wrote *De l'influence des passions sur le bonheur des individus et des nations*, a book that shines through with denunciation of the Year II government's cold and arid violence. She also polemicized with émigrés, branding their feelings of nostalgia for the old order as sterile, when not pernicious.

For this reason, she was ready to return to Paris after Thermidor. Before reopening the salons of the rue du Bac, however, she published a booklet, *Refléxions sur la paix adressées à M. Pitt et aux Français*, where Staël suggested to Britain that the country abandon the émigrés to their fate and make peace with the Republic: renouncing the war would favour the triumph in France of those who, since 1789, had vainly pleaded the cause of moderation. On returning to Paris, she leant a hand to the political career of the man who had accompanied her in exile, Benjamin Constant, whose sincere faith she shared in a republic inspired by the values of 1789, the constitution of which could bring together all patriots, regardless of their previous ideas. Their own liaison, which became a romantic one during their Parisian stay, should have provided an example of how it was possible for those who believed in the values of 1789 to join together: not only had Constant previously applauded the birth of the Republic, but he had also accepted, if not justified, the Terror itself. Their political figures of reference, too, confirmed that differing sensibilities should be no object to establishing a point of contact in the centre, with Staël admiring the circle around Roederer, previously monarchic and Feuillant, while Constant was closer to the former republican and Girondine, Louvet. It was a political line – one that envisaged making extremists on both sides irrelevant – that forced them to put aside their liberalism when the Directory first launched a crackdown aimed at the monarchists and then the neo-Jacobins. For both, the risk that the Republic could once again lose itself in the tumult of factionalism outweighed individual freedom and this explains why Brumaire seemed to both the solution to the agonizing problem of a government torn apart by party struggles. However, she was to be greatly disillusioned by the First Consul, who rejected her proposals for reviving the idea of a constitutional republic. In the autumn of 1803, a decades-long exile began, as, separated from Constant, she returned to Switzerland, as well as travelling a great deal in Italy and Germany. She also made a long stay in England, from where she followed the convulsive final phases of Napoleon's fall and the return, through the means of a *Charte*, of the Bourbon dynasty. Only then, having returned to France, did she decide to put pen to paper with a work on the French Revolution, which took stock, in the aftermath of the return of the legitimate monarchy, of what that long period had signified and, above all, where it might still lead.[80]

It seems clear, then, that the work was not a historical reflection, but a reflection of a political nature on events that had recently occurred, one that therefore had close links with the works that, over the previous years, had been breathlessly trying to make a contribution to the meaning of 1789 and everything that followed. Judgement should therefore be reversed, with the *Considérations* removed from its place as the first historiographic work on 1789, to be seen rather as the last effort of a period where a number of writers had attempted to explain a swath of history that still seemed to leave its mark on the present moment.

The structure of the work itself suggests this shift in perspective, on the one hand yoking together the entire period 1789–1815, on the other, starting with the first developments of the revolution and closing with the hope that Restoration France may emulate British freedom. It develops, however, through the depiction of two contrasting figures: on the one side, Necker – the much loved father whose daughter praises his lucidity of analysis in relation to the various political situations that one after the other emerged; and on the other, Napoleon Bonaparte, described as the revelatory representative of the many authoritarian tendencies that France had experienced over the years. The decision to entrust the task of summarizing the whole of recent French history to these two particular figures also sounds like a sort of admission of responsibility. Unlike her father, who at the time of the radicalization of the political process had withdrawn into Swiss exile, from where he had regarded the developments of 1789 with intense alarm, the daughter had instead believed that the revolutionary movement was governable. Thus, she had first placed her hope in the constitutional monarchy and then in the Directorial Republic, and she had also taken a keen interest in Bonaparte's coup d'état.

The *Considérations* is thus a tribute to her father's foresight: while demonstrating generosity and dedication, to the extent of putting the good of France before the interests of the legitimate dynasty, he had always refused to believe that the constitutional monarchy and the republic, in the form they had taken through the constitutions of 1791 and 1795, could ensure the need for balance demonstrated by French society in the aftermath of 1789. In praising the work and ideas of her father, in other words, the daughter reveals the full range of her self-criticism, admitting the many mistakes she had made – mostly relating, however, to the Directory period, when she had chosen to side with the Republic and thus severed her destiny from that of her parent.

At that point, the definitive political separation from her father had taken place: just as Staël and Constant were attempting to gather together all the moderate, and even monarchist, circles around the idea of the Republic, Necker published a work with the generic title *De la Révolution française*. Here, all the criticism he had previously directed at the work of the Constituent Assembly was confirmed point by point, but with no concession of credit offered towards the post-Robespierrist period.[81] At the beginning of 1796, Necker had still not shifted from the position he had adopted when writing after the coming into force of the 1791 constitution, when he had predicted an inevitable disagreement between the executive and the legislative bodies and to a certain extent forecast the democraticist direction of the Terror. His reconstruction of the events, from the crisis of 1788 up to the days of Year IV, thus followed a very linear path: it was emphasized that, at the basis of the disasters following 1789, there lay only the presumption of the Constituent Assembly in rejecting the English model and venturing out into unknown territory, from where there was escape. Staël herself, on the other hand, had different ideas, accepting both the monarchist constitution of 1791 and then also the republican one of 1795: true though it was that father and daughter had both been monarchists, the former had followed them into defeat, while the latter had continued to believe that the cause of liberty remained a living spirit in French politics.

The two had also disagreed on another point: in the aftermath of Brumaire, Staël had placed a great deal of faith in the Consulate while Necker would go no further than a fleeting encounter in Switzerland with Bonaparte. In 1802, publishing a commentary on the text of the constitution of the Year VIII that followed the Brumaire watershed, he gave a detailed report on how the traditional aporia between the executive and legislative bodies had still found no solution and to what extent the new constitution favoured the rise of despotism – only foreshadowing the return, and under the wrong terms to boot, of the institution of monarchy.

Taken as a whole, the revolutionary period brought Staël, apparently always in the wrong, to make a great distinction between herself and her father: her heartfelt portrait of Necker, as it appears in the *Considérations*, has the tone of a regretful homage to a person misunderstood, not only by the whole of France but most of all by his own daughter. This explains why she made her father the authentic interpreter of 1789 – first presenting him as the architect of a turning point for liberty, since, only in France's interest, he had agreed to put an end to the old order in which he had made his career, hoping to establish a constitutional monarchy along English lines, where order and property replaced privilege as bastions of stability. Then, having described the reasons that led to his unjust exile, she involves her father in subsequent revolutionary events as one who understood from afar the direction in which the revolution was going and who tried in vain to suggest measures to set the mistaken course right. Unsurprisingly, he is regularly evoked for having fought equally against the Constituent Assembly and the Convention, against the Directory and Bonaparte, and for having always firmly indicated how the failure to resolve the constitutional problem was the cause of the loss of liberty. In this way, this use of her father's figure acquired a precise value: Necker, as Staël explicitly acknowledges, was the person who would certainly have accompanied France into liberty's promised land, had the serious and repeated inadequacies of the country's political class not forced him into exile, from where his words fell on deaf ears.

This belief, which comes up repeatedly in the *Considérations*, finds full expression when Necker is vaunted as the inspirer of the *Charte* graciously granted by Louis XVIII in 1814. It was an idea with no basis in reality, but it made it possible to close the circle of the entire revolutionary history, linking the Restoration to 1789 and reading the whole sequence of events as a tortuous process that yet concluded in terms that her father had had in mind since the convocation of the Estates General. In light of this circular reading of revolutionary events, the traditional contrast between 1789 and 1793 – which the *Considérations* would be the first to introduce into the historiographic panorama – turns out to a large extent to be the artificial construction of a host of implicated readers. More precisely, the text distinguishes between an ephemeral moment of freedom (in 1789) and a lengthy succession of errors, horrors and missed opportunities, where the revolutionary government and the Terror are just moments – terrible moments, of course, but sporadic – in a story that covers a much longer arc of time. Indeed, in this context, where 1789 ideally stretches a hand out to 1814, criticism gathers even more closely around the Post-Robespierrist season, when the continual conflict between the executive and the Councils had ended up convincing Staël, like many others, that Brumaire was an intervention in the name of stability rather than the return of despotism in military guise. In this way, however, she certainly did not limit itself, as traditionally indicated, to setting 1789 up in opposition to 1793: she perceived an irreconcilable contrast between the constitutional monarchy and the Republic, no longer distinguishing within the latter between its democratic and liberal aspects.

It was an acknowledgement of failure, of course, but in rethinking the significance of the whole Republican period there was also something more, because the thread of despotism, which ran from the Terror to Bonaparte, led Staël to greatly underestimate the period of the Directory in which she had initially believed. It is certainly no coincidence, after all, that the *Considérations* devotes little space to the period when the Year III constitution was concretely put into practice, relegating it to the role of a brief parenthesis between Year II and 1799. This decision, however, should be highlighted in terms of its polemical intent to attack those who had believed a liberal republic possible, without realizing that the expression was an oxymoron and that only in the framework of a (legitimate) constitutional monarchy would it have been possible to bring 1789's struggle for freedom to a conclusion.

Staël's *Considérations* also thus opens the season of the Directory's historiographical misfortunes: it was considered an inadequate and precarious political system, destined to finish with the triumph of authoritarianism – and, from this point of view, it should not be underestimated that her criticism of the implementation of the Year III constitution was also an implicit admission of guilt. This brought about a nascent dispute with Benjamin Constant, who had shared faith with his lover first in the Directorial Republic and then in the Consulate, but who, on the occasion of the Hundred Days, unlike Staël, had remained attracted by Napoleon's promises.[82] The fact that Constant had already, in the revolutionary years, offered a decisive contribution to the identity of French nineteenth-century liberalism, and had certainly been greatly influenced in the formulation of his ideas by Staël's suggestions, should not obscure the reality that his political career had been very different, not only at the beginning of the revolutionary events but also at the end of the Napoleonic period; in this context, too, Staël's work implicitly distanced itself from certain of her partner's choices.

Having dealt a blow to Constant's political path, criticism in the *Considérations* then swiftly moved on to assail the whole period governed by the Year III constitution, which had believed it possible to escape the turmoil of Robespierrism without tackling the profound truth of a monarchy that could not be eliminated from France's social and cultural scene. The target of Staël's polemic, in other words, became Republican political culture, both in the violent aspects of the Terror and in the only apparently moderate context of the Directory. This explains why her book, which was so very successful in the 1820s and which certainly made the new liberal generations aware of the values of 1789, met with dissent from many of her own generation. Those on the left saw her energetic defence of Necker as harking back to traditional criticism of the democratization process of the revolution; while the right perceived the return of the old monarchist dream of making short work of the revolution by importing a political model from across the Channel.[83]

Prominent among the latter is the work by Louis de Bonald who, very shortly after the appearance of the *Considérations*, published his *Observations sur l'ouvrage de Mme de Staël*.[84] It developed a resolute critique of her liberalism, embodied by her praise of Necker on the one hand and of British political virtues on the other. According to Bonald, the two things went together, given that, by praising her father's farsightedness, Baroness de Staël confirmed the need for the revision of the old constitution in 1788, and to legitimize, within the framework of the desired renewal, the reference to the English model. In this way, familial affection ended up coinciding with political aspiration, and Madame de Staël's posthumous work offered itself as a sort of breviary for all those who wanted to turn the *Charte* into an instrument to prevent the Restoration from becoming a simple return to the past. The polemic launched by Bonald, which only apparently took up de Maistre's traditionalism line by line, fell within a very different political context, becoming an instrument in the hands of French political extremists with regard to the need to limit as far as possible a constitution that would allow the old monarchy to return to the political scene and to demand a total liberalization of the regime resulting from the Restoration.

Jean-Charles Bailleul was also quickly into print with criticism of Staël's work, but this seemed to have less political impact.[85] A former member of the Convention, he had immediately glimpsed in her writings, and was very worried by, the clear intention to expunge the Republic from France's political tradition. He was keen to restore political honour to the Republic, which seemed, in those times of restoration, destined for oblivion. However, his desire to refute Staël's arguments led him into the same territory: despite not having been a supporter of Robespierre, and indeed having suffered personally during the Terror, he too made the Republican period a kind of inevitable consequence of 1789, entirely ignoring its various phases and their different political profiles. In his view, the resistance to change manifested by the privileged classes had been so strong that patriotism had in turn had to be increasingly aggressive in order to win out. In this standoff between an *ancien régime* past and a democratic future, where freedom and equality came about through the elimination of feudalism, Bailleul placed the birth of the republic – a sort of inevitable consequence of the unacceptable resistance shown by the forces of the old order. It was a perspective that also easily allowed him to dismiss the myth of Necker circulated by his daughter: to introduce – as Necker had wanted to do – a Chamber of Peers that would give the nobility a level of political satisfaction would only have meant, in the aftermath of 1789, delivering the revolution into the hands of its most ruthless foe.

In this light, from the political action of Mirabeau, who not by chance had broken away from the monarchists, to the radicalization of the political process initiated by the Girondins – where the border war against emigrant armies was also portrayed as a defence of the revolution from dangerous aggression – everything held together, with the Terror itself becoming an integral part of the revolutionary narrative. And yet, his desire to retrace the line of Staël's work, in order to carefully dismantle all her claims, ended up working against Bailleul, unable as he was to focus to any great extent on the period of the Directory, in which so much of his own belief had been placed. The result thus, in some ways, came across as contradictory: Bailleul, while still a living example of that republicanism which, during the years of the Year III constitution, had attempted to stabilize the new order within a context of liberty, found himself forced to dwell chiefly on the first revolutionary period. He ended up, therefore, concurring with Staël's ideas, and her great insistence on how the manner of its origin and the first stages of its development had had an irreversibly formational impact on the Republic.

Curiously, Bailleul's criticisms ended up lending credence to the idea that the clash was between the supporter of a 1789 which, despite a host of difficulties, continued to resurface, and one nostalgic for 1793, who exalted the work of the whole revolution, but retained a deep dedication to the cult of republican firmness and vigour embodied by the Terror. Thus, the confrontation was narrowed down to a strict contrast between 1789 and 1793, between a liberal world capable of rising from its ashes and a concealed republicanism, which the lack of freedom restrained within nostalgia and regret. It goes without saying that at the dawn of the shift towards romanticism – when, in France, the liberal generation, by making a historical object of the revolution, was able to place it at the centre of the 1820s cultural panorama – the advantage seemed to be all on the side of the supporters of 1789. However, the defeat of the republicans was even more profound: by accepting the confrontation with respect to 1793, which sacrificed everything in the following years, the period of democracy ended up being restricted to Year II alone.

2

Confronting France's revolutionary past, 1815–47

The 1820s were an important turning point in the historiography of the French Revolution: many of the actors of the revolution published their *Mémoires*, the political significance of which soon became clear as it encouraged the appearance of the first scholarly works, written by a young generation of historians who wished to distance themselves from their predecessors. Within the span of a few years, works by Thierry, Guizot, Mignet and finally Thiers came out in quick succession, all of them suggesting, notwithstanding their different viewpoints, that the French Revolution had been not so much the random outcome of circumstances, as the result of a historical process spanning several centuries, which had led, in time, to the gradual emancipation of the Third Estate, the history of which now came to be identified with that of the whole nation. These historians therefore saw the revolution of 1830 and the liberal monarchy of Louis Philippe d'Orleans (1830–48) as the conclusion of a path that had begun almost half a century earlier, which put the final seal on the alliance between the French Crown and its people. Their positions were at once disputed by those with republican ideals, mindful as they were that the French Revolution had encouraged demands for social and political renewal soon to appear under the guise of democracy. This position – popularized by, among others, Buonarroti and Laponneraye – entailed the glorification of Robespierre, whose messianic features were now being portrayed by Buchez and Roux in their monumental history of the Revolution written in the early 1830s. A decade later, the poet Lamartine would demolish such arguments, through a re-appraisal of the positions of the republican circles that had opposed Robespierre. However, the most lucid critique of the rehabilitation of Robespierre and the Terror came from England, through the work of Thomas Carlyle, whose deep influence on historiography in English would focus on the denunciation of the frightful contradiction of a revolutionary movement which, having sprung in the name of liberty, would soon drown in the blood of the guillotine.

1. A political history of the French Restoration

After the last adventure of the Hundred Days and the definitive fall of the Napoleonic star, it seemed that France, with the *Charte* generously granted by Louis XVIII, had returned to the first period of the revolution, when the Constituent Assembly had really believed it was ending the regenerative surge of 1789 through a renewed agreement between sovereign and people. The monarchist dream of a France that took its British neighbour as a political model seemed, after the violence of the Republican and Empire periods, about to become reality, albeit one seriously delayed.[1] This was what Staël's *Considérations* suggested: but this was also indicated by the French political class at the beginning of the Restoration – a class where men were found who, despite different outlooks that had once been in conflict with one another, had decided, often for lack of anything better, to come to agreement on the hypothesis of a political system characterized by the safeguard of a system of liberty. It was a curious experiment, which linked back to the experience of the first revolutionary period without officially admitting it by means of the odd stratagem of an octroyed constitution. The participants included men of all previous seasons: Feuillants and Jacobins, Republicans and Bonapartists, Moderates and Radicals, they all took the opportunity to take part in the political game, finding themselves elbow to elbow in resistance against the extremists – the latter instead eager to restrict as far as possible the exercise of freedom made possible by the constitution. And yet, for the most part, the members of the faction that is usually, by mere convention, defined as liberal, consisted not so much of men of the first revolutionary period, as those who, more generically, and regardless of their actual attitude towards the revolution, had realized in 1789 that the *ancien régime* was no longer a recoverable political system.[2]

A perfect example in this regard is offered by René de Chateaubriand, who in the early years of the Restoration returned to a political arena where his presence had in the past been fairly desultory. At the time of the outbreak of the revolution, the young nobleman from Brittany had in fact preferred to remain aloof without, however, opposing the new direction the country was taking. He then decided, in 1791, to travel to the New World, in search of a freedom that he thought he would not be able to find in France. He returned home in the early months of 1792 and soon fled the process of democratization taking place there in order to rush to enlist in the army of émigrés in Koblenz. However, a wound sustained in an exchange of fire allowed him to retire from the enterprise at an early stage. He found refuge in England, where, in 1797, he published *Essai sur les revolutions*,[3] in which the ancient and modern world were brought together in the context of a carefully organized repetition of events, with the developments of 1789 assigned the original key role as an epigone of the republics of the classical age.[4]

As for many other aristocrats in exile, Chateaubriand's return to France took place after Brumaire and in the early nineteenth century his approval of the Bonapartist course would go hand in hand with the decision to offer a truly cultural contribution to the new order. In 1802, at the same time as the Concordat signed by the First Consul, Chateubriand brought out *Le génie du Christianisme*, where, in line with the romantic canon already proposed with *Atala* and in contrast to the spirit of the eighteenth century, he reiterated the profound part played by Catholicism in the French identity, while indirectly confirming the complete faith he placed in the work of social and cultural remodelling carried out by Bonaparte.[5] The assassination of the Duke of Enghien, however, interrupted the writer's idyllic relationship with the new Napoleonic order – so much so that, in 1811, although elected to the Académie Française, he could not take his place due to an explicit prohibition by government authorities and had to wait in this regard until the return of the Bourbons.

The Restoration saw him become one of its most prestigious figures and until 1820, before falling prey to reactionarism, he attempted to make a contribution to the new framework of moderate freedom through his journalism, financed by Louis XVIII himself.[6] He sought a balance – something considered by most people to be impossible at the time – between the historical identity of the French nation and liberalism, between the traditional liberties of class and octroyed constitutionalism, between the Crown and the assemblies, between France and Britain, between the national interest and the universalistic aspirations of Catholicism. His political outlook, yoked to the romantic model widely deployed in his literary writings, made Chateaubriand the true reference point for the new liberal generation: many believed they could place their faith in his example, where romantic sensibility was the keystone that supported a rediscovery of the deep roots of French identity. It was on those lines, it seemed, that the construction of a cultural model for France could begin, now that the country, after a quarter of a century, was emerging from the tumultuous consequences of 1789.

In this context, the French Revolution was no less of a problem: those who had wanted it, and experienced it, like those who had violently opposed it, sustained its absolute estrangement from the country's past. For decades, they had insisted on its contradistinction in relation to the many centuries that had gone before, and this was not by chance. For the revolutionaries, history had been an ambiguous discipline and for this reason not a very popular one. In their eyes, to cast your gaze over the French past meant looking back at a sequence of periods of slavery that lasted centuries. There is nothing strange in the fact, therefore, that, in the aftermath of 1789, admiring references to history experienced a sudden decline: the distant past seemed no longer to offer themes that could be applied to the new political-ideological framework, there were no models to proudly return to, there were not even any predictions of the revolution that had so suddenly given freedom back to the French. On the opposing side, after all, the counter-revolutionaries had deployed the study of history as a basis for the good reasons to be put forward regarding the exogenous nature of 1789 with respect to the social fabric of France. In their opinion, the levelling-out authoritarian behaviour of the revolutionaries was tearing apart a centuries-old process that had made French society the particular organism that it was and that no rationalizing intent could have made conform to the Enlightenment spirit of the eighteenth century.[7]

Counter-revolutionary domination in the historical field thus posed a serious problem for the new generation that appeared on the scene in the early years of the Restoration: called upon to endow France with a concrete liberal perspective, it believed it could break out of that impasse by proposing history as the instrument that would make it possible to establish the French identity, while at the same time it could also take stock of the recent revolutionary past. In other words, 1789 and its dramatic consequences had to abandon the agitated terrain of political diatribe and make a resolute entry into the past, shedding its more sulphurous aspects in order to allow a more comprehensive effort to read the French identity. The task was a difficult one in certain respects, because it was a question of putting aside what, in the camp favourably disposed towards 1789, had been repeatedly put forward as a supporting element in a polemical political discourse in order to develop yet one more – one that was in a close line of continuity with the other, but also made it possible to withdraw from the reactionary world its monopoly on the use of history.

The opportunity was offered by the various controversies that had gathered around the recent past, and in this circumstance involuntary aid to the young liberal movement came from the arguments from the reactionary side, exemplified by the harsh criticism mentioned earlier that Bonald had dealt out to Staël's posthumous work. Maistre's colleague and emulator had insisted on the inconsistency of her words when they indicated a sort of continuity between 1789 and France's eighteenth-century past, while at the same time reaffirming the completely original character of the revolution with respect to the continuity that the *ancien régime* had been able to guarantee to French society. Now, Staël's actual words – which certainly had no intention of introducing a new reading of the meaning of 1789 and limited themselves to pointing out how this could find more than one precedent in the political affairs of the eighteenth century – came in useful for a predatory and partisan reading from the new generation of Romantics, as they took the extraordinary opportunity to reread, with a backward-looking procedure as unscrupulous as it is fascinating, the possibility of giving a completely new meaning to the nation's recent past. In fact, there were certain arguments in Staël's writings that, placed in a broader perspective, made it possible to see 1789 as a particular moment that events had been leading up to for centuries, rather than restricting it to the unacceptable semblance of a meteorite plunging suddenly down into the old order's peaceful social development. In Staël's work, it was possible to read (and greatly expand upon) the quest for liberty in France as a long-standing one. Certainly, the devastating force that accompanied it in 1789 was something wholly new, but this was a vehemence that came only after centuries of profound stimulus had been working in that direction. For this precise reason, Staël's writings were greatly encouraging in terms of a reading of the French Revolution that made it sound inevitable and at the same time very widespread. The sudden explosion of collective madness in the context of an icy rationalism melted into the thrilling stages of the final transitional moment of a centuries-long search for freedom. Here, the eighteenth century lost every trait of exceptional extraneousness with regard to the history of France, returning – as Victor Cousin noted in those years[8] – to stand as one of the many periods that, since the sun had set on the Middle Ages, had led to the successful affirmation of modernity. In this context, where the problem of the meaning of 1789 within French history deeply stirred the political-cultural commitment of the new generation of the 1820s, the great French historiography of the early nineteenth century found its first impulse.

The basis was provided by the writings of Augustin Thierry, who, starting in 1817, published a series of articles in certain journals of the time which were then, between 1827 and 1828, collected in the *Lettres sur l'histoire de France*.[9] Protesting against the tendency of a large part of the eighteenth century to look only forward, turning away from memories of backwardness and despotism, he urged a radical review of France's past, going back to the ancient Celtic world to unearth a tradition of liberty that *ancien régime* authoritarianism – which revolutionary voices had so often attacked – had so successfully managed to obscure. There began, in the wake of the romantic sensibility exemplified by Chateaubriand's literary work, a quest back through time – one which would make it possible to portray French history no longer as the feeding ground for the egotism of the old order's privileged classes, but rather the context in which to reconstruct a history of national freedom. It was a framework with no reassuring premises: the violence of the past was clear in Thierry's mind, characterized as a war of conquest, destined to break up the social world into winners and losers, oppressors and oppressed.[10] This picture, admirably outlined in 1825 in his *Histoire de la conquête de l'Angleterre par ler normands*, also supported his reconstruction of French history, where the conflict between the Romanized Gauls and the Franks seemed to him to initiate a history of violence and abuse of power – with the disturbing mosaic of the Napoleonic period constituting only the newest piece.[11] Nonetheless, to rebalance this vision of history in the context of dramatic social contrast, there was the belief that this conflict, destined as it was to forge a variety of groups and subjects, was for this reason a factor of progress. This belief was supported by a strong sense of nationalism, which inspired him to see in the great collective movements both an instrument of liberation and at the same time a recomposition of social contexts. This gave rise to his intention to task the writing of history with the responsibility of restoring a sense and a line of continuity to a centuries-old narrative that the French example would otherwise have devalued as ferocious examples of violence.

This was the terrain on which his encounter took place with the contents of Staël's posthumous writings. He expanded dramatically upon the latter, transforming a centuries-old era of egotism and privilege into a world where examples of resistance to despotism had always been present.[12] The rediscovery of local freedoms and municipal prerogatives, the praise bestowed upon Jacques Bonhomme and the many signs of collective resistance that had never entirely been lacking in French history formed a reading aimed at rebalancing a history which had been painted as one of simple oppression. It also became above all the occasion to demonstrate that the rejection of despotism – something the history of the victors (also adopted by the revolutionaries) had wisely erased from the collective memory – had finally returned to galvanize the political destiny of the nation. The past of violence and abuse was thus absorbed into a prospect of liberty and in this context the Third Estate, for too long making its sudden appearance on the scene only in the summer of 1789, returned to invigorate French social matters, assuming a role in this regard that the glorified groups of privilege had never occupied.

In this way, history merged with constitutional belief and Thierry's work, in which he distanced himself equally from both revolutionary rationalism and counter-revolutionary pastism, provided the liberal option with the assurance of a historical confirmation that until then had always been lacking. The strength of his proposition lay in that very ability to call upon the distant past as an instrument of political struggle for the present and as an auspice for the future: historical method became political strategy and made it possible to solve the dilemma of 1789 by portraying it as the culmination of a process of liberation from the chains of despotism, freeing it from the oppressive grip of counter-revolutionary polemics.

This was not a completely new idea: in the revolutionary years there were plenty of voices, especially in the provinces, which sought to transform the Celtic past into a reliable antecedent to contrast the feudalism transplanted into Roman Gaul by the invasion of the Franks. However, those attempts soon broke apart under the impact of the events of 1793, when the so-called federalist revolt forced a return to present times and to expunge any reference to an antiquity whose otherness, in relation to French unity, seemed to indicate it sought to subvert the indivisibility of the general will. Now, however, quite apart from the extraordinarily evocative power of his pen, it was an easy matter for Thierry to demonstrate that past of diversity and otherness had formed the backbone of the Third Estate. Only its triumph in 1789 had made it possible for the latter to form itself into a nation and to gather together into its own organism the other, quantitatively miniscule, parts of the society of the old order.[13]

His ideas thus clashed violently with the mellow portrayal of the *ancien régime* as a place of orderly social interaction that remained in circulation throughout the years of the Restoration. Against this eulogy for bygone times, Thierry evoked instead a past of great transformations, barely controlled by despotism, before the Third Estate found the strength to turn itself into a nation. His exaltation of history thus became a topic of polemical confrontation with those who had insisted on the past as a means to encourage the return to the peaceful times of the old order. His contribution to placing his political opponents of the moment in serious difficulty was decisive: history, until then the trump card of those who contested the abstractness of 1789, became, thanks to Thierry's writings, concrete proof of the plausibility of the liberal outlook. This process of reappropriation of the past constituted a decisive outcome in relation to the reactionary movement, although the latter would nevertheless continue to unsettle France's political modernity.

Problems, however, came hard on the heels of this process: 1789's return to the role of watershed in the nation's social development also involved reflection on what had immediately followed the birth of the nation and the nightmare of 1793 also – it could hardly have been otherwise – returned to disturb Thierry's writings. He was careful to distinguish the period of freedom from that of the Terror and he emphasized the moment of the Constituent Assembly with respect to that of the other assemblies: in short, he carried over to his own work the distinctions that Staël had tersely accomplished in this regard. But further than this he could not go: the Terror remained a self-destructive process from which nothing could be saved and 1793 a sort of excrescence on the healthy body of a nation that only wished to establish a framework of liberty in compliance with the law. In other words, the era inaugurated by the Republic was an attack on the newly achieved unity of the French people and therefore a violent interruption of the liberation process. The result for the young nation, with a sort of ricochet effect, was to have to endure the serious consequences of Napoleonic authoritarianism.

In a scenario of this kind, it is easy to understand why, during the 1830s, despite having greeted the July Revolution as representing the complete fulfilment of what 1789 had only hinted at, Thierry returned to the problem of the Third Estate, this time in a systematic way. The republican protest that followed the days of July 1830 and the state of deep socio-political tension that always accompanied the years of the Orleanist monarchy mounted a dramatic challenge to his progressive and unitary idea of the historical process. Not surprisingly, the revolution of 1848, where the lack of consistency in the unity of the French people was revealed, induced him to look worriedly at a social world in whose national homogeneity he had too emphatically believed.

In this, his political – and at the same time cultural – trajectory was very similar to that of François Guizot, who appeared on the French scene in the early years of the Restoration, when, from his chair at the Collège de France, he made historical reconstruction an instrument for the militant expression of his own liberalism. Speaking out with reference to the dramatic political situation of 1820, when the first fragile period of freedom ensured by the constitution of 1814 seemed to be placed in doubt by the vigorous return of the extremists, Guizot published a highly successful work,[14] in which the nation's past was deployed to make clear allusion to the tensions of the present. The events of the moment, which showed how the non-acceptance of 1789 still weighed heavily on French liberty, prompted him to go back to the nation's distant past, rereading the eighteenth-century controversy concerning the origins of France in terms of a violent confrontation between two peoples that, for centuries at a time, had been distinct and opposed.[15]

Inverting the words of Boulanvilliers, he appropriated those of Sieyes, in order to recall that the struggle for freedom had found an epochal – and for this reason violent – moment of transition in 1789, when the Third Estate, heir to the peoples of Roman Gaul, had settled accounts with an aristocracy that claimed direct descent from the conquering Franks. The revolutionary events thus seemed to bear witness to a violent, conflict-ridden past, testified to by the clashes that soon took place following the meeting of the representatives of the three orders in the national assembly of 1789. In this way, Guizot could portray the revolution as the final act of a narrative that had lasted centuries and demonstrate how the subversion of the *ancien régime*, rather than something imposed from the heights of eighteenth-century rationalism, was simply the conclusion of a clear historical process.

By launching his successful course of lessons at the Collège de France – which, not coincidentally, cost him the temporary suspension of his professorship – he was thus able to recollocate the revolution in history and make of the latter an instrument for legitimizing the demand for representative institutions in nineteenth-century France.[16] His decision to link 1789 to the extraordinary attempt to finally achieve, after centuries of fragmentation, a cohesive social order, had multiple points of contact with the positions concurrently expressed by Thierry: the conception of history as a sequence of violent social antagonisms; the certainty that a French nation came into existence only thanks to the crucial events of 1789; an interest in the British political model, which since 1688 seemed to have found an extraordinary equilibrium between the needs of the various subjects present on the scene; the auspices for a liberalism that would swiftly shed its subversive character with the definitive establishment of representative legislation. All these ideas united the two in the context of a quest for progress, albeit one that was extremely prudent where popular sovereignty was concerned.

Rejection of revolutionary tendencies and the open denunciation of Rousseau's political discourse –which led Guizot to adopt the approach suggested by Staël – were the reason why, in his political ideas, the example he sought came from across the Channel.[17] In England, the disaster of 1640 had been subsumed in 1688, allowing its society to maintain its national past while at the same time perfecting a system of freedom. In France, on the other hand, 1789's epochal moment of transition had been polluted by the demands of the patriots that the past be cancelled, as if this was a necessary step in achieving victory over feudalism and absolutism.

Hence, as Thierry indicated at the same time, the lack of any point of reference in the new political culture and the rapid authoritarian tendency of a political process that had been initiated in the name of freedom. It was not, of course, a stale revival of monarchical discourse and even less a lingering nostalgia for Necker's ideas that suggested this interest in England's 1688, but rather the worry that the unsolved problem of 1789, in the form it took until the years of the Restoration, imposed other points of reference. Thus, if Guizot's attention to the history of England always prevailed over his focus on national events, it remains true that the disastrous results of 1789 were at the centre of his concerns and prompted the construction of a model of social development that would release France from the extraordinary conflict that had tormented it for so long into the embrace of a fully representative political society.

It was this context that gave rise to Guizot's strenuous defence of a *Charte*, which appeared to him the only instrument that could strengthen the link between the Crown and the parliamentary system and channel the tensions within French society into a logic of orderly progress. The turning point of 1830 apparently proved Guizot right and he was at once ready to take over the leadership of the country under the banner of Louis Philippe's new monarchy. Moreover, the glorious days of the month of July, marked by the sudden return to the scene of the veteran Lafayette, were to suggest that France was, as in 1789, once again the leader of European renewal, drawing ever closer to that British model which appeared to Guizot as the only point of comparison. The Third Estate now seemed to be fully a nation and in that precise context it was possible to identify a *juste milieu* around which to build a prudently inclusive society, its moderate culture smoothing out the excess of acrimony that the revolution of 1830 and the republican insurgencies of the following years seemed to predict.

For this reason, although the social terrain of France proved prone to landslides, the revolution of 1848, which demonstrated all the fragility of Guizot's political model and re-emphasized France's irremediable otherness with respect to Britain, still shocked and embittered him, prompting a London exile from which he thundered against democracy and the perverse outcome of the revolutionary myth in the national consciousness. In this way, Guizot's distrust of exalting 1789 in any way was reinforced, once again in line with Thierry: while it certainly remained an epochal moment in the history of civilization in France and (continental) Europe, it had also infected the connective tissue of the new nation with the poison of a destructive desire in relation to the collective past – a poison that had since then prevented the past and present of French society from being held together and had, as a result, also polluted its future.

Even after 1848, for Thierry as for Guizot, there remained the refuge of history, envisaged as the only antidote to exaggerated rationalistic declamation and to the insurrectional eructations of a large part of the French world. And, in retrospect, this was the decisive contribution that the two made to the study of the revolution, even though neither ever made a detailed analysis of the subject. Both, however, returned 1789 to its time and its national context, making it the culmination of a long-lived struggle in the – never completely fulfilled – quest for liberty. Their battle was a victorious one, though by no means decisive, with respect to the conservative creed that had placed all its hopes on history in order to dismiss 1789 as a phenomenon extraneous to French tradition.

Not surprisingly, Bonald had glimpsed the extent of the danger in their work with regard to the equilibrium of a reactionary interpretation of 1789, when, in his criticism of Staël's book, he said he was concerned that history could also be useful to supporters of the revolution. And even more brilliantly, in the same years Maistre mentioned the same dangerous tendency, pointing out that the new liberal spirit was looking for precedents for the revolution in a French past that, in relation to the present, was as plausibly relevant as the Trojan War. And of course, the extremists looked to these ingenious counter-revolutionary writers when, responding to the new slogans of liberalism, they refused to find in the past any foretaste of the violence that followed 1789. In 1820, in an interesting work in prompt response to Guizot, a convinced pastist, hiding behind the initials PLB, challenged his opponents on their own ground.[18] He protested against the reconstruction of a centuries-old history of violence between conquerors and vanquished, suggesting instead that the French identity was founded on a tradition of feudality. This would, in the context of both privilege and inequality, yet welcomed with serenity by all, have successfully provided the basis for a harmonious social order – one that the humblest classes especially would have accepted with enthusiasm.

This perspective, which informed a large part of reactionary writing in the decades to come, was destined to drag with it pastism's traditional positions: Masonic conspiracy, the perverse action of the Enlightenment, the spirit of insubordination aroused by philosophy, the wholly authoritarian presumption of inflicting violence upon a people deeply convinced of the traditional values. And to a certain extent it ended up prevailing even against those who, while regarding liberalism's robust return with great suspicion, nevertheless were so completely subordinate towards the Crown as not to forget that the *Charte*, the target of much counter-revolutionary censure, was in any case something freely adopted by Louis XVIII and should therefore always and in all circumstances be respected precisely for this reason.

These legitimist positions were summed up perfectly by Lacretelle, a writer whom we have seen making history his speciality in the years of the Empire, but who – his monarchical vocation revived by the Restoration – was soon looking back at the revolution. At the very beginning of the 1820s, shaken by the revolution's strong re-emergence in southern Europe, he undertook a history of the Constituent Assembly to replace Rabaut's *Précis* from long before, a work he had previously continued but to which he had never considered it opportune to return. Now, motivated by the necessity to criticize the work of the first revolutionary assembly, he underlined that many of the evils that still tormented France at that moment were derived from the decisions which that particular body had made. Lacretelle was to repropose this critical belittling of 1789 shortly thereafter, this time in another work dedicated entirely to the revolutionary period,[19] and then bring it to perfection many years later, in the mid-1840s, with a piece dedicated to the Napoleonic era.[20] Overall, they were not works of great originality: aiming to translate the political proposal put forward with regard to the Crown into historical terms, they thus possessed all the limits of an approach displaying complete subordination to the discourse of the regime whose cause they were intended to serve.

For this reason, openly counter-revolutionary polemic showed itself to be a much deeper proposition, free as it was from any direct compliance with the monarchy, especially when, in the aftermath of the 1830 revolution, this assumed a liberal identity. It went on to build a reactionary ideological universe that was destined to play a significant part in nineteenth-century society. Rather than the writing of historians, soon forced on to the defensive as they found their territory invaded by the young liberal generation, the supporters of 1789 had far more to fear from the deepest feelings of a society that was still in many ways very traditional. Its tenacity in the face of the liberal watershed of 1830, depriving it of any dynastic reference, was indirect confirmation of this.

2. The force of things

During the 1820s, traditionalism never abandoned its commitment to erasing the revolution from France's past, but it would no longer be able to regain that position of advantage in historical terms that it had managed to acquire between 1789 and 1815. In fact, it was the beginning of a long period of submission for reactionary thinkers faced with an approach to the revolution which, during the Restoration, made it its aim to distinguish the era of liberty from the period of the Terror, and indicated in the supporters of the latter a paltry minority of those who had greeted the 1789 watershed with enthusiasm. An example among those still present on the political scene was provided by Jean Denis Lanjuinais, a member of the Chamber of Peers, but, at the time of the great revolution, first in the Constituent Assembly and then the National Convention. In the aftermath of 1815, however, he denied his loyalty to the Republic and described his Girondist political past as a simple tactical device, given that his authentic position had always been that of a constitutional monarchist.[21] This was demonstrated, he said, by the fact that he had been a bitter adversary of the Montagnards and the Terror, that he had shown himself to be – after suffering dramatic persecution and having been reinstated as a public representative – constantly in opposition to the liberticidal policy of the Directory and that he had, conveniently hiding an initial support for Bonapartism, been an opponent of Napoleonic despotism. His battle in favour of liberty at the time of the Restoration – when it was best forgotten that Lanjuinais had actually, at the time of Napoleon's sudden return from Elba, presided over the so-called Chamber of the Hundred Days – made him the living personification of how the new generation of the 1820s saw the link between past and present. Hostile to the conservative swing of 1820, Lanjuinais, in his parliamentary allegiance, would always cling firmly to the line of continuity between 1789 and 1814 on which the young liberal movement intended to build its political identity.[22]

In those same years, the many volumes of the *Collection des mémoires* took on the task of illustrating to readers how the political path that Lanjuinais had been lucky enough to follow in its entirety would have been shared by many other revolutionaries, had not the violence of the political struggle and the appalling season of terror intervened to crush their intentions.[23] It was not only the case of Bailly, the mayor of Paris ready to resign from his post as soon as the political process had let moderation fall by the wayside and, not coincidentally, put to death during the Terror,[24] that offered enlightenment with regard to the monarchical and liberal identity of the revolution: presenting the memoirs of the Girondin Louvet, for example, the editors of the initiative took it upon themselves to present him in the unlikely guise of a secret supporter of the king, with only the fear of being assassinated by his opponents provoking his repeated proclamations of republicanism.[25] The operation was transparent: it was a question of diverting the great revolutionary river back along the course of its constitutional and monarchical channel, leaving the republican and terrorist current to end up as the work of just a few – a very few, in fact – who had therefore constituted only an infectious excrescence on the otherwise healthy body of the political society that emerged from 1789.

In this context, where the first phase of the revolution prevailed in such a significant way over 1793 to the point of being able to rehabilitate a considerable number of the men who were, however, also active on the republican scene, the first historiographic reconstructions that took advantage of the controversy were destined to take shape, flourishing around Staël's posthumous work. Between 1823 and 1830, Adolphe Thiers published his weighty *Histoire de la Révolution française* in ten volumes,[26] which was joined, in 1824, by a slighter volume, the *Histoire de la Révolution française depuis 1789 jusqu'en 1814* by François Mignet.[27] The two men, both Provençals, were friends and politically close in their opinions, engaged throughout the 1820s in journalism that opposed the reactionary direction the Crown was taking. Their respective works, which aimed to legitimize ideas in favour of liberalism, were thus intended to distance them from the passions still present among the survivors of those events, while at the same time make use of them as a point of support to construct a political proposition that sanctioned the irreversibility of France after 1789.[28]

Like any radically innovative initiative, this sounds like an apparently simple operation: it was a question of keeping the lesson of Staël's posthumous writings in mind, while nonetheless combining them with the many objections raised in their regard by the former Convention member Jean-Charles Bailleul in order to settle accounts with the arguments of the reactionary faction, a la Bonald. It would then be possible to outline, within the framework of a liberal resolution, a reconstruction of events where the contraposition between 1789 and 1793 was finally elided. In other words, Mignet and Thiers, with the differences that will be shown further on, started their reconstructions strong in the conviction that 1789 should remain unmatched as a revolutionary event and the founding act of modern France. Precisely because of its nature as a decisive moment of transition on the path to modernity, it could not even be ruined by the chaotic descent into horror that followed the period of freedom. Bailleul, with his harsh criticism of Staël,[29] came in useful therefore in terms of establishing a distance from the latter when she vainly attempted to portray the revolution as a dream shattered all too quickly. Both Mignet and Thiers thus proposed to reconcile two positions that were forever poles apart, the contrasting nature of which the events of the revolution had only served to exacerbate. The circumstances of the 1820s, however, made it possible to bring these natures together under one banner in order to defend the new order from the aggressive re-emergence of pastism.

As an operation it was a somewhat acrobatic one: holding together monarchists and republicans, liberals and democrats, in defence of the common value of 1789 from the sinister shadow of reaction. But it was an experiment that could be attempted in historiographical terms precisely because, as we have seen, when Bailleul launched his critical salvo against Staël's posthumous work, he had made more than one mistake in the credit he had given to the liberal period. Essentially, he failed to make the birth of the Republic a period that was something quite new compared to that of the constitutional monarchy. Indeed, by accepting a sort of continuity of the revolutionary project, rather than insisting on the fracture between a 'before' the monarchy and an 'after', Bailleul had unwittingly offered the two young liberals a great deal of grist to their mill: it became simple for them – in line with the rediscovery of liberty that was properly of the Restoration period – to conclude that the revolution was a watershed that had been prepared for some time and was unavoidable. Nothing could oppose it, and only the resistance of the most backward sectors of French society had forced it to the extremes of violence that had resulted in the dramatic death of Louis XVI.

In other words, Bailleul's defence of 1793 against Staël's reiterated accusations became, for Mignet as for Thiers, an unrepeatable opportunity to transport the whole democratic movement into the great revolutionary concourse and to demonstrate that, if republicanism had acquired consensus starting from 1791, this success was the result of the foolish aversion of a cowardly and pernicious aristocracy, which had generated the monster of the Terror with its own violent resistance to change. Democracy, in other words, was the direction taken by the revolution thanks to the privileged classes, who had tried to stand in opposition to the onsurge of freedom. The Terror that followed, for so long uncontainable, notwithstanding the horrors it had produced, had nevertheless come in handy for the revolution in terms of tackling the formidable challenges it had to face.[30]

It was, in this context, Mignet who indicated the line to be followed. His small book, partly because of its modest size, was suited to the fostering of a clarifying schematism. This would soon earn him the accusation of reconstructing everything in the light of historical fatalism – an insistent determinism, in other words, according to which the events of 1789 were the logical consequence of a multiplicity of premises all destined to produce that specific result. Mignet had already demonstrated his way of reading history, where the continuous intertwining of cause and effect unfolded under the auspices of an irreversible tendency towards human progress: in 1821, writing about feudalism, he had described this institution – one that had always symbolized the *ancien régime* and absolute monarchy – as a necessary stage on the path to social improvement.[31] Echoing the political-cultural testament of Condorcet, he would always define his own public commitment in terms of history's civilizing function.

In the years immediately following, Mignet began to give free history courses to the members of a Parisian bourgeoisie who eyed the authoritarian direction that the Villèle ministry was taking with great suspicion. Between 1822 and 1823, he achieved great success with some lessons where, recalling the events of the Catholic League, it was easy for the public to see the connection with the reactionary position held at the time by Catholic extremists. The year after, he moved on to deal with the history of Britain, introducing a clear analogy between the Stuart Restoration and that of the Bourbons in order to conclude that the inadequacies of the present time, very similar to those of 1660, would inevitably lead to a move towards liberalism, always along the lines indicated by England in 1688.

On the basis of these premises, it should not be surprising that his writings dedicated at the same time to 1789 were dominated by an overt determinism, which allowed Mignet to present the revolution as the inevitable conclusion of a historical and social process foreshadowed throughout the whole of the eighteenth century.[32] The consequences of such a lapidary proposition were not insignificant: the decision to describe 1789 as the natural outcome of French social progress meant that revolution was no longer the exceptional and extraordinary moment that had hitherto featured in the writings of both its admirers and its detractors. It now took on the guise of an event where inevitability went hand in hand with normality. There was therefore no doubt that the revolution had been prepared for some time and that the convocation of the Estates General, together with the decision to establish a national assembly, met the concrete social needs of a broad collective front, one with expectations that the old order was incapable of fulfilling. From this point of view, 1789 lost all its destructive aspects and appeared in a more reassuring form as the completion of a transformation process that had been underway for a long period.

The liberal divergence of 1789 was therefore hailed as the dawn of the new France, the moment in which a world that had become too restrictive fell away to make room for a statehood in line with the profound needs of the new French society. It remained to be explained why a phenomenon so profound, and apparently so widely expected and desired, degenerated so quickly into liberticidal violence. Mignet had no doubts in this regard, indicating in the privileged classes, and in their insensate and gratuitous resistance to change, the rapid transformation from a first revolution – monarchical and liberal – to a second, republican and democratic, which soon degenerated into the Terror. This reading allowed him to make a distinction between a necessary revolution, 1789, and another that was a mere consequence of the sudden difficulties of the middle classes in the face of the aristocracy's aggressive response. In this way, 1793 found a logic and, at the same time, an explanation: it grew out of the appeal of the middle classes to the people, so that the old order could be defeated. It became violent because the revolutionary process itself forced it to take that form, where the clash between old and new took place in street fighting and at the same time on the frontiers.

On the one hand, the flight to Varennes had favoured the return to the streets of a people who had already been predominant at the time of the Bastille – to which the Constituent Assembly, however, had responded with the shootings on the Champ de Mars. On the other hand, the threat of the émigrés in Koblenz had suggested a military solution, and around this the weight of the popular masses had inevitably grown in the revolutionary process. The uprising in the streets of 10 August 1792, and the Republic, had been the inevitable consequences of a political process that the resistance of the *ancien régime*, partly in the form of frontier aggression, had transformed from peaceful and conciliatory into violent and transgressive. Nonetheless, the Terror, notwithstanding the obvious ferocity with which it had been conducted, had had an important function: with the brute force of popular involvement, it had swept away the ancient vestiges of the past, making the ruins of the old society the basis for the reorganization that was the principal virtue of the Napoleonic era.

In this way, according to Mignet, the books could be balanced and 1814, seen as a return to a constitutional context that France had only experienced for a short period at the start of the revolutionary process, constituted a new beginning. It deserved defending and safeguarding from the political pastism of the ministries of the 1820s, which in turn seemed a disturbing revival of the resistance shown at the time by the privileged classes to the events of 1789. The difference, which shone through the whole significance of Mignet's discourse, was in the learning experience that the most educated part of French society had, in the meantime, undergone, at the cost of incalculable pain: it was not possible to rely on the popular masses, whose ignorance prevented them from participating responsibly in the political process and who too often fell prey to passionate impulse and violent externalization. For this reason, it was necessary for the middle classes to return to the scene as central figures, emulating 1789 without repeating its mistakes. And it was therefore necessary that every revolution, should the force of things drag events in that direction, had the most responsible part of society involved in guiding the political process, with popular intervention greatly limited, never forgetting to act on behalf of the general interest and doing everything accordingly to ensure that the revolution came to a prompt and positive conclusion. Hence the warning for the future: through this reconstruction of the revolutionary and Napoleonic years, it was necessary for the French middle class to take charge of its own history once again and believe in its ability to be the sole leader – even though a period of insurrection might be required – of the process of renewal to which France was irreversibly called.

The courageous nature of this reconstruction of recent national history, which set itself the task of countering bit by bit the conservative attempt to cage the *Charte* within a framework that offered extremely limited concession to freedom of action and thought, cannot be ignored. It is in the light of this particular reading of the revolutionary event – with the past called upon to illuminate the political action of the present time – that the success of Mignet's work must be seen, with two editions coming out in 1824, others in 1826 and 1827, while being translated into a number of other languages at the same time.

Adolphe Thiers, meanwhile, had been working on his own far weightier effort, also destined for a great deal of success, in which he set out to illustrate in detail the story of the revolutionary decade that Mignet had only schematically outlined.[33] The premises remained the same: on the eve of 1789, the situation in France was chaotic, and some event of a revolutionary kind seemed almost inevitable. The last years of King Louis's reign revealed, in worrying terms, the absence of a true constitution, and provided a compendium of the type of usurping activity that the monarchy had been indulging in for too long. Feudality had degenerated into aristocratic parasitism, parliaments were incapable of becoming promoters of a juridical order, there was conflict between the various state bodies. Faced with all this, the disaffection of mature public opinion was growing, ready to challenge the very foundations of the legitimacy of the old order, but at the same time unable to make an impact from within through the vital and urgent work required in order to re-establish the social pact.

It was precisely the fact that the active forces in French society found it impossible to assume an executive function that indicated a stalemate from which many attempted to escape through dogmatic decisions. The protests of the aristocracy were an example of this, which paved the way for criticism of the monarchy and ended up fostering the protest of these forces in society, ready to adopt the constitutionalization of the established order as the principal means for a reconstitution of the social structure on a profoundly transformed basis. The revolution grew out of this aporia between a world closed up into itself – which almost everyone recognized as unacceptable in the obviously despotic form it had assumed – and a malaise so widespread that it was unable to take the form of orderly transformation. The inevitable result was revolution, which immediately, in the absence of guiding reforms, developed into a test of strength between the guarantors of a past that was no longer serviceable and the promoters of a change to which the violence of the classes still in power was itself an obstacle.

For this reason, all the phases that followed the dawn of 1789 were marked by an impetuousness as dizzying as it was destructive – one that overwhelmed, despite the nostalgia expressed by Staël, the reforming spirit of Necker, the only figure that tried to gather all the objections to the new order together within the framework of a policy of moderate renewal. The decision of the traditional aristocracy to wage immediate war on the will of the National Assembly opened the way, with the storming of the Bastille, for a people hitherto the subject of evocation and cajolery, but never actually called to the aid of the Constituent Assembly. After July 14, the die was cast: only a much more energetic personality than Necker could have ferried France safely away from the coast of a new order without further turmoil. Instead, the victory of the Geneva banker meant that the way was clear for the extraordinary test of will offered by the assembly, ready, in its to-the-death confrontation with the forces of the past, to burn all the boats that might still have allowed it to return to the harbour of France's historical-political tradition.

With popular support now seeming to be an inevitable precondition, the Constituent Assembly put an end to the old regime, where the destruction of privileges implied the rejection of a Chamber of Peers, the abjuration of the English constitutional example and setting sail on the open sea of unicameralism. And yet, for Thiers the error lay not so much in the search for a solution different to the constitutional model across the Channel, but in the confident expectation – a legacy from the tradition of the old order – that a sovereign, once absolute, could accept the diminution of their own prerogatives, and that a people, gratified by the prospect of playing a leading role, could soon be reconfined in submission to the new power groups. In his opinion, the explanation for the radicalization of the political process, activated not by chance by the flight to Varennes and the shootings on the Champ de Mars, lay precisely in the Constituent Assembly's fatal error of, rather unexpectedly, taking upon itself a moderating function in the political process, having already made a decisive contribution to the full unleashing of the revolutionary force. The attempt to retrace their steps, renouncing the republican solution to give power back to a king who had blatantly disavowed his actions, proved fatal to the members of the Constituent Assembly, who soon scuttled their own vessel to take advantage of a new national representative body, the Legislative Assembly. This was dominated by the Girondins, who in turn interpreted the spirit of the revolution by challenging the king and the émigrés through choosing to go to war. However, they were soon forced to step aside when the republican solution, forged in the blood of August 10 and the September Massacres, made it clear that their forces were too weak to resist the surge of revolutionary violence.

On this basis, a revaluation of the figure of Danton took shape in Thiers's work, a historiographical operation destined to nourish the imaginary of historians up to the first half of the twentieth century. Although explicitly accused of having direct responsibility in the September Massacres, he is portrayed by Thiers, in the dramatic moments of the first republican days, as the only promoter of decisive action, a sort of political Atlas capable of bearing the entire weight of Revolutionary France on his shoulders. And the nature of his subsequent fall – restricted to his hesitation in the face of the decisive confrontation with the Committee of Public Safety – provided the guidelines for reading all the revolutionary events that follow: hesitation, lack of determination, the sudden collapse in the face of a perpetually changing political framework, decided first the fall of the Girondins and then Robespierre's, then the defeat of the Thermidorians, the futility of the days 13 Vendemiaire and 18 Fructidor, as well as the progressive exhaustion of the Directorial Republic through the actions of Bonaparte.

At the base of this reconstruction of the revolutionary events was a disenchanted study – in the France of the restored Bourbons – of the Republican period itself, seen as an inevitable (and therefore fully understandable) stage faced with the political legacy left by the works of the Constituent Assembly. Thiers's reconstruction was based on the acknowledgement that only a politics of force was an instrument of concrete action in the revolutionary tumult and that setting the past at a distance in order to rush on to the construction of a new order could take place only through that medium. The Constituent Assembly's mistake was, therefore, in seeking a path of moderation without having yet completed its demolition of the old order and, above all, without having placed popular agitation under its control. The Girondins' mistake was to believe that the revolution would purify itself of its intolerance merely because they denounced it in a loud voice. Danton's mistake – the only figure to resort to violence as a political choice and not as retaliation dictated by hatred – was to think his supposed popularity would protect him from the attacks of the Committee of Public Safety. Robespierre, meanwhile, got everything wrong, scorning the resistance of a Convention which the revolutionary government, in its own brutal deployment of reason of state, assigning the solution of political problems to Fouquier Tinville, Public prosecutor to the Revolutionary Tribunal, had reduced to a mere ratifying body for decisions taken elsewhere.

With the politics of force identified as the only instrument for the re-foundation of order and society, the Year II period returned to the centre of revolutionary events and was forever cleansed of the accusation of constituting a sudden and incomprehensible deviation: it was instead the culminating act of a process of subversion of the old order around which France would build its own specific modernity. For this reason, in Thiers's work it was clear that Thermidor was the turning point in the revolutionary process:

the political earthquake following 1789 seemed suddenly to subside at that juncture, and the turbulent plebs were for the first time repudiated by the Convention, which in Prairial Year III would definitively settle accounts with the popular movement. From that moment on, nevertheless, Thiers's version seemed to fall off, with the events of the Directorial Republic sketched out rather schematically and almost inevitably plunging into that blind alley from which, so very ambiguously, Bonapartism had to save it.

The work was a huge success, as shown by the many reprints and translations, and ended up shaping the image of the revolution in the minds of the new generations attracted to the political sphere in a way that went even beyond the intentions of its writer. Thiers's work, and Mignet's, so exceeded the expectations of their respective authors, because the invitation to France at that time to experience 1789 as something of its own became the recounting of a national tradition that until then had been hidden away but which now no-one could speak out against. However, as always happens in the case of any exaggerated victory, their triumph ended up overflowing the reassuring margins that Thiers and Mignet had wanted to set themselves: the decision to make the revolution an irresistible historical event, logical and necessary at the same time, generated unexpected enthusiasm among the new generations, enormously fascinated by the ineluctability innate in human history that these occurrences seemed to indicate. The insistence on the presumed obligatory nature of certain stages – which above all the wilful linearity of Mignet's work heavily emphasized – ended up, albeit turned on its head, by having something in common with the finalistic perspective illustrated at the time by the great counter-revolutionary writers, suggesting once again a providential dimension in late eighteenth-century events. The Terror, which Maistre had outlined in terms of an eschatological design, thus returned to the centre of attention. It took on, in the memory of a heroic era, the shadings of a fresh beginning, which at the time only the phenomenon of de-Christianization had clumsily tried to propose.

Now, however, the very pages of Mignet and Thiers, where they insisted on the essential deference of the nation to that traumatic period, seemed to rehabilitate Jacobinism and Year II, Robespierre and the revolutionary government, Marat and the *buveurs de sang*. They introduced into youthful French society an idea of the revolution destined to translate into the myth of a Year II cut short before its time – one to which, animated by a messianic spirit, it was necessary to return and give shape to. The work of the two young liberals thus had an effect that was not at all expected, much less desired, something which was proved in the aftermath of the 1830 Revolution, which Mignet and Thiers experienced as the manifestation of their political commitment in favour of a France reconciled around its recent history.

In reality, the return of the tricolour flag, the reappearance of Lafayette, the handover from the fugitive Charles X to Louis Philippe, who represented the dynastic branch that had always been more accepting of 1789, seemed to be the realization of their proposal for a France ready to start over, where everything had been brought to a halt thanks to the obstinate resistance of the privileged classes. In reality, the fact that in the Glorious Days of July the people of Paris had once again made their presence felt, once again decisively for the fate of the revolution, meant that not everything would be resolved through a simple change of dynasty and the complete confirmation of the new France's liberal identity.

The test arrived immediately: the new order, although it claimed to have promptly put an end to the revolution, was soon undermined from the left by a republican movement that explicitly looked to 1792 as the historical precedent on which to base its own program of opposition. They had read, in the pages of Mignet and Thiers, about a late-eighteenth-century political event where the social question had made its appearance.

It is no coincidence that the two, destined to receive so much from the new Orleanist order – one occupying important positions in cultural institutions and the other doing the same in the world of politics – were soon disappointed by the political perspectives that opened up after 1830. They always considered it to be the only political system that allowed French society a balanced growth, with an unpreparedness in the lower ranks that forced the elites to look after the common good mainly by themselves. Instead, the period of liberty seemed to be once more accompanied by an era of conflict, this time in terms of the clash with a working class ready to give an extraordinary social profile to the myth of a democratic republic. The order to which Thiers looked, where material and moral force had never to be separated, and which the liberal turning point of 1830 should have irreversibly guaranteed, seemed instead the immediate subject of protest.

He tried to oppose this wave first with government mechanisms aimed at dominating the protests, then, forced to take a discreet step back by the onset of dissension with the sovereign, taking refuge, in the last years of the July monarchy, waiting for better times, in the composition of his monumental *Histoire du Consulat et de l'Empire*.[34] Here, the Napoleonic era was portrayed as the continuation and conclusion of his previous work on the revolution. The work, started in 1845 and completed only in 1862, was greatly influenced by its author's parallel political experience. Neither 1848 nor the years of the Second Empire were able to shift him from the arena of parliamentary struggle: unlike Guizot and Thierry, but also Mignet himself, all quite stunned by the collapse of the Orleanist monarchy, abandoned survivors of a political era irremediably past, Thiers never failed to read the present moment with acumen and flexibility. Suffering heavy defeats, but invariably overcoming them, he became – shortly after the tragic repression of the Commune, which he would always be criticized for – the founder of a republican order that shared nothing with the aspirations of the democratic movement. And it is not an exaggeration to notice that in this extraordinary political longevity, from criticism of the illiberal anguish of the Restoration to the birth of a bourgeois Third Republic, the example of the tumultuous course of the great revolution – where the current could not be opposed, but, abandoning yourself to it, you could hope to find a sheltered position downstream – always came in useful in terms of repositioning himself on the political scene. First in 1848, when Louis Philippe's fall brought him back to the political sphere as the champion of a party of order that proposed to fight republican socialism, then in the years of the Second Empire, when, after a brief exile in England, he represented parliamentary opposition to Napoleon III, and finally, after Sedan, when he signed the surrender to Bismarck and, freed from the Parisian people's thirst for resistance, he laid the foundations of a profoundly conservative republican system.

Throughout these times, as mentioned before, the example of the great revolution was constantly evoked in order to introduce easy analogies with the present moment. In 1848, Thiers recalled how the triumphs of 1789 had been followed by the democratistic shift that even intended to call property into question. In the years of the Second Empire, when completing his history of the Napoleonic era, he was careful to suggest that lack of freedom constituted a limit that would inevitably lead to the great Corsican's downfall (and, in the future, also his nephew's). On the whole, in the aftermath of 1870, having seen his prophecies fulfilled, it was not difficult for him to envisage the republic as the lesser of possible evils. An institutional structure, in other words, that was anything but democratic – prudent, indeed, in matters of civil and social rights – but that nevertheless knew how to counteract the authoritarian seductiveness towards which French society, still to a great extent lacking in experience, never missed an opportunity to demonstrate its vulnerability.

And yet, for the lover of English liberty, the hour of triumph, with Thiers now in his eighties, was also the moment of political-ideological disaster. France would never again be comparable to Great Britain, the constitutional model across the Channel that many of his generation – Mignet, Thierry, Guizot – had gazed upon with anxious admiration remained a mere mirage and France, after decades of convulsion and revolution, seemed only at the starting point, still confronted by the decisions that the Constituent Assembly should have made in the summer of 1791, only to be sabotaged by its weakness in the face of the political situation.

3. The fiefs of the Mountain

The success of French liberal historiography of the 1820s overshadowed the fact that, in those same years, the revolution was also a reason for bearing witness and was evoked to remember the political-ideological path taken by the generation of that epochal moment of transition. Often the easy conclusion that prevailed was that the Restoration had erased from the political scene almost all the revolutionaries who had coexisted, on more or less comfortable terms, with the Napoleonic years. Those who had dared to sign the death sentence of Louis XVI were sent into exile, or else were removed from the public sphere, induced to take refuge in writing, almost always nostalgic in form, about their distant, glorious past.

In reality, this was an image long nurtured by those involved themselves, who often had a direct interest in covering their tracks, if only because on the tortuous path that led from 1789 to 1814 they had often shown themselves open to hasty compromise – something that would make it easy for them to be accused not only of being a violent, atheist and subversive generation but also traitorous. It was therefore better for many of them to retire, for want of a good alternative, to a secluded life, made up of writing and nostalgia, far from the clamour of practical politics, to await possibly more congenial times. But it is worthwhile adding at once that this homeland exile constituted only an officially declared motivation, because – each in their own way, depending on their actions – apart from regret and lament, there was never any lack of hope of returning to the political game, precisely by appealing to revolutionary and democratic precedent.

For this reason, it would be misleading to consider that in the 1820s the changing of the generational guard had already taken place: in that same period, there were many signs of intellectual vivacity on the part of the now elderly revolutionaries, offering sparkling evidence of their political longevity and their ability, even beyond the turning point of 1830, to influence the guidelines of French democracy.

This political perspective in the name of defending revolutionary values translated into the intention of demonstrating that the Terror was only a painful (and in some ways necessary) parenthesis in the context of a republican event that should be interpreted in a completely different way.[35] In this light, it was above all those members of parliament who had refused to vote for the death penalty during the trial of the king who could make their voices heard – those who, having made that decision, were able to demonstrate, in the years of the Restoration, their substantial extraneousness to the violence of Year II. Bailleul's, as we have seen, was an authoritative voice in this sense, though he nevertheless limited himself to point-by-point contestation of Staël's ideas without attempting an overall reconstruction of events. Jacques Antoine Dulaure, however, a former Convention member hostile to the Montagnards, had promptly adopted the same line, and since 1815 had been involved in journalism aimed at distinguishing between the Terror and the Republican periods. In his first work, he reiterated how the degeneration of the revolutionary process into the maelstrom of violence was an obligatory response to counter-revolutionary aggression.[36] He followed this, between 1823 and 1825, with a weighty effort on the revolution, clearly keen to emphasize that the Republican era had nothing in common with the excesses of Year II. From this specific perspective, the Directory period took on significant importance, where democracy, having returned to the scene thanks to the Convention's courage during the Thermidor coup d'état, had then experienced a period of concrete realization, only to be abruptly interrupted, once more through the use of violence, by General Bonaparte.

In the context of a confused and prolix account where attention to crucial revolutionary moments deliberately took precedence over critical reflection, Dulaure's writings did, however, suggest another possible outcome to revolutionary events if only the violence of privileged groups – first, the Montagnards, then Bonaparte – had not repeatedly interrupted a trajectory of liberty that belonged not only to 1789 but had also been celebrated with the Republican moment of 1792. His work, therefore, summarized the testimony of certain groups – essentially Republican, regardless of the decision of some to coexist with the Empire – who intended to take advantage of the newly rediscovered freedom to demonstrate that this was a model that had certainly not been expunged from the memory of French politics – something that Restoration writers instead, especially those on the liberal side, invariably liked to state.

There were those, however, who spoke out against these intentions to distance the Terror from Republican tradition in the name of a liberty-promoting 1792 and a Directory era in which democracy was allowed to thrive. Leading Year II figures, most of them forced into exile after having committed the sin of regicide, they intended instead to hold firm to the sacred nature of the period of revolutionary government.

In this particular context, a testimony of great importance is provided by the *Conspiration pour l'égalité, dite de Babeuf*, published in 1828 by Philippe Buonarroti in exile in Brussels.[37] Buonarroti, who in those years was a reference point for secret republican associations not only in France but also in Italy, had a history of fervent Jacobinism without, however, ever managing to turn this enthusiasm into a successful political career.[38] He had held modest government posts at the time of Year II and his main moment of notoriety certainly derived from the discovery of the Babeuf's conspiracy, when, arrested as one of its leaders, he managed to escape the death sentence. It is not known why, at the end of the 1820s, Buonarroti decided to return to that long-ago episode, but it seems certain that he wished to be part of the revival of interest in the revolution that until then had benefitted the liberal supporters of 1789 or, albeit to a much more limited extent, those who sought to distinguish the experience of the Republic from that of the Terror.

His book, was, in fact, a muster call to the Robespierrist front, clearly stating as it did that Republicanism had found concrete form only in Year II, when the democratic revolution had moved from the political to the social and had also laid the foundations to overturn the unjust economic structure inherited from the old order. The example of the conspiracy hatched by Babeuf – a man who in his time had applauded the fall of Robespierre, only to quickly change his mind in the light of the Directory's reactionary policies – seemed to Buonarroti the crowning proof that all the authentically revolutionary forces had immediately understood what a terrible mistake Thermidor had been. While the *Conspiration* therefore dealt with Babeuf's unfortunate attempt at a coup, in reality Buonarroti's pen was guided by his Montagnard faith, with the result that his work included open praise of the figure of Robespierre, who, he suggested, had known better than any anyone else how to interpret the profound significance of the revolution.

In this context, a long note that served as a preamble included an initial reconstruction of the revolutionary events, which confirmed the accusations against the men of 1789, the simple expression of selfish plutocratic interests, and – the Girondins above all – those of 1792, condemned for a superficial republicanism, destined to vanish abruptly when faced with a challenge from the people that prompted them to make a common front with the aristocracy. It is difficult to judge the success of the work, which certainly benefitted greatly from the sudden revolutionary blaze of July 1830, when the Parisian people once again moved centre stage and seemed to turn the clock of French history back to 1789. In the years immediately following, it then became clear that the claims of Louis Philippe's supporters to ascribe the profound unrest – social, too, in nature – that had escalated during the Restoration merely to the change of dynasty proved to be groundless. The worker problem exploded in 1831, in Lyons, with the revolt of the *canuts*, the silk workers, ready to rebel against an unfair economic system that sacrificed artisanal workshops to the advantage of those who restricted themselves to trading in the finished product. Then, in 1834, there were street riots again, in both Paris and Lyon, where a new republicanism, led by a generation of young people, went through a baptism of fire, knowing they could count on the massive participation of the working class.

The troubled existence of the July monarchy – the result, in Remusat's words, of an almost perfect revolution, which immediately ended with the triumph of the Charter – showed how those rosy predictions were without foundation: throughout its time, the regime was constantly opposed by a democratic opposition which regarded the working class as hugely important and which, as is well known, succeeded in overwhelming the crown with the barricades of February 1848. This opposition to liberalism was plural in nature, merging sensibilities and aspirations that were very different from each other: nevertheless, all the components of French democracy that emerged from 1830 looked back openly to the heroic precedent of the First Republic and in that context forcefully emphasized, as a precedent to refer to, the Parisian people's relationship with Jacobinism.

In 1833, when the *Société des droits de l'homme* was founded, one acute observer, the socialist typographer Pierre Leroux, wrote that it was divided between the Danton line and the Robespierre line and his decision to define the various forms of the new republicanism by making use of these two figures had a precise significance. On the one hand, there were those who, following on from Danton, wanted to reach a compromise with the workers without giving themselves up to sectarian logic; on the other, those who, looking back to Robespierre, referred to 1793 as nothing more than an amplification of Year II and the Terror. It must be said that the many variations on French republicanism of that time could not be encompassed by those two groupings alone: but the fact that in the *Société des droits de l'homme* there was no space for the Girondins speaks volumes about how the reading of events of the great revolution centred only around 1793. The Directory period that followed was dismissed as the poisoned fruit of traitorous Thermidor and all responsibility for the loss of the Republic was laid at the door of the Girondins, viewed first as the promoters of an imprudent war and then as those who had derived a great deal of advantage from the consequences of Thermidor.

It was from this angle that Buonarroti's *Conspiration* was read, and it was reprinted promptly in Paris in 1830, immediately becoming a renewed reason for reflection for the young democrats able to benefit from the new spaces for manoeuvre that the triumph of liberalism had opened up to them. In this way, Buonarroti's work, precisely because of the passionate interpretations it provoked, became something other than the bitter testimony of a revolutionary survivor forced to chase the hope of a new Year II through the underground world of secret societies. The different political paths taken by readers of the work, however, involved appropriations of various kinds, with a meeting point found in the centrality of the figure of Robespierre. For the reason mentioned earlier, this would assume different forms according to the moment: champion of social justice and standard bearer of democracy, but also the symbol of a politics dominated by a profound spiritualism. All his responsibility was cancelled out by the revolutionary martyrdom suffered during Thermidor, in order that his dedication to the common cause might be valorized instead.

Immediately after the July revolution, the young Albert Laponneraye, who had been close to Buonarroti in the past and was a great frequenter of French prisons for political reasons, ventured into similar territory. In the autumn of 1831, in the wake of the workers' revolt in Lyon, he proposed a public course dealing with the history of France from 1789 to 1830, expressly reserved for workers in the capital.[39] The move sounded like a class response to the initiatives carried out by Mignet at the time and was banned by the police after just a few weeks, with the accusation of inciting social hatred. It cannot be said that those in charge of public order for the occasion were distracted to the point of misrepresenting Laponneraye's words: he had started with the figure of Christ as the founder of freedom, inspirer of equality and promoter of brotherhood. However, he immediately launched into a very violent attack on Catholicism, attributing to it all the backwardness of southern Europe and, in this particular case, the failure of the great revolution in France – and then concluding that the work that remained interrupted in Year II should be resumed and taken to its natural conclusion.[40]

Laponneraye's decision to express a certain benevolence towards Christianity – particularly in its reformed aspect – was the consequence of the new political framework made possible by the Glorious July Days and the troubles in the Catholic world that would soon lead Lamennais to abandon the counter-revolutionary sphere for that of social democracy. The presence of a strong religious element in the working class, which had once again become a leading figure on the political, as well as social, scene, forced Laponneraye to formulate a programme of action very different from the one hitherto pursued in Carbonari conventicles. The 1830 revolution had suddenly brought back to life the revolutionary vitality of the Parisian people, who, albeit in a confused way – crying out *Vive la Charte!* now and then with no great reason – had returned to the fore and had since given proof, especially with the Lyonnais insurrection of 1831, of having no intention of abandoning their newly recaptured terrain.

Therefore, in the authoritarian, sectarian universe, of which Laponneraye, as a worthy pupil of Buonarroti, was a significant exponent, there was the need to come to agreement with that world, accepting its spiritual universe, provided that it would support a precise programme and an equally unquestionable political guide. In Laponneraye's eyes, the solution – already very clear in his lessons and taking definitive shape in 1838 with the publication of a history of the French Revolution – began with a close analogy between 1789 and 1830: both bourgeois revolutions, dictated by the selfish interests of the privileged classes, they had produced a superficial form of liberty through constitutional decrees for the exclusive use of the few. Those who had taken power in 1789 were the same as those who, thanks to 1830, had finally returned to the leadership of France, after the peaceful purgatory of the years of the Restoration. The analogy, however, gave some hope for the future: the fact that the 1791 constitution had soon been overwhelmed by the popular insurrection of August 10 raised the possibility that of 1814, too, foolishly endorsed by all the revolutionaries of 1830, could soon suffer the same fate. This was what Laponneraye wanted to say explicitly in his lectures, when – writing from prison – he noted that 'one died soon after its birth, the other ... we shall see'.[41]

The analogies, however, did not end here and went on to tackle the republican camp itself, where distinction was made, following what Buonarroti had once asserted, between the Montagnards and the Girondins. The latter, republicans of a superficial kind, happy to grant democracy to the people while nevertheless claiming to be the only ones suitable to lead it, were in turn the forerunners of many republicans of the time, because 'today, how many men usurp the title of republican, who are basically only Girondins in the full force of the term'.[42] In this constant game of moving back and forth between 1789 and 1830, Laponneraye was thus constructing, thanks to the example of what had gone before, the proposal for a social revolution. Bearing in mind Buonarroti's indication, this subordinated Babeuf to Robespierre –political, rather than communist, aspirations; the insurrectional vanguard rather than the working class. The result was to make the Incorruptible the point of reference for an egalitarian programme destined, through dictatorship, to win out over its many, inevitable, enemies.

The radicalism of the social programme was closely connected to exaltation of the revolutionary dictatorship exemplified by the Terror of Year II, and made up a combination destined to dominate the ideological universe of a significant part of the French republican left throughout the entire nineteenth century and beyond. A further contribution in this regard was provided, roughly in the same years as Laponneraye's work, by the mammoth and cumbersome *Histoire parlementaire de la Révolution française*, which, started in 1834, at the time of its conclusion, in 1839, ran to 40 volumes.[43] It was, at least in appearance, a work of erudition, aimed at furnishing the scholar with a plurality of sources otherwise difficult to find, such as official reports, records of parliamentary sessions and extracts from the main newspapers of the time. However, this voluminous presentation of contemporary information was held together by a prose commentary that put forward an original interpretation, comparing the revolution to the mission of Catholicism, with Jacobinism employed as the political religion to exemplify this connection. The promoters of the initiative were two republicans, Philippe Buchez and Pierre Roux, who had been constant thorns in the side of the Restoration police authorities since the 1820s, when Buchez in particular had galvinized certain Carbonari groups, with even an unlikely attempt to raise an insurrection that had cost him a period of detention. The July revolution had surprised them in the middle of a process of revising their respective cultural ideas: after an initial adherence to the values of Saint-Simonianism, both had returned to the Catholic faith. The experience of the July revolution, which soon ground to a halt in a political structure that merely protected the interests of the most privileged economic groups, had convinced them that there was no connection at all between 1830 and the great revolution. It was necessary, therefore, to return to the latter in order to define its authentic and profound objectives, which the monarchy of Louis Philippe tried to confine to a new system of freedom dedicated to the protection of property and trade.

Buchez and Roux thought instead that 1789 had begun a process of liberation, based on the triad of liberty, equality and brotherhood, which, not surprisingly, translated the moral universe of Christianity into political terms.[44] This reversal of positions took place through the full acceptance of revolutionary modernity, seen as the natural conclusion of a process aimed at building a just society. In this way, the two could say that they were part of the tradition favourable to 1789 and its developments while at the same time proposing the return of the Catholic world in a revolutionary context: the revolution was no longer a meteorite crashing unexpectedly into French earth, and was not even the product of random and unpredictable circumstances attributable to economic reasons or to the malevolence of specific groups and individuals, but the natural conclusion of all humanity's profound design.

These were words that had on their side, above all, the strength of the spirituality that sustained them: their conclusion was the call to gather, under the banner of a

Christian revolution, all the main issues relative to the national events particular to the cultural debate of the time. In a brief history of France placed at the start of the work, Buchez and Roux, in their turn, opposed the thesis of the Frankish conquest, arguing that the French people rose out of the desire both to protect the inhabitants of Roman Gaul from the newcomers and by the strenuous defence of their religiosity. The nation was therefore born already Christian, a trait that would always be preserved, so much so that it was reproposed in 1789 through the intervention of the people: this was, according to both, the fundamental reason for the revolution. Not surprisingly, it was immediately opposed by a selfish and anti-working class bourgeoisie, ready to rest their case entirely on the defence of individuality, forgetting that the perspective must instead be quite the opposite one: reminding a nation – which regarded all forms of individualism with great suspicion – of its Christian duty.

In this light, the denunciation of the National Assembly initiated by Buchez and Roux was complete: in the change to a Constituent Assembly, they saw only the attempt to found an order ruled by the few. Taking the proclamation of their adversaries as their own – that is, that what 1789 had begun, 1830 had brought to fruition – Buchez and Roux could therefore erase the liberal moment entirely, to state that only with the Republic, and only through an even deeper popular involvement, did the revolution show its true face. In this way, bridges were definitively burned in relation to the eighteenth-century bourgeois and Protestant tradition, which insisted on individuality rather than recognizing the homogeneity of the French people. Precisely for this reason, mistrust of the Girondins ran deep: the latters' superficial republicanism hid – as, at the time that Buchez and Roux were writing, did that of many of Louis Philippe's self-styled opponents – an individualism destined to exhaust itself in the selfish defence of specific interests, all to the detriment of France's historical mission.

In this context, accusations of federalism rained down on Brissot and his associates, while the Mountain became the party of the nation, its armed resistance to foreign powers equated with the superhuman effort of those who, in the name of a decision to favour modernity, were called upon to fight against all the united defenders of the old order. This tenacious battle between two prospects, one of redemption and the other of slavery, thus overshadowed the iniquities that occurred in France in Year II. The responsibility for these iniquities, however – always in the eyes of Buchez and Roux – could be laid at the door of many others rather than Robespierre: in the pages of commentary on the collected texts, the two took care to point their fingers at the corrupt and lascivious Danton, or at the de-Christianizing Hébert – both to blame for many of the tragedies that occurred – while Robespierre, who had fought against them and, rightly, put them to death, was regarded as the one great supporter of a revolution in the name of morality.

For this reason, Thermidor marked the end of French society's redemption process: from that moment, instead, all of France began its descent into the inferno of individualism, ready to regain that place achieved in the events of 1789 and which had been temporarily removed by the impact of the people's force under Montagnard leadership. Even Bonapartism, which also, according to Buchez and Roux, enjoyed some popular consensus at first, did nothing in this regard. Very little separated the Empire, and then the Restoration, in terms of defending vested selfishness and the usual privileged classes – the aristocracy and bourgeoisie finding a way rub along together where common pecuniary advantage was the prize – then got their hands on the patrimony-based monarchy of Louis Philippe. A new revolution was unambiguously demanded by the two writers in order to bring the events of 1789 to a successful outcome.

Overall, then, this bulky compendium reflected the reading of events proposed only a few years before by Buonarroti, calling for a profound religiosity to reconstitute, in the context of yet another revolution, a society that politics and economics had unacceptably split apart. However, producing such an enormous effort, the explicit intent of Buchez and Roux was to prepare the ground for future historians of the revolution, who would thus be able to return to Year II with the concrete evidence of Montagnard actions in front of them rather than the copious slander produced against Jacobinism by liberal reconstructions.

Buchez and Roux soon had their own followers, as Etienne Cabet began the publication of his history of the revolution in 1839, where the two writers were duly cited.[45] Above all, though, the work responded to their invitation to write a democratic history of the revolution, which would even things out with the liberal accounts then in circulation. Cabet's declared polemical objective was in fact Thiers's writings, and this open conflict is made even more interesting if one bears in mind that the author of the *Histoire populaire* had come round to democracy rather late in the day and no longer young, being already forty-two at the time of the July Revolution, when he had promptly thrown his lot in with the new order so as to receive a government post in Corsica.

Elected to the Chamber in 1831, but swiftly passing over to the opposition in the wake of the social revolt that seemed to be sweeping through France, Cabet had gradually radicalized his opinions – so much so, that he went first to prison and then into voluntary exile in England. He developed an interest in Owen's socialist theories and set about rereading the recent history of France in a way that opposed the liberal interpretation.[46] The fact that Cabet had shared the ideological universe of Mignet and Thiers before locking horns with them makes it possible to read between the lines of his work to grasp that the liberal interpretation of the revolution constituted a point of reference, even before becoming a matter of contention, for those who, on the republican left, were seeking another reading of the developments following on from 1789.

Cabet's positions were in fact clear: in the four volumes that made up his work, he relied heavily upon the documentation made available by Buchez and Roux, while at the same time following Thiers's interpretative blueprint, both in the division between the revolutionary and Napoleonic periods, and in the indication of 1793 as the culminating moment in the process of overthrowing the overall stasis of the *ancien régime*. In this context, he reiterated all the criticisms of the Constitutional period, agreeing with Thiers on the radicalization of the political process following the failed flight to Varennes. He then broached a controversial matter with his illustrious predecessor on the interpretation of republican events: in this regard, in the face of the terrible massacres that occurred in this history, Cabet fully justified what happened in early September 1792 in Paris and had words of understanding for every manifestation of popular anger. He was, meanwhile, still involved in disagreement with Thiers, very hard on the Girondins and, if possible, denouncing Thiers's clear sympathy for Danton, even tougher in his attitude towards the latter.

Cabet's conclusion, needless to say, was fulsome praise for the Mountain, described as the only political party that had been able to interpret the collective aspiration to profound social palingenesis. He portrayed Robespierre with emotion, repeatedly defending him from the malevolent accusations of all the false revolutionaries: the Incorruptible was thus presented as the authentic guide of the people, more democratic and republican than any other, both prudent and energetic at the same time, generous even to his enemies and rightly inflexible in the light of his country's needs. Cabet showed a certain perplexity only with regard to Robespierre's lack of acceptance of an equitable distribution of wealth: this, however, he put off to the continuation of his narrative and in particular to the Babeuf's conspiracy, where, after mentioning the example of Buonarroti with affection and conveying his admiration for the conspirators, he could not, however, avoid establishing a clear distance between himself and the ideas of the conspiracy's promoters – ideas that to him seemed improvised and cumbersome, locked into the framework of an eighteenth-century philosophy that was no longer applicable.

In this way, suggesting that in that specific context things were still to be initiated, Cabet could hold fast to the cultural tradition of the Restoration in which he had grown up and which for a long time he had also shared: the history of humanity was one constantly oriented towards progress, and in this France played an important role, given that historically it had never failed to fight for freedom. The year 1789 had proved decisive in terms of disposing of the old order, but the revolution had failed precisely because privileged groups had managed to bring its impetuous course to a halt. The democrats themselves – to whom Cabet paid due homage – still bore a great deal of responsibility, the most important being that of holding back, rather than supporting, the people's instinct for complete equality. The result was that the Montagnards, too, in impeding that particular prospect, had ended up pulling away from the collective needs of French society – in turn losing their way and involuntarily allowing class egoism to thwart the revolution. Cabet did not meet with a great deal of consensus here – his communism, which would soon induce him to take the messianic step of founding some colonies in the United States, meant he could not expect convinced support from those who firmly insisted on the importance of the Robespierrist example.

And yet, although there were clearly contrasting motives in the French radical left itself, there was no shortage of volunteers who tried to make everything, or almost everything, fit together. One of these worth mentioning was Alphonse Esquiros, Laponneraye's successor running the journal *La Voix du people*: on the very eve of February 1848's days of insurrection, he published a history of the Montagnards, in which a certain amount of mediation was attempted in relation to the various voices that all referred back to the lesson of Year II.[47]

It is pointless to add anything else to the fact that it overstates its praise of Year II and the extraordinary task the Convention set itself: more interesting, instead, to observe how the exaltation of the Montagnards – and, obviously, the figure of Robespierre in particular – was carried out by trying to centre reflection around the contemporary political situation, which saw Louis Philippe's reign in increasing difficulty as it faced unprecedented social challenge. For this reason, while continuing to extol the Year II Convention and aligning his work with the memoirs of former Convention members and the testimonies of survivors that he was familiar with, Esquiros nevertheless tried, somehow trimming away the sides, to recompose the field of consensus around Robespierre alone. He recognized the role of Christianity, the creator of liberty and brotherhood, while at the same time denying that Catholicism or the spread of new religious morality had led to 1789. While he denounced the dreadful violence of the Terror, he was careful to underline the extraordinary state of difficulty the Convention found itself in when organizing the resistance to foreign armies. In addition, while complaining about the social iniquity of the Orleanist monarchy, he avoided any suggestion of a utopian descent into the world of communism that would indicate that Robespierre's programme held any prospect for solving the problem. Esquiros restored 1793 to the will of the revolutionary vanguard alone, which – had Thermidor not intervened – with no religious mediation, and simply through its awareness of the terrifying social contradictions, would have successfully brought the revolution to a conclusion. He could thus play with the analogy to the present moment and envisage a precise programme for the insurrectionary government that would overthrow the July monarchy.[48]

In other words, in his proposal for a return to the heroic example of 1793, there was the warning that no social question, raised though it might be, could ever be resolved without a reliable political guide, inevitably destined, in the short term, to assume a dictatorial function. This was the matter over which large sections of the radical left would clash with yet another part of the democratic movement, who saw this recourse to Year II as a worrying revival of the issues and programmes that had brought about the failure of the First Republic.

4. Political hermaphrodites

On 12 November 1830, a meeting was organized in New York in support of the recent revolution in France. James Monroe, former president of the United States, the political figure who in the years of the great revolution had been closest to republican France, took the floor for the occasion. His words, however, were cold comfort to overseas democrats: the old companion of the revolutionary of two worlds, Tom Paine, spoke with respect for Lafayette alone, and even underlined the difference between the brute materiality that led to the ruin of 1789 and the luminous wisdom that seemed instead to inspire 1830. Not only that: although in the course of the meeting it was decided to make November 25, the date in 1783 when British troops had permanently abandoned New York, a city holiday in honour of the French Revolution, it became clear that the brotherhood between the two countries did not involve any similarity between their political systems.[49] The many meetings of the trade associations, which all confirmed their participation in the commemorative parade, in their official acceptance texts of the invitation made no reference to the Parisian workers who had fought on the streets of the French capital. On November 27, then, while participation of public and authorities in the event was indeed extraordinary, the official speaker, Samuel Gouverneur, Monroe's nephew, was careful to point out that all the merit of the affirmation of freedom in the world was due to America's 1776, even though the constitutional king of France, Louis Philippe, still deserved the sincere applause 'of the only republic on earth'.

In short, French republicans had lost the opportunity to regain their only possible international reference point and America's dismissal of them to the advantage of the Orleans political system would be maintained for the entire duration of the July monarchy. Again, in 1847, in a speech on the usefulness of history, William Cabell Rives, a Virginia politician and great admirer of Madison, who would later end his political career on the side of the Confederates, pointed out all the glaring differences between the two revolutions in order to suggest that only in 1830 had France properly set out on the path to freedom.[50]

It goes without saying that the French democratic movement was not damaged so much by American exceptionalism and the devotion always shown overseas towards Lafayette, but by the specific equation between Republic and Terror which, from the last years of the eighteenth century, had begun to dominate political discourse in the United States. The fact that, following 1830, Robespierre's reputation was favourably re-evaluated by at least a part of the republican movement then contributed to further isolating French democratism and placed those who rejected the equivalence between the First Republic and the Year II government in a situation of serious difficulty.

And yet, there were certainly no lack of republicans in France ready to resolutely distance themselves from the Terror after the revolution of 1830: the flight of Charles X seemed to reawaken the hope of a complete overturning of the institutional order and the voices of the *juste milieu*, always ready to provide the Orleanist solution with a broad consensus, blared too loudly not to conceal more than one concern in this regard.[51] One of those hoping for a rapid change in the constitutional order was Léon Gallois, a journalist with a turbulent background in Restoration Paris, who, on the very cusp of July, printed his *Histoire pittoresque de la Révolution française*, in which his intention to sever the period of democracy from the dark memories of the Terror was stated directly at the outset.[52] According to Gallois, Bourbon France was plagued by a reactionary spirit that did everything possible to discredit the great revolution and to persecute its few survivors: the time had therefore come for a popular work, something that would be welcomed by most of the French that would look back and clarify the excess of falsehoods in circulation.

Gallois's intention was to demonstrate, in the wake of what early romantic historiography had repeatedly indicated, the inevitability of revolutionary violence, the dramatic backlash to the obstinate resistance opposed by the privileged classes towards every small change. However the author did not intend to conceal anything terrible that had happened and even had he preferred to remain silent with regard to the horrors that did occur, he still believed it was possible to write a history of the great revolution where the grandiose nature of both tasks and results prevailed over the ignominy of the violence that had also been perpetrated. In this context, it was evident that Gallois relied on his acquaintance with some of the men who had been participants in those distant events and who, not by chance, had expressed more than one reservation with regard to romantic historiography – too inclined, in their eyes, to underline the violent divisions in the republican camp. One of these was Bertrand Barère, who exhorted Gallois to continue working on a history of the events that followed 1789 which would testify to the new generations the extraordinary effort made by the entire republican political class, regardless of the factional struggles that had greatly hindered revolutionary action.[53]

Another former Convention member would have agreed on this point, despite, as a declared Girondin at the time, being an opponent of Barère, and then expelled and persecuted by the assembly after the dramatic insurrectionary days of 31 May and 2 June 1793. This was Jacques Antoine Dulaure, whose frenetic activity as a writer on various topics in the Restoration years has already been mentioned. Having always remained a republican, in the aftermath of 1830, availing himself of the help of some collaborators (all with a previous background in opposition politics), he started to go on with his previous work on the revolution. In 1834, his history of the Restoration and the revolution of 1830 came out, where the July Days were proposed as the natural continuation of August 10 instead of 1789 and whose main purpose was to demonstrate how nothing of Louis Philippe's monarchy could be compared to the previous revolutionary events.

In his introduction, he suggested that to opposition circles the change of dynasty appeared as a mere stratagem, because the task of his work was to denounce the line of continuity between the Orleanist monarchy and the Restoration and

> to teach the vast majority of our fellow citizens, deprived of all political rights, of any participation in the management of their own affairs, what this false semblance of representative government really was, with the help of which a handful of intriguers and traitors has, for fifteen years, insulted all our national glories and tried to make us retreat towards an oligarchic regime hostile to all social progress.[54]

These words said everything with regard to the wish that 1830 would mark the unstoppable and aggressive return of a political society that the Bourbon dynasty had unsuccessfully sought to contextualize under the flag of the fleur-de-lis. However, the spectre of the Terror was an obstacle – one that had to be removed by demonstrating that in the meantime the great work of revolutionizing society excluded the return of that kind of coercive violence. From this point on, for Dulaure, the lesson had to be that every survivor of the Convention had to set acrimony aside in order to join forces against the enemies who were once again in power. With regard to this, it seemed to him that one point of balance between the different positions in the republican camp was the recognition of popular sovereignty – that is, of universal suffrage. This would be the natural republican antidote to any authoritarian shortcut that would inevitably once more end up evoking the Year II government and the Terror.

The most ambitious attempt to find an understanding between the various republican groupings, however, was that of Armand Marrast, another republican journalist, who in 1836 published a book devoted to the Revolution.[55] This work again emphasized the revolution's extraordinary feat of social renewal and dealt with the Terror in terms of a necessary violence which, thanks to the progress made in the meantime, would no longer be necessary. In this regard, Marrast believed he was facing the issue introduced by liberal historiography head-on, outstripping even Thiers's interpretation – which blamed aristocratic resistance for engendering the Terror – on his own ground. In his eyes, the historians of those years had indeed grasped the point, but had failed to develop it – they had not taken the trouble to conduct a detailed examination of what the old order really was and of the skein of violence and privilege the revolution had to bring to an end.

In a long introduction, which constituted a sort of premise around which to intertwine and explain all subsequent revolutionary events, Marrast was thus able to give a dramatic account of an *ancien régime* where oppression and violence were the rule of the day and where every attempt at change – even a timid one – was duly doomed to failure. This context explained the excessive violence of the revolutionary process which, in Marrast's case, too, was exorcized by the complacent certainty that the great progress made by French society prevented its repetition. The problem remained, nevertheless, of republican writing that seemed to be making a grave mistake, adulating the figure of Robespierre and as a consequence favouring the biased ideas of their opponents regarding the immutability of democratic politics.

For this reason, with the intention of trying to strike a balance between the various voices of republican politics, Marrast made a clear choice in favour of Danton, a towering presence in the desperate hour of his homeland's threatened invasion and a figure who, later, would never agree to acquiesce to Robespierre's repressive policy. His attention to Danton, however, presented as the champion of the cause of French democracy, risked becoming a proof of weakness rather than a central figure around which various democratic representatives could be gathered. One republican was set up in opposition to another, which therefore ended up dividing the democratic camp, and there was essential acceptance of the perspective indicated by Thiers, who in turn had praised the Incorruptible's adversary. In short, the fact that non-Robespierrist republican circles adopted as their own a figure that appealed to liberal writers exposed Marrast and those who shared his interpretation to the easy accusation that little or nothing, apart from declarations of principle, distinguished their republicanism from the political ideas of many of the *juste milieu*. The insinuation was an inconsistent one, but at the same time compelling: it was difficult to escape the joint siege of Robespierre exegetists on the one hand and the followers of an intensely nationalistic liberalism on the other.

However, still in the republican camp, radical groups that gazed on Year II with veneration also had a mirror-image problem, because only reaching a compromise with all the republican components would allow them to emerge from the isolation in which they found themselves. For this reason, beyond the controversies of the moment and regardless of judgement on the Terror, everyone believed that the construction of a democratic perspective depended on overcoming past divisions and everyone insisted on the need to rebuild the republican front by putting aside all rancour and disagreement once and for all. Léon Gallois appeared to make an attempt in this direction with a work started in 1834, printing the first pages of *Histoire de la Convention nationale*, which he intended to constitute a turning point in the dispute within the republican ranks.[56]

His work, an editorial success that would be republished over the following years, was conceived along the lines of Thiers's writings – the latter having been, in the years of the Restoration, for the whole generation that went through the baptism of fire of 1830, not only the champion of free speech, but also the person who had restored political honour to the Convention. His undisputed historiographical authority was immediately evoked by Gallois to note that a history expressly dedicated to the first republican assembly was still lacking and that his ambition was therefore to restore those formidable events and characters to the direct judgement of the reader. To do this, however, it was necessary to sweep away the excessive amount of slander and backbiting that had accumulated over time with regard to the assembly and in order to do *this* – again, in Gallois's opinion – it was not necessary for his own judgement to intervene repeatedly with regard to the events each time they were presented.

However, if the intent really was to restore an image that fully corresponded to the truth of the Convention, the result was contradictory, to say the least. The seven volumes published were in fact a tale of the rise and fall of the Mountain, whose political activity and terrible decisions the author was always careful to justify. The other members of the assembly eliminated one by one from the scene, from the Girondins to Danton, were treated with great admiration, and their sincere republicanism certainly given proper political recognition; but they ended up under repeated accusation for, at certain times, not having taken into due consideration the dramatic conditions that France found itself in and for this reason having provoked the violent reaction against them.

The Girondins, in particular, even though Gallois took immense care to show his great appreciation of them, were accused of having deliberately put the Republic at risk with their stubborn battle against Robespierre and even of having favoured the federalist revolt in a vain attempt to take swift revenge on the people of Paris. Danton, in turn, whose patriotism was duly praised in certain passages of the work, was certainly not exempt from a critical comment or two, being accused of failing to interpret the political scenario correctly in 1794 and of letting violence get the upper hand when he allowed the Hébertists to go to the scaffold. In short, the fact that he had been silent at the time allowed Gallois to greatly play down the complaisant campaign that his group tried to initiate against the authoritarian direction that the Terror was taking and made it possible for him to conclude that it was Danton's approval of the repression against Hébert that had ended up favouring the backlash against his own person.

In this way, even within the context of ostentatious republicanism, Gallois's work was not very different from that of Thiers, who had distanced himself from Robespierre but had certainly not hesitated to be sharply critical in relation to the Girondins. In point of fact, in the *Histoire de la Convention nationale*, the author's desire was a worthy one – to bring an end to resentment and division in order to pay sincere homage to all those who had served in the Convention: but, all in all, in his praise he followed almost to the letter the recommendations made to him by former Convention members, who opposed Mignet and Thiers precisely because their writings thwarted the survivors' wish to present history with the image of a Convention substantially united in its revolutionary objectives. Not surprisingly, Barère had always urged Gallois on in the enterprise, hoping that his history would put an end to dispute once and for all and, in the judgement of posterity, bestow upon the Convention a political unanimity that – and this was impossible to deny – had swiftly faded away during the course of its work.

Overall, Gallois's good intentions were lost to so great an extent because the desire to re-establish an understanding between the parties did so through the declared political supremacy of the Montagnards. In other words, even in the 1840s, the rules that the post-Robespierrist Convention was given at the time, to welcome back members previously expelled while forcing them to forget the insults they had suffered, still seemed to be in wide circulation – so much so, as to have an influence on the first reconstructions of its parliamentary action. It does, after all, seem rather emblematic that the first history of the Convention should come to an end with Thermidor, excluding the following period, forgetting that the same assembly had won out over the people's movement in Year III, and in 1795 had provided France with a constitution that governed political life in the years immediately following, clearly demonstrating therefore responsibility in the political system after the removal of the revolutionary government.

All this, however, says that, even for the democrats of the new generation, the First Republic remained the one that owed its existence to the insurrection of August 10 and that collapsed after the immense difficulties of Thermidor, when a large number of its members had, in some ways incomprehensibly, chosen the path of political suicide. From this point of view, there was no space for the Directory period, and the reference to the First Republic remained delimited to its first phase, when the new order had failed to stabilize itself – a failure due to internal conflict, frighteningly intertwined with the resistance of the privileged classes and the aggression of foreign powers.

If, in terms of referencing the political experience of the First Republic, the room for manoeuvre thus shrank, the evocative power of that distant period actually expanded: the question soon became one of how to build a new 1792, which would restore the period of democracy lost long before. In these terms, the reference to the First Republic was decisive: it indicated what form of new order the first democrats, like the many people disappointed in Louis Philippe's monarchy, were looking for or were at least willing to accept.

In this context, the question of the relationship between democracy and Christianity, characterized by the Saint-Simonian apostolate and Lamennais' break with the church, once again came to the fore, immediately after the first workers' protests, as a social issue. And so, as we have seen, a Catholic and revolutionary political generation flourished at the same time, with France's Christian identity employed as the justificatory element in its claim to shape the future for the whole of Europe. Not everyone was in agreement with regard to the religious identity of the renewal policy, including those who recognized the centrality of the Christian revival in France. Still in the 1840s, when the relationship between religion and revolution seemed to revive unanimist and coercive practices, Edgar Quinet made a speech at the Collège de France to indicate that the spirit of Catholicism favoured the cult of the Incorruptible, which seemed to dominate republicanism.[57] He also wanted to oppose, with the image of a pope-like Robespierre, a change of an all-embracing kind destined to form a dramatic obstacle in the search for the individual and libertarian identity of the revolutionary process. In his words, there returned the dilemma that the republican movement had been struggling with since its re-composition in the aftermath of 1830: those who proposed Robespierrism in terms of a great movement of social palingenesis found it difficult to coexist with those who doubted that the revolutionary vitality of the sovereign people could find expression in the sort of authoritarian structure that reference to the Year II government invoked.

This conflict resulted in the extraordinary publishing year of 1847, with one Parisian announcement after another heralding the release of three monumental works on the French Revolution. The first to appear was that of the leading scholar of the time, Lamartine,[58] followed not long after by the works of Jules Michelet[59] – the Collège de France lecturer regarded as the most prestigious intellectual of the day – and Louis Blanc,[60] the socialist politician who, better than any other, symbolized the relationship between democracy and the social question in the context of referencing Year II.

While inevitably proffered, the juxtaposition of these three works is actually completely unwarranted: only Lamartine's *Histoire des girondins* was completed in 1847; the other two, just beginning, stretched out across the following years, to be much affected, therefore, by those events that, revolutionary first, then Bonapartist later, occurred in France. In other words, the works of Michelet and Blanc, while originating in the same cultural climate as that of Lamartine, developed through a very different political scenario and soon ended up losing that direct connection with the period of the July monarchy that a dating of 1847 might suggest.

The case of the *Histoire des Girondins*, on the other hand, is quite different, remaining as it did entirely within the cultural debate following the 1830 revolution.[61] It was indeed, in the intentions of its author, a sort of solution to the problem of democratic opposition in France, which the diatribes regarding the 1792 precedent had repeatedly brought to light. How Lamartine tackled the preceding revolutionary period does indicate, after all, that it was politics and not a passion for history that dictated such sudden interest. He came to history late, after a successful career as a poet in the 1820s, and only after the 1830 revolution had stirred in him the desire for an even more significant role in public life. His enthusiasm for the July Days, however, had run only along liberal lines, with no involvement with republicanism – even at the beginning of the 1840s, Lamartine seemed to believe in the task of the Orleanist monarchy to bring peace to the French in the name of a return to the profound values of 1789. The turning point took place on the occasion of the parliamentary debate of 1843, when he announced that he was no longer in agreement with the majority that he had hitherto supported. At the same time, he began his work on the revolution.

The two things were certainly related, but it would be ungenerous to conclude that his decision was dictated only by political – or, even worse, financial – calculation. Rather, he was convinced that it was his duty as a writer to overcome the aporia still present in French society and to propose a solution to the political problem of how to lead society as a whole to fully embrace the values of freedom and equality inherent in the message of 1789. Lamartine's work, then, arose out of the confident (and in some ways presumptuous) expectation that he could make a decisive contribution to dissolving conflict in French politics through a work that would gather the various political groupings of the time around the values of the great revolution. However, his work took more than four years to complete and when it was finally printed – selling extraordinarily well – it was in all probability a different creature from its author's initial intentions: aggrandisement of 1789 had, under the weight of the political moment, turned into a specific republican political proposal for the France of the time.

The chronological parenthesis itself was to suggest the change of strategy, starting with Mirabeau's death and concluding with Robespierre's: it is precisely this decision to emphasize the demise of two key figures that is meant to evoke the incompleteness of the revolutionary process. With Mirabeau's death, the dream of a constitutional monarchy was lost; with Robespierre's execution, hope for a social republic came to an end. Between these two events, however, there had taken place the most passionate attempt to give shape to a radical transformation of French society, and this, in the context of the Republic, had led to the practice of democracy. Lamartine decided to deploy his characters on this terrain, where the Girondins are certainly present, especially in the portraits of Brissot and Vergniaud, but are not the only leading figures in the story – in some ways, even greater attention is reserved for their adversaries, where Robespierre stands out, but Danton, too, gets his share of the limelight.

Saint-Domingue and the September Massacres. The idea was to present the birth of the Republic as a natural continuation of the revolutionary universal ideals of 1789, and it is in this context that all its main characters move, even though Lamartine never misses an opportunity to underline their unpreparedness (and therefore weakness) in the face of such an onerous task.

In fact, nobody in his pages escapes unscathed by criticism and comment: Louis XVI and Lafayette are of a disarming political fragility; the Girondins, animated by the best of intentions, never have a clear view of the situation in which they intend to intervene and must bear the serious responsibility of having unleashed a war in which the revolution would consume itself; the Montagnards manage to handle the dramatic moment of Year II, but their ranks include characters as atrocious as Marat, or as venal as Danton, while their guide Robespierre is responsible for an authoritarian form of politics and for having confused revolutionary spirituality with the cult of the Goddess of Reason. A set of other characters revolve around these figures – this includes numerous women and particular prominence is assigned to Charlotte Corday's generous gesture – and all of them come together to compose a picture that is chaotic and formidable at the same time, where an entire society seems to be on the verge of achieving an extraordinary result – epochal change – only in the end to lose its way entirely.

Apart from the dramatization, which gave Lamartine his own personal publishing Austerlitz, his pages were supported by a clear design, aimed at bringing together the fragmented opposition to Louis Philippe within the framework of a precise political line. In the first place, he declared that the Republic constituted the natural continuation of the universalistic values of 1789 and therefore suggested that this particular institutional form would be much better than a monarchy in terms of carrying out such a programme. Immediately after this, he was careful to note that the violence that had also marked the short life of the First Republic was the consequence of a series of mistakes almost all made during the previous constitutional period – such as the Civil Constitution of the Clergy, the gaps in the constitution of 1791 and the deplorable decision to go to war. In other words, the Republic had inherited an already deteriorated political situation, where, as he said, it was an easy time for sedition and revolution to become confused. In this context, the horror of the September Massacres – and, subsequently, the worst features of the Terror – were limited to the abominable actions of a handful of people and Lamartine was careful to repeatedly distinguish the profound nature of the Republic from the dramatic debacles to which it was brought by the weakness of political leadership.

Overall, in fact, in the republican field, too, people's inadequacy in the face of their daunting task regularly prevailed over their resolution. But precisely an awareness of the unpreparedness of the republican political class made that ill-fated experience one to learn from, as long as the new France took proper care not to repeat its mistakes. On the one hand, therefore, violence had to be rejected: this meant the prompt exclusion from revolutionary circles not only of thugs and assassins, but also of the political mentality, similar to Marat's, that incited people to slaughter. There had to be an equally firm attitude with regard to war – the Girondins had promoted war with heedless revolutionary enthusiasm and were not, therefore, exempt from severe criticism.

In the light of these preclusions, a renewed adherence to the great universal values of freedom and equality had instead to be established – including social values, those which in Year II had found a sincere form of expression. Robespierre, the embodiment of such an attempt, nevertheless failed, when, to seek popularity, he set out on the easy path of government authoritarianism, sacrificing first the Girondins and then Danton in the name of maintaining republican purity. In this context, however, the Girondins, defeated, and to a great extent responsible for their own defeat, returned as the leading figures in the historical narrative, their dramatic political experience summing up both the grandeur and limitations of the entire revolutionary process. And from there, therefore, taking into account what seemed possible, and everything that had instead been lost, it was necessary to start again.

However, if the republican ideal – defined as the practice of political democracy in the context of legality – was not in question, it remained to establish the point of equilibrium on which the different opposition groups to Louis Philippe could converge. In this regard, the way in which Lamartine presented the precedent of the First Republic spoke volumes for his specific political proposal: it was a question of mediating between the Girondins and the Montagnards, abandoning the warlike nature of the former and the repeated temptation to resort to violence of the latter, in order to identify a common centre in political democracy. Needless to say, extremist circles had to be excluded from this perspective – those circles which, in the 1840s, were a source of great worry to Louis Philippe's police – while a hand was extended to the Robespierrists, as long as the latter rejected any desire to re-adopt the violence and authoritarianism of the revolutionary government.

The message, as shown by the extraordinary success of the work, did not go unnoticed: already in the Banquet Campaign, the first sign of the tempest destined to overwhelm the Guizot government and the entire Orleanist monarchy, the democratic opposition would repeatedly praise Lamartine precisely for having definitively rehabilitated Robespierre and for thus having bestowed a sense of completeness on the democratism of Year II. The author, however, remained largely indifferent to this acclaim, preferring instead to emphasize the risks that an excess of sentimentality towards 1793 could mean losing sight of the return to 1789 that should constitute the objective of every good democrat. In other words, it must have been clear to Lamartine, with 1848 at the door, that his proposal for a republicanism capable of leaving behind the paraphernalia of Year II to fall back on the reassuring framework of 1789 was encountering strong resistance and that his work, instead of reinforcing that prospect, had ended up providing support for many in their strenuous defence of Year II.

Shortly thereafter, 1848 would give shape to Lamartine's expectations, but also to his concerns. While his *Histoire des Girondins* succeeded in the intention of constituting a political platform for the period of democracy ushered in by the February 1848 revolution – and, not surprisingly, its author would be foreign minister in the first executive of the Second Republic – his proposal was freighted with the ambiguity that had dominated all democratic historiography in the years of Louis Philippe. Beyond Robespierre was a void soon filled by Bonapartism and even Lamartine would not countenance any resurgence of influence from the Directory period. It was a rejection which French politics would pay a heavy price for during the dramatic events of the Second Republic.

5. *Anarchie française*

In 1831, in the aftermath of the revolution, after having sworn fidelity, not without some hesitation, to the new regime, Alexis de Tocqueville, a young aristocrat from a legitimist family, embarked on a trip to the United States, charged by the government of Louis Philippe to study the American prison system. He would return after a few months, delivering the requested report, but above all retaining the memory of a cultural experience that would live with him forever. In the following years, he was in direct contact with an incandescent political situation where France seemed poised between liberty and ruin. Extremely worried by the aggression of social protest, he looked back at the American political model in order to draw a picture of representative democracy where admiration is tempered by doubt that such a point of equilibrium could really be established in Europe.[62] His work *La démocratie en Amérique*, however, would take some time to actually see the light of day (the first volume is from 1835, while the second had to wait until 1840)[63] and the prolonged duration of its composition means that the work is something more than an impression of the moment. In the end, it is influenced much more than it might seem by the parallel developments in French politics: the situation in which Tocqueville launched – and many years later concluded – his work had in fact taken on the sad hues of an Orleanist monarchy unable to make much of a dent in a society that was still to a large extent corporatist, and which, from below, through the magic term 'association', raised more than one serious obstacle to the affirmation of a complete system of liberty.

All those who had fought against the reactionary rule of Charles X since the 1820s, and who had so enthusiastically welcomed the Glorious July Days, found themselves following the same anxious line of thought as de Tocqueville. Thierry and Guizot, Mignet and Thiers – with their very different levels of responsibility – all looked on in astonishment at the huge difficulties of Louis Philippe's France and soon all had to agree that what had seemed like the spring of a new period of freedom had instead turned out to be a winter of political confrontation and social conflict. It was clear to all of them that there was a profound imbalance between the cultural model they had managed to instil in the French society of the time and its translation into a concrete government project. History's deployment in full support of the cause of freedom, which should have reconciled all of France with its past, had instead had the opposite effect of exasperating the situations of conflict and had even handed over to the parties involved a myriad of topics of argument that had not previously been available to them. Proof of this was the referencing of the great revolution, which (almost) all the main figures on the political scene of the time considered the founding moment of French modernity, but which certainly did not constitute a shared value, since the republicans – by going back to the basic ideas of the works by Mignet and Thiers – had found there supporting evidence for their attempt to overthrow the Louis Philippe monarchy.

The reference to the great revolution had exacerbated the conflicts. The liberals were inspired by 1789, the republicans such as Lamartine looked to 1792, while the ultra-radicals and first socialists were galvanized by the political experience of Year II. The obstacles encountered by the Orleanist monarchy in proposing a hegemonic reading of the revolution of 1789 made it possible, from the legitimist and conservative point of view, to participate in the historiographical debates of the 1830s. To be called into question in particular was the entirely positive reading of the revolutionary decade that Mignet and Thiers had proposed, as a sterile pretension to enclose in teleological terms the whole history of France. The writings of Cyprien Desmarais, a legitimist historian who accepted the constitution as an integral part of the historical mission of the Bourbons, bear witness to this interpretive approach, which led to consider the Revolution of 1830 as responsible for this abyss of anarchy and populism in which France had unfortunately sunk.

In his work, published in 1834, Desmarais reviewed the main works devoted to the revolution of 1789, taking up what Chateaubriand had written against the teleological reading proposed by Mignet and Thiers.[64] These two authors, as claimed by Desmarais, had developed the classic thesis according to which circumstances excused all the misdeeds of the revolutionary process, precisely to avoid admitting that any popular intervention in the political sphere invariably constituted a disturbing element of the social order. Were this conviction adopted, the author could say that the revolutionary elites who, in 1789, had appealed to the people, should be held responsible for what happened thereafter.

This radical criticism of the two liberal historians was accompanied by a systematic review of the errors they had committed not only in their interpretation of the Terror, but also of the first years of the Revolution, when it had been claimed to legitimize the new constitution by popular sovereignty. To strengthen his positions, Desmarais also appealed to Burke, from whom he quoted large extracts to show his extraordinary clairvoyance about subsequent political events in France. Desmarais could then recover the theses of Mme de Staël, which had formerly been aimed at a radical renewal of the Constituents. This rereading of the *Considerations on the French Revolution* in an anti-liberal perspective was shared by another staunch legitimist, Eugène Labaume. His work, published in 1834, went so far as to assert that to explain the course of the Revolution as it was postulated by Thiers and Mignet was to justify the crimes of Marat and Robespierre.[65]

The words of Desmarais and Labaume shed light on the progressive weakening of the liberal interpretative proposal, which, however, at the same time, remained, at a European level, an essential reference, both for those who wanted to propose a reading of the Revolution as a founding moment of modernity and for those who considered it a historiographical source that had to be called into question only for its political implications.

It was the volcanic nature of French politics of those years that would end up weakening the interpretative offering of the new liberal historiography, which, straddling the 1830s, was also an obligatory reference for those throughout Europe who wanted to relegate readings that demonized 1789 to their upper shelves. The fluctuating fortunes of Mignet and Thiers outside France – where, initially acclaimed, they were then repeatedly accused of having constructed an absolutist interpretation of the revolutionary events – speak volumes about to what extent, in this irregular process of references to their works, a decisive role was played by the impossible liberal balance of Orleanist France at that time. The relaunch of Anglo-American exceptionalism as well as the plurality of voices in the rest of Europe aimed at building a national past in which the revolutionary and Napoleonic periods were rightly traced back to a mere – albeit very significant – parenthesis, meant that the historiographical value of the works by Mignet and Thiers was in line with the changing attitude held outside France with respect to the experience of the July monarchy.

At first, not surprisingly, when their works had seemed a timely witness to French liberalism's courageous resistance to the reactionary direction of Charles X, reference to Mignet and Thiers had been useful in terms of clearing the field of portrayals of an old order that still, in a Europe emerging from the Napoleonic storm, seemed to aspire to dictating the cultural line. In Italy, for example, even in 1827, a well-known Pisan jurist such as Francesco Forti, who worked on the *Antologia* of Gian Pietro Viesseux, could dismiss Pietro Manzi's history of the French Revolution which had appeared in Tuscany just the year before,[66] as an old instrument of times irremediably past. It was Thiers's work that convinced him of the extent to which Manzi's writings – a show of disapproval, in accordance with the counter-revolutionary line, of the movement towards liberty countenanced by the Estates General – belonged to a genre of idle polemicism. Thiers, in Forti's opinion, had once and for all demolished the arguments of 'men of limited vision' who usually blamed 'the French revolution on philosophers, on Necker, on the Duke of Orleans or on English gold'.[67]

Similarly, this time in Great Britain, harsh criticism had been dealt out to a very popular biography of Napoleon printed in 1827 and written by Walter Scott at the height of his success. Reviewing it the following year, John Stuart Mill, who had for some time been passionate about French politics and culture, had carefully pointed out that the first part of Scott's work, entirely dedicated to the revolutionary decade, was utterly wrong-headed, in supine thrall to the conservative reading of 1789 that Burke had managed to impose as Britain's authentic interpretative version.[68]

Mill's stern criticism essentially reproached the great Scottish novelist for considering the English model a suitable basis for drawing comparisons, obviously negative in tone, in relation to every other tradition. It accused him of an unbearably Tory approach to the events that originated in 1789 and showed exactly why the French cultural renewal of the 1820s had met with such acclaim in its native land. The radical and libertarian philosopher made no secret of his devotion to the revolution in its first, thrilling phase and, with youthful enthusiasm, presented himself as a follower of the Girondins, having in all probability familiarized himself with the events through reading the aforementioned work by Dulaure. Stirred by a passion that never entirely faded over the years, he had been careful to present the most recent examples of French historiography to the British public, reviewing Mignet's work in laudatory terms in 1826 and the year after singing the praises of Dulaure, whose monumental history of Paris seemed to him a wonderful illustration of how it was possible, while talking about the capital of France, to write a history of European civilization as a whole.[69] The 1830 watershed – Mill was present as an eyewitness in its early stages – further convinced him that political modernity was to be found in France and prompted him to consider writing his own history of the revolution, which in all probability would have twinned July 1789 with that of 1830. While he mentioned this idea in his correspondence, nothing concrete ever came of it and it soon slipped from his intellectual horizon, the usual reason for this sudden change of perspective being given as his meeting with Carlyle, in September 1831: he essentially handed custody of the enterprise over to the Scottish historian, helping the project along through provision of materials and reading lists.[70]

And yet, Mill's interest in the revolution, which went hand in hand with his severe criticism of the conservatism of British politics, never entirely disappeared, finding the opportunity to emerge as he mounted a resistance to the conservative wave repeatedly stirred up by British pens where 1789 was concerned throughout the entire July monarchy. Thus, in 1833, Mill published a vitriolic review of the recently successful *History of Europe during the French Revolution* by Archibald Alison:[71] it seemed to Mill a mere reconstruction of British military triumph, dominated by an intolerable Tory spirit and, in substance, despite its detailed up-to-date bibliography, it actually failed to understand the real significance of 1789.[72] The fact that Mill renounced his intention of writing a history of the revolution, but did not miss a chance to lash out at those who attempted the task from positions opposed to his own, suggests that other factors still intervened to discourage him from the undertaking, announced though it was several times. First of all, the certainty that his position was a minority one in Britain, but perhaps – and even more so – an equally strong conviction that his passion for freedom and for a democracy resolutely distant from any form of political authoritarianism was not a very popular proposition in Paris either.

France's peculiar political situation, where the king Louis Philippe monarchy soon appeared to betray the great hope of renewal engendered by the street riots in 1830 and the sudden explosion of social issues, certainly prompted Mill to take an interest in the Saint-Simonian reading of French history. It should not be forgotten, however, that, behind this decision, there lay the rejection of his beloved Girondins by almost all the republicans of the time. His insistence on the ideas of a political party that nobody, in French democratism, seemed any longer intent on reinstating as the basis of a renewed strategy of liberty convinced him that he was on the sidelines of the political and historiographical debate as it was over the Channel, and this led him to abandon a project that he already knew had no support in Britain.

On the other hand, it is no coincidence that his renunciation of the enterprise coincided with the start of the first contestation, from the left, of the Mignet and Thiers works on which he laid such store. An example of an approach critical of liberal historians for an unacceptable reading of the republican period was, for example, provided in dramatic form by Georg Büchner in Germany. In 1835 he completed *Dantons Tod*, a fierce reconstruction of the violent political conflict in Year II Paris, where, while the main character is the champion of the Indulgents, the author is beyond any doubt on the side of Robespierre the Incorruptible.[73]

The play was in fact in line with the interest in the figure of Robespierre, brought back into favour by the rise of republicanism in France, and constitutes a clear political choice by Buchner in the confrontation, within the European democracy of the time, between Robespierrist radicalism and a republicanism that found its spokesman in Danton. However, the latter's character appears to be largely inspired by the description in Thiers, with Buchner exaggerating the salient features of the portrait of the revolutionary that the historian had provided. The play thus overworked the tired and worn theme of a Danton unable to understand that his moment was in eclipse, transforming into personal tragedy what Thiers had formulated in the context of a cyclonic revolutionary process. Until here, nonetheless, the perspective was that of a left-wing critique of the fundamental work of the liberal historians: their overall reconstruction of events was, however, appreciated. Within the framework of a marked ideological approach, it was employed to denounce a policy of moderation that would be the utter ruin of the social revolutionary thrust inherent in the tumultuous evolution of Year II.

Criticism of Thiers, however, also began to run along openly conservative lines, as a result of the difficulties encountered by the Orleanist monarchy in stabilizing the radical change of 1789 around a constitutional model. The wholly positive reading of the revolutionary decade that Mignet and Thiers had brought to the historiographical debate was thus soon forthrightly contested as a sterile claim to enclose France's entire history within finalistic terms. To return to Italy, for example, in the early 1830s, in the last years of his adventurous existence, Lazzaro Papi, a curious figure, part intrepid explorer and part official historian for the Tuscan House of Lorraine, published a section of a weighty piece of work intended to give a detailed picture of events in France from the crisis of the old order to the return of the Bourbons.[74] The interpretative framework was set out from the first pages, where Papi noted that the development of the revolution was undoubtedly the consequence of the irresponsible resistance of the aristocracy, but above all of the members of the Constituent Assembly themselves, who, in a frenzy to wholly subvert the traditional order, encouraged an impulsive population to take to the streets. This handed things over to the demagogues, whose lust for power and wealth led to the creation of factions, with the result that political manoeuvring turned into opportunities for massacre and revenge. The whole of France was inevitably dragged into tyranny, first under Robespierre and then Napoleon. There was certainly nothing original in Papi's ideas, but, some time later, when it became clear after 1848 that French history seemed to be repeating itself – first, revolution, then subjection to tyranny – there was no shortage of those who sought sustenance from his words in order to distinguish the parallel Italian events from those in Paris. In 1853, in Turin, the mustering place for Italian patriotism after the defeat that followed to the national revolution of 1848, Papi's work was again presented to the public with a warning from the publishers, where a direct comparison was introduced between his work and that of Thiers:

> We will not say that Thiers's work is defeated by that of Papi's for abundance of facts and wealth of documents, but it is certain that the Italian writer dominates the French in a more just and dispassionate appreciation of men and things, and for that sacred impetus of the heart with which he feels and colours virtue and crime, misfortune and pain, which the pen of the Frenchman recounts with a kind of cynical impassivity permeated with fatalism.[75]

Such words returned to a critique of the liberal historical school which liked to claim – Mignet as well as Thiers – that detachment in the analysis of events should foster understanding and consequently open the way to the possibility of mastering them. In the context of the open rejection of the determinism of the two champions of liberal historiography, there is no doubt that the lion's share was taken by English-speaking historians. Many of them, in the years of the July monarchy, as republican fever rose in France, banded together against the malevolent influence of 1789 and insisted on the responsibility, especially of Thiers, for spreading an interpretation aimed at justifying the revolutionary path in each and every case, even when it plunged into the fearful abyss of violence and despotism.

The first sign that the climate in this regard was changing is offered by the 1832 parliamentary debate on the revision of the electoral system that pitted John Croker against Thomas Babington Macaulay in the House of Lords. Macaulay was in favour of approving the reform, recalling that in France, in 1789, precisely because it had opposed strenuous resistance to any change, the aristocracy had experienced a disaster that Britain had instead still managed to avoid. There is no doubt that his words held reminiscences of reading Madame de Staël's work, as well that of Thiers himself and therefore, in essence, constituted a significant acceptance of the new political direction of Louis Philippe's France. Croker, though, in response, as someone with a keen interest in 1789 – so much so that he accumulated a collection of documents still today the pride of the British Museum – attacked him heavily, even questioning whether he knew what he was talking about. Emphasizing that the French aristocracy had been condemned by their compliant pusillanimity rather than stolid determination, he urged strenuous resistance to be offered to any change, and reiterated, following on from Burke, that nothing could be saved of what had occurred across the Channel since 1789.

On this occasion, the match was won by Macaulay, with the reform surviving parliamentary resistance from the more conservative sectors. Croker abandoned his seat rather than live with an electoral law that he both despised and greatly feared and for some time the Whig party, having, in part thanks to Macaulay, overcome this difficult parliamentary moment, tried to re-establish a political link with the new liberal France. It is no coincidence, for example, that in 1837 James McIntosh's *Vindiciae gallicae* was reprinted, a work that, in the aftermath of 1789, represented a voice in favour of the constitutional change in France and which, initially with great success, held its own against Burke's *Reflections*.

However, the developments in French politics and the tensions that began to agitate British society in the 1840s soon had the effect of restoring Croker's opinions to political grace. Any further attempt to democratize political life was swiftly brought to a halt by pointing a trembling finger at French political instability, and it became an easy thing to state that, following the example over the Channel, any further change would irreversibly alter the admirable constitutional balance of 1688. Burke thus returned to the centre of the scene, because, regardless of the political opinions of the writers and without distinguishing too much between Whigs and Tories, everyone agreed on the need to reaffirm British exceptionality. It was necessary, at the same time, to be highly critical of the French historiography responsible for the cynical justificationism of every iniquity perpetrated by the revolution in order to safeguard 1789 as the founding act of French modernity.

A clear position in this context is offered by William Smyth, regius professor of history at Cambridge, who, an elderly man in 1840, published his *Lectures on the French Revolution*, intended to represent a summation of his decades of teaching and the interest he had always had in 1789.[76] Given his age, he had experienced the last decade of the eighteenth century at first hand, when he had openly sided with liberal developments in France and played no part in the demonizing campaign of 1789 promoted by Burke. But a lot of water had flowed under the bridges of English politics by 1840 and Smyth's ideas – he still identified as a Whig, but shared little or nothing with the spirit of the nineteenth century – were dramatically affected not only by the Napoleonic years but, and to a far greater extent, by the revolutionary revival in France in the 1830s. During the parliamentary debate in which Croker went head to head with Macaulay, Smyth, such a firm opponent of Burke's opinions in his youth, showed that he was now very much in sympathy with them: he made it clear that the British constitution was an intangible thing and warned that electoral reform was a prelude to its overthrow. In this light, his lessons on the Revolution sounded like an admonition aimed at preventing the outbreak of a rebellion as an unexpected backlash of a reforming policy. But what is important to underline is the fact that his reading of revolutionary events, while rejecting the cornerstones of conservative ideas, in reality, marked as it was by the experience of Napoleonic despotism and the apparently impracticability of the exercise of freedom in France, ended up in that particular frame of reference. Thus, Smyth maintained certain assumptions of late eighteenth-century Whig tradition, believing as he did that the revolution was the product of stolid parliamentary resistance, indicating the misgovernment of Louis XVI as the main reason for the revolutionary explosion, and even understanding the intervention of the people in July 1789. At the same time, however, while continuing to remain distinct from traditionally conservative readings, he nevertheless agreed on the danger of the revolutionary event as a whole and he employed earnest words to avert, albeit in different forms, its repetition.[77]

In other words, regardless of opinion in domestic politics, everyone, whether Whig or Tory, agreed on the need to confront the threat of French contagion. This attitude involved a renewed exaltation of British political specificity accompanied – it could hardly have been otherwise – by condemnation of a cynical and self-absolving French historiography, which it became absolutely necessary to keep at a safe distance. It seems significant that, during the 1840s, British histories of the French Revolution came one after another, all having in common the condemnation of the works of Mignet and Thiers, held responsible for the worrying return to favour of Year II in the French political society of the time. The success of Carlyle's work, as will shortly be seen, was also a reason for so much interest, but perhaps even more so was the concern to reiterate that French liberals like Thiers could never have emulated British exceptionalism. It was a distancing mechanism that sounded like a form of reassurance with regard to the fact that it would be impossible for Gallic madness to arrive on British shores.

Thus, in 1842, again in Cambridge university circles, the reverend Frederich Fysh,[78] a great expert on the significance of prophecies that followed one after the other down through history, published his own reading of the revolution. Here, resolute condemnation of the Terror – a sort of Satanish reign – was accompanied by much loud protest against Mignet and Thiers, branding their repeated recourse to the extreme circumstances that had imposed certain dramatic decisions as completely 'unworthy of a reflecting man, much less is it to be endured when coming from a historian'. In the years immediately following, others thronged to lend a helping hand along similar lines: in 1844, it was the turn of Scottish writer Charles MacFarlane who, in the attempt to emulate Walter Scott, wrote his own voluminous history of the revolution.[79] The Republic and the Terror were proposed as 1789's descent into hell and Mignet and Thiers were duly evoked (and soundly thrashed) whenever they tried even simply to understand why the violence of the people and of the government had ended up prevailing over the ingenuous auspices of liberty. Even more conservative in tone was Frederica Rowan, who also grappled with the subject in 1844, making it clear that universal suffrage lay at the basis of French anarchy and that, once again, Thiers bore grave responsibility for claiming to justify something that could only possibly be reacted to with disgusted condemnation.[80] All in all, these writings would not deserve a glance if they did not suggest, appearing hastily as they did roughly all in the same years, that it was Carlyle's work, composed between 1834 and 1837[81] and greeted with immense enthusiasm by both critics and public, that prompted a conservative reading of the events in France.[82]

This point is not undisputed: Carlyle's *Revolution* met with agreement on both sides and in the opinions of subsequent generations of historians, too, it maintained an ambiguous consensus, on one side regarded as settling accounts with Burke and, on the other, as allowing the latter's ideas to continue to dominate the British view of 1789 throughout the nineteenth century and beyond. The interpretative perspective of the 1840s outlined earlier speaks volumes about how, independently of the author's opinions – though this was not a problem he ever actually considered – his work was a useful one, from the years immediately following, in terms of rejecting the reasons for the revolution themselves, of consequently relaunching the particularity and primacy of the English model and therefore, albeit indirectly, of restoring the shine to Burke's traditionalist discourse. This does not mean, of course, that Carlyle actually took up Burke's arguments – his own assumptions were diametrically opposite to those of the Irish statesman's. As his friend Mill pointed out in an enthusiastic review, the work's basis was the belief that a centuries-old lie had ruled France – which was that the *ancien régime* was a fair and legitimate power structure, while instead it was an oppressive system in the hands of a tiny minority of priests and aristocrats who had unjustly appropriated power. Unlike Burke, for whom the traditions of the old order were everything and nothing should ever be allowed to break them, Carlyle believed instead that the revolution took place as the all too understandable reaction of the excluded – it made little difference whether, as subjects, they were deserving or heinous – to the revelation of an enormous lie which, for a tremendously long period of time, had shored up the social equilibrium across the Channel.

And yet, beyond the initial premise, which substantially justified 1789 in the name of a feeling of rejection and revenge deemed inevitable in the face of the crime to which it was a reaction, Carlyle's reading of the events that soon followed was one of clear disparagement. The three books which made up the work had revealing titles: *Bastille, Constitution, Guillotine*. The revolutionary events, running from 1789 to Year II, unfolded therefore along a path that emphasized collective disdain with regard to Court misgovernment, which became the protest of an armed population only thanks to the weakness of Louis XVI. A constitutional solution was vainly attempted, but the violent revolt against the Crown would plunge all of French society into the inferno of the Terror.

In other words, if called upon to express an overall opinion with respect to the results of 1789, Carlyle, while showing that he understood the reasons for the revolution, would not hesitate to pronounce a stern judgement. His friend Mill reproached him for this – very discreetly – when, on the one hand, he praised Carlyle's poetic force, which also made his history of the revolution a masterpiece in literary terms, while, on the other, hastening to declare that he disagreed with the Scots writer's ideas on more than one point. Hyppolite Taine reproached him for the same thing in an essay published in 1864, writing that the strong influence of Scottish Puritanism had prevented Carlyle from grasping the profound significance of the revolutionary struggle, with the result that, in his reconstruction, while the prose was majestic, no effort was made to understand the deep mechanisms of the revolutionary process.

At around the same time, Jules Michelet pronounced his own stern judgement on Carlyle's work, accusing him of making a nonchalant, if inadequate, use of sources and not even attempting to grasp the deep feelings that, during the political events of the late eighteenth century, stirred within the French people. These accusations were in some ways not all mistaken: Carlyle's declared aim had been to astound readers, laying before their eyes what he himself had felt when confronted with eyewitness accounts and documents of the time, which gave a dramatic and at the time same epic picture of events in vertiginous motion. His sources had in fact been above all contemporary testimonies, collected in the *Moniteur*, in the collection of *Choix des rapports, opinions et discours*, as well as in the memoirs published during the Restoration and particularly in the monumental work by Buchez and Roux. This did not mean, however, that he had any interest in revolutionary historiography: he knew Mignet and Thiers, but regarded them rather snobbishly: their reconstructions while rigorous, seemed cold and detached and completely devoid of that sense of giddy ferment that had certainly been conveyed by those caught up in the events and which Carlyle intended to reproduce in all their most searching detail. He appreciated the documentary efforts of Buchez and Roux, which he counted on heavily for his own reconstruction, but nothing more – he felt too distant from their Catholic identity and their messianic wish for a new revolution to arrive as soon as possible. In Carlyle's view, the great descriptive scenes, where famous characters and obscure commoners were equally presented, formed the authentic tools available to historians to illuminate the tumultuous nature of the political process and in this context he obtained the better results, taking care to let the combined images dominate over his commentary on the individual phases of revolutionary history. This is why his work was met with consensus even in the circles of the revolution's most ardent supporters: he was careful not to lean openly towards any particular group, without ever forgetting to indicate the reasons that lay behind the dramatic situations of the revolutionary process: thus, the September Massacres grew out of the fear of invasion, Danton perhaps bore responsibility but had not made it the instrument for his own personal gain; Louis XVI met with an unfortunate end, but his fate was not so different from that previously suffered by Charles I in England; and, above all, the many victims of the Terror were, in hindsight, small beer compared to those accumulated by other sovereigns and other wars.

This search for impartiality, however, around which his treatment of events was made to turn, was not always successful. When it came to illustrating the character of individual figures, Carlyle's political preferences immediately reappeared. From the opening pages, on the occasion of the meeting of the Estates General, the figures of Mirabeau and Robespierre are produced, seeming to represent the extremes in the scale of values established by the author: the former leading to the ephemeral triumph of the revolutionary movement over the fragile authority of the Crown, the latter seeming to stir up from the depths the movements of the *sans-culottes* – often portrayed as a monster from Tartarus spewed out directly onto the political scene. Along these lines, especially in the English-speaking world, where Carlyle's work was an immediate success, it is not difficult to conclude that nothing of substance was grasped of what Alphonse Aulard, on the eve of the First World War, aspired to discern in it in favour of the revolution. There prevailed, rather, a widespread discourse in Britain that saw the 1789 revolution as an unlikely emulation of that of 1688, and the figure of Mirabeau, soon portrayed as the unfortunate exponent of a revolt launched in the name of freedom, confirmed, in reality, how distant from revolutionary France the British political model remained. Hence, the insistence on the republican degeneration of the revolution; the rejection once more of the democratization of the political process; the demonization of the Terror; and the criticism of Year II, whose violence and paroxysms Carlyle so brilliantly succeeded in capturing. This is also the context for the criticism directed at Mignet and Thiers, who had deliberately attempted the gruelling task of rehabilitating Year II in the belief that in this way it was possible, once and for all, to settle accounts with tradition; and also, in the final analysis, for the hymn of praise that soon unravelled in favour of a United Kingdom that, since 1789, had strenuously resisted every wrong move made by European politics. At bottom, nevertheless, duly documented by the modest historiographical operations of the 1840s, there was anguish, stirred up by the fear that the British political model, too, could emerge overwhelmed by a social crisis brought to the tipping point by its neighbour across the Channel. In the snobbery towards the monarchy of Louis Philippe and those who sang his praises, in the aggrandisement of the unattainable perfection of the English political model, there was the terrible anxiety that the situations depicted in Carlyle's writings were soon destined to be repeated, and not only in France. The success of his work was intertwined with the malaise of a society increasingly dominated by inequality.

3

From national myth to the myth of nations, 1848–75

The political crisis of 1848, starting with the fall of Louis Philippe's regime, and ending three years later with Louis Bonaparte's coup, represented a momentous time for the renewal of the studies devoted to the Great Revolution, a mirror through which the most heated issues of the time could be raised. Writing about 1789 did not only imply passing judgement – often negative – on the protagonists of the present, it also meant investigating the reasons for the continuous political instability seemingly characterizing France, inviting reflections on the relationship between modernity and revolution. The three different levels overlap, which explains the copious abundance of historical studies – in terms of both publishing and intellectual development – which, marking this part of the century, towered over by Michelet and his work. His *Histoire de la Révolution* is structured around the idea that the revolution was a refoundation of the political identity of the French nation thanks to the action of a 'People' capable of turning into an engine of progress destined to encompass the whole of Europe.

Michelet's monumental work was soon subjected nevertheless to harsh criticism by the representatives of a multifarious republican front. In addition to Blanc and Hamel, ever ready to highlight the limits of the Revolution's regenerative effects which Michelet had instead praised, the most vigorous criticism, albeit for different reasons, came from Tocqueville and Quinet, who both insisted on the heavy influence of the *ancien régime* on the development of the Revolution. However, whereas the former, a Norman aristocrat, saw in Bonaparte's actions the fulfilment of the social levelling begun under the *ancien régime*, Quinet, with his republican (and moral) intransigence, insisted instead on the ambiguities and the contradictions of the Revolution, which, to his mind, had led to the use of terrorist-like blind violence. The risks involved in a glorification of 1789 would be highlighted by both Mazzini and Marx, for whom the French Revolution had only been the first step on the road to a profound social upheaval. Finally, the last and most radical opposition took shape in the German-speaking world through Von Sybel, who countered Michelet's revolution of freedom with the revolution of the Nation, of which Bismarck's Germany was, to his mind, the incarnation.

1. The social contract of the nation

For Lamartine, too, his Austerlitz triumph would shortly be followed by a Waterloo: however, he was very wrong to indicate the aftermath of the publication of the *Histoire des Girondins* as his moment of victory. In fact, the work's success showed that the time of consensus had just begun, with the culmination coming soon, when the February 1848 revolution catapulted him to the leadership of the new republic's provisional government, while universal male suffrage for the new assembly, held in April, saw him elected in over ten departments.[1]

For the occasion, Lamartine illustrated his ideal of a French society cleansed of conflict and bound by a spirit of unity to reduce the macroscopic social contradictions which the Louis Philippe monarchy had instead casually exploited. In the few weeks of his government, Lamartine confirmed his preference for a capitalism based mainly on small ownership, which, not requiring large individual shares, fostered the progressive reabsorption of economic inequalities within the framework of a nation of owners. In this light, it is easy to understand why he accepted the presence of Louis Blanc and of a worker, Albert, in his government and gave his personal assent to the decision to open national workshops that would cushion the drama of unemployment. It was a decision that seemed to be a concrete foreshadowing of the right-to-work issue which, by now only in parliamentary circles, he would focus on with determination in the following months. Nonetheless, the violent street uprising of June 1848, brutally confirming the profound divisions and conflict in French society, all too soon made it clear how wrong Lamartine was and prompted his rapid disappearance from public life.

In December 1848, on the occasion of the presidential elections with universal male suffrage, his candidacy came last in the voters' choice by a good margin – overwhelmed by the magic of a surname. It was the end of a short-lived political career, which saw Lamartine unsuccessfully attempt to avoid repeating the errors of the First Republic in the Second. While the pacifism of his foreign policy, which led him to refuse support for republican uprisings in Italy and Germany, represented the translation of his strident criticism of Girondin adventurism to the political sphere, it offered no advantage to the young French democracy, which was soon isolated and encircled by the whole of Europe.

Yet, if the arrival on the scene of an unknown Bonaparte marked the collapse of his political adventure, throughout the long years of the Second Empire Lamartine would repeatedly go back to that decisive turning point in his public career. It is no coincidence that his self-criticism in relation to his government decisions ended up taking him back to the realm of historiography: in 1861, just after the return of a Bonaparte army to Italian soil, he published a rereading of his *Histoire des girondins*,[2] where critical reflection on the history and significance of Paris's 1848 accompanied a commentary on the First Republic that was very different from the one he had offered many years before.[3] Returning to his work published in 1847, Lamartine now seemed to make a painful distinction between fraternity and social justice – a hendiadys which had previously been the guiding star of his perilous navigation through the troubled waters of politics. The tragedy of 1848, where the dream of bringing the French nation together once again in the name of republican values had been overwhelmed by insurrection in the streets, led him to pass a much sadder sentence on the work of the Convention: its constitution of Year I now seemed to him an artificial construction, the result of an obstinate authoritarianism, which, in the light of reality, had proved to be inconsistent. The political figure of Robespierre, who in 1847 had prevailed over the naive generosity of the Girondins, was now regarded as less significant: Lamartine defended himself from the insinuation that he too had succumbed to the fascination of the Incorruptible and his repeated denunciation of Robespierre's fanaticism came in useful in terms of launching a polemical attack on liberal historiography itself. Thiers's youthful enthusiasm was thus repeatedly evoked to point out how much harm the disinterest in the morality, or lack of morality, of political attitudes had done to the French public spirit and to suggest the need to distinguish in the Terror not only a period of intolerable exploitation and frightening violence, but also an instrument that, pulverizing the political body, was inevitably destined to ruin national unity.

In some ways, Lamartine's argument against the Montagnards of 1848 – which first, with the street rioting in June, and then by having Raspail as a candidate in the December elections, bore serious and evident responsibilities for the republican defeat – ended up reviving the historical role of the Girondins, this time in far more convinced terms. In Lamartine's later version, while they had certainly committed devastating mistakes, it was to their merit that they had known how to stem fanaticism: the entire first period of the Republic, August 10 to the days of 31 May and 2 June 1793, was thus proposed as the unfortunate attempt to found a new social pact; working against this was not only the unpreparedness of the people of France but also the knowing calculation of those who wished to gain advantage from division. In this context, although in later years Lamartine changed his mind about many things, his rejection of Orleanism remained indestructible, and he confirmed that it was the main culprit for widening the social fracture in France on the eve of 1848. It was the anguished awareness of a serious lack of social unity, the perception, in other words, of how much the French nation lacked the unity that the search for fraternity should instead have promoted, that led Lamartine to express a sense of understanding towards Bonapartism. After all, the authoritarian direction Louis Napoleon had taken had been in line with the search, albeit from above and with coercive systems, of that concordant unity of the French that the Orleanist monarchy had opposed and the Republic had not managed to transform into a prospect of liberty.

In these terms, it is not difficult to conclude that Lamartine's constant attention to the revolution was intertwined with the developments of French politics. The aggressive return of Napoleonism suggested an obsessive to and from of analogies between 1789 and 1848, between Brumaire and 2 December 1851, between the role in the history of modern France of the uncle on the one hand and the nephew on the other.

In this context, it is worth reading the other two works by Michelet and Blanc: their first sections, as mentioned earlier, were printed in 1847, but their conclusions arrived much later. There was a difference, however: while Blanc interrupted his work at the outbreak of the February Revolution, only to resume it in London exile after the defeat of the democratic and social republic, the writing and publication of Michelet's *Histoire de la Révolution* extended from February 1847 to August 1853, accompanying the entire period of the Second Republic to come to an end in what was by then the Second Empire. Unlike Lamartine's endeavour, which held out hope of a revolution in the near future, Michelet's long and tormented work conveyed to the contemporary reader the enthusiasm and disillusionment of republicanism: in short, past and present found a way to intertwine in the context of a detailed dialogue between history and politics. The first two volumes, reconstructing revolutionary events up to the flight to Varennes, came out in 1847, without enjoying Lamartine's resounding success, while the third, available from October 1848, took the reader from the Champ de Mars shootings to the eve of August 10. Volumes four and five, appearing not long after between 1849 and 1850, dealt with the dramatic events of the first republican phase and stressed the dramatic divisions between political parties, ending with the expulsion of the Girondins from the Convention. The last two volumes, published in 1853, when Michelet, refusing to swear loyalty to the Empire, had been removed from office and had retired near Nantes, illustrated the events of the revolutionary government and concluded with Thermidor.

In the temporal arc of its writing, the work thus took on a precise significance: it started with the glorification of a period of liberty, in which, against the selfishness of the Louis Philippe monarchy and the sectarianism of many of its opponents, it wanted to celebrate the leading political role of the Parisian people; it ended, collapsed beneath the impact of the concomitant political events of the Second Republic, with painful reflection on the serious responsibilities of a political class incapable of interpreting the profound sentiment of the nation – and, for this reason, inevitably destined to lose democracy in the narrow alley of government authoritarianism. Michelet's work thus accompanied the expectations and drama of the republican movement from the moment of its return to the scene in the aftermath of 1830, but was also blent with its author's personal experience. As the son of a small Jacobin printer, he had experienced the memory of the revolution as a family saga and he had had its significance in the construction of French identity in mind ever since he had started his monumental *Histoire de France*.[4] But the genesis of his work, in particular, foundered in the political moment of the 1840s, when it became clear to many that the Louis Philippe monarchy was increasingly turning in a conservative direction, deliberately setting aside the great expectations of renewal that had at first favoured its rise. It is no coincidence, then, that in 1843, having published the sixth volume of his *Histoire de France*, and while he was writing its successor, he interrupted the enterprise at the time of Charles VIII, throwing himself into the task of writing a history of the revolution that, strictly speaking, should have formed the conclusion to the work. In 1845, when he decided to make 1789 the subject of his lessons, it could be said that divorce from the July monarchy was complete. Not that this was at all inevitable: at the time of the glorious days of the Parisian July, Michelet had applauded the change of dynasty, which seemed to him an overwhelming opportunity to revivify the achievements of the Great Revolution. It also opened up to him the dawn of a brilliant career, first in the archival field, when he was invited to direct the manuscript section of the National Archives, and then in teaching, when, in 1838, he was appointed to the chair of history at the Collège de France. In this context, the image of the revolution in terms of a collective event accompanied the birth of the myth of the people as the only leading figure in processes of historical transformation. The history of revolutions thus came to identify itself with a history of the people – an equivalence conveyed to him by the revolution of 1830, which appeared to him 'sans héros', given that, ultimately, it was society as a whole that had produced the leap forward in modernity. In this way, the revolutionary event was shorn of its traits as a violent rupture and could instead be viewed as an active subject in the process of continuity of historical evolution.[5]

Up to this moment, nevertheless, Michelet remained in the stream of the historiographical liberal tradition, which in the same years, through Thierry and Guizot, had continued to emphasize the same theme. However, the accentuation of his interest in history understood in terms of a path to freedom soon prompted him to establish a ranking of nations, assigning France primacy in Europe in political-cultural terms, making it a point of reference for all other peoples.[6] This superiority, which reflected the historical role played by the French nation during the revolution, suggested two decisive guidelines for Michelet's writings and teaching: on the one hand, it convinced him that 1789 was the arrival point of a narrative that had lasted centuries, something he had set about reconstructing through his composition of the *Histoire de France* – which explains why it was a relatively easy matter for him to stop halfway through this lengthy work to tackle the revolution and then subsequently once again take up the argument that he had, for about a decade, laid aside. On the other hand, the emphasis on French centrality in the historical context of Europe led him to distance himself from the Anglo-American model, suggesting that nothing about 1688 and 1776 could be compared to 1789.

There had matured, around this last point, an irreconcilable break with the liberal world which Michelet had for some time remained close to: while Thiers never concealed a sort of envious admiration for the English political model and Tocqueville lauded the American example, Michelet suggested constructing a history of liberty entirely dictated along internal lines – one that freed France from any position of subservience and rendered it conscious of the historical mission to which it had not only been called, but which it had already been duly working towards for centuries. In this way, the 1789 revolution became an event of universal significance that nonetheless developed out of a truly national basis and placed France at the centre of the historical evolution towards freedom: all its previous history had to be read in the light of this future liberty, while nothing after 1789 could prevent it from representing the point of reference for other peoples in search of authentic freedom. Thus, in the many preceding centuries, monarchs had presented themselves as the expression of a 'national' interest against the corruption and 'liberties' of the nobles and in their action against local resistance they had ended up, albeit indirectly, fostering a growing awareness among sections of the people. From another direction, the Church, too, had exercised a positive function, favouring and legitimizing, at a strictly religious level, the representation of a 'spiritual' will in the national community. These two forces thus created the conditions for the people of France to be constituted over time as an autonomous political subject: on the one hand, centralization, clearly privileged by the Anglo-Saxon model of local self-government, had made possible a situation where a national community founded on the unity of all territorial communities had taken shape; on the other hand, the moral contents of Christianity, instilled through the Catholic monarchy, had allowed the birth of an original spirituality around which the exemplarity of the French people could be based.

This scenario had reached completion in the early 1840s, when Michelet came to the conclusion that the Orleanist monarchy had exhausted its galvanizing function and had to stop moving in a liberal and anti-national direction. As is well known, the official date when he took a step into the world of militant politics was April 1843, when, in agreement with his great friend Edgar Quinet, he launched a fierce attack on the Jesuits in favour of the freedom of teaching. In this context, through the publication that same year of *Des Jesuites* and in another work that soon followed entitled *Du prêtre*,[7] he had recourse to the revolution in order to illustrate how 1789 had nothing in common with Christianity: the universalistic principle of justice that fomented it was even opposed to the Christian theological idea of grace. In the meantime, he had started his work on the revolution, just preceded, in 1846, by the publication of *Le Peuple*, where the reasons behind his interruption of the *Histoire de France* to jump forward to 1789 and his new political direction were promptly made explicit through identifying the French people with the revolution.[8]

It was the strict dependence on the historical process that began with 1789 that made the French people one and indivisible. Beyond any possible party division, the community that passed through the extraordinary patriotic ordeal constituted a spiritual unicum, based on an irrepressible collective desire for freedom – something which the harsh law of social and economic structures had no power against. The French identity had in fact grown out of overcoming the traditional hierarchical model of the *ancien régime* and had coalesced with the dramatic crucible of a patriotic war, when, beyond the factional struggles and the errors and horrors that followed it, the French people had presented all of Europe with a model of social integration thanks to the successful nationalization of the ancient community spirit.

All this demonstrated how the revolution's impetuous course had not only destroyed the old regime in order but also had fruitfully set out to build a new society.[9] It was held together by a yearning for freedom, capable of dissolving rank and class and then reassembling them in a community of equals, where disparity would be eliminated in an ideal world of small owners and producers, in cities and, above all, in the countryside. This admirable example of social and cultural equilibrium had, however, been profoundly crippled by the Napoleonic period, which, apart from official proclamations to take peasant property into account, had only made decisions in the interest of big capital, while the Restoration had managed to make things even worse. Finally, Louis Philippe had turned his back on the ideals that had brought him to the throne: in the aftermath of 1830, instead of halting the drift towards selfish individualism shown by the elites of the time, he had actually employed inequality as a buttress to his monarchy, demonstrating that the Glorious July Days, when the people had returned to the centre of things, had been betrayed. Needless to say, at the end of this work, Michelet, who proved he knew the social reality of France as well as that of Britain, who took a stand for artisanal workshops against the merchants in possession of the systems of product distribution, could focus on the issue of national specificity. He rejected the example from across the Channel to suggest that French society should return to a free association of individual subjects made equal by patriotism – in other words, by a common belonging to a common framework of civil values. It is worth underlining, in this regard, that Michelet had come to interpret in his own terms the magic word that fascinated the best minds of France and Europe at that time, 'association'. This had constituted the obligatory term of reference for those who opposed Louis Philippe, but in his *Peuple* it turned into something other than the Saint-Simonian model and something very different from the ideal of the first socialists, becoming the representation of a secular religion which had its natural end in republicanism. The first two volumes of the *Histoire de la Révolution française* took their lead from this perspective, where the dense introduction that accompanied them was responsible for defining his idea of the meaning of 1789: the revolution constituted the definitive affirmation of justice among men through an act of faith in a brotherhood born from an awareness of mutual commitment.[10] In this context, 1789 marked an epochal date in a universal sense: only in that astonishing year had the two great principles of history had a dramatic impact on the French scene – on the one hand Christianity, on the other, revolution. While the former had legitimized the monarchy of divine right (and therefore absolutism), the latter instead involved the forewarning of an extraordinary process of emancipation. It thus followed closely that the *ancien régime* was tyranny in the name of the religious concept of grace, while the revolution represented the process of the restitution of justice among men.

From this point of view, Michelet could laconically assert the alternative nature of the revolution in relation to Christianity and that 1789, precisely because age-old mental structures had been overturned, constituted a *unicum*, which could not be compared to any other political precedent, let alone be translated into the limiting framework of social history. Thus the myth of the revolution came to maturity as an all-encompassing event, in which the people became the collective protagonist of a colossal process of transformation – a process that the political and cultural elites of the time had been called upon to follow along with, even before taking the lead. In short, precisely because the birth of modern democracy was the product of an innate sentiment of justice destined to oppose the religious concept, and had allowed the human spirit to emerge from the condition of subjection to royal, as well as theological and priestly, oppression, the French people became a chosen nation – their example was to be followed, even though ultimately no other community could be set alongside them.

These premises, which animated his introductory pages, found a strictly historiographic stance towards the end of the second volume, dated 10 November 1847, where Michelet summarized the spirit of the work. Here he made his purpose clear, one already rendered explicit in some notes made at the end of the first volume, to take an equal stand against liberal, Christian and socialist historiographic tradition, to suggest that 1789 was the triumph of popular sovereignty. He could thus demonstrate that the French Revolution, on the one hand, was nothing at all like a repetition of 1688, which in itself seemed to him a small political upheaval limited to its British island setting, and, on the other, did not initiate, indeed excluded, a period of social conflict: instead, it initiated a collective regeneration that assigned the new nation with the responsibility of taking charge of all human progress. In short, for Michelet, popular sovereignty became the guiding star of revolutionary navigation, the point of reference that he would always bear in mind throughout the course of his work. Nevertheless, it might be said that he owes lasting historiographical success to the first two volumes alone, given that in those pages there is concrete articulation of what he had undertaken to illustrate, in other places before, and in the long introduction later. He notes, in fact, at the end of the second volume, that the events narrated were composed of a first part – where the people, given voice for the first time through the convocation of the Estates General, took the situation in hand and, with an extraordinary and unpredictable proof of political intuition, reclaimed a sovereignty that the federations of 1790 were unrepeatable testimony to – and another, where the fraternal impulse of those demonstrations concealed the discontent of the reality of betrayal and resistance, of selfishness and specific interests. At the bottom of all this, there was the summer of 1791, when bewilderment following the king's flight was followed by the popular will to go it alone and adopt a republican solution. It is not difficult to see Michelet's wish for an imminent re-emergence of popular awareness in this scenario, entirely occupying his version as it does, where the people, suddenly united, are the leading player and are extolled as the true political subject around which the whirlwind of events is woven. Thus, the violence goes largely unremarked – in regard to which the descendants of Foulon and Bertier would vainly ask for respect for their dead – to be laid at the door of a handful of troublemakers representative of the general will. The moments in which the first revolutionary figures appear, with Mirabeau acting as master of ceremonies and Desmoulins urging the crowd on to insurrection, are presented as demonstrating the ability of individuals to read and correctly interpret the popular will.

In fact, July 14 is not the result of a strategy drawn up at a table by a group of insurrectionists, but a free, sudden and unified descent of the people onto the political field, which, storming the Bastille, breaks open the walls of the old order. Not surprisingly, again according to Michelet, the night of August 4 originates from that shining example of a rediscovered harmony of minds, which also legally sanctions the already rediscovered unity of all the French people, given that the privileged ranks themselves decide to let them freely converge. The October Days should be read in this light, a sort of female rerun of July 14: the popular demonstration that took the citizens of Paris to Versailles and their joyful return escorting the royal family mark another stage, again in Michelet's eyes, of that popular protagonism that finds its apotheosis in the federations of July 1790. Even in the smallest municipalities, all the people gathered together to swear loyalty to the nation, thus bringing to an end a centuries-old process of political emancipation.

There remained the problem of the quickly visible involution from the extraordinary political successes of the first revolutionary year and in this regard Michelet had preceding historiographical tradition on his side, which had immediately identified powerful obstacles to a prompt stabilization of the new order in Court intrigue, the resistance – soon, too, from an armed aristocracy – and non-acceptance of the *fait accompli* by the high religious hierarchies. However, to his mind, those things that were reasons for understanding, if not justifying, the violent direction of the political trajectory became an occasion to focus on the issue of popular participation and to demonstrate the extraordinary proof of maturity of the French people who, abandoned by their own king with his flight to Varennes, showed this maturity to the point of demonstrating that they were already prepared to take destiny into their own hands. The second volume came to an end here, but Michelet took care to insert a long final note in which, distancing himself from opinion favourable to the Terror and sensitive to the connection between Christianity and revolution, he returned to insist on the irreconcilability of the two terms and on the profound popular dissent in relation to Year II. His was a choice of terrain where politics and historiography supported one another: the latter meant silencing the fideistic reconstructions that, under a downpour of published documents, enlivened the comments in Buchez and Roux's *Histoire parlementaire*, while the former indicated the need to sweep away the feet from under the allied competitors so that the events of the Great Revolution could direct opposition to Louis Philippe in a socialist context.

In the meantime, French daily life had been lacerated by another revolution and preparation of the third volume was accompanied by the drama of the first republican months, where initial collective enthusiasm was soon followed by political conflict and the people's revolt in June. The work was published in October 1848, when the dream of brotherhood had already been shattered in June's street battles. Michelet had been an eyewitness to this – a barricade was erected in the street where he lived, and when the violence was over he wandered around a Paris made ghostly by the dead on the roads.

The pages he was working on were thus hugely influenced by what was happening around him at the time: the drama of June 1848 spilled out across the description of the shootings on the Champ de Mars, for which Michelet implausibly blamed monarchical intrigue, as well as the unpreparedness of Lafayette and the units of the national guard. In this way, the account of long-ago 1791 was an implicit indictment of General Cavaignac, who had played such a big part in the repression of the recent revolt: it was almost as if, reviving an event, even from a moment so distant in time, dealing with the inadequacy of those who were called upon to face the spontaneity of the masses, could remove the spectre of popular immaturity that he had instead seen taking place in front of him and which, had it been confirmed, even if only in the past, would have ended up seeing his entire reconstruction founder. The opposite situation, meanwhile, the temptation to make the past a point of reference for decisions in the present time, appeared in the pages dedicated to the debate on war. Here, his taking a stand against Robespierre and essentially becoming a spokesman for the crusade for freedom evoked by the Girondins say everything about how Michelet criticized the neutrality of the new republican executives with respect to the contemporary dramas of the Italian and Polish revolutions. It was an issue that was largely avoided by subsequent historiographical periods, which would gladly leave the warlike features of the revolution in the background, but for Michelet the impulse to go to war for freedom was a decisive one, both for substantiating the patriotic dimension of the French people and for demonstrating that, still, in 1792, the revolutionary political class, or at least the best part of it, had its finger on the pulse of popular feeling and knew how to interpret it correctly.

This theme continued on into the fourth volume, published in 1849, where the issue of popular patriotism again came to the fore: the day of August 10 – on the eve of which, in 1848, in an atmosphere of tension and trepidation, he had laid down his pen – was represented as a decisive continuation of July 14 and the turn towards republicanism was consequently envisaged as the natural conclusion of a political path initiated in 1789 in the name of collective awareness.

These pages therefore represent a crossroads: on one side, the popular uprising leading to the Republic is painted in the same colours as the other parallel movement, as if to draw a line of continuity between August 1792 and February 1848; on the other, a similar correspondence seems to be drawn in the first, heartfelt pages dealing with the Convention's difficulties in maintaining the extraordinary abundance of collective expectation inherited from triumph over the monarchy. Michelet thus began a journey through the revolution's loss of popular consensus, which would find shape in subsequent volumes. All of these were marked, in turn, by an awareness of the dramatic involution that took place in the Second Republic, soon to have a Bonaparte at the helm, and too afraid of popular enthusiasm not to press, through its own parliamentary representation, abruptly on the brakes. This is the part of Michelet's work that was least valued by later critics, who always tended to focus on the first two volumes, those published in 1847, while treating the hundreds of subsequent pages in a very general way. It does not seem an exaggeration to suggest, therefore, that the first two books alone would have been sufficient to establish Michelet's extraordinary fame in the context of revolutionary historiography. These volumes contain the aggrandisement of the revolution as a collective event and the depiction of popular sovereignty in terms of a French nation, redefined into a community of the free and the equal, irreversibly led to forge the republican myth. However, in the remaining volumes, Michelet's narrative mastery shines out even more, founded among other things on a knowledge of sources that no one else could have mastered so successfully and on an ability to marshal a depth of detail that no one else, until revolutionary history became a matter of university study, could have equalled. These books constituted the other face of the work, where hope for the future gives way to bitterness with regard to the present. In those many pages, Michelet, through an accurate description of the political events leading up to Thermidor, illustrates the concrete facts that caused the Convention to lose control of the situation and – apart from the extraordinary, duly highlighted, moments of heroism – to fail, in a definitive manner, to carry out its duty as the emissary of the nation that the sovereign people had assigned to it with their vote.

However, none of Michelet's pages could escape the whirlwind rhythm of French politics and the turn towards conservativism that followed the failed radical-socialist demonstration of June 1849. The fact that the Second Republic soon closed in upon itself, renouncing a policy of full popular participation, was plain to see in the dramatic sequence of divisions that soon took place in the republican camp, where Michelet seemed to distance himself from the Girondins, who had unnecessarily heightened tension with the Montagnards. He identified Danton, above all, as the revolutionary figure who seemed to have an even better sense than the others of the nation's deep feelings and of that call for a supreme effort against enemies both external and internal. In this context, Michelet recorded the dramatic loss of consensus as bit by bit republican events seemed to get bogged down in party struggles and to lose sight of that crowning patriotic endeavour which the foreign armies and the Vendée demanded of the nation. The days of 31 May and 2 June 1793 were criticized, but at the same time read as an obligatory moment of transition for the Republic to survive.

And yet, this is the moment when Michelet seems to interrupt his writing, overwhelmed, on a personal level, too, by the coup d'état – which would soon deprive him of his teaching post and archival position for refusing to swear loyalty to the Second Empire. He moved near Nantes, to the solitude of a voluntary retreat, where he composed the last part of his work. The authoritarian involution is dealt with with a sense of shock and dismay as he testifies to the drama of a Republic by now on the downward slope of government despotism: the Terror is a consequence, but also an instrument of acceleration of a popular disaffection destined to overturn the preceding years' extraordinary hope of freedom. In this framework, Michelet's criticisms of a revolutionary policy that abandons great popular vision to wither in the activity of small cabals find their ultimate form.

The choice seems to be in contradiction to his constantly repeated homage to the Convention: in his pages on the assembly following the expulsion of the Girondins, while abhorring their inexperience and despising the demonstrations of a minority in the name of the sovereign people, while underlining in this regard the ambiguities of the Montagnards and Robespierre's sectarianism, he never fails to pay homage to the deputies, who managed to keep afloat a vessel destined otherwise to vanish beneath the waves of the counter-revolution. And yet, alongside due homage to those who had saved France, Michelet depicts a progressive and ineluctable narrowing of revolutionary inspiration: federations are replaced by factions, the people by the Jacobins, Danton, with his overwhelming personality and acute ability to interpret the collective sentiment, by the mystical pedagogy of Robespierre. And all this while, in parallel, the government of national sovereignty is overlaid by the authoritarianism of the few in the name of the general interest.

It was a perspective that led towards the aggressive return of the religious authoritarianism that Michelet glimpsed in the person of Robespierre, whose momentary triumph seemed to him to definitively dash the hopes – burgeoning in 1789, but sublimated in 1792 – of a democracy characterized by justice and brotherhood. It is no coincidence that Michelet's work ends – here, apparently at least, in line with the historiographical tradition of the time – with the fall of the Incorruptible. For Michelet, too, after Thermidor there was nothing more worth telling and the last period of the Convention, as well as the Directory years, was deliberately set aside, as if they were an insignificant parenthesis to Bonaparte's arrival on the scene. He would never completely return to this point, not even when, much later, he would begin writing about the years that followed: he was forestalled from producing a convinced version of the rest of his history by the certainty that selfishness, individualism and sectarianism had never abandoned the terrain regained thanks to the fragility of the first democratic political class and that writing about France under the Directory was merely going over old ground.

2. Robespierre, or the supreme pontiff

In the long years of the Second Empire, after committing himself to a ten-year study of revolutionary events, Michelet resumed working at a good pace on his *Histoire de*

France, returning to rejoin 1867 to the revolution through pages dedicated to the reign of Louis XVI.[11] Shortly thereafter, nevertheless, it was time for a second edition of his *Révolution* and for the occasion the author had to find a way to take into consideration works that, alongside his own, had shed new light on 1789.[12] It was time to take stock of the revival of the figure of the Incorruptible, to whom Ernest Hamel had dedicated a biography in 1865.[13] It seemed to Michelet, however, that Hamel veered away from straightforward admiring praise to venture along the ruinous path of legend. In that weighty tome, the figure of Robespierre seemed to him to assume the contours of a Messiah, descending to the revolutionary land in order to free France from the individualism ratified by 1789: Christianity and socialism, often intersecting with one another, seemed to him the two terms that formed the basis for Robespierre's aggrandisement – but it was precisely this choice that, as seen earlier, clashed with Michelet's profound conviction that the revolution had been an alternative to one as well as to the other. In the ostentation of the Incorruptible there was a preliminary political choice, clearly authoritarian in nature, which led to an less than scrupulous use of history – one that legitimized a particular line of conduct and confirmed, in the past, the correctness of what the present had instead taken on the task of denying.

Michelet's argument with regard to a socialist reading of the revolution – one not too cordially reciprocated – was not, however, new: it had already been deployed before 1848, when, with the release of its first two volumes, he had officially criticized the *Histoire parlamentaire* of Buchez and Roux with great severity. In his opinion, it was a weighty and commendable work, certainly useful thanks to its reproduction of particular documents, but misleading in more than one respect, given that it was dominated by the bias of foreseeing revolutionary events in socialist terms. Michelet thought the two editors had wanted to repropose the idea of contrasting 1793 with 1789, hypothesizing that the unbridled liberal individualism of the Constituent Assembly had obscured Year II, where the socialist perspective was instead clearly highlighted. It was an artificial and sectarian construction, however, into which, without any foundation, they intended to fit the historical role of the individual personalities, as well as the very meaning of certain testimonies also reproduced. And yet, what still seemed to worry Michelet on the eve of 1848, was the popularity that the *Histoire parlamentaire* appeared to enjoy: with their works – on which he prudently suspended judgement – Lamartine, Esquiros and Blanc seemed to him to be all too reliant on Buchez and Roux's collection of documents and in some ways even take their perspective as their very basis. He could not overlook the fact that his own position was very distant both from the prejudice favouring the French clergy, which was largely absolved of any responsibility for 1789 and its developments, and from the passion shown towards the experiment of Year II. Michelet not only believed that French clerical opposition had played a nefarious role in the work of destroying newly regained national unity, but that the Terror had also contributed a great deal in this regard – with its unacceptable policies it had brought round many who had previously applauded the Republic to the counter-revolutionary cause.

We can see here the abyss that separated Michelet from other historians of the revolution: he claimed to be the only one to have tackled the subject from below, placing the people alone at the centre of his version and in this way returning to praise the meaning of eighteenth-century philosophy – something others unjustly neglected. It seemed to him to unjustly sum up the French spirit while at the same time rejecting Robespierrism, which others instead made much of, dismissing it as an example of the sort of sectarianism destined to ruin national unity. It was an enormous schism, a written prediction that, shortly thereafter, the democrats of 1848 would in turn soon go their separate ways on the grounds of political practice and would thus prove unable to escape from the doldrums of factionalism in which the First Republic had already foundered.

Michelet certainly had all this in mind when, during the 1850s, deprived of his professorship at the Collège de France and removed from direction of the National Archives, he found a way to follow, albeit from a distance, the development of Louis Blanc's work, which seemed to him – as he would say in the introduction to his new edition of the *Révolution* referred to above – to epitomize an interpretation favourable to the Terror, and which would only further aggravate the difficult cause of French democracy. And then, to divide Michelet from Blanc, there was an argument entirely internal to the historiographical field: the latter, who resumed writing roughly when the former brought his work to a conclusion, used it to a large extent as a basis, without depriving himself, however, of the satisfaction of criticizing it on several occasions in order to demonstrate his adversary's fragility in detail, even in the field of documentation, where his expertise was widely recognized. The two also had family histories that did nothing to draw them closer together: Michelet was the son of a Jacobin in revolutionary Paris, Blanc came from a legitimist line – a grandfather had lost his head to the guillotine and his father came close to doing so. Blanc had been educated in the Catholic faith, Michelet's education had been patriotic – skilfully put to good use after 1830, when the new regime had greatly valued him. In the same period, meanwhile, the legitimist Blanc family had lost the pension granted to his father and fallen on hard times. In the field of historiography, their respective political reference points divided them in an irreconcilable manner: Blanc became a republican, gravitating into the orbit of a world that favoured the precedent of Year II which had Robespierre as its symbol, while Michelet would always be accused of being sympathetic towards Danton – perhaps to discredit his trenchant arguments against the Incorruptible.

In any case, the two, on the eve of 1848, in the sphere of historical studies, encapsulated the extent to which the various republican groupings differed in the field of political practice: and it is not an exaggeration to conclude that Lamartine, also in historiographical terms, with his *Histoire des Girondins*, intended to build a bridge between the two camps, reconnecting the division between Dantonists and Robespierrists that Leroux had in his time indicated ran across republican circles.

Division was present, however, in the field of historical reconstruction, too, and, since 1847, insurmountable: the work of Louis Blanc was a foothold for a political activist, and his writing was aimed at achieving a specific programme of social renewal, which could hardly have been limited to mere republican egalitarianism. His *Histoire de la Révolution française* came out of an intense period of journalistic activity, which had led the young Catholic and legitimist Blanc to translate his rejection of 1830s turn towards liberalism into socialist terms.[14] This decision was clear from the simultaneous publication of two works in 1840: one, taking stock of ten years of liberal monarchy, firmly denounced the selfish and classist spirit that inspired Louis Philippe's reign; the other, criticizing uncontrolled capitalism, proposed a profound renewal of the economic order through the state application of rigid stabilizing manoeuvres to productive activities.[15] The meeting point of the two arguments was the thaumaturgical value of universal suffrage, which on the one hand would put an end to the excessive power of economic potentates and, on the other, through a profound democratization of administrative power, induce state interventionism that would remedy the oppressive exploitation of labour by trading groups.

Blanc's socialism thus grew out of a concrete reading of the labour issue that emerged in France after 1830. He was careful to interpret the active presence of a working class which in the cities had organized itself around the themes of associationism and cooperative movements and intended to give a concrete answer to the workforce made up of artisan proprietors who lacked the opportunity to trade on their own. His vision of things, however, required a strong, centralizing state, with a rigid leadership that could dissolve particularistic resistances in the context of a project to reorganize the entire socio-economic structure. In this light, Blanc decided to write his own history of the French Revolution, where the years from 1789 to 1794 seemed to foretell the present period and to constitute a sure foothold to identify in the recent past a reason to feel encouraged about the future.[16] The dramatic confrontation between liberalism and democracy that characterized the France of Louis Philippe – and where nothing suggested that one, by agreeing to enlarge suffrage, and the other, by admitting the rules of political freedom, could find reconciliation – was thus brought back to its origins, the year 1789. Then, from the ashes of an old corporatist regime, a new order based on individuality had arisen – which soon, however, became egoistic itself, the certain forerunner of what the Orleans monarchy had only brought to perfection. Blanc believed, in fact, that the history not only of France, but of the whole of Europe, had been guided by the principles of authority and individualism, both of which could be traced back to the Christian experience in terms of Catholicism and Protestantism. The latter, nonetheless, soon left the religious sphere to make its mark on the process of the secularization of society, which had reached its peak in 1789, with the Declaration of Human Rights and in the work of the Constituent Assembly, when the bourgeois world, ready to dominate the nineteenth century, had assumed a definite form. For this reason, Blanc, appealing to the lexicon of the Great Revolution but from a different perspective to Michelet's, made brotherhood the fulcrum of his argument, in order to knit together the fracture between the two previous principles through a synthesis of both. This would give rise to the birth of a new society, rendered homogeneous and supportive by the waning of individualism within a social order whose harmony obviously had nothing in common with the structure of *ancien régime* privilege.

For this reason, in 1847, Blanc was already at a distance not only from Lamartine, who he regarded as little more than a novelist, but above all from Michelet, whose position was now even more radical than in the past: as we have seen, in his opinion 1789 marked the conquest of a new world, and its emblem was the night of August 4, when the Constituent Assembly had burned the bridges of the old order that they had crossed to get there. In Blanc's eyes, however, it was precisely the dramatic social tensions within a France emerging miserably and brutishly from the revolution that demonstrated the complexity of the 1789 phenomenon. He found it impossible to share Michelet's vision of only one revolution, believing that two had to be seen, 'one up in arms against the other'. The people of France had certainly given repeated evidence of their generous enthusiasm, and this was soon joined by another impulse, more powerful and at the same time more deaf, which had allowed individualism to win out over the spirit of community.

Brotherhood, which for Michelet was an accomplished fact in 1790 in a nationalizing context, for Blanc instead meant something quite different: in particular, it was the only possible response to the aporia of a world that, in the transition from the old regime to the new order, had lost its traditional social values as well as the best part of its religious identity. In other words, what for Michelet was a conquest that was unfortunately lost, for Blanc was, much more modestly, an aspiration that had found both vigour and sudden death in Year II: the revolutionary government seemed to put an end to individualism and selfishness with its economic policy decisions, but the most backward part of the Convention had responded to these decisions with Thermidor. Robespierre's fall did not, however, exclude the fact that this was the point from which it was necessary to start again – from Year II, in other words, when it seemed that a new social order, different and more just than the traditional regime, could be consolidated to the detriment of the anarchist fury of liberalism.

This was the message that, on the eve of 1848, Blanc's work intended to propose to the French left of the time: the first volume was a harsh indictment of individualism, its origins traced back to the religious sphere – the Hussites, forerunners of the Jacobins as the bearers of brotherhood against authority, were soon crushed, just as the Anabaptists were shortly after. Calvin, whose doctrine of predestination was accused of being for the exclusive use of the feudal nobility, was in turn replaced by Luther, who, however, only affirmed the dignity of the revolt of conscience, while harshly condemning rebellion dictated by material need. The result was the swift spread of individualism in politics as well, whose triumphs were sanctioned by the balance finally found by Henry IV and the birth of a bourgeoisie ready to adopt it as their own philosophy.

The whole last part of the first volume was in fact devoted to the developing fortunes of that new class in France under the old regime, while the second, also published in 1847, started with the prophecy of two revolutions, one soon victorious in the name of Voltaire, the other just as quickly ending in catastrophe in the name of Rousseau. The following pages promptly began their discussion of the first, concluding with the episode of the night of August 4: where Michelet had emphasized the point of no return of the nationalization process, Blanc instead saw the triumph of bourgeois selfishness, given that the majority of Constituent Assembly members turned a deaf ear to the proposal to accompany the declaration of rights with one of duties and carried straight on when voices were raised to point out the need to take into consideration the suffering of the people.

Hence the inevitability of yet another revolution, which promised to improve on 1789's strictly bourgeois version and which would raise humanity to results never before achieved. With these words, Blanc interrupted his discussion and there is no doubt that, by writing about the past with his mind on the present, he proved himself to be a good prophet: the need for still another revolution after the wholly bourgeois example of 1830 would appear very soon. For Blanc, well known for some time in the ranks of radical opposition to Louis Philippe, it was time to lay down his pen and assume the role of statesman.

In the February 1848 provisional government, Blanc appeared as the representative of the extreme left and, partly to limit its range of action, partly to satisfy worker protests, he was called upon to chair the Luxembourg commission charged with improving the workers' living conditions. Despite some decisions – such as the ten-hour day in Paris and the abolition of the *livret* – Blanc did not gain a great deal from the work carried out: in the April elections for the Constituent Assembly, he was the last of the Parisians elected, with the result that he was promptly excluded from the new executive. His participation on May 15 in the demonstration in support of the revolutions in Europe, where demonstrators circulated his name for a new government, and then in the workers' June Days, put an end to his political career. Swiftly deprived of parliamentary immunity, he sought refuge in England, where he would remain for over twenty years, and in the midst of a life of hardship, in the rooms of the British Museum, find his way back to his history of the revolution.

It was a question of picking up the thread of a narrative that the events that had taken place in the meantime inevitably put in a different light and that the democratic diaspora made even more dramatic. From the collapse of the Second Republic, Blanc had once more received confirmation of the existence of a class struggle between the bourgeoisie and the people – the Great Revolution had been its starting point and 1848 another painful chapter. In this light, it went without saying that the events of 1793, in contrast to what liberal writers were still trying to say, were not an expedient to cope with circumstances, but a new and more complete phase of the centuries-old liberation process of the lower classes, who in the revolutionary government had found new political protagonists able to take charge of their specific interests.

Blanc's pages soon gave themselves over to the exaltation of an authoritarian solution, which from above, thanks to certain impartial figures, had launched a policy of remediation with regard to social problems. The statehood that appeared on the scene in Year II thanks to the desperate efforts of the Convention thus became a progressive model whose example should not be forgotten: as guarantor of an equality based on the new concept of brotherhood, it represented the true point of reference for any future political initiative. Blanc's *Histoire* thus became a work where the interpretation in a light favourable to Robespierre could not be separated from a socialist perspective: in this context, nonetheless, it was necessary to provide a reading of the Incorruptible that, while sympathetic towards him, was at the same time distinct from previous apologias for the Terror.

The aim of Blanc's work thus became that of demonstrating that the revolutionary government was something different and that the violence of Year II had nothing in common with Robespierrism. It seemed a titanic undertaking, but Blanc set out by trying to underline that the violence was a legacy of the old order and that the counter-revolutionaries themselves had first contributed to its unleashing. His justification for the Terror thus ended up being dictated by circumstances, as liberal historians had already written. But this did not mean that Robespierre's proposal for government was itself part of the exceptional nature of the events. On the contrary, in Blanc's view, the Incorruptible represented the alternative to the Terror – he was the promoter of a political line that aimed to heal the wounds of society without facile recourse to violence. The Incorruptible, he wrote, had only been a victim of the dynamics of events, where, in the course of Year II, the Hébertists – who were charged with full responsibility for the Terror – temporarily prevailed.

In this context, where the reckless ultraradicals of Year II seemed to resemble the extremists of 1848, it went without saying that Blanc saw great merit in the agreement between Robespierre and Danton and unsurprisingly he regrets the former's decision to send the Indulgents to their deaths. And yet, this was a necessary step to put an end to factional struggles, and constituted the supreme sacrifice for the new order to triumph. This is demonstrated by the fact that, in Blanc's view, Robespierre was extraneous to the laws of Prairial Year II, which others within the Convention – especially those who would later put him to death in Thermidor – were instead ardently in favour of. In this way, the books were balanced: Robespierrism was something quite different from the Terror, which instead was identified with the selfish policies of the worst sections of the Convention, ready and willing to repress popular protest with unprecedented violence when, desperate with hunger, the Parisian people rebelled in Prairial Year III.

Thus, the events of the First Republic – it was not by chance that, to signify bourgeois triumph, in Blanc's work they came to a close with that episode – chimed with those of the second. In 1848, too, in fact, as the provisional government attempted to establish a new social order (and where a follower of Robespierre had tried to introduce concrete measures in favour of the people), it was followed by a back-stabbing assembly, which preferred carnage in the street rather than surrender even slightly the intention of maintaining a bourgeois grip on the working class. The June Days of 1848 thus became a sad repetition of Prairial Year III, with the shadow of the Terror falling across both their tragic outcomes, ready to lash out at every dissenting voice, with the reaction of Thermidor on one hand and the expulsion of the socialist left on the other,.

It is, however, a perspective that suggests that in Blanc's pages there was a conflict entirely internal to the republicanism of the time, destined to have repercussions in historiographic terms, too: while not neglecting to harshly attack liberal writers, he would criticize republican writers above all, having a great deal to reproach them for with regard to concrete political decisions. The *Histoire des girondins* was thus the target of his ire, but so, especially, was Michelet: while his work had been of great use to Blanc, he saw Michelet as dominated by an anti-Robespierrist (and therefore anti-socialist) prejudice, encapsulating the sensibility of a bourgeois republic destined to be easy prey for whichever Bonaparte happened to be in power. It has been noted that Blanc made a clear distinction between Lamartine and Michelet: the former, he thought, was essentially a writer of fiction, very inclined to embellish historical events that his scruples and seriousness as a scholar were responsible for restoring to the world of truth. Michelet, on the other hand, often praised as a valuable historian, was regularly criticized when it came to summing up the meaning of Year II and to reaffirming the primacy of Robespierre among the various republican groupings that were soon to clash violently with one another.

There is evidence that the harshness of historiographical confrontation went hand in hand with the recriminations and reciprocal accusations that circulated in the camp of the defeated republicans in the fact that Blanc was late in entering into direct argument with Michelet. In volume six – published in 1854, when the latter's work was finished – he differed in opinion concerning the debate between Brissot and Robespierre with regard to the war on the Jacobins, detailing point by point the correctness of the Incorruptible's positions, but he believed that the argument between the two revolutionaries had to be considered with greater fairness of judgement and seemed only to be amazed at Michelet's error. He still praised the latter's work, with admiring words in another passage regarding the fact that only an excessive love for freedom had dragged the republicans into a fight with each other.

For the occasion, nonetheless, Blanc began the tactic of introducing some concluding pages to certain chapters to point up the differences in his interpretation compared to others. This decision, repeated over the course of the final volumes, makes it possible to understand the reasons for dissent that increasingly distanced him from Michelet. His criticism exploded when it came to expressing an opinion on the September Massacres: in this case, he also dedicated pages and pages to Lamartine's reconstruction, denouncing its inventiveness and license. But the real target of his attack was Michelet, whom he accused of having deliberately misrepresented the facts in order to place responsibility for what happened on Robespierre, insinuate suspicions about the Parisian Commune and transform what had only been the irresistible delirium of a moment of fear into a deliberate plan of execution. The good intentions of the previous volume thus soon ended up crumbling away when the story touched on the first republican period and dealt with the first dramatic issue of violence within the revolutionary political dynamic. At this point, Blanc, in response to the criticisms rained down upon Robespierre's head, did not hesitate to channel them over to Danton, in turn insinuating more than one doubt about the latter's responsibility for the unrelenting horror.

From that moment on, his Robespierrism became almost inflexible and the other two authors were consequently made the subject of repeated attacks. The high point was reached during the trial and execution of the Girondins, when Blanc showed contempt for Lamartine's claim of making those condemned to death so insouciant that, on the cart to the scaffold, they gave the contents of their pockets to the people. He pointed out that the gesture, accompanied by the cry of 'A nous, amis!', was instead the desperate attempt to create enough turmoil to allow them to escape. For the occasion, he also judged Michelet himself with severity, accusing him of having forgotten the duties of a historian in order to swiftly, and with bias, come to the aid of a party he had looked upon with sympathy since the days of Brissot's warmongering.

Blanc made use of the same argument when it was time to deal with Danton's death: accusing Michelet of being the head of those historians favourable towards Robespierre's adversary, he proceeded to clear the ground of the many accusations directed at the Incorruptible, demonstrating their artificiality and explaining the collapse of the Indulgents as the inevitable need to prevent the campaign for moderation from opening the way to reaction and the loss of the Republic. Blanc criticized Michelet once again in the last volumes, especially when the former endeavoured to demonstrate – the first of all the revolution's historians to do so – Robespierre's intention to put an end to the Terror: he had not been responsible for its beginnings and had always had profound reservations about how it was managed. This was the conclusion to which his preceding pages had been leading, where Blanc had already hotly contested Michelet's opinion that Robespierre had made himself into a sort of pontiff of the Republic and had resorted to mysticism to forge an effective instrument of power. The decision to separate the fate of the Incorruptible from the Terror was also a response to the personal drama of a Robespierrist whose family had suffered terribly from the unrestrained use of the guillotine. Apart from this private aspect, however, Blanc had the acute perception that only establishing a certain distance from violence as a system of government could provide a definitive citizenship for Robespierre and Jacobinism as a whole within the pantheon of a democratic and social republic. For this reason, he took care to distinguish between Robespierrism and Hébertist extremism, turning over responsibility for the violent direction of the revolutionary process to those who, during Year II, had seemed to get the better of the Incorruptible. Unsurprisingly, in his *Histoire* he was very harsh towards the Cordeliers – as already mentioned, he charged them with serious responsibility for the explosion of violence that would tear down the republican edifice to the benefit of bourgeois egotism.

So, if it is true that Blanc's *Histoire* indicated that the revolution was now a disputed legacy even on the left, his decision to insist on the Jacobin and socialist identity of 1793 had the effect not only of destroying Michelet's dream of unanimity (and ultimately that of Lamartine himself) but also of deepening the split within the extreme left.[17] The insistence with which he distanced himself from the Cordeliers and praised the alleged repressive action of Robespierre and Danton against them was not, moreover, designed to pacify souls in the republican camp. The fracture, in other words, which had already appeared in the years of the Louis Philippe monarchy, went on deepening throughout 1848 and demonstrated not only the plural identity of the French left, but that it had to struggle too hard to find points of agreement. In the years of the Second Empire, it was the historiographical field that was responsible for confirming these oppositions, as Michelet and Blanc came to loggerheads: the latter, aggrandizing Robespierre, criticized the 'asocialist' republicanism which Michelet had provided with an extraordinary voice. Michelet, for his part, at the time of the second edition of his work in 1868, was careful to respond in kind, mentioning Blanc's work more than once in the new pages dedicated to the Robespierre's tyranny. Tension was not limited to these two particular adversaries: in addition to Lamartine, who had already changed his mind with regard to 1793, other groups – some extremist, others socialist, yet others libertarian – laid claim to the revolutionary legacy without being seduced by the authoritarian myth of the Year II government. A fine example of this is offered by Gustave Tridon's *Les Hébertistes*, where the author took a stand against the criticism so freely spread first by Thiers,[18] but then also by Blanc, regarding the Cordeliers in Year II. Curiously, the author seemed instead to make a partial exception for Michelet, conceding the fact that he had at least defended Chaumette, procurator of the Commune of Paris from slander. In this way, anti-Robespierrism – in the sense of a rejection of leader-driven and inevitably authoritarian politics – demonstrated great vitality not only on the right, but also to the left of Louis Blanc himself, with examples provided by Auguste Blanqui on the one hand (Tridon himself was a staunch supporter) and Pierre-Joseph Proudhon on the other.[19]

In this atmosphere of violent tension and bitter conflict, there were those who emphasized the bourgeois nature of so much republicanism, as well as the utopian aspect of the various groups within French socialism: apart from the validity of the assertions, applause came – from the right – for such a mishmash of positions and ideas.[20] After all, given the bad press that Year II seemed to have on a collective level, the identification of 1793 with the birth date of the contemporary left was an equivalence worthy of underlining and putting your name to.

3. Reconnecting the thread of the past

Autumn 1850, Sorrento: Alexis de Tocqueville found there temporary refuge to treat the tuberculosis that had recently afflicted him and in the quiet of the Amalfi coast, to give some meaning to his days, he decided to transcribe the memories that thronged his mind. The topic was the recent events in France, and his intention was to trace the steps that had led up to them as well as the dramatic developments thereafter.[21] As a witness, there was none better: since 1839, having won a seat in the Normandy of his birth, his life had been a parliamentary one.[22] Soon drawn to the more liberal part of Orleanism, he had, however, seen the July monarchy meet with increasingly intense contestation and it had been all too easy for him, at the beginning of 1848, to prophesy, in a parliamentary speech, the imminent catastrophe that was about to strike the throne of Louis Philippe.[23] He had been distressed at first by the February Revolution, with Parisian workers making a threatening appearance on the scene, but it was only the consternation of a moment: he immediately realized that universal suffrage, rather than favouring the most radical fringes, would actually help set France, if not Paris, back on an even keel. On Easter Day, a rainy April 23, he had accompanied local peasants to their first vote, where, at the end of a short speech, in which he suggested that they listen to nobody else apart from him, he was triumphantly re-elected. Back in Paris, he was a witness to the June Days, and was greatly struck by the fact that the bloody street battles were suddenly assuming the nature of a working-class rebellion.[24] The class struggle seemed to him to have made its appearance in a way both majestic and terrifying: Tocqueville had observed in the many armed workers a horde still in need of civilization, which nonetheless considered its condition illegitimate and which demanded as a right from the new republican order what was only the fruit of the capricious fantasies of socialist preachers. And yet, that destructive wave that tore through the whole social framework, driven on by new slogans and with the old insurrectionism of the sans-culottes coming quickly to the surface, was soon followed by Louis Napoleon's electoral triumph in December. The suggestion was that February 1848 had not been another revolution at all, but was only the continuation of one that had never in fact ended – that of 1789. What his father's generation had seen begin, in other words, was an earthquake destined to destabilize the political structure of France, and he himself despaired to ever see its conclusion.

It was a sense of disorientation – faced with a political sickness that had arrived in France in the late eighteenth century and never eradicated thereafter – destined to afflict not only a refined aristocrat like Tocqueville, but also that multiform bourgeois world which had long based its hopes on the liberalism of the July Monarchy.[25] Not by chance, at the same time as these notes – which should have remained strictly confidential – interest in Year II and in the role of the Convention took hold again, this time on the right, as if the events of 1848 suggested it was time to put aside the portrayal, despite its enthusiasm for the work the Convention had carried out, given at the time by Mignet and Thiers. The time had come when it seemed necessary to say loud and clear how little or nothing had to be saved from Year II: while resistance at the borders had allowed France to survive, it had also linked it to a perennial condition of instability. At that moment, the perverse mechanism of popular intervention in freely elected assemblies had been activated, and France's political dialectic was no longer allowed to breathe.

It was a conviction that was soon in circulation, as shown by the fact that the first part of Brugière de Barante's *Histoire de la Convention* was published in 1851 – the author being a baron, who many years before had been part of the liberal opposition to Charles X and who had greeted Louis Philippe's ascent to the throne as the full realization of his political ideals. Forced to end his diplomatic career following the revolution of 1848, withdrawing into a cloistered life,[26] he quickly targeted the work of Thiers, whom he charged with more than one responsibility for the collapse of the French monarchy. He also underlined that the aspect of the Convention that the other had most extolled – the indomitable spirit of resistance in the face of the foreign invasion – was largely questionable: the men who had led France during Year II were those who had dragged France vainly into the military ordeal, who had not known how to manage military operations and who had only taken advantage of an extraordinary national effort to which they had actually contributed nothing. In contrast with a result that was none of their doing, there was disaster in terms of public order and legislation, while liberty and prosperity had dramatically vanished. Barante could thus suggest that it was time to move away from reconstructions that acquitted the Convention, as Mignet's and Thiers's did, to once again favour condemnation: the goal of the Convention was to perpetuate itself in power through the cynical calculation of tearing an entire society up by its roots.[27]

Barante's ideas reflected the anxious bewilderment of many of Louis Philippe's supporters confronted with the unpredictable events of 1848, which had begun with the reckless disobedience of the Parisian populace and come to a conclusion in the name of the Napoleonic myth. This was what Augustin Thierry shortly confirmed by republishing his history of the Third Estate in 1853,[28] suggesting that the disaster of 1848 had caused him to entertain great doubts with regard to his previous reconstruction of French history. National events seemed to repeat themselves regularly, and the many vicissitudes of 1848 were there to suggest the resumption of a comparison between Robespierre and Bonaparte that the years of the Restoration had proposed from the beginning.

In the years of the Second Empire, Louis Mortimer-Ternaux – another liberal deputy at the time of the Louis Philippe monarchy, who then moved on to vigorously defend a politically conservative and socially reactionary republic and was also an obstinate opponent of Louis Napoleon's coup d'état – made a decision along similar lines, setting himself, simply for his own enjoyment, to carry out extraordinary archival research into the Terror.[29] The purpose was clearly stated from the very beginning, where the author noted that demagogy and despotism were two sides of the same coin – one that in France never went out of circulation. In this way, for Mortimer-Ternaux, returning to 1793, when in liberty's name liberty itself had been sacrificed to the violence of the streets, was to recall the rebellious populace and barricades of 1848, from which Bonapartist populism had made its forceful return. Similarly, the success of Louis Napoleon Bonaparte referred back to that of his uncle, who had been able to exploit to his own advantage the political desert that the period of the Terror had bequeathed to France. In his view, too, there was no doubt that the great revolutionary historiography of previous years, especially the liberal perspective of Thiers, carried serious responsibilities: with the aim of endowing the political affairs of modern France with a sort of unity, it had ended up restoring the rights of citizenship to the period of the Terror, which had brought to the country only infinite and lasting mourning.

For Mortimer-Ternaux, too, after all, the merits of the revolutionary government in terms of defending the homeland from foreign aggression were an artificial construction, soon deployed to its own advantage by historiography wishing to make Robespierrism its point of reference, but wholly unable to resist the first small puff of historical truth: because what emerged from his meticulous archival research was instead a period of tyranny and violence that had risked engulfing the French nation rather than defending it from attack. In line with Barante's reconstruction, Mortimer-Ternaux could also therefore conclude that France had found in itself alone the strength to resist the foreign offensive and the demolition of social coexistence triggered by the revolutionary government. Napoleon would shortly benefit from that generous and sudden impulse – one which no one had paved the way for and which no one, for some time, would be able to build on, or even to exploit. In any case, Napoleonism, in the properly Bonapartist aspect assumed on the occasion of the events following 1848, was the key to rereading the entire modern history of France, with the result that the revolution, in its initial phase predicated on the idea of liberty, gave way to an outcome shaped entirely within the trajectory of despotism.

These were considerations, after all, circulating among those who had once placed their faith in Louis Philippe and had then decided in favour of the republic, as long as it kept its distance from the maelstrom of populism and extremism in which the most radical groups intended to plunge it. Tocqueville himself was prominent here, and at the time of his sojourn in Amalfi seemed to have predicted far in advance what the others would metabolize only in the period immediately following the December 2 coup d'état. In his Sorrento retreat, Tocqueville already seemed to have a clear idea of how the Second Republic would end and while he noted down his freshest memories he also allowed his thoughts to form an overall reconstruction of recent French history. It was, in fact, his reflections on recent events that prompted him to consider a broader portrayal of the French past in the light of an affair both worrying and seemingly without end. Tocqueville's loyalty to the republic was sincere and had strengthened in the aftermath of the drama of June 1848, when it seemed to him an essential requirement to take the side of General Cavaignac, soon to be accused of being the butcher of the Parisian insurgents, but in reality the only figure who could halt the terrifying movement towards the total collapse of every socio-political class.

Thus, Tocqueville did not hesitate to side with the general in the name of a moderate and orderly republic, one that supported a policy of progress without detracting from the liberal framework inherited from 1830. And yet, while remaining in his place and taking on an enormous amount of parliamentary work, aware that the success of the new order was at stake in its formational phase, he had before him the clear perception that the defeat of the workers was a muster call to the less mature part of French society. Consequently, the schism that had opened up in the republican camp would inevitably be recomposed in terms wholly unfavourable to an authentic prospect of freedom. Tocqueville knew that reaction to the Parisian events would take the shape of a further conservative wave rushing in from the provinces to collide with the capital's precarious political balance. He had no doubt, in the second part of that terrible year, that Cavaignac's candidacy for the presidency of the republic was both extremely fragile and the only card that could be played by a republic that wished to remain true to itself. But he himself could not believe the result of December 1848, when the glamour of a name handed victory to a stranger – not only in the conservative circles of peasant France but also in the working-class banlieues of the large cities.

The plebiscite election of Louis Napoleon demonstrated to Tocqueville that France's past had never actually come to an end and the 1849 elections for the Legislative further confirmed that the conservative recovery following the drama of June 1848 was very strong. Nevertheless, he was sincere in taking part in the attempt to build a conservative republic and agreed to be part of Odilon Barrot's executive, leading the foreign ministry until October 1849 and thus taking responsibility for the expedition to Rome which returned temporal power to Pope Pius IX. Barrot's resignation momentarily returned him to parliamentary life and it was then that he decided to travel to Italy, where reflection on recent events expanded to include painful consideration of the exceptionality of French politics. His experience of government, placing him in close contact with Louis Napoleon, had confirmed his suspicion that the new Bonaparte had swiftly grasped the country's need for a guide and the captivating power of a name and had convinced Tocqueville of how difficult it would be to prevent him from emulating his uncle.

As is known, having returned to parliamentary life in 1851, Tocqueville did not give up, unsuccessfully attempting to get the assembly to approve a constitutional amendment that would allow Louis Napoleon to stand again for the presidency of the republic while preventing him from resorting to a show of strength against the deputies. The failure of this move, soundly rejected by the chamber, led to the coup d'état and the temporary arrest of Tocqueville himself, who had sided with the deputies ready to resist President Bonaparte. It was something he had been preparing for for some time: in his days on the Amalfi coast, it was the writing of his memoirs that had led him to reread, in the light of a Bonapartism felt to be looming closely on the horizon, the entire course of national events between the eighteenth and nineteenth centuries. It has been said that in 1850 the drama that began in 1789 did not seem to him to have reached a final conclusion: the Revolution, the Republic, the Empire, the Restoration, the July monarchy and, lastly, another Republic still seemed to be so many phases of a narrative that lacked a proper epilogue – even if this seemed to be taking shape with the arrival of yet another

Bonaparte. This impression impelled him to go back to the recent history of France to highlight when, how and where revolutionary events, rather than coming to an end, had instead coiled in upon themselves and become lost in the meanderings of a menacing déjà vu. Spurred on by political passion, and somehow predicting an imminent new Brumaire, Tocqueville wanted to carve out a precise space in France's recent past, with special emphasis on the Napoleonic decade – a period when it seemed to him that the alternating revolutionary events had found a conclusion, albeit a provisional one. It was, nonetheless, a point of equilibrium that was rife with danger: the democratic, levelling-out thrust that had overwhelmed the monarchy and denied the republic a life of any length was, in his view, transformed into an intensified form of centralization, destined to dramatically obliterate any degree of freedom, inherent in the revolution though this was.

All this seemed clear in Sorrento, when Tocqueville, writing to his friends Kergorlay and Beaumont, confided to them his desire to write about the Empire. He described it as the power structure that, although soon torn apart, would continue to condition civil life in modern France up to and including 1848. The starting point was provided by the Bonapartist ghost that returned to hover over the France of the Second Republic and unsurprisingly Tocqueville quickly set to work, draughting some sketches awaiting completion (his usual writing technique) that dealt with two aspects that seemed crucial to him: on the one hand, the reasons that induced France to surrender itself to Bonaparte in 1799 and, on the other, why the end of the Republic – which, in his view, took place with the Brumaire coup d'état – did not, however, spell the end of the revolution. These were two significant elements, where the tension (and anxiety) of the present were reflected in the past and seemed to suggest the revival, in modernized form, of 1799. The two aspects, while dealt with separately, came together in Tocqueville's idea, stated and restated, that government centralization – the instrument that had allowed the dream of a liberal revolution to be shattered in such a short time – was created through the work of Napoleon. Up to that moment, this was nothing new in Tocqueville's thoughts: he had been articulating his convictions in this regard, drawing fire from more than one adversary in the Orleanist establishment, since 1842, when, on the occasion of entering the Académie Française, he had already indicated this line of continuity.

However, in the aftermath of 1848, with the June Days and the plebiscite election of a new Bonaparte weighing heavily upon him, the picture was becoming, if possible, even clearer: the revolutionary narrative seemed to assume a compactness that liberal historiography had long denied. He could now openly reject the Directorial Republic, which appeared to him – unlike Staël and Constant – not simply a prelude to Napoleon's seizure of power, but actually directly responsible for it. Certainly not by chance, he suggested that only after Thermidor did armies assume a political profile, destined to accompany the republic's death throes and at the same time keep revolutionary hope alive. The image of an army of patriots, so successful in France's political tradition in the early nineteenth century, was therefore for Tocqueville the representation of a sensational misunderstanding: it was not love of the Republic, but of the revolution, that had inspired the group of generals from which, by a curious play of circumstances, Bonaparte himself would emerge.

Tocqueville's liberal perspective was therefore very different from that of his predecessors.[30] After 1850, due to the pressure of contemporary events, he no longer had – if he ever really did have – any confidence in the republic, which seemed to him a sort of, in some ways inevitable, parenthesis on the road to Bonapartism. The year 1799 seemed to him to offer the harsh confirmation that the period of liberty in the revolutionary decade had been very short: from the very beginning, the destiny laid out for 1789 was something different, something far more than a mere choice regarding freedom. This approach led Tocqueville to weld the revolutionary and Napoleonic periods closely together to form a kind of inseparable block, whereas all his predecessors had instead been careful, due to an excessive love of liberty, to distinguish between different phases and periods. It is worth pointing out, then, that a perspective of this kind was destined to emerge further strengthened by the events following his return to France. In 1851, the failure of his work of constitutional mediation, the coup d'état, the useless parliamentary resistance which he himself been a part of had all made a powerful contribution to sending him back to the pleasures of his study. At the same time, however, they had done a great deal to reinforce his idea that Bonapartism was an even more powerful phenomenon than he had previously believed and therefore derived from a greater distance in time – from a period, in other words, that could not be limited to just one decade, even one with such a devastating, revolutionary character.

It is no coincidence that in December 1852, in parallel with the plebiscite that sanctioned the birth of the Second Empire, there is an annotation that is often mentioned in historiography, to the effect that Tocqueville had decided to return Thibaudeau's *Mémoires* to the library,[31] taken out on loan not long before. He had not looked through it yet, convinced he would read it at a later moment, when it would be time to deal with the revolutionary period. The note in some ways constitutes conclusive evidence, revealing that, in the meantime, Tocqueville had changed his plan of work, convincing himself that he should not limit his attention to revolutionary times: it was necessary to go even further back, investigating those events of much longer duration that were covered by the vague term *ancien régime*. This gave rise to *L'Ancien Régime et la Révolution*, which he dedicated himself to throughout the 1850s. It was the result of in-depth archival research in both Paris and the provinces, of study trips to Britain and Germany, of wide-ranging reading and an extraordinary knowledge of the old order's political, administrative and socio-economic life. But death overtook him in 1857 and prevented him from completing it. The result is that what remains today is only the first part, dedicated to the period prior to 1789, while the study of the revolution itself amounts to just a few sketches that he intended to elaborate in much greater detail.[32]

And yet, this incompleteness does not interfere with either the ingenuity of his interpretation or the originality of his conclusions: in these pages, the idea for the first time appeared that the prefect of police was the direct descendant of the *intendant* of the old order – that centralization, in other words, was the work of the *ancien régime* and that the revolution and the Napoleonic regime that followed had only taken over and perfected a system that had been in operation on French territory for some time. It was a perspective that came freighted with many other insightful observations: the tendency towards centralization, which went along with a movement towards absolutism, had brought about a profound levelling-out of society and in some way prepared the way for an egalitarian direction; the devitalization of the political role traditionally assigned to the aristocracy, without a corresponding reduction in privileges, had transformed the nobility into a caste, closed in upon itself and deaf to any prospect of change; the new power structure thus disillusioned the great majority of French peasantry, ready to rebel against an order that suddenly seemed to have deviated from the paternalism on which its social consensus was based; centralization, while allowing the aristocracy numerous advantageous positions, had nevertheless fostered an equality of conditions within the Third Estate which liberal aspirations took advantage of in order to move away from the traditional government framework; for this reason, all the attempts at reform of the last few decades of the eighteenth century had not only failed but in their ineffectiveness had acted as instruments that accelerated the old order's plunge towards crisis. In this context, Tocqueville offered a powerful description of the various social forces and their divergent interests, transforming the contrasts that inevitably arose from the majestic history of a social evolution, where continuity and severance between the old order and the revolution found complete explanation.

This was the basis for a reading of the pre-revolutionary period (1787–9) which, with great clarity, Tocqueville first identified as a historical moment in its own right, where the reforming drive of the Crown had broken against the wall of an administrative revolution that would accompany, and greatly condition, the political revolution. While the convergence of these conclusions was destined to have a decisive effect on how 1789 was read in the context of its time, it soon led to the concealment of the impulse that had prompted Tocqueville's journey back in time. Going back to the origins of the old order, which constitutes the extraordinary result of his research, all connection was lost with the political motivations that had prompted this kind of path as it established itself as a gigantic historiographical operation which, thereafter, no scholar of the *ancien régime* could ignore. And yet, if it is true that the overall result ended up dissipating the contemporary thought that had encouraged Tocqueville to set out on his perilous expedition, historiographical catharsis should not prevent us from grasping what his work ended up implying, in France at that time and in the context of the developments of a tradition of studies regarding the revolution. Thus, it is first worth emphasizing that his effort entered into direct collision with the work of those who had instead indicated in 1789 the advent of a completely new period – one that severed any link with the past. Tocqueville's work swept away all those that had gone before, whether revolutionary or not, whether more strictly liberal in tone or more exquisitely republican: the distance he had established in relation to them was enormous. He perceived in French modernity not only a persistent opposition to the values of liberty to which he would always remain faithful but also a worrying line of continuity with an *ancien régime* that immediately – that is, since the taking of the Bastille – had been the target of so much destructive language.

His work was, in other words, something different from, and opposite to, those that in the years immediately before had packed revolutionary shelves: it could not have been a more radical move away from Michelet and from those who, albeit with varying emphases, had made 1789 the date of modern France's birth. The origins of the modern nation were no longer located in an irrepressible search for freedom, but, far more ominously, in a propensity towards egalitarianism through means of a centralizing system. However, it was not so much on republican historiography that Tocqueville's work had such a devastating effect – it ended up being much more destructive in relation to liberal reconstructions, suggesting as it did that the period of liberty had not collapsed due to resistance offered by the aristocracy or the demagogy of the democratic tribunes: instead, its brief, faltering existence was due to the fact that it arose in a cultural, political and social framework that looked in an opposite direction. The arguments traditionally put forward – the revolution as a period of freedom destined to die out because of the mistakes of its own protagonists, or the shortcomings of the aristocracy, or the weakness of the Crown – turned out to be trivial matters compared to a reading that, turning the connection between *ancien régime* and 1789 on its head, pointed at continuity as the key to solving the enigma of France's distorted political modernity.

From this specific perspective, Tocqueville's work had a decisive impact, bringing to a close the era of Thiers, Mignet and Staël and indicating how little there remained to cling to for those who rejected the aggrandisement of 1793. The work thus became a furious testimony to how the December 2 coup d'état had inflicted a fatal blow on the liberal cultural model that, among many difficulties, the Restoration had nevertheless initiated. The collapse of a Second Republic mired in conservativism – so much so that it reversed course on universal suffrage in the vain hope of stabilizing the new order at a more limited level – had occurred when faced with the irresistible appeal of the Bonapartes, which suggested that the contorted series of events that had begun in 1789 could find an explanation only by denying that the new France had arisen out of a yearning for liberty. Tocqueville's position was therefore a far more desecratory one than that even of Barante or Mortimer-Ternaux: they had criticized Thiers, basing their arguments on the Parisian events of 1848 in order to show that 1789 should be kept quite distinct from 1793, in that it was necessary to separate the positive moment of an illusory freedom from the dark aftermath of violence and despotism. Tocqueville, on the other hand, had shown that hope was useless not only from the turning point of the Estates General, but also from the period of the Directory – the entire history of the revolution began in the name of an egalitarianism nourished by the power of an old order that could never have allowed the dream of liberty to become concrete reality.

And yet, even before Thiers – who Tocqueville treated with reserve, if not contempt – his real target was the first liberals, Constant and Staël, who, in different times and in different ways, had nevertheless believed they could discern profound traces of freedom throughout the entire revolutionary decade. Now, however, it was clear that Tocqueville's work denied all this: the journey he had undertaken in search of democracy in his, and America's, youth ended many years later in his own land and the result was disheartening on more than one level. Democracy was confirmed as belonging across the Atlantic – in the old continent, in France, where the old order had spread its web further and better, it could only be a matter of plebiscitary distortion, where first the uncle, and then the nephew, found it easy to establish a system of power in which egalitarianism clearly prevailed over the cause of freedom.

It was a discourse that once again had an impact on the political situation of the moment, and this explains why Tocqueville's work was highly successful in the years of the Second Empire, only, instead, in the aftermath of the birth of the Third Republic, to meet with swift, even if only apparent, oblivion. In any case, the liberal Tocqueville succeeded in the involuntary enterprise of sinking the historiographical tradition that was the embodiment of his own values and which, not surprisingly, from the years of the Second Empire, was rapidly lost to sight. Even more, the turn towards conservativism of a liberalism in an Orleanist framework manifested itself with even greater clarity in the aftermath of 1870, when yet another revolutionary event following the defeat at Sedan convinced many that 1789 had brought down some form of political curse on the whole of France. It was a curious destiny, Tocqueville's, who never wrote directly about revolution, but whose ingenious reconstruction of the connection between the *ancien régime* and 1789 played a decisive part in eliminating from the scene for entire decades a liberal tradition within which revolutionary historiography had taken its first steps.

4. Democracy in exile

L'Ancien Régime et la Révolution enjoyed a great deal of publishing success in the years of the Second Empire: the first two editions in 1856 were followed by a third in 1857 and a fourth in 1859, while the two fragments dedicated to 1789 were printed with his correspondence by his friend Gustave de Beaumont for the first time in 1861. Curiously, the historiographical fortunes of Tocqueville ran alongside those of Adolphe Thiers: forced into silence in his turn after December 2, the first historian of the Revolution had returned to his studies and had brought to completion the continuation of his work began long before, the *Histoire du consulat et de l'Empire*. In no fewer than twenty volumes, this had been started in 1845, continued with some difficulty during the years of the Second Republic and finished, with the printing of the last nine volumes, between 1856 and 1860. The works by Tocqueville and Thiers were poles apart: the former used the First Empire to demonstrate that the crisis of France's political and social system was a long-standing one, while the latter, rejecting Bonapartism, did not hide his admiration for Napoleon's genius and politics of power.

There was no contest between the two writers in strictly publishing terms: Thiers's argument, especially in the years of the Second Empire, was destined for great success. The Bonapartists gladly passed over the author's liberalism to be captivated by his discourse on national *grandeur*, while conservative circles also appreciated his work – although distancing itself from plebiscitary logic, it insisted on the need for a system of order. Only the Republicans were critical, very worried as they were by Thiers's sales: they seemed to endorse the role of Bonapartism in the country's destiny and explained everything about how the magic of the name bestowed complete stability upon the Second Empire. In their eyes, Thiers was unacceptable – he pointed out that the Napoleonic years were linked to the revolutionary era and noted that all together they had led to France's primacy in Europe, something that not even the Restoration was able to remove.

This reading of the revolution and Bonapartism in the name of continuity seemed to them an attack on the nation: Bonaparte's coup d'état was only the death throes of the hope raised in 1789 and the ominous foreshadowing of what his nephew would accomplish in 1851 against the Second Republic. In short, Thiers represented the Republicans' main polemical target – not only did he bear serious responsibility for the ultraconservative direction taken by the Second Republic, he also tasked himself, through his writings, with legitimizing the historical significance of the Bonaparte family's coups d'état.

The Republicans actually knew that Thiers's work closed with a note of criticism towards the Napoleonic experiment, a sort of political judgement on the Second Empire, but his stance against the December 2 regime did not cancel his enthusiasm for *la grandeur*, thanks to which myth the nephew was able to inherit the legacy of his uncle.

In 1862, from his London exile, Louis Blanc, as the conclusion of his history of the French revolution was coming out, had in fact accused Thiers of ambiguous liberalism and being essentially complicit in December 2. Other republicans in exile also took the same line: in 1863, another member of the 1848 Constituent Assembly, the Alsatian Victor Chauffour-Kestner,[33] thundered against the unacceptable ideas in Thiers's work, where rejection of authoritarianism was accompanied by the extolling of Napoleonic military operations, and nothing was said of what the latter had contributed to the military oppression of the whole of Europe. Another republican forced into exile in Switzerland, Jules Barni, during lectures held in Geneva in 1863, also targeted Thiers's work, dedicating a meticulously critical review to it to reiterate how wrong he was in his judgement of the emperor: Napoleon, it had to be said, together with Madame de Staël, was the first in the serried ranks of nineteenth-century counter-revolutionaries.[34]

Also from Swiss exile, another 1848 parliamentarian, Edgar Quinet, commented on Thiers's work to demonstrate the suspicious similarity of its patriotism to Bonapartist rhetoric. In 1862, he described Napoleon's last military campaign, carefully distancing himself from the account offered by Thiers, which seemed to him dominated by 'inexplicable fatality', as if the 'oddness of fate' had unexpectedly put an end to a period of triumphs that was otherwise destined to continue indefinitely. For Quinet, central to Thiers's reconstruction was a 'méthode asiatique', where energy and strength ruled the scene and the disaster to which Napoleon had led France was reduced to the level of a perverse trick of fate. And this was an unacceptable reading, because it seemed to validate, hidden under the guise of heroism and grandeur, the political minority of France that emerged from the 1789 watershed.[35]

For this reason, criticism of Thiers was accompanied by a rereading of Tocqueville's work, which seemed to Quinet very useful for demonstrating how the theory of circumstances was a weak justification for the distortion of the revolutionary process. In this light, he returned, again in 1862, to *L'Ancien Régime et la Révolution*, which in 1856, at the time of publication, had instead seemed to him of little account – commenting about it, in a letter to his friend Michelet, in terms of condescension. At that time, Tocqueville's work had suffered from the political acrimony between the two – Quinet having reproached him for endorsing, as foreign minister, the expedition against the Roman Republic of 1849 and for contributing to the cancellation of democracy in Italy. Now, in 1862, having read Tocqueville's posthumously published fragments on the revolution, it was his concern regarding the wide public consensus of Thiers's latest work that prompted Quinet to look for support in Tocqueville's writings. Suddenly, continuity between *ancien régime* and revolution offered truth and enlightenment, making it possible to read 1789 in broadly depreciative terms as an event that had proved unable to overcome the substantially archaic consequences of the past.[36]

From here, it was a short step to contrast Tocqueville with Thiers and demonstrate the fragility of the liberal tradition in the 1789 reading. Overall, it was a brilliant operation: Tocqueville, the champion of liberalism, was reclaimed, with an admiration that did not conceal a very different historiographical project, to be deployed against his own political stance. The tactic took on the semblance of a settling of scores with the entire republican right, which Quinet believed bore serious responsibility for Louis Napoleon's rise. In a properly historiographical context, however, it was a perspective that also made it possible to revise left-wing readings: in Quinet's opinion, these had become bewitched by the theory of circumstances that Thiers had circulated in order to validate the period of revolutionary government and had ended up being imprisoned by it. Tocqueville's work therefore became a useful foothold from which to consider the distorted manner in which everyone, first the right, then the left, had looked at 1789 up to that moment.

For Quinet, in other words, *L'Ancien Régime et la Révolution* was the missing link in terms of giving complete form to a consideration of the consequences of the Great Revolution's failure in France's social and political development. The goal was an ambitious one: to write a history of the revolution as an interpretative essay, where detailed description of events gave way to reflection on the individual phases of the revolutionary process. This meant taking up what had previously been written on the subject to provide a description that was substantially different and never before attempted, where reflection on the revolutionary decade made it possible to explain a variety of elements: the weakness rather than strength of nineteenth-century France, the frustrations of democracy even more than its ambitions, the need to build a new republican perspective rather than languish in the poignant memory of its long-ago (and ephemeral) triumphs.

La Révolution saw the light of day in 1865, not long after the works by Tocqueville and Thiers and was in turn a great success.[37] The title, deliberately laconic, says everything about the centrality of 1789 to subsequent developments in French history. It was not, however, a work that came out of nowhere, nor was it merely the protest of a republican outlaw against a homeland tradition that was always prepared to compromise with Bonapartist enticement – exile had only strengthened, and offered an unrepeatable opportunity to develop, certain ideas that Quinet had entertained even before 1848. *La Révolution* was, rather, the result of long-standing contemplation, originating in the years of the republican challenge to the Louis Philippe monarchy, filtered through the political experience of the Second Republic and finally revisited during exile.[38]

Quinet, too, belonged to that generation of 1830, enthusiastic about the return of the revolution and soon disillusioned by Louis Philippe's quick turn towards conservativism. In his cultural journey, the July Revolution had represented moving away from the passion for Herder and for the German world inherited from Staël's reading, while in political terms his romantic education soon turned into passionate patriotism. At first, the example of the Great Revolution remained the one acclaimed by liberal historiography – so much so, that, even in 1835, being part of the republican sphere went together with the rediscovery of France's political mission in Europe and inspired his verses in praise of Napoleon, seen as continuing the democratic wars of the revolution and as the promoter of various national causes.

It was still a politically ambiguous attitude, which soon became clear in his opposition to the Louis Philippe regime. Rejection of the July monarchy led him to denounce Cousin's eclecticism as a fig leaf for the egotistic and anti-national solution in which Orleanism had imprisoned French society. Hence the impulse to react towards the moral bankruptcy of the nation on which the fortunes of the bourgeois world rested and the denunciation of the nefarious role played in this regard by the Catholic Church – always at the centre of French life and always responsible, in Quinet's eyes, for the nation's lack of moral renewal. Son of a Protestant, who had brought him up in the Catholic faith, this was something he would constantly emphasize, pointing to the social backwardness of France in the lack of religious reform and suggesting that the various regimes, including the revolutionary government, had never tackled the problem – had, indeed, counted on Catholic liturgy to ensure an easy, but fallacious, stability. These ideas were formulated for the first time in the polemic against the Jesuits conducted together with Michelet in 1843 from the lecture halls of the Collège de France. Quinet developed them the following year in a series of lectures against ultramontanism and brought them to final form in 1845, when in yet another course he tied the thread of social and religious revolutions around the great occasion – soon lost – of 1789.

Immediately published under the title *Le Christianisme et la révolution française*, those lessons grew out of an examination of how the church of Rome had betrayed the profound values of Christianity.[39] For Quinet, however, it was an abandonment that had had limited effects: evangelical morality was maintained in the community of believers and had animated the renewal force of French society in 1789. In other words, the revolution had once again given voice to the hope, always present in Christianity, that the word of God would find form in earthly life rather than be consigned only to the world beyond. To this point, Quinet's positions reflected those already existing for some time on the French republican left and were not particularly innovative. However, his specific way of looking at the connection between 1789 and a collective expectation with certain traits of messianism made them original: in his view, moral and social revolt had soon turned into a political revolution, but in that transformation the Catholic Church's positions of dominance had remained intact, with the result that its control over France's religious universe had greatly restricted the breadth of renewal.

It was precisely this contradiction that weighed so dramatically on the developments of 1789: the revolution, originating in the name of pacification between state and church, instead, with even greater intensity, once again put forward reasons for friction. French politics thus ended up quickly absorbing the poison of intolerance that centuries and centuries of religious prejudice had spread throughout the moral body of the nation. The entire revolutionary process was irremediably marked by this, the path to freedom deviating into political violence and dictatorship. Robespierre expressed the desire to be the pontiff of a new religion, one form of fideism took the place of another and political dissent replaced religious heresy as a crime against society.

Quinet's attack on the church, however, also spilled over into the republican camp – his target included those, like Buchez and Roux, who considered Catholicism to be allied with the values of the revolution and made a sort of civil religion of Robespierrism. In Quinet's eyes, however, the French Revolution taught something else: the violence, intolerance and dictatorship that emerged in 1793 were unacceptable, the purges suffered first by the Girondins and then by Danton formed a wretched tide of blood in which the Republic had been lost. The Terror was a system of government that echoed those found in Catholic countries fuelled by religious intolerance, the cult of the Supreme Being a pernicious state religion which simply replaced the one that had gone before.

Quinet had nothing in common therefore with the most radical republican circles: his goal was to demonstrate that the heinous influence of intolerance had ruined a revolution that in its intentions – even in the crusade for freedom initiated by Brissot and only carried on by Bonaparte – meant to respond to the message of original Christianity. The conclusion, in the face of the failure of 1789, remained, however, open to a prospect of republican recovery. Quinet reiterated that, for the future, the revolutionary enthusiasm of the Constituent Assembly should act as a guideline – purified, however, of the abstractionisms that had harmed the progress of the nation to such a great extent – together with the patriotic value of the Convention, as long as it was detached from the political violence that accompanied its action, and the universalist crusade carried across Europe by Bonaparte, liberated in turn from its despotic features.

The work gave Quinet notoriety, so much so that the Catholic hierarchy complained to the government, ready to put pressure on the Collège de France to call him back into line. In response, he controversially resigned and threw himself into political life. Failing to win in the 1846 election, he intended to stand again on the occasion of the revolution of 1848, when, while reinstated to the Collège de France, he preferred to take a seat in the Constituent Assembly. With the tragedy of June 1848, however, Quinet immediately moved away from the more radical groups, siding with the Cavaignac government. He was convinced that the popular uprising was a prelude to a reactionary coup – so much so, that in December he vainly supported his candidate against Louis Napoleon. Re-elected to the Legislative in 1849, Quinet tried to oppose the conservative direction of the Second Republic and criticized the expedition against the Roman Republic. In his *Révolutions d'Italie*, written for the occasion, he noted that it was wrong to focus on the liberalism of Pius IX, given that the presence of the papacy prevented rather than favoured the democratization of the peninsula. In the educational field, he then tried to launch a free, secular education project, while, in the political sphere, he held firm to the ideal of a democratic and social republic – something shattered, however, by the December 2 coup d'état.[40]

Forced into exile, first in Belgium, then Switzerland, Quinet always refused to return to France. In the years of the Second Empire he reflected on the defeat suffered by the Republicans on December 2, 1851, soon returning to the uncle's triumphs to understand those of the nephew. The awareness of a dramatic continuity in the history of modern France thus induced him to go back to 1789, reassembling it in its entirety, from the convocation of the Estates General to the Brumaire coup d'état, in order to bring to light the reasons for the repeated defeats of democracy.

La Révolution, in other words, was the natural development, following the failure of the Second Republic, of the ideas produced in his Collège de France lectures in and after 1845.[41] This was not so much because he insisted that lack of moral and religious reform was the basis of the failure of 1789, but because the dramatic conclusion of 1848 prompted Quinet to take up again and develop the criticisms that even then had not spared republican circles that continued in their praise of the Terror and Robespierrism. The arrival on the scene of another Bonaparte seemed to him concrete evidence of how the past of the Great Revolution had also weighed too heavily on 1848 and left its mark on the inauspicious outcome. French society seemed to Quinet to be based frighteningly around an inadequacy of political order that had its roots in the revolution and without its removal there was no future for democracy. In other words, writing about 1789 and its dramatic conclusion in Brumaire, Quinet wanted to talk to those republicans who had survived the meteorite impact of the second Bonaparte to show them how to unravel the dramatic tangle in which, starting from 1799, French democracy had remained entrapped. For this reason, taking up a tradition that, not coincidentally, began in the years of the Directory, he proposed his writings as a sort of philosophical history of the revolution. Detailed description of events thus gave way to reflection on the main phases of the revolution, so that the inadequacies of the republican political class destined to frustrate the French people's will for renewal would emerge more clearly.

The work flowed quickly over the events therefore: what interested Quinet was the possibility, through reference to the individual moments of the political process, to show where, and above all how, the revolutionary ruling class had missed its appointment with history. For this reason, the work was inspired by the political inadequacy of the king and his minister Necker, both mistakenly convinced that the Estates General, by providing a response to the financial crisis, could quickly bring a halt to the crisis of the *ancien régime*. In Quinet's view, however, convening the assemblies of orders made it possible for an entire society – one that had been waiting for palingenesis for such a long time – to distance itself from royal authority. Following in Michelet's footsteps, 1789 was for Quinet, too, a people's affair above all: the storming of the Bastille and the days of October had taken the political movement well beyond the expectations of those who were only interested in civil reform.

The Constituent Assembly, then, played its part through the subversion of the old order, but it was an operation that included many decisive errors. One of these was the administrative reform of 1790, which had ended up favouring the centralization of government; another, the Civil Constitution of the Clergy, the deleterious coup de grâce of what was an inherently mistaken approach to the religious question. The freedom of belief and worship sanctioned by the Constituent Assembly seemed to Quinet a mere ploy to avoid committing to wide-ranging religious reform, with the result that the refusal to intervene meant that the old political order was able to remain on the scene under another guise. The Civil Constitution of the Clergy summed up this dramatic ambiguity: on the one hand, it freed curates from the oppression of religious hierarchies, but, on the other, it allowed traditional spirituality to remain a presence and thus condition the new order. They were measures that betrayed the inexperience and arrogance of the Constituent Assembly, brought into a collision course with the Crown by Mirabeau's skilful politicking, but soon in difficulty following its guide's sudden death. Judgement on the first revolutionary assembly, extolled until then in all revolutionary reconstructions for its work subverting absolutism, was thus defined in terms of bitter disillusionment as a result of the excessive inadequacies demonstrated.

The Constituent Assembly had waged war on the Crown relying on popular support, but it had avoided a moral reform that would allow it to become the expression of the entire nation. The consequences were devastating, because the assembly was not able to exercise control over the people's new remoteness from the monarchy. The failure became clear on the occasion of the flight to Varennes: the assembly demanded that the king be brought back to Paris, rather than letting him escape, but at the same time, out of touch with popular sentiment, it was obliged to use force against protesters on the Champ de Mars. At the time of its dissolution, the Constituent Assembly therefore left a bleak legacy to the nation, having unwittingly succeeded in reconnecting a close alliance between traditional powers without providing any kind of counterbalance. With a Court by now openly counter-revolutionary, and a church outraged by intolerable intrusiveness into its internal organization, what was required was a monarchical constitution, but the people were no longer ready to accept this.

When the Legislative Assembly met, in other words, the civil war was already underway and the Girondins' decision to go to war was for Quinet an inevitable response to the hostilities that the Court itself had secretly initiated some time before. However, the military challenge to Europe had the effect of destabilizing the assembly and plunging it into factional conflict, creating room to manoeuvre for the intervention of the Parisian crowd. The day of 20 June 1792, when the people erupted into the Tuileries to protest against the indictment of the Girondin ministers, was a decisive step in this regard. At that point, the assembly's ability to keep a grip on revolutionary spontaneity failed and the Republic, destined to be born a few weeks later, suddenly appeared to lack a sure political guide. The day of August 10 marked the end of the Legislative Assembly and the birth of the Convention, but the power vacuum favoured the September Massacres and the rise of demagogues such as Santerre, the commander of the National Guard, who would later be one of the 'little employees of the Empire'. *La Gironde*, though it came to power, was never able to stabilize the new order: at the beginning of 1793, the Montagnards easily managed to obtain the death of Louis XVI, letting it be thought that in that way 'everything would become simple. Europe would be terrified, the war cut short, victory decisive, abundance assured, parties resigned or extinct. So did illusion mingle with hate.'

For Quinet, instead, it was a decision that paved the way for the opposing solution of political chaos, where everything was soon overwhelmed by violence. The days of 31 May and 2 June 1793, when, up in arms, the sections obtained the political elimination of the Girondins, marked the point of no return: the real revolutionary party, which had no intention of retaining anything of the old regime, gave way to those who were willing to come to terms with the pastist mentality of the Parisian crowd in order to stay in power. The fall of the Girondins thus led to truly revolutionary ideas being set aside: French regeneration would pass through a system imposed from above and profoundly authoritarian, directly inherited from the *ancien régime*.

Tocqueville's thesis was thus useful for contesting at root the interpretation of republican parties in conflict for the first time, the Girondins fully rehabilitated, the Montagnards condemned without appeal. Robespierre, after all, also bore the blame for having theorized the Terror system, intending to promise freedom at some point in the future, when no enemies were left on the political scene. In this way, nonetheless, in Quinet's view, virtue was once again a matter for the few, who had the prerogative of leading the nation through dictatorship to happiness. Here was the dramatic contradiction between a goal never before achieved and the systems to accomplish it, which remained brutally old-fashioned, rooted as they were in the intolerance of the old order. Religious traditionalism, officially rejected, in reality repositioned itself at the centre of revolutionary moral life and stretched its sinister shadow over the Republic's destinies.[42]

In this way, the Terror was not the result of circumstances – as everyone, since the times of the histories of Mignet and Thiers, had rushed to report – but rather of a shrewd calculation to limit expectations, showing a willingness to accept everything from the old order in order to emerge victorious from the difficult political conflict in progress. The result of the revolt of the French provinces against the expulsion of the Girondins from the Convention proved this: accusations of federalism and counter-revolution flew hither and thither, but they were only a fragile mask to conceal the proposal to put an end to all dissent. Fear, which drove the people of Paris to act, rather than being the consequence of the political inability of the revolutionaries to respond to the crisis, was actually transformed into a system of government. At that point, superstition and ignorance came back into play: in the violence of 1793, the intolerance of past centuries re-emerged – it had always suggested putting an end to all dissent to safeguard the purity of the French people and the revolution became one more step in a line of continuity with the violence that, since the times of the wars of religion, the *ancien régime* had orchestrated to the detriment of the free will of the people.

For this reason the revolution was overtaken by fragmentation – consensus drained away and the fragile body of the Republic suffered the consequences. The decision to put an end to the Terror and overthrow Robespierre was an important one, but organized by a discredited ruling class, which, with only coercive means to obtain consent, could not therefore found a true system of liberty. Unlike his predecessors, who had made the fall of Robespierre the conclusion of the revolutionary trajectory, Quinet believed that the years of the Directory were just as important in terms of understanding the profound reasons behind revolutionary failure: they alone made it possible to read the Brumaire coup d'état as an authoritarian development that had long been circulating within the revolutionary process.

It was precisely this phase of the revolutionary event, little emphasized up to then, that Quinet used to draw an analogy with the Second Republic, with the Directory becoming a clear foreshadowing of that fragile regime of freedom that followed the June 1848 Parisian repression. In 1799, Bonaparte's sword brought back the servitude of the old order – an event, in Quinet's view, that grew out of the choice of the post-Terror political body to prefer military power to the free exercise of a democracy that might be guided by the more radical fringes. This reading, where the Directory period became the only prolonged moment of the republican exercise of liberty, reflected the drama of the coup that Quinet had experienced first-hand. In 1851, the spectre of the next legislative elections had convinced many in moderate circles to support – or at least not to impede to too great an extent – the coup d'état; and, in 1799, the two Parisian councils had preferred to let Bonaparte through in order to curb the electoral rise of the radical left. What was valid for Brumaire was also applicable to December 2: the responsibility for the rise to power of both uncle and nephew fell squarely on the shoulders of the moderate sphere, ready and willing to forget the advantages of freedom in exchange for the guarantee of privileges accumulated up to that moment.

For this reason, the analogy between the Directorial Republic and the one that emerged from the popular uprising of 1848 was also transferred to the institutional sphere: both fell due to an improper exercise of freedom, intending as they did to found an alternative system to despotism, while nonetheless lacking the social basis which a model of that kind required to survive. In other words, the end of both republics arose from the contradiction that the system of liberty was entrusted to a ruling class unable to defend itself from the challenges it had to inevitably face from the exercise of democracy. In this context, in the antinomy between the unpreparedness of the elites and popular expectations lay the failure of the First and Second Republics, giving way to the same brutal mechanism of appropriation of power by the two Bonapartes.

In this way, Quinet's analysis spared no one: not the people who, abandoned to themselves, had become easy victims for schemers and rogues, and not the ruling classes, who had struggled to imagine a politics of freedom and, having achieved it, had not been able to exercise it – preferring, in both 1799 and 1851, to bow to a soldier's blade. His conclusion was dishearteningly lucid: the Napoleonic dynasty was not the result of treason lurking constantly in the shadows, but the consequence of a policy, going back to 1793, which, through deploying the Terror as a liberating tool to break the shackles of the *ancien régime*, had ended up re-establishing absolutism within the new order.

La Révolution was a great success, though it would cloud the close friendship between Quinet and Michelet and bring down a storm of ferocious criticism on its author. This came above all from the left, who rightly read in the description of the Parisian insurrection days of 1793 the birth date of that revolutionary spontaneity that would also show itself in such a bad light in the spring of 1848. Louis Blanc, who had just completed his own history of the revolution, was keen to have his say, reiterating the exceptionality of the Terror, and Alphonse Peyrat, a journalist who in June 1848 had defended the reasons of the insurgents against the republican assembly, took the same line. With different emphases, the friend of a lifetime, Jules Michelet, and a young republican destined for great things, Jules Ferry, instead undertook to defend Quinet, underlining that the connection between 1793 and Brumaire was an important aspect of *La Révolution*.

That publicistic climate, which inflamed Parisian circles in the last years of the Second Empire, was reproposed by François Furet many years later in the light of a dramatic clash regarding the fate of the French left. He wrote that the diatribe opposed those who held firm to the Montagnard nature of the French left and those who, mindful of the repeated defeats suffered, underlined the need for a liberal revision of their political tradition. It seems difficult to agree on this point, however, because the reason for the dispute was not so much about 1793 as 1799: for Quinet, Bonaparte's rise indicated the return of that authoritarian and despotic spirit that France had already experienced in 1793; for Blanc, the collapse of Robespierre had instead opened the way to Brumaire.

The disagreement, in short, ended up hinging on the Directory period, with Quinet reading it as the time of an impossible equilibrium, given that the ruling class that had emerged from the Terror maintained all the elements of weakness that had made it possible. Blanc rejected any approach in this regard – the revolutionary dream had been shattered with Thermidor and nothing in the following period foretold a different end from that of the muster call beneath a general's banner.

For this reason, it seems to be possible to exclude that the confrontation was between liberal and pro-Terror republicans: and instead of a late-in-the-day return to the scene of the conflict between Girondins and Montagnards, the argument was wholly internal to a democratic world far more united than controversy might indicate in the rejection of a liberalism with its constant and invariably egotistic traits, whether in a legitimist context or in favour of the recurrent temptation of Bonapartism.

The proof lies in the fact that, in the aftermath of Sedan, in the dramatic situation of the Parisian Commune, all the participants in the dispute found themselves on the same side, fighting the repressive decisions of a revenant Thiers but refusing to support Parisian insurrectionalism. For Quinet, for Blanc and Peyrat, for Hamel himself, who had even written a biography of Robespierre, with differences put aside, the time would come to build a new Republic from the far left parliamentary benches – a republic that would learn from the excessive number of failures suffered by revolutionary politics. Despite the differences, which never entirely went away, they all remained resolute in their intention of building a Republic – a democratic one, however, rejecting any liberal influence. Quinet, making use of Tocqueville's work, had indicated the way to keep liberalism at a distance.

5. Sonderweg: *The rejected legacy*

The Bonapartist conclusion of the 1848 revolution seemed to put an end to the admiration for France's historical-political past which the February Days, a signal and hope for the rebellion of peoples throughout Europe, had previously taken to its apex. The Second Republic's fate was a strange one: its origins and developments placed France at the centre of democratic revolutions, but coming to an end with the entrancing Bonaparte name had the effect of bearing out those who, throughout Europe, blamed France for a policy of unacceptable hegemony. It was the narrative of political modernity itself that suffered: if 1848 exalted the red thread that tied together

1793, 1830 and the February Revolution in the name of social democracy, December 2 instead demonstrated that France had launched, but was unable to complete, renewal in the name of freedom. In the words of Giuseppe Ferrari, an Italian patriot with close connections to France's democratic movement who refused to lose hope, even after Louis Napoleon's coup, the 'risen Napoleon' was not reactionary darkness so much as 'progress without freedom, democracy without discussion, revolution without revolutionaries'.[43]

It was a position that was difficult to sustain and one that Giuseppe Mazzini, the standard bearer of Italian republicanism, decided immediately must be demolished. In his opinion, December 2 was nothing more than a coup d'état, destined to kill the Republic. The Bonapartist triumph that brought the revolution to an end convinced him that France had already exhausted its historical task and was no longer 'Europe's spearhead of progress'.[44] Mazzini had reached this conclusion in 1850 in exile in London, where he had been forced to take refuge when French troops had put an end to the Roman Republic. For the occasion, he had insisted that each nation, depending on its historical-cultural specificity, needed to seek its own path to democracy and this direction meant that little or nothing could now be recognized of the French legacy.[45] Mazzini had decided that the Italian idea had to replace the memory of the Great Revolution, so that a Europe of nationalities might be born, in the sense of a group of democratic associations between equals gathered in the framework of a unitary state under the aegis of a written constitution. In the attempt to impose his own concept of revolution, however, Mazzini encountered a powerful obstacle in the unsparing efforts of Marx to put an end to the contradiction of a socialism which, in France specifically, still at the time of the Second Republic, had focused on the nation to build a valid alternative to capitalism and liberalism. In the European left as a whole, there took shape an opposition between those who still believed in patriotism and those who, considering that model definitively overcome by the class struggle, followed the path of proletarian internationalism. Over and above the results of a clash that dragged on until the First World War, it is worth mentioning here that the positions of both sides grew out of the collapse of the myth of the First Republic in the revolutionary imaginary. Year II became in the eyes of most a moment of liberation that was quickly betrayed, as, specifically due to the Bonapartist victory, some saw it as little more than a simple phase in the triumphal march of the unacceptable bourgeois class and others claimed that it bore serious responsibility for the wretched conclusion of the democratic undertaking. The results of 1848 in France, however, were a decisive turning point, because previously both Mazzini and Marx – and therefore the whole European left – had repeatedly spoken of their enthusiasm for the Great Revolution and had looked with interest at the political struggle on French soil.

It was in Marseille, in 1831, in the political climate following the July Revolution, that Mazzini founded *Giovine Italia*, a party whose guidelines followed the political and social programme of French democracy. He admired the First Republic and was careful to place it at the foundation of political modernity. It was no coincidence that the *Giovine Italia* statute prevented those over the age of forty from joining, since they were therefore born before the fateful year of 1792. The disagreements within French republicanism suggested to Mazzini how he should interpret the revolutionary events:

with the aim of conquering hegemony within Italian democracy, where the Latomian and Carbonari tradition was still in the majority, he took the side of those who had no nostalgia for Year II, attacking Buonarroti and his emulators as exponents of a world that no longer existed. He rejected the lure of collectivism and Babuvism and indicated the correct path for the Italian revolution in the urban proletariat's consensus for the path of worker associationism. For this reason, after an initial phase which included praise for the way things were handled during the Terror, Mazzini's opinion of the revolutionary government soon turned harsh, following the programmatic lines of French circles that rejected any kind of authoritarian perspective. His decision to build an Italian nationality centred on patriotism and the creation of a unitary state was a clear homage to the First Republic. His idea to found *Giovine Europa* in Switzerland in 1835, an association that was supposed to bring together all oppressed nationalities, also reflected the intention of expanding the French republican model throughout the continent.

Mazzini's intention to bind nationality and cosmopolitanism together through a political decision in favour of the Democratic Republic produced excellent results over time and found him ready for the February Revolution. The idea of a democratic revolution throughout Europe passed without too much damage through the Caudine Forks of the June 1848 repression and the electoral triumph of Louis Bonaparte, to reach its peak in June 1849, when the left-wing 'démoc-soc', led by Ledru-Rollin, tried vainly to bring aid with a street demonstration to the Roman Republic, attacked by French troops. Despite the defeat, Mazzini continued to look with sympathy at democratic circles in France, hoping with them that, once Louis Napoleon Bonaparte's mandate ended, the 1852 elections would mark the triumph of the democratic left. The December 2 coup convinced him, however, that nothing more could be expected from Paris. He was worried that a history that had already been seen should return in such a dark guise and was distressed that many Italian republicans, until just a short time before his companions in adventure, were ready to succumb to Bonapartist allure and wait for the new Napoleon and his armies to descend once again on the peninsula. In this context, during the 1850s, Mazzini began to move away from the French revolutionary model and from then on he began to intensify his attack, attributing to France the claim of a revolutionary primacy that was stolen away from it by history itself.

However, it is no coincidence that, in parallel with the new positions assumed by Mazzini, Marx also revised his own, arriving at a historical judgement on the French Revolution that had not previously been quite as clear to him. He had arrived in France in the early 1840s and had positioned himself opposite to Mazzini in the political debate within republicanism. The Italian looked to the circles of social democracy, and did not hide his great admiration for Leroux, while Marx was interested in the Babuvist circles, which in those years kept alive the idea of armed insurrection against Louis Philippe. In 1844, Marx had even begun considering his own history of the French Revolution, which would surpass previous efforts in the German language and take as its reference French historiography of the time – so, on the one hand, the works of Thiers and Mignet and, on the other, those of Buonarroti, Buchez and Roux and Cabet. The project soon ran aground, but the reading he carried out in the meantime led him to the idea of 1789 as a bourgeois revolution, to be overcome through social emancipation leading to a communist revolution.[46]

It was a perspective that promptly inspired reference to the Great Revolution, in which judgement regarding historical phases and characters was often contradictory: hence he admired Robespierre, but also hinted at his role as a forerunner of Bonaparte; he proposed the Terror as a political instrument, while also seeing a role for it in terms of a new social order. However, nothing could predict that clarity of purpose with regard to the historical role of the French bourgeoisie that Marx established only in 1848, when, faced with a revolution on German soil, he introduced the concept to demonstrate that, beyond the Rhine, revolutionaries were locked into a pastist logic and lacked the clarity of intent shown by their neighbours in 1789. During 1848, faced with the events in France and Germany, Marx insisted on the precedent of 1789 until the December 2 coup led him to break with French revolutionary tradition.

The fact that another Bonaparte was in power seemed to him to confirm that nothing more was to be expected from the French political tradition and that Jacobinism – which he had previously regarded with sympathy – was now something distinct and in some ways opposed to socialism. He thus announced, in 1852, that while Bonaparte had brought statism to perfection, it was in reality a process with long-standing roots in French history – a process in which the Terror had played a decisive role. His conclusion was similar to Mazzini's, even though from an opposing point of view: the French Revolution had nothing in common with a revolutionary outlook, which should have focused on the future rather than remain imprisoned in the memory of a past that the wretched class-based society itself had produced.

On similar lines, in the years of the Second Empire, there were also significant exponents of French socialism – utopian, in Marx's view, because it had engaged in a bitter polemical duel for the primacy of the revolutionary left. The obligatory reference can only be to the work of Pierre-Joseph Proudhon, who published his own political manifesto in 1863.[47] Here, he abandoned the prejudice on the need for a governing body, indicating federalism as the only way to overcome the government centralism which the two Napoleons had equally inherited from the experience of the revolutionary government. It is worth remembering here that, in the years of the Second Empire, in France as in Europe, throughout the whole radical and socialist left there was a prevailing polemical discourse regarding the Year II government, directed against the statist matrix of many democrats and contrasted by the value of anti-Robespierrist standpoints that were also present in 1793. This rejection of a state deemed irreversibly centralistic stamped its mark on a large part of the European left, in its socialist and radical aspects, and demonstrated its worth on the occasion of the collapse of the Second Empire.

On the matter of the Commune, the various left-wing groups would again split – this time definitively. For radical democratic groups, the Parisian events seemed to confirm a streak of violence and intolerance in the genetic character of modern French politics. An elderly Mazzini returned to speak in order to denounce the ominous results of unacceptable class struggle in the Communard revolt – something he had been warning against since 1848, given that it threatened the unity of the nation which alone could bring about the vanquishing of social inequalities.[48] Marx, on the other hand, saw the embryo of a new revolutionary state in the Parisian revolt and was quick to condemn the patriotism that the capital's workers appeared to demonstrate: the proletarian triumph in Paris seemed to him shadowed by the threat that the followers of republican mythology would commandeer the new political direction and channel it into a patriotic war. In such circumstances, Marx had no doubts:

> The French workmen must perform their duties as citizens; but, at the same time, they must not allow themselves to be swayed by the national *souvenirs* of 1792, as the French peasant allowed themselves to be deluded by the national *souvenirs* of the First Empire. They have not to recapitulate the past, but to build up the future.[49]

The invitation to remain distinct from the French population of 1792 and to ignore the sirens of the past, however glorious, served Marx to thwart the continuation of a Franco-Prussian conflict which seemed to him to place the future of both proletariats in doubt, pressing them towards a patriotic infatuation in which both would inevitably be lost. In any case, his invitation to set revolutionary memory aside went hand in hand with those put forward by Proudhon for France and Mazzini for Italy, and all played their part in rejecting revolutionary tradition.

This sharp left-wing criticism of the 1789 revolutionary model had profound consequences in the historiographical field, benefitting those who missed no opportunity to see revolution and Bonapartism as one entity and to complain, consequently, of a sensational lack of liberalism in the political life of modern France. This trend was not new, having fuelled liberal opposition to the Second Empire: in 1858, Pierre Lanfrey, a journalist at the time close to Lamartine, had for example published an essay, where he emphasized concern that France seemed to be in the tight grip of its past, given that throughout the nineteenth century it had continued to follow the political models of the revolutionary decade. Thus, the Restoration had been a return to the first monarchical phase of the revolution, the July period a resumption of constitutional monarchy and 1848 a revival of the republican phase, with even the Montagnard aspect incorporated, since for Lanfrey socialism was just a 'repetition without originality'.[50] Bonapartism, meanwhile, was in line with what had already happened in Brumaire, compensating as it did for the lack of stabilization of freedom. Here, the old litany returned regarding the inadequacy of the Directory, implausibly compared, frankly, to the Legislative Assembly that in 1849 sent its army against the Roman Republic and in 1851 tried vainly to resist Louis Napoleon. Lanfrey's political message was clear: the Republic had failed once again – it had not been able to establish liberty and, faced with these difficulties, French society had responded first with popular insurrection and then with loyalty to the Bonaparte name.

The following year, Ernest Renan reprinted his *Essais de critique et de morale* with a preface in which he backdated to 1851 the observation that the values of 1789, which he said he had believed in up to then, were only a combination of egotism and violence.[51] It was an indictment against an individualism from which any morality had been stripped away: hence his exhortation to renounce the revolutionary myth once and for all. His march towards the Second Empire took place in light of this – so much so that, by the end of the 1860s, his loyalty to the liberal direction of Napoleon

III made him say that the task of the new France was specifically to put a final end to the revolutionary dream by denouncing the excessive number of errors that followed. These ideas were the last act with which supporters of the Second Empire tried to cleanse Bonapartism of the repeated accusation that it was a continuation of Year II authoritarianism. However, in search of a liberal identity for Napoleon III's regime, Renan's words were not directed only at national public opinion – they were also a response to the criticism that had, from a large part of Europe, poured down on the authoritarian nature that French politics had quickly assumed.

This distancing – after Paris had been the political centre of Europe in the years of the July monarchy – was certainly the consequence of the failure of national revolutions, which had led to the crisis of democratic groups and favoured the rise of national movements with conservative features, immediately brought in to oppose the French model. The Italian case is exemplary from this point of view: Mazzini's attempt to move away from the attractions of the Great Revolution led him to adopt a long-standing national discourse, which, since the years of the First Empire, to escape the asphyxiating Napoleonic embrace, had emphasized Italian cultural primacy in relation to France. In the first half of the nineteenth century, this idea – while it arose in circles close to revolutionary standpoints – soon migrated to conservative spheres, where it stimulated the growth of a national sentiment that was a long way from French democratism. In 1848, the supporters of a national revolution with monarchical and conservative features gathered around Vincenzo Gioberti, promoter of a re-evaluation of the Italian moral and cultural tradition, who envisaged the political end of the Italian republicans:

> the future will tell whether its consequences will be good or bad. I tend to believe it will be good for several reasons [. . .] but the act itself is brutal, wicked, infamous [. . .]. That a state born in this way can achieve solidity is a chimera. However, if it manages to overcome the initial conflicts it will last for a period of time less short than many believe [. . .]. Evil in this case will be compensated for us by great good, that is, by the death of Mazzinianism[52]

His words – where one can glimpse the desire to confuse the various aspects of the Italian democratic movement with Bonapartism – soon found confirmation in the following years, when Mazzinianism faced divisions and difficulties, while more conservative circles took advantage of these complications to reaffirm the claim of the Italian national movement's autochthonous nature. The result was the progressive permeability of Mazzinian patriotism towards a nationalism that had based its historical representation on Italian primacy and for this reason had always affirmed its total extraneousness from the French political-cultural heritage. On the eve of Italian unity, the voices stating that the national revolution owed nothing to the French event had by now multiplied and one of these voices was that of Alessandro Manzoni, whose commitment to Italian unity was not only a matter of linguistic interest, but also took the form of historical reconstruction.

In a piece written in 1859, but published posthumously,[53] commenting on the expulsion of Austria from the heart of Italy thanks to the help of Napoleon III, he contrasted the Italian revolution with 1789 and suggested its superiority: it had managed to avoid popular violence and had been able to translate into a plan of liberty what in France had instead lost its bearings first in the Terror and then in Napoleonism. Manzoni could thus conclude that the Italian national movement was an autonomous process, whose roots lay in the reforming policy of the eighteenth century. Liberty had already been initiated when the French invaded the peninsula in 1796, and while they promoted it formally, they hindered it in practice. Thus, the way was open to suggest a specific Italian path to political modernity – the national movement adopted the guise of liberalism with conservative social traits, with the pride (and the arrogance) of those who wanted to free themselves from an embarrassing past, resolutely rejecting the idea of any debt (even though abundantly run up at the time) with 1789.

This spurning of the French Revolution, the result of the conservative path taken by Italian unity, appears even more clamorously in Germany. There, too, the 1830 revolution had intervened to stir the waters of a Restoration, where, in fact, in some southern states, constitutionalization was already a fait accompli. For this reason, interest in France's revolutionary events soon made a return to German publishing: in 1834, Karl Friedrich Ernst Ludwig started a general history of the previous fifty years where the French Revolution, suddenly present again in 1830, occupied the lion's share[54] and, at the beginning of 1840, Wilhelm Wachsmuth began a weighty work on the history of France in the revolutionary era, which would even inspire Marx to study the subject.[55]

This interest spanned all the years of the July monarchy, involving a wide ideological spectrum, which ranged from the more or less markedly liberal positions of Karl von Rotteck and Karl Theodor Welcker to the radicalism – as we have seen – of the young Georg Büchner. Both these positions were destined to become largely minority in the framework of a German intellectual world in which historicism, characterizing itself as fully supporting a nation state, soon placed itself at the centre of political discussion. In the aftermath of 1830, voices claiming that freedom came before unity became less and less stentorian and the example of the French Revolution, a constant presence in intellectual confrontation of the time, became rather a point of reference in a contrary sense – a warning of how late-eighteenth-century rationalism, believing that it could apply the same institutional model to all peoples and all societies without distinction, had failed miserably.

It was no coincidence that, in 1832, Leopold von Ranke was called to run a government paper that intended to silence all dissent from the left, but also from the right, in the name of an administrative state that knew how to keep well away from the insurrectionary turmoil of France.[56] In the following years, more than a few historians, almost all of them directly involved in the revolutionary events of 1848, played a part in supporting a politics of liberty in which the reference point seemed to be Great Britain rather than France.[57]

In this regard, the most emblematic case is that of Friedrich Christoph Dahlmann, who, in 1845, following a previous history of the English revolution, completed a history of the French Revolution up to the advent of the Republic.[58] The homage to Mirabeau, seen as the figure who, for a moment, seemed about to provide France with a model of freedom on the English example, tells us everything about Dahlmann's lack of interest in democracy and universal suffrage – especially given that, at that the same time, he sang the praises of the Reformation. The latter, in Dahlmann's opinion, was to be placed before the late-eighteenth-century Atlantic revolutions as a moment of liberation, further confirming the tenuous nature of his references to other countries and that historicist zeal urged him to seek the key to German modernity in a strictly national context. After all, it is no coincidence that Dahlmann, and many others with him, such as Gervinus, Droysen, Waitz, Duncker, Haym, Häusser and Mommsen himself, entered the political arena in 1848, sitting in the Frankfurt Parliament and contributing forcefully to setting the national question at the centre of the Germanic political landscape.[59] The events of the revolution in Germany soon brought about the exclusion of the Greater Germany solution, including Austria, to fall back on the Lesser Germany concept under Prussian leadership. This led the large historicist contingent to strike a blow for Germanic specificity. Dahlmann, for example in 1855, unearthed an archaic commitment from the Hohenzollern dynasty in favour of unity. This change in tone rewarded Prussia's rapid rise in the Germanic context, as did the effects of the failure of 1848 in France, which had shown that Germany could expect nothing from its powerful neighbour. Fear of democracy and socialism, anxiety about the aggressive return of the workers to the social panorama and an ending once more in the name of a Napoleon were all reasons that prompted Germany patriots to search within the country itself for a solution to the national problem.

In this context, just after Louis Napoleon's coup d'état, Heinrich von Sybel, a historian trained at the Ranke school and with liberal views, offered the German public a history of the French Revolution that extended to cover the whole of Europe.[60] Von Sybel had a markedly political background and made no secret of the fact that he considered the historical discipline as a sort of present-time laboratory. Rhenish, constitutional in sentiment, he had sat in the Parliament of Hesse and during 1848 he had taken an aggressive line with Austria, whose composition as a multinational empire seemed to prevent it from having any role in a strictly German sphere.[61] According to his own testimony, he had taken an interest in 1789 because he was afraid that Germany's 1848 could go down the same road as the Parisian revolution. Hostile to any form of socialism, sceptical of the dogma of popular sovereignty, it seems that his main intention was to produce a pamphlet in which any French-style cajolery was rejected on the grounds of historical truth. Subsequent events – above all Louis Napoleon's coup – convinced him of the need to expand his thesis and the huge number of printed sources consulted, followed by peregrinations through Europe's most important archives, were all pulled together throughout the years of the Second Empire to form his monumental work. Beginning in 1853 and ending with the fifth and last volume in 1871, the work ran parallel to the process of German unification under the Prussian aegis. However, the book – which was translated into French and English and consecrated the author as the first historian to make full use of archival sources[62] – also accompanied the trajectory of the Second Empire, the target of von Sybel's unsparing criticism: he considered it the deformed realization of that French political model which, since 1789, had sacrificed freedom in the name of equality – and a misunderstood form of equality at that. The work deserves to be read from this perspective: begun in response to the Parisian days of February 1848, the *Geschichte der Revoltionszeit* became an open and obstinate protest against 1789 as a founding moment of political modernity in Europe. It claimed to replace that centrality with the birth, in the same years, of a new statehood marked by the overcoming of the old order through the principle of nationality. In this way, revolutionary France was only one of the outcomes of the eighteenth century's cultural developments: von Sybel was careful to put 1789 and its developments on the same level as the partition of Poland on the one hand and the end of the Holy Roman Empire on the other. In political terms, the intent was clear: to belittle the significance of the revolution by underlining the rise of Prussia through the building of a German nation state with the partition of Poland, on the one hand, and, on the other, the (well-deserved) eclipse of the Habsburgs in the Germanic world.

This manifest intention, however, was sustained by a historical method of huge significance, which made it possible for von Sybel to go beyond the modest limits, albeit necessary, of an international history of the modern world, to produce an imposing choral fresco of economic and social history with a detailed reconstruction of European events in the revolutionary and Napoleonic years. The merits of Prussian power politics – the resistance to revolutionary influence and the liberation of many Germans from the Polish yoke – were coupled with the responsibilities of the Habsburgs, ready to make deals with the Jacobin Republic, to the detriment of other Germans, in order to take possession, thanks to the treaty of Campoformio, of Venetian territories. But the historical merits of the Prussian Hohenzollern dynasty were revived above all through a far-flung comparison with the revolutionary history of France. In this regard, von Sybel's reading followed a linear path that led him to consider 1789 as an important (but not unique) moment of fracture with the *ancien régime*, which was not followed by the balanced construction of a new order.

Indeed, the subversion of the old regime soon became a battle against the right to property itself – which brought to the fore the worst part of French society, prepared to go to any lengths to take possession of a leading role. Social revolution consequently turned political and the work of the Constituent Assembly became the premise for Year II's violent and despotic egalitarianism to find its own affirmation. Von Sybel's words were therefore the annihilation of the moderate and liberal historiography of a de Staël; in his opinion, 1789 and 1793 were not opposed, but closely linked. What distanced him from Mignet and Thiers, too, was the fact that he saw no sign of heroism in revolutionary events. More prosaically, the actions of 1789 were the seed from which Year II's cankered flower would bloom. Along similar lines, there is no doubt on von Sybel's part that the fall of Robespierre and the end of the revolutionary government certainly could not change the course of the revolution: the Year III constitution seemed to him as inconsistent as that of 1791, while the Directory period was a brief interlude between revolutionary convulsions and onslaughts destined to be channelled into Bonapartist militarism.

Ultimately, what seemed important to von Sybel in 1789 was precisely the translation from the structure of an old order to a militarily organized state. In such a context, the French case naturally flanked the Prussian one, with the historian preferring the latter – it was capable of giving a stable and hierarchical form to a society that had remained irreversibly shaken and fragmented since the revolution of 1789. On the other hand –

and here von Sybel's nationalism gave the most obvious proof of itself – Bonapartism's aggressive return, with the figure of Louis Napoleon taking the place lost by his uncle, was the concrete proof of an irremediable French diversity: its political model was wholly unexportable – certainly not across the border to Germany. There, in fact, a different historical path had been followed, divided between acknowledgement of the end of the Holy Roman Empire and the rise against Austria of a Prussia that immediately opposed the revolutionary horde arriving from France. Over the years of writing the work, political events – the rise of Bismarck, the birth of a German Reich thanks to military victory over Austria and then France – confirmed von Sybel in his claim that the myth of the French Revolution should be cancelled once and for all, to be replaced with that of nationality; which, however, found its most complete expression on German soil alone. In this way, his lengthy work constituted, especially after the defeat at Sedan, a sure point of reference for those throughout Europe who contested French primacy and sought their own ways to nationhood. But at the same time it was a sign of triumph for the historicist school, making his *Geschichte der Revolutionszeit* a touchstone for others. In France, all this was a reminder that the political and cultural primacy of former times had vanished and that, for a country stunned by the defeat of the Second Empire, it was imperative to come to terms with its many revolutionary pasts.

4

A republican history?, 1875–1914

Whereas for a long time criticism of the revolution had been confined to condemnation and to a revival of the foundational texts of the counter-revolution, the years following the humiliating defeat at Sedan and the Commune mark a turning point. Under the influence of Positivism, the study of history underwent a profound renewal in its methodology which led to a new interpretation of the causes underlying the crisis of the French national model when compared to the German one. The most brilliant example in this sense is represented by Taine's work, joining as it does a critique of individualism and of democracy with a thorough reading of historical sources. His work constitutes a firm reference point intellectually for all those who disputed the common opinion of the emerging and still fragile Third Republic. Taine's considerable legacy was taken up and perpetuated by *Action française*, as well as by anti-revolutionary historians such as Sciout and Cochin. Taine's work was harshly criticized, instead, by Alphonse Aulard, who, starting from the 1880s, had established himself as the leading figure in the field of academic and republican historiography. Seeing his academic work as a civic mission, Aulard encouraged the publication of important archival sources on the basis of which he fostered the renewal of the political history of the revolution, seen as a long process of democratic apprenticeship, whose fulfilment was being achieved by the Third Republic. His interpretation quickly established itself as the classic one, both within and without France, even though, at broadly the same time, the socialist Jaurès was proposing a different interpretation, inspired by Marxist materialism and more attuned to social factors, which challenged Aulard's in several respects. Once more, on the threshold of the twentieth century, politics and history found themselves inextricably tied: the shadow of the Great revolution following in the path of the rising struggles in mass society and of the new revolutionary stirrings. Jaurès's intervention gave rise to a heated debate which soon transcended national borders, leading to the writing of new histories of the Revolution: from Kautsky to Kropoktin, via Salvemini in Italy.

1. The poisoned seed of national history

Von Sybel's work, which placed 1789 and the rise of Prussia on the same level, certainly could not hope to meet with widespread favour in France, but its pages provided an example of a historical method to which a doff of the hat was obligatory. Although his work was much criticized for erasing French supremacy from the late eighteenth century, a translation was carried out and the first two volumes saw the light of day between 1869 and 1870. The initiative grew out of the acknowledgement that Prussia had by now achieved supremacy in the German world thanks to the military triumph over Austria in 1866 and that von Sybel's survey of the historical process of Europe had been duly confirmed by recent international events. However, no one could foresee that his divinatory powers would soon be applied to France as well and the collapse of the Second Empire made it impossible to continue with the printing of the translation.

In fact, the Commune seemed to confirm von Sybel's intuition that France was clinging to the past: the memory of 1792, of republican patriotism and democratic warfare, strengthened the resistance of the people of Paris and ended up overflowing into popular violence and civil war. Von Sybel himself was one of the first to denounce the Commune for a dangerous sense of déjà vu in the direction of anarchy: he immediately proclaimed the historical rights of Germany over Alsace and Lorraine, drew a gloomy picture of modern France's historical course and emotionally saluted the rebirth of the Reich. The latter was founded on the principle of nationhood, but at the same time was organized around a bureaucratic and military system capable of keeping social unrest in check.[1]

For this reason, the third volume of von Sybel's translation had to wait until 1876 to be published and another ten years passed before the last three volumes were printed between 1885 and 1888. Meanwhile, France went through a difficult process of stabilization, with the Republic surviving by a hair's breadth in 1875. The clash was not only between monarchists (in Legitimist, Orleanist and Napoleonic guise) and the republicans, but had a direct impact on the latter: the memory of the Commune led many to accuse the new republican political class of opportunism and fostered the attractions of anti-parliamentarianism. There was even a miniature Bonaparte in the picture: between 1887 and 1889, the Revanchist general Boulanger repeatedly exploited universal suffrage to get himself elected at every national by-election and, in the name of Caesarism, launch his own challenge to French democracy.

In such a context, there was a strong temptation to see recent history as an unresolved issue and criticism of the new republican political society favoured von Sybel's return to the bookshops. His work applauded harsh judgement on 1789: referring to Burke and Maistre, to whom he had previously dedicated some studies,[2] he related only the destructive aspects of the French Revolution, its merits in subverting the *ancien régime* erased by an inability to fill the power vacuum that opened up with the collapse of divine-right monarchy.

This prospect greatly excited Legitimist circles, all firmly counter-revolutionary in nature, but it could not convince Orleanist groups, whose liberalism instead led them to denounce the Republic (and the Bonapartism that followed) only for moving away from the policy of liberty announced by 1789. It is no coincidence, on the other hand, that, at the same time as the publication of Sybel's translation, Tocqueville's work was reprinted, in 1877 and then again in 1887.[3] Orphans of the monarchy and very fearful of Boulangism, liberal circles thus wanted to state that, in France, Napoleonic centralism was the only rock upon which every policy of freedom had always broken.

It was a concern that also occupied the mind of Hyppolite Taine, whose *Origines de la France contemporaine*, however, in the same years, contributed decisively to cancelling the liberal political culture in which he, too, had been educated. The structure of this very successful work and the publication dates of its seven volumes are worth mentioning here: the first volume, dedicated to the crisis of the old order, was published in 1875; the following three, all regarding revolutionary events, came out in 1878, 1881 and 1884; while the last three, which should have dealt with nineteenth-century France, remained unfinished. Taine only managed to publish the first of these, in 1890, while the second and the third came out, posthumously, in 1901.[4] If these publication dates are cross-referenced with those of Tocqueville's reprints and Sybel's French translation, the coincidences are singular: Taine, who always professed admiration for Tocqueville and who followed him in the subdivision of his own work, certainly found a way to familiarize himself with Sybel's work too, since the translation of the first two volumes was already available at the time of the appearance of the first volume of the *Origines*. Sybel's translation, in turn, was relaunched by Taine's success – after the enforced halt following the Franco-Prussian war, the third volume followed on from the printing of the *Origines* and the other three, too, came out after Taine's writings on the Revolution.

This all shows that, between the 1870s and 1880s, a fierce confrontation took place within the liberal camp, where criticism of the revolution went almost unchallenged and set aside Thiers's fatalistic reading once and for all.

The architect of this particular cycle, with lasting effects on Europe's intellectual landscape, did not, however, have a historical background: in the early 1870s, Hyppolite Taine was above all known for a history of the English literature[5] where, partly on the basis of an amateur passion for anatomy, he had suggested that the cause of certain types of behaviour depended on the same rules that dominated the natural world. Enough, anyway, to swiftly be classified by religious hierarchies as a dangerous liberal, and, at the time, they were not even wrong: Taine had already shown interest in the subject of the revolution, having read Carlyle in the years of the July monarchy. He accused the Scottish writer of moralism, contrasting him with Thiers, whose political project he followed even after the 1848 revolution, when the decisions of the Legislative Assembly reassured him that popular revolt and attack on property could be contained. Conservative before being liberal, Taine reacted to December 2 coup d'état with disgust, even though his opposition to Napoleon III was soon mitigated by satisfaction at the return of social order immediately promoted by the Second Empire.[6]

In the meantime, however, also due to the political situation, his interest in history had grown and he was very passionate about having the discipline abandon its merely descriptive character and rise to the rank of a science – one capable of revealing the profound laws that regulated certain events. He was convinced that, in this way, the historian would be able not only to read the past according to correct causal links, but, in the same way, be able to predict the future as well. History would become capable of revealing the general rules of human behaviour if it were founded on certain elements which, cross-referenced with one another, would make it possible to understand the general features of the evolution of any given social process.[7] Taine identified three causal factors: race, understood as a sort of national character and based on a temperament transmitted by heritage; milieu, the set of socio-political conditions in which collective behaviour unfolded; and moment, being the point of connection between the two previous factors.[8]

These ideas, developed at the time of the Second Empire, seemed to him brutally confirmed by the Commune and the civil war following the Sedan disaster. He had harsh words for the revolutionary spirit that had once more overwhelmed the capital, but those events, which certainly troubled him from a political point of view, fascinated him, too – confirming as they did his hypothesis that self-destructive tendencies had been at work for some time deep within the French social body. The events he witnessed, in other words, spoke of a nation still entangled in the contradictions of 1789 and prompted him, through a study of the Great Revolution, to identify the general rules of social life in modern France. What followed on from the collapse of Sedan consequently opened up the possibility of discovering the profound laws governing the political evil that had plagued France for too long.

Les Origines took shape in the aftermath of the Commune, in a country once more poised between monarchy and republic – a work begun under the influence of Tocqueville, whose unfinished plan was taken up to explain the events of the nineteenth century through the study of the *ancien régime* and the revolution. For Taine, too, in fact, the government centralization wanted by the French Crown was the key to interpreting 1789; and he also saw the revolution not as a break with the past, but rather as a revelation of its profound influence. However, Taine took it upon himself to take this perspective – something only suggested by Tocqueville – to its extreme consequences, and by delving into revolutionary events, starting from a situation of disintegrating traditional powers, he soon came to dismiss any hypothesis that France could emulate the English model. The abolition of privilege and control over the monarchy, instead of favouring a liberal direction, had instead plunged the country into catastrophe, the best soon silenced by pressure exerted from the streets and the worst, dominated by charlatans and adventurers, soon taking the lead in the political process.

The Constituent Assembly, constantly acclaimed by liberal historiography as the only body that could have ended the revolution, became, in Taine's work, the main force responsible for its momentum: with its authoritarian and generalizing spirit, it had destroyed what history had spread throughout society and territory – by abolishing distinction, it had demolished the principle of hierarchy. After all, emphasis on the violence in the summer of 1789, something Taine made much of, served to certify the collapse of all forms of government and the dissolution of all social ties. It was what, in his view, would continue shortly thereafter, when the revolution brought only dissolution. Refusing to deal with issues, however decisive, such as war, finance or conflict with ecclesiastical hierarchies, Taine showed interest only in power itself and excluded the idea that it had taken on monstrous form, something all liberal historiography agreed on, only in the aftermath of extraordinary circumstances.

With truth as his protection, he could thus conclude that nothing justified the terroristic and violent direction of the revolution: Year II was not the terrible reaction to an equally threatening challenge, but the natural conclusion of the process started in 1789. In a sense diametrically opposed to Thiers, revolutionary government was not the degenerate continuation of revolutionary spirit, but its natural consequence. But if the dynamics of the Revolution appeared disfigured, this did not mean that they were inexplicable: they were the fruit of a collective madness that had taken advantage of social decomposition and were revealed both in the behaviour of the revolutionary crowds, the unclean populace, and in that of their political leaders, the Jacobins, whose psychology Taine described in clinical terms. The revolution thus became the conscious project of a handful of deranged figures who profited from the psychosomatic degeneration of the rebellious multitudes.

The work caused a sensation: Taine dismissed the myth of the French Revolution which previous authors – liberals and democrats, conservatives and radicals – had helped to forge and his pages seemed to revive, with the expressive force of an iron-clad interpretative system, the best of what counter-revolutionary writers had stated long before. However, the *Origines* was not the sudden, robust return of a long-standing tradition – its points of reference were, in fact very close in time. On the one hand, Tocqueville was certainly a presence, but, on the other, Mortimer-Ternaux was no less important, with his outright condemnation of the Terror, and, above all, his patient archival excavation work. Taine's choice to combine the two authors had an air of careful deliberation to it, but had the merit of launching a denunciation of the diseased nature of revolutionary reality without rushing into the vague embrace of the world of pastism. Rather, the confident use of Tocqueville allowed Taine to follow in the wake of a liberal world and to give quite a different shape to a decision that could otherwise have been mistaken for mere traditionalism. Intelligent and balanced, inspired by an inexplicit conservatism, his writing was decisive: aiming ambitiously for the heights, it made it possible for him, alternating between description of panoramic collectivity and individual circumstance, of psychological detail and street rioting, to offer a linear reading, in some ways all too consequential and yet constantly fascinating, of the modern history of France.

Its basis was the injustice of the old order: however, the loosening of the hierarchical structure of the *ancien régime* had allowed the nature of the French people to come to the fore and to imprint on public life an abstract and rational conception of man and a politics modelled on the mathematical example of the metric system. In this way, in Taine's eyes, eighteenth-century philosophy had become a sort of new religion, galvanized by the illusory (and soon devastating) belief that the regeneration of man was truly possible and that Enlightenment progress would soon bring forth the paradise of a just (and equal) society. The fact that all the new philosophical principles were libertarian and aimed at the freedom of a humanity dominated by the basest instincts had thus opened the way for the triumph of Rousseau's ideas: in 1789, popular sovereignty had taken over from all forms of authority and made it possible for the bestial violence of the people to become an instrument of change.

In presenting such a scenario, Taine distorted Tocqueville's discourse, showing that not only 1789, but also everything that followed, namely 1793, originated with the old order: devoid of the support of social hierarchy, traditional society disintegrated and individualism, in other times contained and neutralized, was then free to fight for power. Jacobinism, according to Taine, had played a linking role in this regard: it had homologated, in the ideological terms of Rousseauian democracy, the various individuals who had found the strength to rise to prominence from the subversion of the *ancien régime*. He did not differentiate, therefore, in the revolutionary field, between the multiple groups that came to power from time to time, while the individual figures who had taken the lead in events seemed to Taine to be united by irredeemable pathologies: Marat was dominated by homicidal mania; Danton was a savage swindler who made the dictatorship of the frenzied an opportunity to excel; Robespierre, a nullity, spurred on to becoming a virtuous rhetorician by a monstrous doctrine of violence. Thermidor itself thus ended up in a line of continuity with the previous revolutionary phases, as one of the many stages through which the revolutionary spirit had devoured its followers. The death of Robespierre, in other words, simply confirmed that a destructive logic always and only governed the revolutionaries, for whom the physical elimination of the opponent remained the dogma of the new political action.

The anarchy denounced by Taine at several points was based on this assumption: for this reason, in the face of the arbitrariness and oppression that had become the fundamental tools of a rootless power, the time would come for the military – the only force that, in the revolutionary decade, had, albeit with difficulty, held firm to the hierarchical template of their identity. The sword of Bonaparte – this was the meaning of the last part of Taine's work, which remained unfinished – would thus be responsible for slicing through the knot of anarchy. But the return to order and France's entrance into modernity involved, as a counterblow to the lawlessness of the Terror, the construction of a statehood that would impose itself on every intermediate body, destroying local identities and the spirit of a small country in the name of a perverse individualism.

Taine's ideas, supported by meticulous work in the Parisian archives, validated, albeit indirectly, von Sybel's immediately before him: both suggested that anarchy dictated the revolutionary process and denied that liberty was the basic premise for the subversion of the old order. The German historian himself remarked on this with satisfaction in a review of Taine's first two volumes: in von Sybel's opinion, with his thorough exploration of the archive papers, Taine had only confirmed his thesis that the Constituent Assembly had introduced a distortion into the social equilibrium and that in 1789 all the conditions therefore existed for the direction of the new French order.[9]

Self-certifying one's own merits could not, however, be accepted coolly on the French side of the Rhine, implying as it did that the French Revolution, too, was a subject that the German historical school could exercise its hegemony over. For this reason, Albert Sorel, a Foreign Ministry official who became a university teacher, took it upon himself to answer von Sybel and in his argument also ended up resorting to Taine's work – its mastery was something he would always praise. He developed his ideas in *L'Europe et la Révolution française*, an earnest work of diplomatic history published in several volumes between 1885 and 1904.[10] The title indicates that Sorel drew a comparison between himself and von Sybel, initiating an ex officio defence of France against the other's accusations that the country was directly responsible for the drama throughout Europe that followed the 1792 declaration of war.[11] Sorel, making timely use of Tocqueville, reiterated instead that the events of 1789 and beyond were in the destinies of France and the whole of Europe – that was the direction in which the century was heading. If the revolution had taken shape in France and spread outwards from there to a large part of the continent, in part through violence and conquest, this was due to the fact that France, and no another place, was the most developed country. All this implied that revolutionary foreign policy itself, where an element of fracture with the past might instead have been expected, maintained more than one point of contact with tradition. Also in Sorel's view, frontier defence had been a cause for concern for the monarchy since medieval times and it had never given up the use of the military to assert its rights. The problem lay in the fact that, in past centuries, France's line of diplomatic activity had already fluctuated between caution and subjugating adventurism: Henry IV and Richelieu, on the one hand, treated the Rhine question with care; on the other, Louis XIV's military adventures had borne little fruit and greatly penalized the image of French foreign policy in a European context.

Attentive to the values of 1789, Sorel was thus able to distinguish the Constituent Assembly from other revolutionary bodies: it had made a choice for pacifism, in line with the best tradition of the old order, while the others, dominated by a democratic impulse, had taken an absolutist direction in foreign policy and raced into the war of conquest across the Rhine. It remained to explain why, in the history of France, these two opposing lines existed and why, in the years of the revolution, after an initial equilibrium, the country had plunged into Terror within and, outside, into the overwhelming tumult of war. And here, Sorel paid a worrying price for his great admiration of Taine: he perceived the roots of many revolutionary evils in the worst practices of the *ancien régime* and insinuated that this sliding into self-destructive war was the – in some ways inevitable – conclusion of the corruption inherited from the old order's past. Sorel had no sympathy for the self-absolving theories of the Terror that Thiers, above all, had circulated. He estimated, in fact, that the revolutionary government was not concerned at all with the necessity of defence and that it was instead the construction of an authoritarian power that favoured the organization of the armies' new and devastating power. For this reason, the Terror was in turn the perverse result of the degeneration which power politics had brought to France: instead of public safety, the only intention of the revolutionary government was to perpetuate tyranny. When the threat of invasion vanished, with all pretext gone, it ended up spewing out its power on the Republicans themselves. In other words, the call to arms in defence of the 'homeland in danger' was perfectly in line with Louis XIV's own power politics and formed the rhetorical universe which Jacobinism deployed in order to seize power.

In this way, comparing Tocqueville with Taine, Sorel could sing the praises of the Constituent Assembly against the iniquities of subsequent bodies: but a liberal perspective that did without the reassuring protection of exceptional circumstances to introduce a direct link between *ancien régime* absolutism and revolutionary terrorism was a tricky operation to balance. His attempt to move away from Taine, amending his conclusions in several places and noting that the magnitude of the event prevailed over the atrocity of its crimes, was a fragile procedure, one on which it was impossible to establish a new, genuinely liberal, reading of the revolution. This is proved by the success of Louis Madelin's history of the Revolution, published for the first time in 1911, with numerous reprints and translations ahead of it in the years to come.

The work confirmed Taine's eminence, but the author seemed to prefer the teachings of Albert Sorel, who, in his view, had described a France besieged by European monarchies and had thus restored to its authentic meaning 'the sometimes insane gestures of the besieged, demoralised or exasperated, dejected or overexcited, sometimes to the point of alienation'.[12] Sorel's calm fairness allowed Madelin to paint a picture of revolutionary events that certainly followed the path of liberal historiography, both by Tocqueville and by Taine himself, noting that the old order had exhausted its capabilities and that there was a great deal of truth in the *cahiers des doléances*. Following the ideas of previous authors, he did not demonize 1789, pushing into the summer the move towards violence destined to ruin everyone's great hopes for renewal. Along similar lines to Taine, he was unsparing in his criticism of the Constituent Assembly, especially for its attacks on the Church, which had wounded French sensibilities and left its mark on the country's political and civil affairs. The rest of the work contained nothing original: the revolution toppled into the hell of violence and dictatorship due to a small circle of extremists, quick to take advantage of the chaos to dictate their own law. The Republic arose in the framework of these factional struggles, its degeneration into the Terror partly due to the difficulty in otherwise managing the complex military situation. However, a small group of individuals dominated the scene, a genuine oligarchy ready to take over the state apparatus in the name of revolutionary interest, but in reality devoted only to personal profit. At the basis of this trajectory were internal conflict and factional struggle raised to a system of government, with Thermidor itself representing the apex. However, the stubborn resistance of the Crown, unwilling to come to an agreement on the values of 1789, made it possible for the Republic to survive and then, thanks to its own weakness and rampant corruption, surrender to the embrace of military force.

Madelin's work thus ended up prompting interest in the various conservative circles, which certainly accepted the Third Republic at that point, but regarded with great suspicion its claim of rediscovering its historical origins in the revolutionary decade. His debt to Taine was clear, and he was in broad agreement with right-wing polemical observations that inflamed the reading of the revolution. The result was a work that apparently bore the stamp of a discourse of freedom, but which essentially, dominated as it was by conservative patriotism, greatly reduced the room for manoeuvre for a renewed reading of 1789 from a liberal perspective. In other words, Madelin explained the reasons why Taine's rise had corresponded to Tocqueville's fall – the latter never reprinted until after the Second World War. The confrontation between legitimism and republicanism had now closed down the space for a historiography (and a politics) that could claim to be truly liberal and showed that, between revolution and anti-revolution – in other words, between complete acceptance of the whole decade following 1789 and its overall demonization – it was increasingly difficult to perceive yet another position.

The radicalization of positions that marked the beginning of France's twentieth century would accompany its course for a long time to come.

2. Renewing the counter-revolution

On the eve of the new century, Emile Boutmy, the founder of the *Ecole Libre de Sciences Politiques*, made an accurate assessment of Taine's book: it was a monumental work, which represented an irreplaceable reference point in the French cultural panorama, but it was, at the same time, multifaceted and multiform.[13] For those who approached it, its massiveness made it an easy temptation to take only what appealed to their specific sensibility. These observations clearly explained the wide-ranging success of the *Origines de la France contemporaine*, which had found consensus from both right and left, and soon influenced the positions previously held with regard to the revolution by the various political groups. The first to feel the impact of Taine's work was the legitimist camp, which could still, in the first years following the collapse of Sedan, rely on Jean-Joseph François Poujoulat's history of the revolution.

Poujoulat, hugely nostalgic for the years of the Restoration, had looked upon the Orleanist monarchy with great suspicion and had not surprisingly been an intransigent presence in the political life of the Second Republic, without ever collaborating thereafter with the Second Empire. His work was published for the first time in 1848 and went through six editions up to the end of the 1870s.[14] It rejected any revolutionary enticement and set itself, if possible, even further to the right than the counter-revolutionary writers of the early nineteenth century. In its pages, the history of the old order was never anything other than a tale of liberty: France had never lacked a constitution, and Louis XIV's absolutism had always remained a jealous protector of territorial prerogative as well as of class privilege.

In other words, Poujoulat saw 1789 as a disastrous accident – something that had prevented the orderly development of French civil history. It was, however, precisely this radical rejection of the hopes that had accompanied the convocation of the Estates General that could not, after the Second Empire, find a great deal of popularity with the Legitimist circles themselves. The latter, aware that no other way was then feasible, had vainly tried to reconcile the Count of Chambord, the heir to the throne, with at least some of the values from 1789. Taine's work was thus to provide relief to those who well knew that it was now impossible to present the revolutionary movement as a nightmare from which it was finally possible to awaken. In fact, its pages demonized the direction soon taken by the revolution, but admitted the need for change in the France of 1789. Those who advanced this new right-wing reading of revolutionary events included the promoters of the *Revue des questions historiques* – founded in 1866 by the Marquis du Fresne de Beaucourt, it quickly became the leading historical scholarly publication in France.[15]

The journal had not actually awaited Taine's triumphs in order to devote ample space to the studies of revolutionary history: in the 1870s, some of its collaborators had participated in the initiative of the *Société bibliographique*, an editorial association with an openly Catholic stance, to publish a series entitled *Brochures populaires sur la révolution française*, where, at a modest price, a highly critical reading of 1789 was offered to the general public.[16] One of these collaborators was Maxime de la Rocheterie, an aristocrat from Orleans who had to his name a stalwart rehabilitation of Marie Antoinette.[17] Between 1881 and 1885, from the columns of the *Revue des questions historiques* itself, he hailed Taine's volumes on the Year II government as the instrument that made it possible to dismiss, once and for all, the vulgate favourable to the revolutionary process.

La Rocheterie's words are illuminating with regard to how legitimism drew near to Taine: he developed his ideas about 1789 through reinforcing the distinction between the harbingers of the revolution – necessary and in some ways meritorious – and its developments, which soon degenerated into popular violence. However, despite the many sinister signs of forthcoming anarchy, for La Rocheterie, unlike Taine, the revolutionary process had held out until almost the end of 1791, when the exercise of the constitution had strengthened the monarchy and forced the demagogues to play the war card in order to upset the new equilibrium that was on the point of taking shape. In other words, in La Rocheterie's view, despite the dramatic episodes of popular violence, up to the heinous decision to go to war, the revolution had kept faith with the programme of renewal and the monarchy had in some ways succeeded in managing the difficult transition from old regime to new. Then the 'scum' had intervened – La Rocheterie made no distinction between Girondins and Montagnards – and all together had made a success of the republican plot that led first to the Terror and then to a corrupt and violent regime, the Directory, which in his opinion was in no way different from that of Year II. The triumph of General Bonaparte was thus the inevitable consequence, distancing the French as a whole from a system of power where religious and political persecution went hand in hand.

This perspective was not the only one to stir up right-wing opposition to the young Third Republic. On the occasion of the centenary of 1789, a variety of voices tried to wreck the executive's intention to hail July 14 as the celebration of French modernity.[18] Indeed, the criticism that won the greatest consensus was that of the Bishop of Angers, Monsignor Freppel, who in his often reprinted essay on the Revolution deliberately kept Taine's work at a distance.[19] Was this the legacy of the old resentment that had long made the author of the *Origines* unpopular with religious hierarchies? This is not an idea to be excluded: the work of the prelate – who also knew Tocqueville and did not say he was insensible to modern times – seemed keen to suggest a very different reading of 1789. No longer the starting date of a revolution in some ways unavoidable, as Taine himself admitted, but the moment in which reform should have become more intense and against which the revolution itself brutally intervened. The result was the plummet into violence, where the hope for a period of renewal also gave way to a revolutionary movement with anti-Christian traits. There followed, from this dramatic deviation, everything that had since then weighed so heavily on the country: the despotism of centralization, the inequality of false brotherhood, the worsening of living conditions for both the highest and lowest classes, the dominance of a statehood that had its bastions in public education and militarism. It is hardly surprising that, faced with this situation, Monsignor Freppel asked for the return of France to the Christian tradition, the return of the monarchy, the rebirth of a free local life, the restoration of the corporatist system and the limitation of weaponry. In other words, his way of commemorating the 1789 centenary meant a moving away from the secular cult of the revolution and showed how difficult it still was for the Catholic world to come to terms with the republic.[20]

In 1889 other writers, too, added their denunciation of what had happened a century earlier. Gaston Feugère went back to the classics of the counter-revolution, such as Mallet du Pan and Maistre, to completely reject the revolutionary process,[21] while Paul Baudry put the blame on the fickleness of the French character:[22] increasingly dissatisfied with each successive regime over the course of the century and then in the end accepting the inevitable revival of the monarchy. The scenario even included those who, like Georges Romain, returned to making distinctions between 1793 and 1789 and, to the detriment of Madame de Staël, hurled anathema at the Third Republic and called for the return of the monarchy.[23] These writings, very different one from the other, all had in common with Monsignor Freppel the idea of referring to the past in order to speak of the present: in other words, they made use of 1789 to express an opinion on 1889, on a Republic that in some way had managed to impose itself without, however, enjoying a deep, corresponding social consensus.

This tendency to develop a confrontation, increasingly centred on the first republican experience and the contemporary version, certainly did not begin on the occasion of the centenary and it continued over the following years, accompanying the violent clash between the two ideas of France for which the period of the Third Republic provided the battleground.[24] Not by chance, in this revival of interest in the history of the First Republic, it is above all the Directory that comes in for scrutiny. It is significant that the *Revue des questions historiques* gave ample space to the period governed by the Year III constitution, with several pieces by Victor Pierre and Ludovic Sciout, two scholars who dedicated themselves at the same time to the years of the Directory. Pierre, in numerous essays devoted to the abuse meted out to political and religious opponents, developed a precise parallel between the decisions of the Third Republic and those of the Directory.[25]

Ludovic Sciout's works, which in turn cover the last three decades of the century, did not differ from Pierre's too greatly in terms of theme and basic approach. Sciout, a practicing Catholic, had begun to be interested to the revolution in 1872, writing of the Civil Constitution of the French Clergy during the Revolution, where he adopted the legitimist positions of the immediate aftermath of Sedan.[26] He still distinguished, therefore, between the first revolutionary phase, where liberty could be protected from the catastrophic excesses of the mob, and the subsequent period, dominated, not by chance, by a *pretrophobie* ('priest hatred') that had given rise to the Terror. In Sciout's view, the religious policy decisions of the Constituent Assembly – but even more so those of the Legislative – were the point of no return for the revolutionary process. He believed that attempting to force religious figures to take a civil oath, obliging them to choose between observance to the Roman pontiff and the new France, had prevented

Louis XVI from controlling the situation and thwarted any possible chance for the Crown and the Girondins to come to agreement – the only thing that could have prevented the Terror.

It was a position that reflected the desire for a return to the monarchy under the aegis of prudent liberalism and within the framework of full respect for the freedoms of the Church and Sciout would come back to it again over the following years. He participated in the initiatives of the aforementioned *Société bibliographique* with two pamphlets, *La chute des Girondins* and *Decadi*, where the positions he previously expressed became more radical. On the one hand, he still agreed that the Girondins were the presentable face of the revolutionaries and admitted that, if they had resisted the pressure from the Paris streets, many disasters would have been avoided in 1793.[27] On the other, he was harshly critical of the Decadary Cult, brought in by the Directory, and suggested that the whole revolutionary period following the Civil Constitution of the Clergy was marked by anti-Catholic prejudice.[28] These observations were corroborated by contemporary events, which from the 1880s led the Third Republic to expel the Jesuits and to initiate the secularization of the statehood through the reform of education and the expansion of civil liberties.

It is no coincidence that Sciout's interest then shifted to the Directory, regarded as the Third Republic's natural predecessor precisely because of the rigorous application of the division between state and church. Sciout's collaboration with the *Revue des questions historiques* also began, which continued until his death, due to a stroke in 1900 while attending the international history congress in Moscow. The works he published in the journal were the result of the research he was conducting in relation to the Directory and went more deeply into some of the criticisms traditionally directed at the political system based on the Year III constitution. In this way, Sciout dealt with financial issues and France's aggressive policy towards Sisters republics that it had created out of nothing with its own armies. Between 1895 and 1897, parallel to the developments of the Dreyfus affair, which greatly contributed to radicalizing Sciout's own ideas, his work on the Directory was published. While this certainly refers back to Barante's work, it stands out for its breadth of archival research and above all for the radicalization of his stance.[29]

By now, Sciout had abandoned the prudent liberalism of previous years to start an intense duel with the new republican order, the origins of which he perceived as lying in the Directory period itself. From here, it was an easy matter to move swiftly between past and present, robustly denouncing the exercise of the Year III constitution as a political system where anarchy and administrative despotism came together, where religious persecution reached its apex, where financial turmoil and scandalous bankruptcy operations were a cause of daily concern and above all where coups d'état followed on from one another to allow individual factions to either take power or defend themselves from the onslaught of others. In this context, Sciout could consider that Thiers's historical proposal had come to an end, given that the latter had ventured to treat the Directory in terms of a government that was 'légal and moderate'. Sciout noted that it was instead quite the opposite, since, in line of continuity with Year II, the period following Thermidor had revealed itself to be central to the spread of illegality and tyranny.

The whole text was written with this in mind and was unsparing in its treatment of the main events: Thermidor, instead of a moment of liberation from tyranny, was the simple superimposition of one unscrupulous group upon another; the Year III constitution was a false example of liberty, behind the restricted articles of which power elites dominated political life; religion was oppressed as much as in previous years and release from the Terror had meant nothing in terms of its return to French life; the policy towards dissidents – émigrés and monarchists – remained marked by the most severe repression; the logic of war, on which the republicans had built their fortunes, had actually been relaunched; parliamentary life remained distant from the feelings running deeply in the country; the elections were a simulacrum of the general will, their results annulled under various pretexts; the sacredness of republican institutions was reduced to bargaining chips by individual factions ready to purge to restore a more advantageous political equilibrium; representation had been ignored and vilified by three coups that, from 18 Fructidor of Year V to 30 Prairial of Year VII, had altered the expected balance of power between the legislative and the executive; corruption had devastated public life, and was also exported to Sisters republics, where French troops, instead of freeing the neighbouring peoples, had imposed harsh servitude upon them and carried out systematic dispossession of their resources.

Brumaire itself, after all, which according to the *fable convenue* had put an end to the corrupt directorial regime, was the product of that same political class, which had seen Caesarism as the way out from the impasse of a political system that no longer seemed able to ensure the stability on which fortunes and dominion were based. In this way, in Sciout's eyes, the circle was closed and the Directory really was the antechamber to Caesarism – that is, a political system that, beyond constitutional formalisms, needed to end with a plebiscite as the only way to preserve the ideological structure of the revolution.

Needless to say, such a gloomy picture of the post-Robespierrist period was useful for the reader to draw easy parallels with the present time: Sciout could thus list the great similarities between France at the end of the nineteenth century and the time of the Directory. There were the same political factions, the usual anti-religious fanaticism, the same greed for the property of others in which Babeuf had first distinguished himself, the same decay of manners and morals, the same rejection of the privileged classes, invariably portrayed as unrepentant aristocrats, and, above all, the same parliamentarism. This last continued to be dominated by corruption and pusillanimity, of which the exiguity of the political class was proof, unable to limit social contestation and for this reason its members easily disposed to pass to any grouping that assured them the maintenance of their own income and position.

This long list explains the origins of the bleak reputation that conditioned the Directory era for the twentieth century: Sciout's monumental work became a sort of encyclopaedia of the iniquities that could be ascribed to the Directory and in the times that followed these continued to haunt historical judgement. However, it should be emphasized that this denunciation of the post-Robespierrist period – similar to that of the Terror, but contrasted with that of Year II – is a construction from an anti-revolutionary perspective, which only passed to the left during the twentieth century. Its origins, however, are easily recognizable in the increasingly violent clash between republicans and monarchists that the developments of democracy in France were destined to fuel. All this went unnoticed not only, and not wholly, because Sciout died shortly thereafter, but also because, in the meantime, the counter-revolutionary world had gone through a number of changes and moved away from that particular approach to the revolutionary problem of 1789.

Sciout's text was also entirely dominated by a declared polemic against the democratization of social life promoted by the Third Republic. However, based as it was on the criteria of a thorough archival search in the name of an impersonal quest for truth, over time it was cleansed of its ideological origins to become a reference work for the Directory era, regarded by all twentieth-century historians as a printed source of great importance. While its erudition and positivism eventually made Sciout's work a success, in the immediate future it was soon set aside in counter-revolutionary circles, which, again through the Dreyfus affair, were in turn greatly transformed by the end-of-the-century crisis. Legitimism, as it could still be understood at the beginning of the 1880s, was overtaken at the start of the twentieth century by a new anti-revolutionary generation, swayed by the late nineteenth century's cultural enticements, social Darwinism in particular, with its racial implications, as well as the move away from anti-positivism. Historical scholarship, which in the case of counter-revolutionary studies had relied on Taine to distinguish the dawn moment of 1789 from the horrors that followed the eruption of the frenzied lower classes, seemed to follow the usual liberal line to indulge in polemical discourse against the Directory, forerunner of the Third Republic. But by then it was a discourse from which, except for the denunciation of irreligiousness, there seemed very little worth salvaging. For this reason, in the early years of the twentieth century, while new cultural sensibilities, new scientific horizons and new political movements appeared – first of all on the right, with the *Action française*, founded by Charles Maurras in 1899, making of the Revolution a central issue in its social design[30] – the reading of Taine, too, which remained a point of reference for the counter-revolutionary universe, underwent a profound reinterpretation. It was the consequence of the *Origines*' great success, not only in the field of revolutionary history, where it was an unavoidable text up to the Great War, but above all in the new scientific disciplines – anthropology, psychology, sociology – which came to maturity at the end of the century. Taine's role as an innovator and teacher was, after all, something recognized from many quarters. The responses to the survey carried out in this regard in 1897 by the *Revue blanche* included that of Cesare Lombroso, who treats Taine as the only master after Darwin; of Gabriel Tarde, who praises his great impact on sociology; and of Emile Durkheim, who counts him as one of the initiators of experimental psychology. In this context, it should not be surprising that his historical work on the revolution once again became an issue and, faced with the enthusiasm of the new sciences for its foreshadowing of the role of crowds and political parties, there was a swift response from those who would accept no contamination of the historical discipline.

Alphonse Aulard, of whom more later, was professor of the history of the French Revolution at the Sorbonne. He dedicated two university courses to demolishing Taine on the grounds of scholarship, stressing that his imprecision in the use of sources deprived him of his right to be called a historian and greatly undermined the plausibility of his reconstruction. His decision to wage war on Taine, considered the bastion of the counter-revolutionary political line and therefore the banner around which authors hostile towards 1789 used to gather, nevertheless had the effect of arousing more than one perplexity among those who believed that Taine's work had to be read differently precisely because it revealed very different perspectives from another angle. On the right, Augustin Cochin took on the task of rereading Taine in tune with the new cultural sensibility of the century that had just begun. Cochin was the heir to a dynasty of the Parisian upper middle class who, at the time of the Third Republic, had made a vow of Catholicism and liberalism in the name of Orléanism, thus rejecting first Boulangism and then the *Action française*, while conceding nothing to the new democratic order.[31] A passionate cartographer, he had also inherited from his father Denys a passion for philosophy, distinguishing himself from the positivist scholarship of the time to look with interest at the renewal of the discipline initiated by Emile Boutroux and then Emile Durkheim. In politics, he followed firmly in his family's footsteps, marked by a traditionalism attentive to social issues – although he did, initially, have some sympathy for the *Action française*, given that his first piece of work, dealing with the elections of 1788–9 in Burgundy, came out in 1904 in Maurras's journal.[32] Here, thanks to in-depth study in the provincial archives, he identified a hidden world that had piloted the elections of the Third Estate and suggested the existence of a machine, never publicly revealed, which, through the skilful interweaving of contacts, manoeuvres and blandishments, had managed to predetermine the electoral outcome of the meetings. On these grounds, Cochin considered it appropriate to distance himself from the *Origines*, which seemed to him to have raised the problem, underlining the curious synchrony of the subversive outbursts that occurred in 1789, without elaborating on the reasons. In his opinion, the metaphor employed by Taine – the revolutionary explosion arose from a door that, once opened, rekindled the flame of long-latent protest – explained little or nothing.

The opportunity to return to the point, however, came from the attack Aulard conducted in grand style against Taine's work. Cochin, in the year 1909, promptly intervened in the argument, not so much, as is usually said, to defend the memory of one from the aggression of the other, as to declare the uselessness of the clash, to show how he differed from both, and to conclude that by now the way historical research approached the theme of 1789 should be completely different.[33] His pages began with Aulard's accusations that there had been too many errors in Taine's quotations, and Cochin quickly demonstrated – he who, as a good *chartiste*, presented himself on the book's frontispiece as an archivist-paleographer – how specious his arguments were. Both, in fact, scrupulously examined, had made mistakes and Aulard's almost equalled Taine's: it was evident, said Cochin, that the argument concealed something else, namely two opposite ways of understanding the revolution. He himself, however, rejected both equally, because both were misleading, although in different ways. The proof lay in the idealized image of the people: Taine presented them as stirred by pathological forms of violence that would lead to anarchist activity; Aulard said they were inflamed by a thirst for justice and freedom – both ideas, however, which remained very distant from reality. In Cochin's view, there had to be another reading of the revolutionary population and in this regard a new methodology was required that would make it possible to grasp which general laws had governed the behaviour of individuals during the revolutionary turmoil. In relation to this, Cochin suggested looking at Durkheim's sociology – history, he thought, could benefit greatly from the encounter. There seemed to be a paradox: Cochin was a good Catholic, a traditionalist and a liberal (in other words, with an Orléanism that had more than one doubt in terms of entirely adopting the model of liberty across the Channel). But, deeply hostile to 1789, he should have distanced himself from Durkheim, ideologically poles apart in a way that made him an example of the cultural policy of the Third Republic.

The contradiction, however, brought great advantages. By going against the tide, Cochin, without ceding anything in ideological terms, could settle accounts with his own political side – that is, with all those conservative historians (Cochin included Victor Pierre and Ludovic Sciout here) who, although inspired by a sense of destructiveness towards the political tradition of 1789, in reality had not escaped from the narrative constraints their opponents had placed around the treatment of revolutionary events. Cochin, in other words, with his recourse to an author from the opposing camp, could, on the one hand, challenge republican historiography by overtaking it on its own ground, and, on the other, make a clean sweep of a historiography hostile to 1789 which always seemed to him, however, to be constantly on the defensive with respect to the other.

His idea was to construct a critical history of the revolution, deciding – from the right, of course – to abandon a descriptive line of events and actors in favour of a conceptual analysis of the great cultural and political forces that came into play with 1789. This brought his studies on Burgundy back into the picture, demonstrating as they did the existence of a new subject on the French scene, ready to take the lead in rending France's centuries-old historical fabric. According to Cochin, this impetuous force, the *Sociétés de Pensée*, which became the Jacobin circles with 1789, constituted the real unresolved knot of revolutionary historiography. But, at the beginning of the twentieth century, a methodical study became possible: the historian could make use of the many documents that had in the meantime become available and cross-reference them with ideas coming from the new disciplines – not only the sociology of Durkheim, but also the political science of Bryce and the study of political parties as, above all, the work of Ostrogorski had recently illustrated.

In the latter, Cochin was fascinated by the way the machine managed to manipulate consensus, which seemed to him to confirm the intuition he had had when investigating the Burgundy elections. It matters little that this point in Ostrogorski's work was immediately criticized by both Bryce and Lovell, since his writings could give the reader the (essentially incorrect) impression that the party could do everything, could take care of everything. Cochin, on the other hand, was thrilled with this prospect, which seemed to him to open up a new field of studies on 1789. At the centre there was to be the study of political societies, their organization and functioning, and, on a strictly correlated level, the examination of how and to what extent those groups interacted with, clashed with and prevailed over the rest of public opinion. The conclusion of this new line of study would mark the fact that notice had been served on obsolete revolutionary history, which would renounce the 'generous illusions' of '89, the 'excesses' of '93, this measured, sensible, liberal – derisory – historical literature, which, for a hundred years, has been tinkering with little by little, adorning, assuaging, the terrifying memory, and spreading across the Revolution like moss on ruins.[34]

This was of enormous benefit to the possibility of understanding the extent of 1789's innovativeness – that is, how the protest developed such an overwhelming dynamic that it could so quickly overthrow an order that had lasted centuries. And at the end of this descent into the bowels of revolutionary fact, abandoning all forms of fetishism, it became possible to read the breadth and limits of modern democratic politics, such a daily source of concern for Cochin. The project was an ambitious and fascinating one: it was a question of putting an end to archaic counter-revolutionary polemic in order to channel the result of the new disciplines into the course of traditionalism and consequently challenge, in the context of modern research techniques, a republican historiography that seemed stalled at positivism. It was, however, doomed to remain only a hope: in 1916, the battle of the Somme put an end to Cochin's life and prevented him from completing his work on the *Sociétés de Pensée*.

In the meantime, nevertheless, the critique of republican historiography was enriched by another voice, which the violence of the political struggle in France had impelled to combine sociology and history in reading the political fact. Gustave Le Bon had, in the wake of the anarchist threat, already studied crowds as a subversive political subject at the end of the nineteenth century and in 1912 he published a book where republican historiography came in for a great deal of severe criticism.[35] To Le Bon, who, despite differing from Taine also greatly admired him, those who lauded the revolutionary population, from Michelet to Aulard, had been mistaken in portraying them as a homogeneous, independent subject. On the contrary, the opposite was true: the psychology of crowds taught that they were invariably guided by *meneurs*, leaders who were able to manipulate their intervention on the scene. Here, once again, the echo of the present resounds in 1789: this interpretation of revolutionary crowds reflected trade union protest in the early twentieth century, something that Le Bon believed arose from the tactics of a small group of *meneurs* that directed and dominated the interests of the workers. The basis was, according to Le Bon, the triumph in nineteenth-century France of a Jacobin spirit, characterized by the intention to bend the whole of society to its own specific truth, even through force. This mentality had taken root everywhere, in political parties, in the bourgeois world and in the world of the common people. The result was the violent conflict of the early twentieth century, where revolutionary syndicalism, through strikes and sabotage, had brought France to the edge of the precipice. Ultimately, according to Le Bon, it was a question of acknowledging that historians had failed to interpret the revolution correctly, even transforming street anarchy into a regenerating moment for an entire society. Hence his certainty about having turned the page on the history of the revolution, setting aside the old instrument of patriotism and republicanism to replace it with a detached reading of the psychology of the masses. For Le Bon, too, as for Cochin, the time of republican historiography was over. And yet, shortly thereafter, revolution returned with a vengeance in 1917 Russia, violently reviving the old arguments for and against 1793 which both writers believed had been silenced forever.

3. Speak as a pure democrat

Alphonse Aulard, born in Montbron in 1849, might have been designed specifically to displease Augustin Cochin: he was almost twenty years older than the bourgeois Parisian and in 1871, after trying to defend Paris in the ranks of the *Garde Mobile*, he decided for republicanism in the name of secularism and democracy. A *normalien*, he began his career as a literature teacher in the high schools of Nimes and Nice. After a short period teaching rhetoric in Clermont, he received a doctorate in Paris in 1877 with a thesis on the Italian poet Leopardi and the following year he became *maitre de conference* in Aix and Montpellier. In 1879, he taught courses in French literature and the classics at the universities of Dijon and Poitiers, before becoming a professor of French in Poitiers in 1880.[36] Interest in the revolution came to him late, filtered through his passion for rhetoric, with the result that, in 1882, he edited the speeches to the Constituent Assembly of some of its main figures.[37] This was followed by a second volume in 1886, where the survey expanded to include speakers of the Legislative and of the Convention.[38]

In the meantime, in preparation for this second part of the work, he published a short biography of Danton, whose political role he praised in the crisis of 1792 and whose death he mourned as an incalculable loss for the democratic stabilization of the First Republic.[39] In that same year, after beginning a collaboration with the *Révolution française*, the journal founded in 1881 by Jules Claretie, Aulard obtained his longed-for transfer to Paris to teach rhetoric at the Janson-de-Sailly high school there. The move was dictated by his desire to exploit a political visibility acquired through collaboration with the paper *La Justice*, founded by Georges Clemenceau – Alexandre Millerand, elected to the capital's municipal council in 1885, was also a presence there. The support of both these figures proved to be decisive, and in 1886 the *mairie* of Paris offered to finance him with 12,000 francs – a considerable amount at the time – to teach the history of the Revolution at the Sorbonne.[40] The news caused a scandal in a cultural world which still had significant reservations with regard to 1789. Conservative newspapers, covering the first lesson given by Aulard, sarcastically noted the presence of Clemenceau and Millerand and severely criticized the new professor – toeing the line, in their view, of the patriotic vulgate pushed vigorously by the political watershed of the 1880s. Words that confirm that Aulard's public career had already taken off: in 1886, he took over direction of the *Révolution Française*, while in 1889, on the occasion of the centenary, he received the title of knight of the Legion of Honour. He explained the programme of work that led him to obtain the professorship at the Sorbonne in 1891, preaching the need to combat Orleanist pedantry in order to offer revolutionary studies that were not just a matter of hastily put-together anthologies. He proposed a commitment to the field of scholarly research by placing great importance on archival documents and the publication of original research work.[41]

This working method, developed over four decades, led him to important results: the adoption of the French Revolution as a specific university discipline allowed him, thanks to academic visibility, to offer a contrast to Taine's great success in the country and to challenge von Sybel's scientific primacy in the debate between the great national historical schools. All this was accompanied by a strong commitment to the field of divulgation: Aulard was a regular contributor to the press, especially in the provinces, which gave him a great deal of political prominence. Starting with the Boulangist threat, then passing through the Dreyfus affair and the clash with the Church, there was no dramatic situation in national life that did not see him participating in the front line. The two aspects of his public commitment, academic and civil at the same time, soon ended up intertwining: reference to the revolution was a comfort to him in the idea that the development of political democracy went hand in hand with civil reform, because these alone would make it possible to reactivate a French republican identity that the traditional aristocracy, the myth of legitimism and the conservative paralysis of the countryside had managed to conceal for so long.[42] Central to this militant vision of the profession of historian are, on the one hand, his *Histoire politique de la Révolution française*, of which more later,[43] and, on the other – as has been seen – the polemical pamphlet *Taine historien de la Révolution française*.[44] With the latter, he believed all accounts to be settled with the champion of a hellfire reading of the revolution, which earned him both hierarchical ascent to the Legion of Honour and, as has been seen, robust protest from Cochin.

There is no doubt that the latter was right when, writing on the crisis of revolutionary historiography, he indicated Aulard as the standard-bearer of a historical method he called 'republican defense'. It was not a term introduced at random: Cochin revived the definition chosen in 1899, in the midst of the Dreyfus crisis, by Waldeck-Rousseau to define his own executive, which featured, for the first time, a socialist – Millerand, in fact, who represented Aulard's true political support. Cochin was wrong, however, to suggest that Aulard was a late-coming follower of Michelet, as if democratic historiography had experienced no tensions and contradictions and had always based its individuality around the myth of 1793. Throughout the years of the Third Republic, democratic reference to the revolution had been articulated in a variety of ways, and the *Histoire politique* was an attempt to identify a new point of equilibrium around which the many and hitherto opposed republican groups might gather.[45]

At the beginning, in fact, republican pedagogy had had to deal with the nightmare of the civil war that followed the Commune and had had to work to ensure that the image of the First Republic was not tainted by comparison with recent events. But how was it possible to propose the revolution as an example to a republic that was still in the balance, if the ominous testimony of party struggle and popular violence arrived precisely from 1793 and Year II? How was it possible to separate the Paris of 1871 – the scene of the bloodiest social conflict of the century – from the Paris that had first launched the violence in the late eighteenth century? As a task, for republicans called upon to defend the memory of 1792 in order to illuminate a fragile democracy's difficult present, it was something at the limits of the possible. First of all, it was urgent to find unity between the opponents of the monarchy and in this regard the protagonists of violent clashes in the recent past immediately set an example: Louis Blanc and Edgar

Quinet, different in everything in their ideas about 1793, instead found themselves on the same side in terms of distancing themselves from the attempted Parisian insurrection after Sedan. They also both wished for conciliation between the parties, which would come late – amnesty for the Communards was granted in 1880 – passing through a silence that was of little help in healing the wounds. However, it was the very evocation of the First Republic that caused the problem: the present time invited a revolutionary analogy with the Commune, which everyone – even its most resolute opponents – admitted had its origins in turn in the initial democratic period in France. For this reason, in the aftermath of 1870, selective intervention was necessary within the intricate events that followed 1792, distinguishing the shining examples of struggle against privilege and resistance to foreign armies from intolerable events such as popular violence and the annihilation of liberty. The operation was initiated by those who had been active on the subject for some time and who for the occasion hastened to reread the revolutionary events that they had previously described through the lens of the Sedan disaster on the one hand and the drama of the civil war on the other. The first voice raised in defence of 1792 belonged to Hippolyte Carnot, son of National Conventional member Lazare, the organizer of the victory of Year II. In 1872, in the preface to the second volume of his *Revolution Française*, begun in 1867, Carnot *fils* established an equivalence between the Hébertists of Year II and the Communards in order to reiterate the need for republican unity in such a difficult moment.[46]

The same hostility towards factions illuminated the latest work of Ernest Hamel, already encountered as a Robespierre apologist: in 1870, on the eve of the Franco-Prussian war, he had published an essay, which he proposed as a mere synthesis of Blanc's work.[47] It did in fact follow the latter's chronological arc, ending with the Thermidor period, as well as its interpretation in favour of the Montagnards. At any rate, just two years later, in 1872, improbably presenting it as the natural continuation of his previous effort, Hamel also published a concise history of the French Directorial Republic.[48] This was a very different operation: the drama of the Commune led him to re-evaluate the Directory era, which until then had not met with great success in revolutionary historiography. In his opinion, the affair of the First Republic had to be divided into an initial revolutionary phase, directed until its dissolution by the Convention, and another phase which, on the basis of the Year III text, had launched the properly constitutional phase of the new order. And here Hamel displayed all the merits of the Directory period: a far better constitution than all those that would follow it in the nineteenth century, the maintenance of the great principles enshrined by 1789, the division between state and church and a foreign policy of great substance which had led the Republic to sign the victorious peace of Lunéville (1801) and Amiens (1802). To the easy objection that Bonaparte was responsible for these latest results, Hamel was quick to point out that it was the Napoleonic writers that represented France in 1799 as being in the throes of an irreversible crisis: the situation was in fact not compromised at all and the victories of Marengo and Hohenlinden confirmed that the 1799 emergency, skilfully exploited by Bonaparte, was a temporary reversal. The conclusion of Hamel's work was obvious: in the aftermath of 1870, only the Republic could draw France from out of the tumult of defeat and violence, and salvation would come from the example indicated by the constitutional period inaugurated in Year III.

This was also the assertion of another 1848 republican, forced into exile in Chile during the Second Empire, Jean Gustave Courcelle Seneuil.[49] His pages began with Louis Napoleon's coup d'état to go back to that of Brumaire to demonstrate that, in both cases, uncle and nephew had perpetrated violence upon a republican system that had nevertheless proved capable of ushering forward French modernity. From the repudiation of Bonapartism, there emerged a clear-cut link between the Directory period and 1848, which should have constituted the course that the republic could be channelled along following its difficult return to France after 1870. The road, however, was fraught with obstacles, if only because reference to the Directory facilitated accusations of moderatism against the republican generation called upon to found the new order. It also fuelled the denunciations of opportunism on their part and, instead of bringing together, seemed to further divide the many republican groups. Yet, throughout the 1870s and into the 1880s, there prevailed those who, in the past of the First Republic, perceived the origins of a democracy unconnected to Year II authoritarianism and alternative to the figure of Robespierre. A clear trace of this can be found in the many narrative works aimed at a large public published in those years. The *Histoire populaire des revolutions françaises* is exemplary in this regard, published in 1872 by Louis Combes, as is the 1879 work with the same title by Ernest Duvergier.[50] The basic line taken by these works was a simple one: revolutionary history was denoted by a search for freedom that the *ancien régime* had always impeded, but which 1789's unpredictable developments had risked preventing several times, from the right as well as the left. It was a simple and linear way of reproposing the interpretation of the revolution by the new republican ruling class. In the world of scholarship, however, the same political line was put forward by Pierre Laffitte and above all by Alfred Rambaud[51] – the latter not surprisingly head of Prime Minister Jules Ferry's cabinet before going to teach history at the Sorbonne. His judgement was clear with regard to the republican affair: 1792 was kept distinct from Year II, and he praised the move towards democracy, while denouncing the Terror that came hard on its heels. It was a line that on the one hand favoured the posthumous success of the Girondins, indicated as the political group that had best understood how moderation alone could save the Republic, and, on the other, for the same reason, had praise for Thermidor and for the constitutional equilibrium of Year III. The text was an influential one over the following years, given that the revolutionary histories published on the occasion of the centenary greatly emphasized, for example, the merits of the Directory era, proposed as the first – unfortunately missed – opportunity to give the republican order a solid foundation. Thus, in his pages, Edouard Guillon suggested that the Directory had 'inaugurated the regular functioning of the constitutional regime, until it was suspended by the revolutionary dictatorship',[52] while Paul Janet's *Histoire de la Révolution française* noted that 'the Directory was one of the rare moments when France could, had she been wise, set up a legal and liberal regime. It was enough that the public spirit had enough firmness and common sense to find a middle ground between the extreme parties and impose peace on them ... [but it] was not to be'.[53]

This praise for the Directory was intended to counteract the demonization from counter-revolutionary writers which, as has been seen, also accused it of having perfected the policy of religious persecution. However, it actually had the opposite effect: the decision to privilege, in reference to the First Republic, the periods free from factional struggle and popular violence did not appease conservative party opposition. The latter could never, ever, accept a system that claimed the inheritance of the Directory and favoured the aggressive left-wing return of other voices that did not intend to sacrifice the first republican phase. In contrast to Robespierre and the Terror, which remained the point of reference for a minority component of republicanism, the time came for Danton, praised as the champion of resistance to foreign armies and at the same time the bulwark against Year II authoritarianism. It was an idea that soon came to maturity, once more driving the Directory back into the limbo of unacceptable moderatism: already on the occasion of the centenary, the decision to make the 1795 constitution the basis of support for the legitimacy of the Third Republic could be said to be an exhausted one, given that, faced with conservative group threats, many had made the decision to return to the heroic moment of 1793.

This was the basis on which Alphonse Aulard built his success. In the years immediately preceding 1889, arriving finally in Paris, he set up the cultural coordinates of his own renewal programme of revolutionary studies. He began with a standard portrait of Danton, followed by another piece in which he distanced himself from Robespierrism apologists, but his rejection of extremist politics, in line with the political discourse of the moment, soon changed in significance and perspective in parallel to the development of programmes for the centenary celebrations. As director of the *Révolution Française* he assumed patronage of initiatives that, since 1886, had been in development by national and municipal commissions invited to organize 1889.[54] From this fruitful relationship of collaboration with scholars and intellectuals, many of whom were keen to carry out the kind of archival excavation that he encouraged, Aulard started, in 1889 itself, to publish the documents of the Committee of Public Safety and the Jacobin Club.[55]

There were two monumental collections of documents to be used, in the editor's intentions, to reread revolutionary politics, especially in the first republican phase – the phase that the opportunism of the ruling class had tried to brush aside for the benefit of paying homage to the Girondins or of referring to the Directory's constitutional period. The scientific-philological attitude thus went hand in hand with the new interpretative positions assumed by Aulard. This gave his positivism, certainly borrowed from Auguste Comte, a wholly precise meaning as he turned it to support a reading of the revolution as a founding moment of the political system and sociology of the entire West. This French centrality in European modernity gave rise to Aulard's renewed interest in the figure of Danton, which in the 1890s led him to move away from the studies previously initiated by Robinet and Claretie, still wrapped up in the anti-Robespierrist controversy.[56] For Aulard, the figure of Danton was no longer just the defender of Paris from the Prussian offensive or victim of the bloody Terror, but – and above all – the most suitable interpreter of a revolution seen as a radical transformation of the whole of European society.

This new interpretative area was combined with archival research: scholarship meant the possibility of a more accurate and substantial reading of events and made it possible to establish the foundation of documentary evidence for the new role that Aulard intended to give Danton in the context of the revolutionary process. He was not only the protagonist of the move towards republicanism, not only the architect of the August 10 insurrection and the person who had unfortunately closed his eyes to the September Massacres: he was, rather, the real political figure of the new France, the one who had saved it from threats both internal and external. Perhaps to do this he had had to twist the law – as in the case of the expulsion of the Girondins – but his ultimate aim was always to save a revolutionary process that was otherwise destined to break upon the rocks of factional conflict. Not surprisingly, Aulard insisted on the fact that just after the defeat of the Girondins only Danton's policy, had he succeeded in overcoming the internal divisions of the Republicans, could have prevented the Terror: this would have led to a positive outcome for the revolution, since, without the sacrifice of the best part of the ruling class, the Bonapartist threat and the return of the monarchy would certainly have been prevented. Ultimately, as the Centenary was actually going forward, Aulard was developing an interpretative line of the first republican period that, on the one hand, reflected political concerns of the moment, but, on the other, also provided them with an answer, advocating a democracy that was capable of overcoming its internal divisions. The key point lay in the (re)discovery of the figure and work of Danton, who became the crucial figure in a narrative that would certainly have been different had he managed to impose his unitary line with respect to Robespierrist sectarianism. In Aulard's reconstruction, the developments and overall outcome of revolutionary events profited by a strong, new interpretative element, certainly destined to arouse similar levels of dissension and consensus, and yet with definite impact on the attempt to restore complete homogeneity to the history of First Republic. Following this idea, Aulard produced his *Histoire politique de la Révolution française*, published in instalments by the publisher Colin between 1900 and 1901, but previewed from 1896 by his contributions to the *Histoire générale du Ive siècle à nos jours*, edited by Ernest Lavisse and Alfred Rambaud.[57]

Considering the revolution's internal politics from this vantage point, Aulard could define his reading of the revolutionary decade in terms of a movement for freedom, which reached its apex with the taking of the Tuileries and which fell away dramatically not so much after the defeat of the Girondins, for whom the author showed no sympathy, but as a result of factional conflict, which led to the loss of Danton, and therefore to the Terror. In this context, however, there was no sympathy for Thermidor either. The return to freedom after the Robespierrist parenthesis was proposed as the swift triumph of a moderation destined to sacrifice a great deal of previous democratic success: the Year III constitution was seen as a dramatic regression, putting an end to universal suffrage and permitting the pomp of the bourgeoisie while bringing no stability to the republican system. The season of coups, from Fructidor Year V to Prairial Year VII, was stigmatized on the one hand, but largely justified on the other when it intervened to stop the return of the monarchists. Overall, the Directory appeared to be the bloodless heir to a democratic politics traumatized by the violent contortions of Year II and therefore a political system completely incapable of opposing the rise of Bonaparte. On the whole, the synthesis of revolutionary history that Aulard delivered to Lavisse and Rambaud reflected the rise of a political radicalism aimed at restoring completeness to left-wing fragmentation, excluding Robespierre and his authoritarian system without nonetheless sacrificing anything more of the legend of Year II and of the climate that accompanied the enormous efforts of the Convention in the face of the many challenges received. Aulard's reading thus dismissed every possible moderate interpretation of the Republic to reiterate that its decisive moment was between 1793 and 1794, when Danton, with the Girondins defeated, could have provided the new order with stability in freedom – only to be prevented by Robespierre's preference for sectarianism and the shortcut of authoritarianism.

In this shift to the left from previous positions, Aulard had in mind the extent of the challenge from the right to the Third Republic and the need to move the necessary understanding between republican groups even further to the left. For this reason, it was time to abandon the Girondins to their fate and focus on Danton in order to dialogue with those who, bewitched by the revolutionary government, saw what was in his view an improper equivalence between that particular political experiment and Robespierrism. Aulard was even more insistent on this point in his *Histoire politique*, a hymn of praise to the Republic – seen as the natural point of arrival of the process that started in 1789 – but also an attempt to demonstrate the number of deep roots the new institutional order, despite dramatic internal conflict, had managed to put down. Not by chance, the work is divided into four parts: the first illustrated the birth and progress of republicanism at the time of the constitutional monarchy; the second, from 1792 to 1795, examined the properly democratic republic; the third, the bourgeois republic up to Brumaire; and the fourth, the plebiscitary republic up to the birth of empire. Consequently, the work, which the title suggested as dealing with the French Revolution, was actually dedicated to the First Republic, with events reconstructed along precise political coordinates. Guiding Aulard's pen was praise for democratic groups, Danton most of all, the authentic architect of the 1792 turning point, the valiant defender of Paris, the man who had been able to save representation from assault by the sections at the Convention on 31 May 1793, and who would certainly have continued to unite liberty and revolution if only Robespierre had not sacrificed him to his own ideal of an authoritarian democracy.

However, alongside the eulogy of Danton, there was now a particular insistence on the political status of the Republic. The pages dedicated to the period following Robespierrism offer testimony to this, which in previous writings had instead been dismissed as a downward slope that Bonaparte took full advantage of. Now, on the other hand, Aulard could return to the Directory to denounce it once more as a selfish, bourgeois regime, which had sacrificed many of the great democratic conquests of 1792 and could do little when faced with a general's sword. And yet, he also emphasized that the limited remaining spaces of liberty had, however, allowed Year II survivors the possibility of maintaining a political vitality that they would demonstrate until Brumaire (and beyond).

The category of 'democratic republicans', previously introduced to indicate the Directory's left-wing opponents, was here taken up and developed to underline how much had survived, throughout the years of the Directory, of the intensity of political and moral health originating in 1792 – an intensity that neither Thermidor nor the subsequent coups were able to exhaust. In this context, Brumaire was an even more serious disfigurement to democracy because it had a vitality that was too often underestimated: and this explained, again in Aulard's view, why Bonaparte resorted to the plebiscitary solution. Given the lack of consent to his proposal from the majority of Year II survivors, his only chance of success was a malformed surrender to popular sovereignty and to go the way of the plebiscite – a tactic to arrive at Empire. This says a great deal in relation to the extent to which the sacred value of popular sovereignty dominated the French political society that emerged from 1789.

It appears clear at this point that Aulard's reconstruction kept in mind the convulsive, unpredictable and by no means irreversibly established developments of the Third Republic. The monarchist threat, the moderation of a large part of the ruling class, the attempt to slow down the development of civil rights, the confused agitation of extremist circles, the exploits of General Boulanger – everything active in the present of French politics was the product of a centuries-old history and was marked by the ways in which preceding events had taken shape and come to a conclusion. For this reason, the *Histoire politique* became a sort of breviary for the political class of the Third Republic that emerged victorious from the Dreyfus affair and wished to stabilize its success in secularist terms. Needless to say, Aulard was its official historian as well as its gladiator in the arena of cultural confrontation: it was certainly no coincidence that, after the success of his *Histoire politique*, he launched a robust attack on Taine's work, dedicating two monographic courses to dismantling presumptions of scientificity.

In addition to primacy in the field of documentation, Aulard had in mind the possibility of establishing a narrative of the revolution that would become the common heritage of the new France and put an end once and for all not only to counter-revolutionary arguments, but also to those who, memories still haunted by the Commune, continued to deny legitimacy to the new republican order. The Great War seemed the perfect occasion for right and left to fall silent in the name of the *Union Sacrée* and Aulard threw himself headlong into supporting the nation's war effort. In the nearly deserted Sorbonne classrooms, all through the years of conflict, he advocated the image of a revolutionary France which had been (and remained) the standard-bearer for liberty and an example of democracy for the whole of Europe. The outcome of the conflict, of course, seemed to confirm his viewpoint, paving the way for recognition of a parliamentary kind.

4. War on the left

In the field of political commitment, Alphonse Aulard – who had also declared ambitions of impartiality – set himself a specific task in his work: to do away with the reactionary vulgate, to which Taine had offered an excessive number of new arguments, through rallying together all the forces of progress in the name of the revolutionary heritage. However, the results of this strategy were contradictory. He succeeded in bringing the study of the revolution into the university system and transforming the network of research institutes and scholarly societies – which he himself had been instrumental in helping to form – into an element of support to his specific reading of the Revolution and the Republic. No less important was the dialogue on the left: Aulard always maintained excellent relations with Jean Jaurès and showed admiration for the *Histoire socialiste de la Révolution*, which came out, edited by Jaurès, at the same time as his *Histoire politique* and in some way integrated with it in terms of attention to social and economic issues. And yet, otherwise, Aulard's challenge proved impossible to win: right-wing readings of the revolution, as we have seen, maintained vitality and visibility, while the explosion of anarchist attacks and the birth of revolutionary syndicalism encouraged criticism of popular movements.

Furthermore, a large part of the French left was not tempted by Aulard's ecumenical reading of the revolution: in the socialist movement itself, the results were far more uncertain than the publication of Jaurès's opus magnum at first suggested. Up to the Great War, there still circulated a great deal of suspicion with regard to 1789, which seemed only the foundation date of bourgeois dominance.

It could hardly, after all, be otherwise: memory of the Commune remained vivid and meant that the polemic against the bourgeois and opportunist republic could not be peremptorily dismissed. On the occasion of 1889, although amnesty had restored citizenship (but not political honour) to the Communards, the confrontation with a Third Republic propped up on the tips of Thiers's bayonets greatly divided the French left. It is true that the centenary induced Jaurès to accept the revolutionary tradition and make it the supporting platform for his conversion to socialism, but it remains equally indisputable that he landed in a movement where positions towards the Third Republic were for the most part very different: Brousse and Allemane seemed 'possibilists' towards the bourgeois executives, but Granger and Vaillant, standard-bearers of Blanquism, in their contempt for the egotistic republican order had instead allowed themselves to be tempted by the attractions of Boulangism. Jules Guesde, meanwhile, founder of the *Parti Ouvrier Français* (POF), had for his part shown contempt for the general's electoral actions and competed with the anarchists in refusing any participation in the rituals of a plutocratic republic.

If a meeting point could be identified between such different positions, this lay precisely in criticism of 1789, which was mostly viewed as the dawn of bourgeois triumph over the interests of the people.[58] For everyone, the revolution thus remained a historical moment of utmost importance, often attracting authentic veneration, but no one doubted that its potential was soon betrayed. It should therefore not be surprising that in the difficult political journey of the Third Republic, and until the turn of the century watershed marked by the work of Jaurès, there was no overall reconstruction of the revolutionary events from the French socialist world. And it is no coincidence that, in the aftermath of the Centenary, rejection of Third Republic rhetoric remained firm on the French left. For socialist circles 1792, which the politicians of 1889 identified as their point of reference, seemed to be the wretched continuation of the *ancien régime*'s social abuse as well as a foreshadowing of Napoleonic authoritarianism.

The roots of this mistrust went back a long way: from the first socialism, Saint-Simonian in form, up to the political and cultural action of Proudhon, in France's political nineteenth century there was a constant attempt to construct a revolutionary order that would signal its distance from Year II authoritarianism and do away with a Jacobinism accused of having established a centralized state well before Napoleon. This perspective did not, however, exclude a keen eye for revolutionary spontaneity, exemplified by the Parisian uprisings. Syndicalism, legalized in 1884, would always maintain a balance between these two aspects: its main exponents, first Pelloutier and then Lagardelle, claimed they were hostile to the results of the revolution, but looked with admiration on the forms of popular intervention in the Paris of Year II. And, in the aftermath of the centenary, the future theoretician of revolutionary syndicalism, Georges Sorel, looked back to the Jacobin past for the origins of the political and cultural backwardness in which, in his view, the Third Republic was submerged. In those studies, conducted from 1888 to 1892 and dedicated to the action of the revolutionary government in the provinces and to the psychology of François Ducruix, a Year II Jacobin, Sorel also relied heavily on Taine, whose work, he thought, was illuminating in terms of reading the lack of development of French society and politics throughout the nineteenth century.[59] The fact that, once more, Taine's *Origines* was an object of fascination to the left says a great deal about the strength exerted, at the beginning of the twentieth century, from one side of the political spectrum to the other, by the pincer-like grip of the Third Republic's cultural project.

This is the context in which it is worth reading Jean Jaurès's decision to write, for the first time, a history of 1789 imbued with the values of socialism. His intention was to build a cultural platform for a new left in France which would do away with subordination to the German social democratic model on the one hand, and with anarchism and syndicalism on the other. He wished to emphasize a French way to socialism that the democratization of political life following the Dreyfus affair seemed to encourage. Understanding between the various left-wing groups had therefore to arise from full acceptance of the parliamentary political game: it was a decision that would make it possible for the socialist movement to fully claim its membership in the constitutional framework of the Third Republic.[60] Precisely for this reason, in Jaurès's eyes, the choice in favour of 1789 – in other words, to proclaim themselves heirs and continuators of that tradition – played a crucial role for socialism. The lesson he had drawn from the Centenary lay in the definitive affirmation of a cultural and ideological framework instilled with the values of democracy in which socialism too had to find its place – because, from that position, by fully participating in the constitutional life of the Republic, it could soon legitimately reach power. Ultimately, for Jaurès, accepting that the revolution was the birth date, in a positive sense, of modern France, meant opening up great space for manoeuvre for socialism – it would make it possible, through the coming together of all sincerely democratic and republican forces, to oust the conservative groups still in power.

The idea of the *Histoire socialiste de la Révolution française* therefore grew out of a clear political project, which soon, however, came into conflict with the abundant resistance still within the socialist movement. Initially, Jaurès only intended to take care of the editing of the work, reserving the years of the Constituent Assembly to himself and leaving the discussion of subsequent phases to other socialist politicians: the Republic, in the heroic Convention era, to Jules Guesde, and the periods following the fall of Robespierre to Gabriel Deville and Albert Thomas. However, the idea of a choral effort, with all the various facets of socialism represented, was soon shattered by the result of 1899's political turning point. While Jaurès saw in Millerand's participation in the Waldeck-Rousseau executive a first, decisive step in the birth of that new political framework which his *Histoire socialiste* was designed to reinforce, Guesde, faithful to German social democratic directives, refused to endorse a political line that seemed to entail submitting to the advantage of bourgeois interests. The project therefore seemed on the point of collapse, but Jaurès, left alone, relaunched the political-cultural initiative himself, taking on the responsibility of tackling the entire revolutionary story up to Thermidor. The political clash with Guesde, which sheds light on the extent to which Jaurès's ideas were opposed in socialist circles, did, however, allow the latter to define his own specific interpretation of the whole event as it unfolded from 1789.[61]

The *Histoire socialiste* was the result of a plural approach to the revolution,[62] an authentic collective work where, under Jaurès's leadership, different figures set out with the same intention of building a monument to the great source of French political modernity. The work, however, was presented under the auspices of three tutelary deities – Marx, Michelet and Plutarch – apparently difficult to reconcile, but which the political stance of its proponent managed, in a masterly way, to render compatible.[63] The German philosopher offered the opportunity to place the economic question at the centre of the discussion, highlighting its continuous intertwining with the great social and political questions that had come to the fore since 1789. On the one hand, it was a tribute to the socialist tradition that Jaurès laid claim to, though without exaggerating: it was enough for him to rediscover, in this regard, thanks to that attentiveness, a long-unpublished text by Feuillant politician Antoine Barnave, where an economic theory of the revolution was already present, to suggest the great perspectives opened up by a properly materialist approach to the study of history.

Reference to Michelet, on the other hand, was more dense and emphatic. Jaurès had no truck with Michelet's reconstruction of the revolution as a product of poverty, noting that the crisis of 1787–8 interrupted a long period of economic growth. But apart from disagreement over the economic cause, everything about Michelet fascinated him: he considered him to be the authentic historian of 1789, with a mysticism that came in very useful, both to balance the materialism of his work and to endow it with a passionate and committed voice. Finally Plutarch, the example of that antiquity on which the classical culture of the revolutionaries themselves was built, adopted by Jaurès in order to legitimize to the reader the exemplarity of their existence. Overall, it was a proposition intended to summarize the best features of the political nineteenth century in France, glorified by the affirmation of the working people in the context of a liberty that the generous presence of the populace made attentive to the social dimension. For the same reason, it gathered together all the forces of progress of a France that, at the dawn of the twentieth century, set itself the historical task of being the standard bearer of democracy in Europe and the world.

Consequently, the *Histoire socialiste* was only apparently similar to Aulard's *Histoire politique*: if the point of contact was, undoubtedly, the full acceptance by both of Michelet's model and therefore the exaltation of the Republic as a positive conclusion of 1789, for the rest, beyond the personal esteem that existed between the two authors, it was not only the economic element that differentiated the two works. Jaurès insisted to a far greater extent than Aulard on the national dimension of the revolution, his pen travelling across the complex French provinces, illustrating the originality of the impact of 1789 and the plurality of different responses that revolution had ended up inducing. The attention to local realities, over-neglected by a political approach that was highly focused on the Parisian aspect alone, led Jaurès to traverse distant vectors that were at the same time attributable to the desire to emphasize the centrality of the revolution in the birth of modernity. The Vendée, while condemned as a pastist movement, found in his heartfelt pages a popular element that the extremely violent polemical conflict of the whole nineteenth century had largely set aside. The colonies, in particular Saint-Domingue, entered by right into revolutionary history, not only for the consequences they had drawn from 1789 but also for the way in which they in turn had influenced the political sensibility of the homeland. The whole of Europe became the revolutionary cause's field of proselytism and thus put an end to the difficulty of dealing with the German-speaking world that the defeat of 1870 and the triumphs of von Sybel had highlighted in Albert Sorel's work.

And then, with respect to Aulard, he made a decisive choice in the republican period: rather than Danton, whom Jaurès certainly very much appreciated, he favoured Robespierre instead, liberating him from the excessive number of accusations of monstrosity and wickedness that so much Third Republic historiography had, confirming a pre-existing tradition, blown out of all proportion. The differences, however, should not be exaggerated: beyond the contrasting judgements on individual personalities or specific political moments, Jaurès retrieved from Aulard a vital point – and that was the rejection of the Girondins and the certainty that 31 May and 2 June 1793, while brutally mutilating the Convention, did not put an end to the revolution. Indeed, the ability of the assembly to remove a part of itself was praised as the highest sacrifice in the name of the general interest and exalted as the beginning of the era of greatest glory. Dangerous and foolish extremists had unfortunately worked against it, such as Collot, who had massacred workers during the repression in Lyon, and sectarian elements such as the Hébertists. The reasons behind this choice should not be overlooked: selecting from the revolutionary field in this way made it possible, looking forward to the political panorama of the early twentieth century, to trim away the extremities – that is, on the one hand, the republican opportunism recognized in the Girondins and, on the other, the Blanquism revived by anarcho-syndicalist elements attracted by echoes of Hébertism.

The message of the *Histoire socialiste* for the new twentieth-century France was clear: the period of democracy inaugurated by the Waldeck-Rousseau ministry had to grow out of reconstitution within the Jacobin camp, with the followers of Danton and Robespierre abandoning their ancient disputes in the name of a political project finally made viable by the socialist world, bringing to democracy a working populace hitherto over-tempted by the allure of insurrection.

Historiography and politics, however, did not go hand in hand: and this explains why Jaurès's reconstruction, destined to dominate the scene for a large part of the twentieth century, did not initially meet with broad consensus. On publication, the *Histoire socialiste* seemed to position itself as following on from the tradition of statist socialism and to continue (as well as overshadow) Louis Blanc's monumental work – not coincidentally, never reprinted during the twentieth century. Hence the collision course – in the interpretation of many of his readers, if not in the intentions of the author – with Aulard's *Histoire politique*. Although relations between the two remained excellent to the end, the new generations, formed in the climate of the 1890s, saw in Jaurès's proposition an opportunity to interpret the revolution in a far more radical register than the officially sponsored Third Republic version. Jaurès's text, which certainly offered the possibility of a broader and more cogent interpretation of 1789, seemed to lay the positivist reading to rest and to be the most suitable to accompany history's tryst with the new disciplines.

It is no coincidence that Albert Mathiez's break with Aulard, who had agreed to supervise his thesis dedicated to revolutionary religions, developed precisely in this area in the early years of the twentieth century. In his work, Mathiez's debt to the Marxist reading, mediated through Jaurès though it is, appears clear: the religious factor was proposed as a profound bond in society and the basis of the political – so much so as to be a decisive element in the construction of reality in the same way as social and economic data.[64] Here the debt to Durkheim came out: Mathiez, always starting with the example of Jaurès, proposed to raise the stakes of historiographical renewal, opening up revolutionary studies to involve sociology. His aim was to make use of the contribution from the new discipline to give a deeper picture of the fresh way of understanding politics and religiosity that the experience of 1789 had brought to modernity. The idea was to do away with the historiographic tradition of the nineteenth century: and this, as well as the cold reception the jury gave to his work, triggered the disagreement between Mathiez and Aulard, identified (not wrongly) as the most prestigious representative of a positivist approach that, the hope was, would soon throw in the towel.

However, given the disparity of the forces in the field, it was a rather unequal duel. Obliged to adopt a more aggressive stance, Mathiez brought to the field of political argument, too, a reason for differentiation founded on strictly cultural bases. Mathiez saw confirmation in the *Histoire socialiste* of how it was possible to read the political struggle at the time of the First Republic in a different way than the interpretation credited by Aulard and promptly took a stand in favour of Robespierre. In this he did nothing but give voice, again thanks to the work of Jaurès, to a tradition of admiration for the Incorruptible that had traversed the whole of the nineteenth century, but which the Third Republic's cultural policy had deliberately cast a shadow over. However, the decision to restore political honour to Robespierre by contrasting him with Danton, whose venality and corruption were emphasized, involved giving a precise political reading of Jaurès's work. The latter's rediscovery of the founding value of 1793 meant, in Mathiez's view, that socialism entered into direct competition with the radical democracy forged in the years of the Third Republic. Hence his decision to contest Aulard's scientific work as a whole: suffice it to recall that, in 1908, Mathiez wanted to pit his *Annales révolutionnaire* – in 1924 to become the *Annales historiques de la Révolution française* – against the journal directed by Aulard, the *Révolution Française*, and that he also launched an attack on his professor on the occasion of the polemic with Taine. In this case, Mathiez, who also agreed on more than one point with the criticisms that Cochin had already directed at Aulard, did not even bother to hide the political intent that motivated him. In his view, the argument – an end in itself, since it added nothing of scientific interest – simply revealed that Aulard, in attacking Taine, demonstrated an anti-socialist attitude and that both figures were, consequently, in terms of the new perspective of revolutionary studies, equally ineffectual. And yet, in the disagreement with Aulard – which, it is worth remembering, was never endorsed by Jaurès himself and lasted well beyond the First World War – something else, above all, was present: in particular, the concern that, faced with the difficult beginnings of parliamentary collaboration between socialists and republicans, the figures who benefitted from the situation were those, especially the revolutionary syndicalists, who denounced, in Jaurès's action, the clamorous betrayal of proletarian interests.

On this point Mathiez, was not very wrong: the *Histoire socialiste* was certainly not spared criticism from the left. From the moment of its appearance, Jules Guesde, who had opposed the great refusal to Jaurès, thought of making reparations by promoting the translation into French of a booklet by the leading exponent of German Social Democracy, Karl Kautsky, who since 1889 had established, as will shortly be seen, the orthodoxy of the Marxist reading of the revolution.[65] The many circles that did not recognize themselves in the parliamentary turn towards socialism, and who would oppose the birth of the SFIO (*Section Française de l'International ouvriere*, the new socialist party) soon found, however, in the writings of a Russian anarchist exiled to France, Piotr Kropotkin, the basic text with which to reformulate their link to the outcome of 1789. Kropotkin had had the work in mind since his arrival in England in 1886, but, bedevilled by a thousand interruptions, had found it difficult to go on with, and was only able to have it published, at last, in French in 1909.[66] Meanwhile, the failure of the Russian Revolution of 1905, successfully opposed by the Tsar's government, had once more confirmed that 1789 remained the only point of reference for the proletarian class all over Europe.

For this reason, Kropotkin's history followed two main lines that made direct reference to the struggles of the time.[67] On the one hand, he reconstructed a revolutionary development that was very different from the one that had existed up to then; and, on the other, he suggested that in the early years of the revolution – more or less until Thermidor, which for Kropotkin, too, marked the end of all hope – there had taken shape that current of thought, but above all of action, which later, over the course of the nineteenth century, became anarchism. The interpretation thus accompanied the description of a popular protagonism that, with the development of revolutionary events, assumed a physiognomy that differed from the past: on the one hand, the economic conditions on the eve of the revolution were exceptional, but, on the other, mass spontaneity came into contact with the action of the Enlightenment. The people played a significant role, therefore, at the beginning of the revolution and in, Kropotkin's view, organisms of direct democracy were established in the first revolutionary months through the direct impetus of the masses.

The acceleration of the revolutionary process therefore lay with the base, which made it possible to overthrow the old order and also to attempt, even though worker consciousness had not reached complete maturity, the path of proletarian democracy. In contrast, the defeat of the revolution, which Kropotkin put down to Year II and the Terror, stemmed from the desire of the Jacobin bourgeoisie to crush it as a threat through authoritarianism, hypocritically justified by the need to withstand the impact of the counter-revolution. Kropotkin thus had in mind a history of the revolution that had never been attempted before, distinguishing proletarian interests from those of the bourgeoisie by contrasting the *Enragés*, such as Roux and Varlet, and then the Hébertists, to all the parties, including the Montagnards, that succeeded one another in the aftermath of 1789. In this reconstruction, he relied on previous histories – Michelet's, of course, but above all Aulard's and Jaurès's – to establish himself as profoundly distinct from them in terms of his judgement on 1793.

Whereas for republican and socialist historiography this was the revolution's highest point, Kropotkin suggested – joining in with the polemical vein initiated at the time by Proudhon and taken up, among others, by Georges Sorel – that instead all the parties had in mind the destruction of popular dissent and the liquidation of its political vanguard. Year II was not so much the apotheosis of the revolution as the moment of its end: the Terror would not be responsible for saving the republic from the counter-revolution, but for protecting bourgeois interests from the challenge thrown down by the proletarian world. Thus, again according to Kropotkin, republican historiography was mistaken in distinguishing between Girondins and Montagnards and in contrasting Brissot with Danton and both with Robespierre: all were united by a centralizing spirit designed to respond to the threat of the masses towards bourgeois social equilibrium and the inviolability of representation. Far beyond the subversion of the *ancien régime* and beyond the revolutionary action of the Constituent Assembly, the revolution therefore became, immediately after the birth of the Republic, the stage for a left-wing clash – one blithely ignored by patriotic historiography. In the name of the sanctity of republican defence, the proletarian world and its original forms of self-government got the worst of it.

Kropotkin's theses picked up on several points of the Blanquist tradition, which late-nineteenth-century anarchism also took into account to define symbologies and recruit adepts: however they differed from it – and profoundly – in terms of the political perspective that followed. If the interpretation of the Great Revolution was the same – 1789 as the birth of bourgeois oppression – the strategy of revolutionary action that followed was very different. It is no coincidence that while Babeuf had long dominated the imagination of the Blanquist circles, Kropotkin instead judged the conspiracy harshly and even dismissed its promoter as responsible for an impossible relationship between the revolutionary spontaneity of the masses and Robespierrism. The reconstruction of Buonarroti's conspiracy thus found itself in the dock and it was an easy matter for Kropotkin to note that at the time the popular movement was dead and buried and the rediscovery of a Robespierre in defence of the people could do nothing to revive it.

Kropotkin was so aware of offering a new interpretation of 1789 that he also avoided entering into open conflict with those who had preceded him, transforming the great historiographical tradition that went from Michelet to Jaurès into a simple collection of sources he could occasionally resort to when he wanted to legitimize his own ideas. No open controversy appears in his book, therefore, but what Kropotkin had avoided was brought up in the context of a polemical confrontation that lay outside historiographical strictures, in the sphere of revolutionary syndicalism itself. Kropotkin's reconstruction overlapped (and greatly supported) the argument against 1789 (and 1793) by Georges Sorel and Sorel's *Reflexions sur la violence*, which appeared in 1912, was in fact an explicit indictment of Jaurès's politics – it is no coincidence that he mentions the *Histoire socialiste* several times, calling it a 'tedious book'.[68]

Sorel was very hard on the work, but it is important to underline that he examined 'only' the 1,824 pages that Jaurès dedicated to the republican period to represent him as a Montagnard in miniature, 'a supplier of guillotines' and 'capable of terrible ferocity against the vanquished'. Jaurès, in other words, defended the Terror to the last and in this strenuous resistance to the evidence of barbarism managed to justify Danton and his serious involvement in the September Massacres; he also considered the expulsion of the Girondins 'a policy of vigour and wisdom', defended Robespierre and criticized Desmoulins for attacking the unity of national politics. The conclusion of Sorel's examination left no doubt. The *Histoire socialiste* demonstrated that Jaurès was a very different man from the one who had bravely defended Dreyfus: in the meantime, enjoying the trappings of power, he had developed a ferocious theory of the state, which led him, like all parliamentary socialists, to become successor 'to the Inquisition, to the *ancien régime* and to Robespierre'. The conclusion was lapidary: Jaurès's work had to be opposed because it supported the ideas about statehood that had given rise to Year II in all its monstrousness.[69]

5. World conquest

On the occasion of the centenary it seemed that France, despite a thousand difficulties, had found political balance in republican form, rejecting revolutionary violence and authoritarianism in the name of parliamentary democracy. The Republic saw itself as bourgeois, robustly rejecting any reference to 1793 in order to look at the political example of the Girondins and even more so at the Directory era. The following years, up to the turning point following the Dreyfus affair, showed that this was not the case, however, and that the stabilization of the new order, in the face of joint challenges from right and left, could only arise from a political radicalism capable of involving at least a part of the socialist world. At the beginning of the century, this perspective, which revived Year II as the true historical precedent of reference, found precise historiographic form in the works, different though they were, of Aulard and Jaurès. In fact, their two *Histoires* are complementary in more ways than one and indicate the founding value of French modernity in the combination of political democracy and the social question. The relationship between these two positions held steady until the Great War, and this historiographical line soon became an obligatory point to consider for those outside the Hexagon who wished to intervene on revolutionary matters.

The fact, however, that both Aulard and Jaurès insisted on France as champion of political democracy, then and before, constituted an insurmountable limitation to their success outside the country. It is not surprising, therefore, that the reactions of conservative and liberal circles throughout Europe were extremely hostile to the new trend – continuing to set the works of Taine and Sorel against it– and that in the socialist camp itself Marxist orthodoxy viewed with suspicion an operation that seemed prey to the attractions of parliamentarism. The parallel triumphs of national historiographies soon made Aulard's proposition, which reaffirmed French primacy in the construction of modernity, a challenge to remain on guard against, while in turn the success of Marxist internationalism helped restrict the historical approach of Jaurès in terms of a socialism with ambiguous national and parliamentary features.

And yet, the fact that the new historiography was the subject of careful appraisal all over Europe, from right as well as left, shows that, starting from the Centenary and reaching its peak at the turn of the century, the revolution was once more central to international historiographical interest. This attention was fostered by the short-circuiting of the great European socio-economic transformations, which seemed to turn in the direction of proletarian revolution, and the return to the international scene of France as the champion of political democracy. For this reason, Francophobia and anti-parliamentarianism became the two polemical subjects, sometimes even combined, against those who counted on republican values to release European society from the tension that seemed to envelop it. The most significant example in this regard is offered by *Sonderweg* Germany, where, until the fall of the Wilhelminian Empire, liberal historiography held firm to the ideas outlined by von Sybel and, with Carlyle and Taine translated and published several times, insisted on the rejection of the republican identity that the revolution had quickly assumed.

The syntheses proposed in the German-speaking world at the time are thus mostly marked by the rejection of political radicalization, something that war would bring to the Germanic world. This is Albert Scheibe's perspective in *Französische Revolution*, which appeared in 1909,[70] and it was confirmed, from an Austrian vantage point, albeit with a strong emphasis on traditional values, by Franz Zach's work of the same name in 1914.[71] If the new French historiography was therefore – *et pour cause* – completely ignored, it had no better luck on the left, where the Social Democratic Party not only dominated the national scene but also would soon dictate the line to the workers' movement of a large part of continental Europe. Here the reference point was a small book by Karl Kautsky published in Germany on the occasion of the centenary,[72] which was translated into French in 1901 by Edouard Berth as a response, as already mentioned, to Jaurès's *Histoire*.[73]

For a long time Kautsky's work represented a sort of breviary for those who, throughout Europe, had no wish to depart from Marxist orthodoxy. However, it was not a history of the revolution, rejecting a chronological structure and focusing on certain themes – some even before, others after, the revolution itself – to illustrate class antagonism at the time of the Great Revolution and to insist on 1789 as the epiphany of the irreversible rise of the bourgeois class. Starting with the nature of absolute monarchy, Kautsky went on to analyse the privileged classes and their spirit of resistance to centralization; he then moved on to the bourgeoisie and to take a close look at the peasants and *sans-culottes*. This examination of the social actors made it possible for him to highlight the role played by the urban and rural populace in revolutionary developments: without denying the importance of the bourgeois element, his book is rather a recognition of the peasant class and the common people who, at different times and in different ways, provided the revolution with a decisive impetus.

Although Kautsky was careful not to equate the late-eighteenth-century lower classes with those of a century later, neither did he try to hide the analogy with his own time: while the bourgeoisie often had to endure the revolutionary spontaneity of the *sans-culottes*, they managed never to lose control of the situation and ended up, in fact, getting the better of things. For this reason, what had fascinated and frightened a large part of the nineteenth-century left – namely the figure of Robespierre and the drama of Thermidor – were irrelevant to Kautsky: the bourgeois revolution had started long before and was not brought to a halt even by the advent of Bonaparte, who took it upon himself, rather, to export it to large areas of Europe. Jacobinism, a political meeting ground for the lower middle classes and urban proletariat, was thus, in his view, a double-edged sword. On the one hand, it represented the revolutionary impulse, but, on the other, it had soon created a political tradition that weighed heavily on late-nineteenth-century France: contamination with the bourgeois element, in the name of the republic, prevented the formation of a large united and independent workers' party.

Kautsky's account represented a genuine turning point in revolutionary historiography: for the first time, that indistinct people around which Michelet had based his epic, and which even voices more left-wing that his own had not managed to otherwise define, was transformed into a class.[74] For this reason, his book was a success with the European left, and was reprinted several times until the immediate post-war period, when the author returned once more to the example of the French Revolution, this time as a counterattack to the triumph of Bolshevism.[75] Alongside Kautsky's work, however, in the same period, there circulated a real history of the revolution, published on the occasion of the Centenary by another exponent of German Social Democracy, Wilhelm Blos, which constituted the transposition, in strictly narrative terms, of Kautsky's Marxist interpretation. His hefty work running to over 600 pages, was in fact equally inspired by a materialist conception of history, following the line that the revolution had led to the triumph of the bourgeoisie, and in describing the various phases he placed a great deal of emphasis on the intense class struggle.[76] The book was a great success with the public until the 1920s – it sold three times as many copies as Kautsky's work and filled the shelves of German workers' libraries until the Great War and immediately beyond. The work began with the convocation of the Estates General and continued to the end of the Consular Republic, unfolding as a true narrative history. It faithfully followed the course of events to illustrate how great popular expectations were soon betrayed and to what extent the Terror, also a product of the alliance between sans-culottes and lower middle class, had ended up inflicting a death blow on their possibility of diverting the revolutionary process from its inevitable bourgeois conclusion. In this way, the Republic was proposed as a generous experiment when socialist unrest made its first ineffectual appearance: the Parisian sans-culottes, who had driven the revolutionary movement forward since 1789, to the point of overthrowing the monarchy and then overcoming the Girondins, found themselves in difficulty with the Year II revolutionary government. The Terror and Robespierre's Year II authoritarian politics gradually elided them from the scene and prevented them from mobilizing successfully on the occasion of the Thermidor coup, paving the way for reaction. For this reason, in Blos, judgement on the Incorruptible was suspended: returning to address the question on the occasion of the translation of Buonarroti's work on Babeuf, the German socialist politician again underlined the strength of the myth, capable of intriguing the conspirators themselves.[77] In his opinion, the mistaken image of Robespierre as the people's tribune had soon overwhelmed reality and started the egregious cult of the Incorruptible in a large part of the nineteenth-century French left.

This interpretation of the revolution, formulated on the occasion of the centenary, was extremely popular, especially in the following years, when it greatly benefitted from the triumphs of the German social democratic model in early twentieth-century Europe.[78] The works of Kautsky and Blos, translated into several languages, achieved particular success on the left in central-eastern Europe: in Russia, the translation of their works came out on either side of the 1905 revolution, Kautsky in 1903 and Blos in 1906. These were, therefore, the texts which interpreted the revolution for the left in Russia. Needless to say, the socialist universe's interest in 1789 was in sharp contrast to the national tradition, which had long demonized the French Revolution. In the last decades of the nineteenth century, conservative historiography, influenced by Nikolai Liubimov and Vladimir Ger'e, discovered Taine as a point of reference for treating the revolution as a possible element of contagion for Russia.[79]

However, the liberation of the peasants (1861) and then the assassination of Tsar Alexander II (1881) opened up a new way of dealing with 1789, which, taking advantage of the studies developed in France and integrated with original work, soon became part of the historiographical debate of the time. In the last years of the nineteenth century, Nikolai Kareev, Ivan Luchitsky, Maksim Kovalevsky and Aleksandr Onu studied in Paris and through careful archival research made significant contributions, especially with regard to the French peasantry at the time of the revolution.[80] Interest in the peasantry of 1789 reflected, once again, a specific national concern and found lessons in the past to prevent the outbreak of a revolution in Russia at that time.[81] The hope that a reformist policy could somehow halt the decline of Tsarism was, however, never realized as a work of synthesis, because, as a tribute to the founder of the positivist tradition of studies, the task of summarizing revolutionary events was handed over to Aulard's *Histoire politique*, published in Russian in 1902. Jaurès, on the other hand, enjoyed no similar success, totally ignored by socialist circles until the First World War, and remaining, as has been seen, under the ideological aegis of German Social Democracy.

The Italian case was exactly the opposite, where Aulard had no luck at all and was contested by nationalist historiography for having revived, in opposition to Taine, the idea that the revolution had inaugurated a positive new order of things. The *Histoire socialiste*, on the other hand, following in the wake of the Dreyfus affair, was immediately translated, curiously credited with a refined use of historical materialism in the investigation of the economic conditions underlying political-institutional upheavals.[82] The decision to make Jaurès available in Italian was a challenge to the historiographical lines of the time, which on the occasion of the Centenary were divided, on the basis of national political culture, between moderate and radical elements. On the one hand, Ercole Ricotti had published a book where the beneficial events of 1789 were followed only by horror and failure,[83] and Ercole Montefredini had brought out his considerations where modern socialism is even foreshadowed in the violence of 1793.[84]

Along different lines, Carlo Tivaroni instead published the third edition of a history of the French Revolution which appeared for the first time in 1881.[85] It was a detailed narrative of events in France up to the Terror, followed by a brief discussion of the period up to Brumaire, which allowed the author to reject the vulgate according to which the Terror had saved France from destruction. His work translated the political line of the Italian left after the Commune into historiographical terms, and the argument – following the example of 'opportunist' France – was built on the rejection of Year II and revolutionary violence, defined as a disease that had weakened the republican body throughout the nineteenth century. In his rejection of the year 1793, the direct ancestor of Communard violence, Tivaroni contested the centralizing aspect of the new order, denouncing it as a direct anticipation of the Napoleonic model and establishing a direct link between Jacobinism and Bonapartism. He was here, of course, referring to Tocqueville, but above all Taine, overturning the latter's observations, for, in his opinion, in *Les Origines de la France contemporaine*, it was ultimately Jacobin violence alone that was denounced.

In Italy, however, Tivaroni's writings formed part of a much broader reflection on Taine's work, which in the following years would be further developed by Cesare Lombroso – who even underlined the ineffectuality of the Revolution – and by his son-in-law, Guglielmo Ferrero, who instead emphasized the authoritarian and centralizing nature of the revolutionary legacy.[86] These ideas were not original, since, under the influence of Proudhon, the French left had already distanced itself from the myth of Year II. However, in Italy, if not in France, the libertarian stance of the left managed to translate their ideas into a consolidating work on the Revolution, published in 1905 by Gaetano Salvemini.[87] The author, a socialist at that time, set the chronological limits of his work from the summoning of the Estates General to the battle of Valmy. The decision to exclude the period of the revolutionary government and the Terror might seem paradoxical, but his insistence on covering only the years between 1789 and 1792 contained a clear political indication: namely, that the union of all the elements of the Italian left could only be realized on the model of the revolutionary movement until the fall of the monarchy – different opinions with regard to the Terror would always prevent a shared reading of the revolution.

Salvemini's attention was thus entirely on the *destruens* phase of the event that followed 1789, while the *construens* moment, the birth of a new order that would establish the rules of political modernity in continental Europe, was deliberately set aside. The choice was anything but fortuitous: Salvemini was well aware that the Italian left was unanimous in its aversion to the *ancien régime*, but that, at the same time, it had more than one reservation with regard to the modalities of the birth of political democracy. For this reason, by distinguishing the first revolutionary phase from the second, by making Year II the line of demarcation between liberty and authoritarianism, he could thus show his readers that the Brumaire coup d'état and the spread of Bonapartist centralism throughout the entire nineteenth century had not been foreshadowed by the events of 1789 and that the subsequent victory of reaction was simply an unpredictable accident in the revolutionary process.

The most striking aspect of this chronological decision, however, lies in the rejection of the French historiographic tradition, which seemed to him to add the voice of scholarship to the political discourse of Clemenceau, always ready to emphasize the Jacobin period and a consequential interpretation of the whole revolutionary decade.

Salvemini instead believed that it was necessary to move away from a hagiographic reading of this kind, noting that the political process begun by 1789 had not achieved its purpose and that the teaching of the Great Revolution was defined in terms of an incredible event that was nevertheless interrupted. It was no coincidence that the last pages of the work closed with the figure of Bonaparte on the one hand and Babeuf on the other, the former indicating government centralization and authoritarianism as the distorted legacy of the revolution, the latter, the birth of a precocious socialist movement – which, although emerging defeated by the events of the revolutionary years, still had the future on its side.

Salvemini's *Rivoluzione francese* therefore reflected one way for Italian socialism to think about 1789, where the anti-Robespierrist teaching of Proudhon and Georges Sorel remained strong and, to Taine's advantage, it was an approach that prevented interested contemplation of the historiographical renewal in progress in France. In other words, Salvemini's reading was aimed at the Italian left, which in the years at the turn of the century sensed the difficulties of the liberal state, but had no unified line on how to overcome it: and it was a reading that seemed to navigate brilliantly between reformists and maximalists, revolutionary trade unionists and supporters of the parliamentary path, republicans and anarchists, reminding them all of the exhilarating moment when the French proletariat found the strength to destroy an unjust order. At the same time, however, it warned them of the possibility that a future revolution could end up exhausting itself in the revitalized power of the bourgeoisie. So, Italy's troubles at that particular moment in time lay at the basis of the decision to exclude 1793 from the discussion; and this curious amputation of traditional chronology contained the awareness that the subject was still a highly divisive one, not only in Italy, but in France itself.

Although very different in political-cultural terms, the same mechanism can be seen in the way the Revolution was looked at in Great Britain in the years of the Third Republic. In fact, just after the Centenary, Ernest Belfort Bax's adroit summary appeared, following Kautsky's interpretation of 1789 as a harbinger of capitalism, without however being able to leave a lasting mark on the historiographic tradition across the Channel.[88] In the same period, *A History of the French Revolution* by Henry Morse Stephens also came out, with a first volume in 1886 and a second in 1891.[89] A Scots lecturer teaching in both Oxford and Cambridge, Stephens offered a detailed reconstruction of revolutionary events, starting with the Estates General and, rather than halting at Thermidor or Brumaire, continuing to the end of the Consular Republic. His work's originality lay in the fact that it moved away from the hostility towards 1789 that British historiography had accumulated during the nineteenth century. The first volume also earned the distinction of an American edition, for which Stephens wrote a special introduction in which the link between the two Atlantic revolutions was emphasized.[90] At first, his aim seemed limited to the desire to clear the ground once and for all of the many British prejudices towards the French Revolution. In fact, the author wanted to show that the subversion of the old order was governed by an exemplary desire for renewal, which had since then been a feature of liberal politics in Europe and which, in his opinion, the recent period of reform in Great Britain, unfolding in parallel with the writing of his work, was also in some way affected by. Everything suggested that Stephens did not therefore intend to deviate from the traditional approach that contrasted 1789 with 1793. Moreover, in the preface to the US edition, he repeatedly underlined the fact that the decision of the French not to follow the constitutional example of Philadelphia had encouraged the rapid end of liberty. However, in an almost improvised fashion, in the second volume – released, it should be remembered, in 1891 – the consequences of the Centenary were made manifest.

Stephens was now showing great appreciation for Aulard, whose research method, aimed at enhancing archival excavation in the provinces, seemed to open up new possibilities for reading the revolution. Thus, the rejection of 1793 was promptly set aside, with the birth of the republic being read as another attempt at freedom: in other words, the Scottish historian accepted Aulard's progressive vision of the course of events following 1789 and adopted all his positions on Year II. This reading – based on France's new historiographical direction – was also confirmed, in 1893, with a summary of European history at the time of the revolution: here, his praise for the policy of liberty initiated by France's armies supported the structure of the work and corroborated that the theme of nationalism was the result of the democratization process undertaken by the French military alone.[91]

Shortly thereafter, in 1894, Stephens left England to move permanently to the United States, first to Cornell and then to the University of California, where he died in 1919. Here his appreciation of Aulard's historiography found more favourable terrain than in Oxford.[92] As early as 1858, John Abbott had published a history of the French Revolution, which was intended as a tribute to French historiography and aimed to illustrate to the American public the concrete dangers that had succeeded in overwhelming, even recently, France's dream of freedom and equality.[93] The same work came out again in 1876 when it seemed that the Republic was now also an established fact in the old continent. However, in the meantime, Andrew D. White, appointed as a professor of history at the University of Michigan, during the academic years 1859–60 and 1860–1 had delivered the first courses on the French Revolution, but his lectures were followed only in 1875 by the first large work on the French revolutionary years, written by William O'Connor Morris.[94] Then, on the occasion of the Centenary, the Statue of Liberty was carried across the Atlantic to pay homage to the great republic of North America, reviving US interest in the French Revolution. At first, however, a Tocquevillian reading prevailed, which indirectly exalted the exceptionality of the American experiment and emphasized the authoritarian direction that dominated France after the overthrow of the monarchy.

The first comparative studies between the two revolutions should be read in the same light and this also explains why – despite the favourable review of Aulard's work by New History theorist James Robinson[95] – over the following years, American historians only showed specific interest in the first years of the revolution. Fred Morrow Fling, for example, a Mirabeau scholar, started a research programme at the University of Nebraska with the intention of directing some of his numerous students to study the period of the constitutional monarchy. This prudent point of entry into the history of the French Revolution, however, also turned out in practice to be the field on which the drama of the Republic and its radicalism had to be faced. Laura Belle Pfeiffer, in 1912, published her thesis on the June 1792 insurrection, where the people are portrayed as convinced supporters of democratic politics, while Eloise Ellery published a biography of Brissot, still today one of the best work available on the Girondin leader.[96] These monographs show that, in the years immediately preceding the First World War, Aulard's ideas had found full acceptance in the United States. One more example of this is Robert Johnston's deft summary published in 1909,[97] where his reconstruction of events wholly follows the line of teaching laid down by the *Histoire politique* – which was, not surprisingly, translated in the United States just a year later.

There was a parallel edition of Aulard's work in Great Britain and translator Bernard Miall's introduction was certainly shaped by that cultural environment. He took the trouble to explain the main events of the story to the casual reader, foreshadowing a distancing from the Terror, which was not only far from the spirit of the work but also in contrast to university trends across the Atlantic.[98] Miall does explain, however, that the climate in Great Britain was not yet very favourable towards the *Histoire politique*. Just as Stephens was preparing to leave Oxford, a decisive response to his reading, which considered it far too accommodating in relation to the justificationist ideas of French historiography, arrived from the rival city of Cambridge. Between 1895 and 1899, John Emerich Edward Dalberg-Acton, a Catholic aristocrat of firmly liberal principles, gave a series of lectures there, which addressed all the main issues of the Revolution, with a particular focus on the period 1789–93.[99]

But Acton's talks did not come out until 1910, posthumously, under the title of *Lectures on the French Revolution*, and it was preceded by other works, the most interesting of which was the *French Revolution* by liberal politician Charles Edward Mallet, published in 1893.[100] Here, there appeared the clear intention to respond to Stephens with a balanced reading of revolutionary events, where a wary eye was kept on the subject of the Republic. When it was decided, therefore, to publish Acton's lessons, the ground had already been prepared. The work offered a decisive return to the myth of 1789 as the dawning moment – an unfortunately short-lived one – of liberal France, with the author placing eighteenth-century philosophy at the basis of the revolution on the one hand and the example of the American colonial insurrection on the other. In his view, the French revolt against the old order had drawn strength from these two sources and it was a battle for liberty that was initially welcomed by unanimous consent, both inside and outside the Hexagon.

Subsequently, nevertheless, the dramatic and unpredictable nature of revolutionary developments had led many to ask for much more than a balanced constitutional monarchy and the birth of violent political conflict between the warring parties had soon led to the loss of the period of freedom itself, first with the Republic and then the Terror. For Acton, in other words, the defeat of the *monarchiens* had been decisive in deviating Louis XVI's reign from the path of liberty and the 1791 constitution was witness to how the revolution had produced a constitutional system destined to collapse, once again, into despotism. France was unable to emulate Great Britain and the United States and the brutal confrontation between revolutionaries and reactionaries shipwrecked the constitutional era on the rocks of authoritarianism: Robespierre's vicious tyranny was thus simply an anticipation of Napoleon's even more refined version of despotism.

Acton's interpretation was therefore not particularly original, picking up as it did on the liberal discourse celebrated by Staël and Tocqueville, without forgetting Burke.[101] All this, however, was defined in unusual terms by the curious mixture of historiography and morality present in his pages. For Acton, the task of the historian was also, thanks to knowledge of the documents, that of placing himself in the condition of arbiter of past events and expressing a clear moral judgement on the various positions under examination. In this context, considerations regarding circumstances and characters arose, all of which would have a large following in the historiography of the British twentieth century: to give unity and focus to this specific line of thought was the painful consideration that fanatic democratism went hand in hand with calculation and interest and that equality declaimed was the prelude to the loss of freedom.

5

The revolutionary use of history, 1914–45

The shock wave coming on the heels of the Russian Revolution hit the historiography of the Great Revolution fully in the face. Leaving aside the facile play with analogies from which even such great historians as Aulard and Mathiez were not exempt, the debate was strongly influenced by political passions, and brought once again to the surface the dubious role of the French Revolution as the foundational event of political modernity. In Europe after the First World War, it became the event through which could be uncovered the rules governing the development of a revolution, the succession of its various phases, and, inevitably, a foreshadowing of the fate of the revolution in Russia. Between the two world wars, the interpretation of the Revolution of 1789, and even more so of the events of 1793, entailed, indirectly, passing judgement on the Bolshevik revolution. Thanks to such a Zeitgeist, new research methods and themes became established. Social history took its place side by side with political history, while crowds took the place once reserved to assemblies and individuals. Thus, while in the United States and in Great Britain the influence of Aulard's lesson was reaching its zenith, in France his legacy was being disputed by the novel work by Mathiez and Lefebvre. Both historians introduced a new sensibility with regard to labour, seeking to understand its influence on the revolutionary movement while distancing themselves from the Stalinist trends then rampant in the USSR where, as a result, all contrary views had been banished. While being on the opposite end of the spectrum, such an authoritarian view of revolution caught the interest of some personalities in Italian Fascism, which, under the banner of corporativism, was positioning itself as the positive conclusion of the unresolved social tensions that had arisen out of the Great Revolution. Such a view was strongly disputed among reactionary milieus, which took refuge instead in a mythical glorification of the *ancien régime* and whose influential spokesmen in the 1930s were Gaxotte and Bainville. While maintaining their differences, these texts were already a harbinger of the ideological turn of Vichy, pivoting as they did on a retreat into the past to forswear the malignant products of a democracy seen as the poisoned fruit of a Judeo-Masonic conspiracy, as Faÿ tried to prove in France, and Nesta H. Webster in Great Britain.

1. The shadow of 1917

The First World War marked the large-scale revival of the revolutionary myth. In France, war against the central empires and defence from the German invasion immediately offered an opportunity to remember the conflict of freedom that began in 1792, as well as the strenuous resistance, in Year II, to the armies of the coalition of France's enemies. Alphonse Aulard, who had had to withdraw his candidacy for parliament in 1914, immediately returned to blending erudition and patriotism, exhorting love of country in the now almost empty university classrooms and repeatedly suggesting a direct analogy between the world conflict in progress and the war at the time undertaken by the First Republic. Then, in 1917, the Russian revolutions – the first in February that overthrew tsarism, the second in October, which gave power to the Bolsheviks – demonstrated that revolution itself, seen as a huge political overturning of the traditional order and as a social upheaval of equal proportions, was suddenly once again a reality. Its path, too long interrupted by the triumphs of a liberalism with increasingly conservative social features, was set to continue. The memory of Year II thus returned, bringing with it excitement and concern at the same time. The analogy between the revolutionary government and 1917 immediately began to circulate, accompanying not only the rise of the Bolsheviks, but also the subsequent phases, when Lenin dissolved the newly elected Duma (where it was in the minority), pulled out of the war by limiting Russian demands and coming to agreement with the central empires and then organized a revolutionary army, which managed to overcome the military challenge of the White and the Allied intervention. The main figures of 1917 Russia favoured comparisons with the revolution in France: since the 1905 revolution, which had swiftly collapsed, they had seen the sign of an irresistible force of destiny that carried them forward to live out a history whose line had been drawn long before.[1] Even more than followers of the great protagonists who came out of 1789, they could be the prophets of the great mystery of revolutions. And so Robespierre, Bonaparte, the days of insurrection, the struggle between the Girondins and the Montagnards, Thermidor, crowded into the political life of the Russian revolutionaries and became mirrors to read the future in, as well as measuring instruments to evaluate the significance of the events that accompanied the rise and triumph of Stalin.

The historical analogy between 1793 and 1917 had immediately bewitched all of left-wing Europe: the Belgian Henri De Man, a member of the socialist delegation visiting Russia in the early 1920s to verify the amazing event that had occurred in the East, noted that all the main figures of the Bolshevik revolution were certain to go down the same path as 1793. These were ideas in wide circulation since 1917 that had, not without reason, aroused the deep concern of Raoul Labry, responsible for the Institute of French culture in Petrograd: he had ineffectually warned that the reading of Russian events based on the example of the long-ago French Revolution prevented a deeper understanding.[2]

However, particularly in the Hexagon, the attraction of witnessing the spectacle of a new republican and democratic revolution was difficult to escape, as it appeared there on the other side of Europe and soon followed, with all its uncertainties and dramatic stumbles, what was still the glorious example of Year II. This is demonstrated by the passionate interest shown by Aulard in Russian events, following as he did the developments of the February revolution with anxious patriotic participation and at first even wanting to believe that the new order would revive the idea of a war of liberty.

His articles in the *Journal de Russie*, a French news sheet that the Paris government circulated with mixed success in revolutionary Petrograd, showed that the Sorbonne historian, after equating the February revolution with a new August 10, was careful to support the new course in Russia, always putting the cause of the military alliance before any other political reflection. He was not even worried by the events of October, which seemed to him, at least at first, a sort of revival of the days of 31 May and 2 June 1793 – he preferred to gloss over the dissolution of the first democratically elected Duma, putting the need for military conflict over the attack carried out on national representation.[3]

Not surprisingly, disappointment was only profound when Lenin, instead of continuing with the war, drawing inspiration once more from the Year II Jacobins, preferred to abandon the allied camp and make peace with Wilhelminian Germany. At that point, Aulard decided to move away from Bolshevism, accusing it of betraying the interests of the Russian people and of being something different from the French Revolution: it was now clear to him, as he repeatedly said during lessons, that, on the one hand, in the west, the eighteenth-century cultural tradition had led to the triumph of liberty, while, on the other, in the east, under the guise of a process of liberation, the 1917 revolution had only extended the dramatic continuum of the political tradition of violence and barbarism typical of modern Russia.

Aulard reiterated these positions after the war, when, at the end of 1919, he ran for parliament on a radical-socialist list against the National Bloc of Clemenceau and Millerand, his mentors from the distant past. For the occasion, declaring his faith in the work of US president Wilson and in the League of Nations, he announced that he was now resolutely 'anti-Bolshevik – because I am a democrat and I am a democrat because I am French'.[4] In the elderly professor's words there returned the myth of a nationalism founded on the hendiadys of liberty and equality, which the political tradition of the Third Republic had intended to enhance. This declaration of faith led him to reject the idea of 1917 as – as he had described 1793 – a 'constructive revolution': the Bolsheviks had only taken advantage of the precedent of Year II to construct an erroneous and unacceptable genealogy. Beyond appearances and the many attacks from reactionaries, in his opinion, violence and dictatorship had remained extraneous to the revolutionary activity of Year II, given that, even in those moments of enormous drama, the spirit of legality had never failed.

But the elections were a fiasco and Aulard returned once more to the world of academe, remaining for a few years in his position as professor of the history of the French Revolution at the Sorbonne, until 1924 when, vainly resisting retirement, he was not even able to choose his successor. However, he was very involved in public life and a leading member of the *Ligue des droits de l'homme*, where protests soon arose against the authoritarian direction Russia was taking and the rise of Fascism in Italy, and he always used the values of 1789 as a direct reference point to indicate the main path for democratic progress, in France as in Europe. His political life was at an end, however, and revolutionary studies were turning elsewhere. Between the choice of reconnecting the thread between the American and the French Revolution, as Aulard himself tried in vain, and the proposition of making 1793 the starting date of a social revolution that found fulfilment much later in Russia, as advanced by his former pupil and increasingly aggressive rival Albert Mathiez, the latter soon prevailed.

It would be easy with hindsight to underline how the consequences of this approach were a downward slope for France's political and cultural centrality, as it abandoned the claims of having made a mark on, and continuing to illuminate, modernity with its own revolution, to carve out instead a more modest role as an epiphany of humanity's Soviet future. However, this would do a grave disservice to the colossal drama of the First World War, whose violent impact on European society formed the basis of a new and more aggressive way of challenging the alleged linearity of a historical process that followed an irresistible course towards a liberty that seemed the privilege of the wealthy few. This is reflected in the intellectual trajectory of Albert Mathiez, who in the war years reformulated, within a different ideological universe, the many reservations he had accumulated in previous years against the absorption of the French left into the parliamentary system.[5] Mathiez was soon disappointed by the results of the tryst between democracy and socialism, and his devotion to Jaurès had not prevented him from launching a robust polemic against a representative political model that, while validated by elements from the left, involved them in a game of interests in a very different context. Along these lines, even before the outbreak of hostilities, he started his own research on corruption under the Terror, suggesting, with a clear reference to the times, that the Year II Convention, apart from the heroic decisions made under Robespierre's leadership, had shown a serious lack of connection with the profound needs of the working classes.[6] Shortly thereafter, the war provided this particular line of research with further impetus. It is true that his support for the patriotic war was passionate, but the position he adopted was one that eulogized the defensive war of Year II, while the governments of the *Union Sacrée* seemed to him dominated by selfish interests, similar in every respect to those which in 1792 had induced the Girondins to declare war on the whole of Europe.[7]

Rejection of the war executive, which seemed to him to violate national rights, induced him to keep his guard up, once again, towards Aulard, whose support for the war suggested that he was motivated by very different purposes from his own. In the midst of hostilities, while reprinting some articles against Danton,[8] Mathiez relaunched his attack on the *Union Sacrée*, accusing it of emulating Danton's politics, since it likewise sacrificed the general interest in favour of narrow and often unconfessable personal interests. The study of the political and economic life of the individual revolutionaries on which he worked so hard at that time – often denouncing them, as in Danton's case, as being the beneficiaries of financial interests especially intolerable in times of war – thus became an opportunity to note how parliamentary corruption in the Year II Convention had ended up putting an end to Robespierre's democratic experiment. It was easy for Mathiez to relate this to the bleakness of the present moment, suggesting that only a revival of the Year II war policy would allow France to achieve victory over its enemies.

The decision, in 1917, to dedicate, a collection of essays on parliamentary corruption at the time of the Convention to his friend Albert Thomas, in charge of supporting the national war effort, testifies to how Mathiez saw the resistance to foreign aggression shown at the heroic time of Year II as the only acceptable example for the ongoing war.⁹ The primacy of 1793 over 1914 was confirmed in another work, which appeared in 1918, dedicated to the presence of foreigners within revolutionary France. In the introductory pages, the author proposed a comparison between the time of the revolution and his own present times to suggest, once again, that the past should be taken as an example. Between the war of freedom, supported by the elites throughout the whole of Europe, and the war of nationalism, in which fear of German *Kultur's* continental dominance was paramount, for Mathiez the balance was all in favour of the former. Revolutionary France's restrictive policy towards foreigners came very late, in fact, and only when it seemed clear that their presence was that of a financial plutocracy; in 1914, however, the executive had launched repressive measures against them immediately, often to get their hands on their assets, making use of national identity as a basis, through the *Union Sacrée*, for dismissing the class struggle to the advantage of petty racial conflict.¹⁰

It was a short step from parliamentary corruption to the subject of the war economy: the link between Jacobin policy and its social base, which had so fascinated Mathiez since the early twentieth century, emerged more strongly due to the upheavals in Russia. Like Aulard, he was enthusiastic about the news of the revolution and immediately launched a timely parallel between the events of Russia and those of revolutionary France: February was August 10; General Kornilov a new Dumouriez, quick to betrayal; Kerensky a Girondin who, after October, had to step aside without inviting protest; the Bolsheviks the new Montagnards, with everything indicating that they were willing, in emulation of the Year II patriots, to continue the war. The peace of Brest-Litovsk must have greatly disappointed Mathiez who, also in line here with Aulard, supported the Wilson peace process, writing in the American student newspaper in Besançon about the link between the two late-eighteenth-century revolutions.

But then came the post-war period of high prices and misery, of a Versailles peace that treated peoples like merchandise, of a France where opportunists and turncoats celebrated their triumphs to the detriment of the proletarian world and were triumphantly elected to the *Chambre bleue*. The spectacle of the sensational recovery of a conservative world faced with the Soviet bogeyman convinced Mathiez that only Bolshevism could interpret the Jacobin policy that, from lecture hall and newspaper, he had vainly put forward to wartime France. The turn eastward was, however, a reflection of the electoral disappointment of 1919: from the early 1920s, his parallels between Year II and October became closer and closer, and increasingly implausible, leading to the unlikely prospect of Lenin in the guise of a revived Robespierre.¹¹ Mathiez's writings foreshadowed his swift joining of the French Communist Party (PCF), which originated, in the last days of 1920, following the socialist split that took place at the Congress of Tours. His membership did not last long, but it was in this particular period that Mathiez made his explicit attempt to assume the leadership of revolutionary historiography. For the party publishing house, he edited a new edition of Jaurès's *Histoire socialiste* (appearing in eight volumes between 1922 and 1924), where, in the brief introduction, he stated his complete devotion to the socialist politician, defined as 'marvellously evocative' and a brilliant historian of the economic and social crisis that gave birth to the modern world.¹² However, Mathiez, newly communist as he was, believed it useful to employ Jaurès's historiographical legacy as a basis to continue his attack on Aulard: thus he noted, with reason, that Jaurès had come round to Robespierrism in the last period of his life. However, he also maintained – and here the truth lay elsewhere – that Jaurès had never differentiated between him and his old professor and indeed, had he lived, would surely have ended up with a preference for his ideas.

In other words, Mathiez's idea was that his edition of the *Histoire socialiste* would make him the direct heir of Jaurès: the issue he had gone into in greater depth during the war – that is, the essential link between the social question and economic policy established by Year II, with the union between Montagnards and *sans-culottes* – was put forward as the distinctive trait of the *Histoire socialiste*. On this point, Mathiez stretched Jaurès's positions somewhat – the latter had, for a long time, shown little interest in the theme of revolutionary personalities – and, seeing himself as the continuer, rather than interpreter, of the *Histoire socialiste*, ended up with a largely predatory attitude towards the work. In fact, Mathiez's political background lay elsewhere: his Robespierrism shared nothing with Jaurès's ideas and firmly followed the work of Blanc and Hamel, tracing the current of French history up to the monarchy of Louis Philippe, when the Year II myth had attracted converts, and further on to Buonarroti – the latter's introductory pages to the *Conspiration pour l'Egalité*, he had written in 1910, were the 'most impressive and most truthful summary of the history of the Revolution'.[13]

There was more: it was on this exact basis, in post-war France, that Mathiez had then rested the myth of October, given that Buonarroti's work was always a reminder of how Babeuf's communism was a development of the politics of the Incorruptible. In this way, the *Histoire socialiste* had provided Mathiez's positions with the, certainly important, contribution of interest in economic and social history, and nothing more; but the political situation meant that he could present himself as the most authoritative continuer. It's a claim that today sounds to a large extent inappropriate, but in the immediate post-war period political conflict on the left made it possible for Mathiez to present solid credentials in this regard: he had moved away from Aulard and the positivist tradition and he had renewed political history, rediscovering Robespierre to Danton's detriment, the latter's success seeming to him the fig leaf for a school closely linked to the mandarins of the Third Republic. During the war he had shown, by comparing war economies, the frightening differences that existed between Year II's executive of national salvation and the governments of the *Union Sacrée*; and, finally, the triumph of Bolshevism had shown how right he was in emphasizing the combination of Robespierrism and the popular masses as the apex of the revolutionary narrative.[14]

In short, at the beginning of the 1920s, nothing prevented Mathiez from being seen as the new historian of the French Revolution (even though he was hardly new on the scene) and his political leanings did him little harm: always a good French patriot, Mathiez soon left a PCF under strict Moscow control. His studies, frenzied, passionate, went on as before, finding their highest expression in 1927 with his work on the social movements under the Terror, the best example of his interest in social history in the last years of his life.[15] At the same time, nevertheless, Mathiez decided to produce a new history of the revolution, through which he believed he could, on the basis of the new political-cultural sensibility following the war, set the guidelines for a general interpretation of the revolution. This work was carried out between 1922 and 1927, but continued for the rest of his life, to be interrupted with his sudden death in 1932. It amounts to three volumes dedicated to the first phase of the revolution until the fall of Robespierre,[16] and another, in 1929, on the Thermidor period.[17] His lecture notes dealing with the Directory only reached Year V and were published posthumously, in 1934, by Jacques Godechot.[18]

However, Mathiez's commitment in this regard could not be understood without mentioning the *Histoire contemporaine de la France*, the collective work that Ernst Lavisse was commissioned to promote for the publisher Hachette.[19] The original initiative dated back to well before the First World War, but the work only came out afterwards, starting in 1920, when Philippe Sagnac published the first volume, dedicated to the early years of the revolution (1789–92).[20] This was followed by Georges Pariset's second volume, dealing with the republican period up to Brumaire.[21] The two authors, who were not new to revolutionary studies, both followed in Aulard's footsteps: they were careful to underline the unified nature of the revolutionary process, both in its monarchical-constitutional phase – Sagnac took care to emphasize its limits, which would favour the rise of democracy – and in the strictly republican period, where the clash between the different parties was related solely to the political situation and no connection was made to socio-economic class distinction.

Pariset, in particular, kept well away from any re-evaluation of Robespierre and the Terror. In his reconstruction, he was careful not to introduce profound differences between Girondins and Montagnards and contested the revolutionary nature of 31 May and 2 June 1793, defining them as the first in a long series of coups d'état leading to Brumaire. He stressed the authoritarian aspect of Robespierre's personality, described the experiment of the Terror as an emergency government, without closing his eyes to its violence, and interpreted Thermidor as another dramatic moment in the political struggle within the Convention, while refusing to include any hint of reaction. The Year III constitution and the Directory period, which were also indicated as a dramatic decline in revolutionary political life, were once more linked, within their limits, to what had gone before. The result was that, from Fructidor to Brumaire, the coups d'état were the example of a process bogged down in factional conflict – a situation, given the collapse of popular consensus, it was impossible to escape from.

It was an interpretation that Mathiez contested at its very roots in the idea of the unified nature of the political process. In his book, commissioned by the publisher Colin, he proposed fracturing the revolutionary bloc in order to put an end to that unitary vision of the revolutionary political process that had dominated the scene until then – something that Jaurès himself had not wanted to abandon. The decision to emphasize Year II and Buonarroti's reading of the revolution in fact allowed Mathiez to break with the unity of the narrative that followed on from 1789 in order to indicate that the 'great revolution' had contained a number of revolutions, each with its own particular life – and only if this had first been isolated could it be studied and interpreted. All this is evident in his reading of the first phase, from the crisis of the *ancien régime* to the collapse of the monarchy, where he introduces the theme of the 'aristocratic revolt' for the period preceding 1789.

The suggestion that everything had arisen out of a conservative protest made it possible for Mathiez to trim the wings of the liberal interpretation of the revolution and to stress, from the early stages of the upheaval, the importance of popular participation. It is no coincidence that his gaze fell upon the Parisian populace, but also upon the countryside, registering the latter's importance without, however, developing the idea very far. Above all, he took the French provinces into account, where, in his view, municipal revolutions assumed decisive importance in terms of tracing the process of acceleration of democracy in French politics. Apart from the fact that his work was intended to be a student textbook and therefore could not have the breadth and extent of the work of scholarship that he certainly had in mind – without however having the time to write it – his decision indicated a precise interpretative path: he read the years of the Constituent Assembly and the Legislative Assembly as revealing a France moving forward. Its objective, achieved on the occasion of the revolutionary government, was a Republic, of course, but above all a social democracy – one that was willing, in the interests of the majority, to accept more than one imperfection in the exercise of political freedom.

In this way, the linearity of the revolutionary decade emerged to a large extent distorted: for the first time, the graph of its progress experienced headlong upward growth until it reached its apex in Year II, to suddenly precipitate with Thermidor. It soon exhausted itself, with the Year III constitution, in a bourgeois and feigningly constitutional regime – one that dripped with the innocent blood of Babeuf, and with Bonaparte's sabre the nadir of its wretchedness.

It is worthwhile emphasizing the success of this new chronological arc, something that also emerges from other works Mathiez had in preparation for that general history of the revolution which was, nevertheless, never completed.[22] This interpretative slant, minimizing the liberal period and reducing the Directory era to stale and bloodless moderatism, would become a reference point over the following decades and also a framework for others to make use of, if with a very different intensity of interpretative enquiry. However, Mathiez's influence on subsequent reconstructions was profound: from that moment on, the entire history of the revolution would become a social history of the proletarian classes, raising themselves up in search of a new socio-economic order and for this reason soon becoming a competitive ally of a ruling class that in Year II was able to interpret it, at least in part, in terms of expectations and interests.

From the first volume of his history,[23] Mathiez set out to identify those in the patriotic universe who were in sincere agreement with the lower classes and those who had promptly made use of their name, but essentially only to take advantage of their enthusiasm. In this regard, the second volume was exemplary, dedicated entirely to the clash between Girondins and Montagnards, which ended with the expulsion of the former from the Convention. In the description of the vanquished, for example, the impassioned reading of Buonarroti's writings shines through, but also the harsh lesson of the First World War. The Girondins in fact emerge from Mathiez's pages demonized, both when they are described as good bourgeois provincials in league with the selfish interests of France's mercantile groups and when they are accused of having desired hostilities only to boost the profits of speculators and exchange dealers. Continuing the theme of the unscrupulous use of power, he portrays them plotting to silence the Montagnards, even to the detriment of the revolution, and, in the end, throwing off their masks to reveal their true counter-revolutionary nature by fomenting the summer of 1793's federalist revolt throughout France. It was a clean break with respect to a historiographic tradition that, since the mid-nineteenth century, while favouring the Montagnards (though not Robespierre), had often bestowed the honours of war on the Girondins. In this case, too, Mathiez's work laid down an interpretative line that would be enjoy a great deal of success in the decades to come.[24]

Finally, the third volume, entirely dedicated to the activity of the revolutionary government, was the one that Mathiez wanted to crown his whole historiographical journey. In his description of the Terror, he made use of his previous in-depth studies in matters of religious, political and socio-economic history, drawing a picture that was certainly positive, and yet convulsive, of Year II government activity, aggrandized as the culmination of a revolutionary process that imposed a dictatorship so that the virtue of a few could promote the interests of the many.[25]

There remained the problem of the revolutionary legacy after the poli of Thermidor, which put an end to democracy internally and, in foreign policy, instead of peace, promoted a war of conquest with renewed fury. And here, what Mathiez had always sought in his studies of 1789 – the hope that the revolution could return to illuminate the destiny of his own times – came to the surface in the attention he reserved for Babeuf, lingering lengthily on this particular figure in his last, posthumously published, pages. In his description of the first Communist, Mathiez's political trajectory, from a nineteenth-century socialism that had little in common with Jaurès to his quickly abandoned passion for Bolshevism, ended in the acceptance of the dominance, in the present, of another revolutionary fact. On the one hand, Babeuf the convinced Robespierrist was a legacy of nineteenth-century tradition, but, on the other, Babeuf the admirer of Year II and, at the same time, the first communist, confirmed for Mathiez that 1917 was the dawn of a new era – an era that had taken its inspiration from 1793 and had therefore been able to mould the revolutionary events to suit the interpretation that it wanted.

2. The 150th anniversary that never was

Albert Mathiez's academic life was not an easy one: a professor in the provinces, first Besançon and then Dijon, he never managed to get to the Sorbonne – something that he often complained about, because his searches in the Parisian archives suffered greatly. For this reason, he tried in every way to move to the capital. In 1922, at the time of Aulard's retirement, he decided to let him know that, should he place no obstacle in his way, he would certainly put an end to his attacks on his work. Aulard, of course, paid no attention to his proposal and tried to arrange his own successor by nominating Léon Levy Schneider, a professor from Lyon who had produced a biography of Convention member Jean-Bon Saint-André.[26] As frequently happens, a third figure, Philippe Sagnac, who taught in Lille and was also a member of the circle of Aulard's journal, *La Révolution Française*, took advantage of the competition between the two candidates. As we have seen, his candidacy had been given a significant boost by the recent publication, for Lavisse, of the first volume of the *Histoire contemporaine de la France*, dealing with the early part of the revolution.

The decision seemed a final tribute to the elderly professor, whose fortunes were in decline, both because the minister had refused him the extension of his post to seventy-five years and because in the council of the Parisian *mairie* some, recalling Cochin, had accused him of lacking impartiality and had even refused to vote a public display of thanks for him.[27] His post, however, was taken by a scholar with political views that were not very dissimilar to his own and who, in the inaugural lecture held in April 1923, was quick to praise his predecessor. Sagnac noted that Aulard's historiographic method was superior to the German version: it was not ruined by the exaggerated erudition and spirit of domination that was too often typical of the writing of his colleagues across the Rhine. Yet Aulard, whom Sagnac always credited as the founder of a historiography 'both of the nation and of humanity', could not sleep soundly.[28] While the Sorbonne seemed to close ranks around the legacy of his teaching, the cultural climate had changed greatly in the meantime. In that same year, the merger of the *Annales révolutionnaires* with the *Revue historique de la Révolution française et de l'Empire* handed over to the *Société des études robespierristes* the *Annales historiques de la Révolution française* and made Albert Mathiez, the promoter of the initiative, an even more combative rival.

But, more than this, Sagnac was not the right person to fight a battle in the name of Aulard's historiographical purity: his approach was different, he openly admitted that social and economic history could add decisive knowledge with regard to the revolution and his interest in multidisciplinarity also demonstrated an awareness of the international dimension of the events that led him to harbour more than one perplexity regarding the reconstruction, so wholly along internal lines, of his predecessor. Among other things, together with the medievalist Louis Halphen, he had already agreed to edit a series, entitled 'Peuples et civilisations', which the publisher Félix Alcan had proposed to them after the war. The initiative would take shape over the course of the 1920s and promised to present, in contrast with the strictly national interpretation of Lavisse's work, the great historical moments from antiquity to modernity in a form 'both scholarly and wide-ranging', through a narration with an international scope. For the volume on the French Revolution, Sagnac, who could not be involved directly with it given the commitments he had with Hachette, the publisher of Lavisse's *Histoire*, decided to tackle only the last part, dedicated to the meaning of 1789 for European civilization.[29] Meanwhile, he divided the part on the revolutionary decade between Georges Lefebvre, for the period up to Thermidor, and Raymond Guyot, for the Directory period.[30] The latter had discussed his thesis on the peace of Basel (1795) in 1911 under the tutelage of Aulard, while the former, although a little older, had only arrived at discussing his work at the Sorbonne only in 1924. Here, with Aulard already retired but still a presence, Lefebvre had Sagnac himself as supervisor of his work on the Northern peasantry at the time of the revolution. The choice of the two scholars seemed to indicate the desire to offer a general overview of revolutionary history that would bring together the international aspect – neglected since the time of Albert Sorel – with the most recent research regarding France. It certainly shows that Sagnac was not at all controlled in his editorial choices by his predecessor and that he had no intention of devoting himself wholly to the cause of the Aulardian positivist tradition. Confirmation soon came: a few years after taking up his position at the Sorbonne, Sagnac decided to move to Cairo for a three-year stay, from 1926 until the end of 1929, leaving in his place, of all people, Albert Mathiez, who finally realized his dream of arriving in Paris. Thanks to a higher number of students, he now hoped to relaunch his own historiographical discourse.

While Sagnac was still in Egypt, in October 1928, Aulard died. His was a state funeral in all but name, attended by the highest authorities in the Republic, as well as local politicians and administrators, Russian dissidents and Italian anti-fascists (Miliukov and Kerensky on the one hand, Count Sforza on the other) and, of course, the academic world en masse. Mathiez's absence stood out, while Georges Lefebvre sent a message of condolence. The latter, after the discussion of his thesis, had begun to collaborate with the *Annales historiques de la Révolution française*, while continuing to write for Aulard's journal, and was at the time working on the part assigned to him by Sagnac for the new, multi-authored history of the revolution. In the difficult game of balance between Mathiez, Aulard and Sagnac himself, Lefebvre's pages on the first revolutionary years, published in 1930, set out precisely the field he had chosen.[31] While it is true that the book emphasized the international aspect of 1789, and that its purpose was to show the revolution's impact at a European level, the guidelines for the sections dedicated to domestic politics, which set the tone for the whole work, were largely inspired by Mathiez's studies. These were taken into account when he described the need for the Terror, as well as the operational mechanisms of the revolutionary government; when he illustrated the economic policy decisions of the Committee of Public Safety; when he dealt with the frontier victories; and when he passed judgement on the leading figures, where Robespierre's prominence over Danton was increasing. Mathiez himself, on the other hand, was pleased with so much attention – so much so that he wrote with satisfaction that his decades-long research by now dictated the interpretative line of the revolution and had finally eradicated Aulard's 'opportunist' reading. Not only that: the fact that his studies were held in such high regard in a work for the general public convinced him to return with greater enthusiasm to working on the broad general treatment of the revolution that he had had in mind for some time and in which he hoped to lay down the new line of interpretation on the subject. Mathiez worked assiduously on the project, but was never able to bring it to completion – killed by a stroke, in the middle of a lecture at the Sorbonne, on 26 February 1932.

His departure from the scene nevertheless opened the way for his contemporary Lefebvre, who promptly took up his legacy, both as president of the *Société des etudes robespierristes* and as director of the *Annales historiques de la Révolution française*. It was the beginning of a whirlwind ascent, as fast as the initial part of his career had been slow: in 1935, the equally sudden death of Raymond Guyot brought Lefebvre to the Sorbonne, and there, in 1937, with Sagnac's retirement, he took over the role of professor of history of the French Revolution. In the meantime, the closure of Aulard's glorious *Révolution Française* left a clear field for the *Annales historiques de la Révolution française*, which, under Lefebvre's direction, had an easy time of it in terms of dictating the scientific line on the subject. So, in the space of just a handful of years, the doctorate late-comer had become the new prophet of revolutionary studies, claiming the legacy of Aulard's teaching as well as the entire research organization developed by Mathiez. Nothing would previously have predicted all this: for a long time, his professional career had been split between high school teaching and burrowing through provincial archives.[32] His opportunity arrived in the early years of the century, when, following Jaurès's political and cultural ideas, in Lille, where he taught, he had contributed research on the Northern department to a collection of revolutionary documents promoted by the socialist politician. This was the provincial background that, on the eve of the First World War, gave rise to his studies on the working classes in the small town of Bourbourg and provisioning policies in the neighbouring district of Bergues. The war and the looming military front forced Lefebvre to move and interrupted his studies on the revolution, which he resumed with the return of peace, bringing them to a conclusion, as mentioned above, in 1924, at the age of fifty. His thesis on the Northern peasantry at the time of the revolution nevertheless marked a turning point in revolutionary studies: it restored autonomy (and consequently original meaning) to the actions of the peasant masses that previous reconstructions had to a large extent concealed, with the countryside indistinctly blended in to the overall panorama of the revolutionary bloc.[33]

Lefebvre, on the other hand, through minute examination of local historical realities, was able to illustrate the plurality of positions expressed, which he correctly linked to the stratification and internal differentiations of peasant society. This created another way of looking at the politicization of the rural masses, where the traditional political institutions of the Third Estate were set aside to emphasize the multiple forms of ownership, cultivation and rent that would cumulatively contribute to forming the various reactions of the peasants when faced with the new phenomenon that the revolution represented. The research, where statistical detail was combined with geographical representation and economic structure, therefore made it possible to open a new page in the history of 1789: it presented peasant protest in its specificity and incompatibility with a more generic framework and at the same time for the first time managed to fully explain it. The anti-capitalist feelings that stirred this protest and that had encouraged the rural masses to get involved in political activity was for the first time scientifically validated by painstaking research, which made it possible to understand the deep motivations for the protest and why the peasantry had suddenly, in the political situation of 1789, ended up turning in a direction both conservative and progressive. Conservative, because it aimed to stop that policy of liberalization in the economic field that the monarchy, with a great deal of hesitation, had ended up adopting in the last decades of the old order; progressive, because resistance in this regard had made it possible, in the political field, to block the agreement, otherwise already defined, between the enlightened aristocracy and the upper middle classes. The French peasantry, with their revolutionary activism, had thus triumphed over the system of enclosures, inspired by the British precedent, and their resistance in the name of civic rights and small properties, if it had delayed the birth of capitalism in the French countryside, had, however, provided the rural masses with living conditions that were much better than those of their island cousins.

This element, destined to weigh heavily on the social life of modern France, constituted the main accomplishment of Lefebvre's thesis, which demonstrated the importance of the socio-economic dimension in reading political history. He would feel all the more confirmed in his ideas when, having begun his university career in Clermont-Ferrand, he was able, in 1928, following the untimely death of Georges Pariset, to move to the University of Strasbourg. His meeting with Marc Bloch and Lucien Febvre was decisive,[34] urging him in the direction of social history even as he was working on the initial part of the volume on the revolution promoted by Sagnac.[35] These pages of his, which it has been said depended a great deal on Mathiez's work, are nevertheless revealing of how, in any case, Lefebvre sought a meeting point between the originality of his approach to the revolution and the weight of a historiographical tradition that, until then, had looked to political history alone to determine the success of the subject.[36]

It is not surprising, therefore, that his work is in many ways contradictory: on the one hand, there are already certain foreshadowings of future interests, such as the attention to peasant rebellion (up to and including the Vendée), the importance given to the role of working class mentality (even in its most traditional form) in the construction of a new revolutionary ideological universe and the concrete significance of the economic crisis in the political reconfiguration of the urban masses; but on the other hand, these are areas that still seem simply to support a reconstruction of events which, as has been said, follows the line of traditional political history.

However, this was an imbalance that Lefebvre gradually set out to correct during the 1930s, when he produced his best work. First, in 1932, when, with his *La Grande Peur de 1789*, he combined agrarian history and the history of mentalities in a masterful reconstruction of the conspiracy psychosis that spread almost everywhere in France in the year of the revolution.[37] For the occasion, Lefebvre returned to a well-known theme, to turn it on its head – given that, in contrast to Le Bon's observations, it illustrated that moralistic or counter-revolutionary conclusions should not be drawn from collective mobilization. The psychological factor made it possible to reveal the deep mechanisms of the *ancien régime*'s value system and the concrete means of its transformation into a revolutionary context, destined to give yet another significance to collective violence. A few years later, in 1939, on the occasion of the 150th anniversary of the revolution, Lefebvre presented his history of the sensational upheavals of 1789, beginning according to him much earlier, in 1787, to conclude with the October Days in Versailles.[38]

Both works are today regarded as classics of revolutionary historiography, but it is worth emphasizing here that one was the necessary premise of the other. It was the study of the 'great fear' that allowed Lefebvre to break down the unity of the 1789 moment to underline, as he did in the second work, the existence of three distinct, though contemporary, revolutions: one aristocratic, one bourgeois and one working class. In 1789 there had therefore not been a single revolution – as Mathiez and, even earlier, Jaurès had surmised – but a plurality of events destined to intersect with, and influence, one other, without their confluence in the great framework of the drive for change, however, cancelling their own particular originality. He certainly arrived at this result through his research on the peasant world, but also thanks to his ability to master (and recompose) all the historiography of the Third Republic within a new narrative of great originality. He valued the works of his predecessors highly, without modelling himself on anyone: with respect to the anti-revolutionary tradition that arose in the wake of Taine, he agreed both on the largely minority aspect of the revolutionary ruling class and on the uncommon level of violence. He emphasized, nevertheless, that every revolutionary movement needed an elite and that the great merit of the latter was to transform the period of brutality into a political programme capable of overcoming a world of oppression. From Aulard, Lefebvre took the constant reference to the period of liberty, but setting himself apart from it at the same time, underlining that it was the push from below, and also its violence, that had led to revolution. On the other hand, he adopted Mathiez's attention to the working-class movement, while profoundly broadening its dimensions and meaning, demonstrating that, essentially, it was Jaurès's historiographical lesson that he had, always and only, in mind in all his works.

The same thing cannot be entirely said of Lefebvre from a strictly political point of view: while it is true that until 1940 he was a follower of the SFIO, it should not be forgotten that he had previously been a member of Jules Guesde's Socialist party, where distrust of collaboration with bourgeois forces was the order of the day and parliamentary acceptance of the Socialist world was long regarded with great suspicion.[39] There is a clear trace of this political background when he had to deal directly with the political story of the revolution – in the 1930 work, his distrust of the parliamentary version of the revolution had already made a repeated appearance. In those pages, his judgement on the Constituent Assembly is cutting, precisely because class selfishness seemed to dominate every gesture; the same goes for the Legislative Assembly, whose decision to go to war was the product of the understanding between the Feuillants and the Girondins, made possible by the bourgeois nature of both. The Convention does not come out much better: socio-economic decisions make use of popular discontent, but are adopted to support a war economy; the behaviour of the warring parties is wholly dominated by opportunism, aimed at deploying pressure from the streets for their own power games; and the days of 31 May and 2 June 1793 are viewed as a simple settling of accounts within the assembly – so much so, that the same mechanism is also applied to the Thermidor.

It was a perspective that Lefebvre confirmed in 1937 when he wrote *Les Thermidoriens* for Armand Colin, a small book similar to those previously written by Mathiez, whose guidelines he intended to follow.[40] Once again, there emerged his intense hostility towards a parliamentarism aloof from the deepest hopes of the social body and entirely wrapped up in its own bourgeois egotism. Lefebvre distinguished between the revolutionary government and the Convention in order to emphasize that the latter had had to submit to the watershed of the Terror and was forced to accept against its will the elimination of the factions within it. In reality, it found these decisions repugnant, its social nature favouring a compromise between the parties present in the assembly hall – something Thermidor would allow it to put into practice during Year III.

It is therefore no coincidence that in 1936, invited by Sagnac to compose another volume for the *Peuples et civilisations* series, dedicated to the Napoleonic years, he looked with interest at the Consulate experiment. He thought it superior to the Directory, the result of the constitutional work of the Thermidorians, which he was quick to accuse of corruption and ineptitude. In his *Napoléon*, the Bonapartist adventure, including all the Empire years, thus became a direct continuation of the revolutionary period, with the Corsican general, even within the framework of an authoritarian policy, continuing the task that 1789 had only begun. In other words, admiration for the man went hand in hand with contempt for the Directory and led Lefebvre to perceive a certain continuity between the Consulate and the Committee of Public Safety, given that both government experiments had set aside parliamentary practice, an obstacle to profound change in the country.[41] For Lefebvre, the revolution was too enormous an event to be enclosed within a context involving individual freedom alone. In his view, in the process of subverting the *ancien régime*, other victories had to take precedence: the right to existence and the abolition of feudality came before individual freedom, an observation, valid for 1789 as for 1793, that justified admiration for Robespierre and explained his attention to Bonaparte. There was a profound trace of Guedism in Lefebvre's political culture, highly suspicious as he always was of the system of power on which the parliamentarism of the Third Republic had rested.

However, during the 1930s, this substantial distrust of bourgeois democracy was nourished by a dismayed examination of French society and politics between the two world wars, their fragility and shortcomings a constant presence for Lefebvre as he worked on his interpretation of revolutionary dynamics. But this distrust also inspired a parallel political commitment, with deep connections to the left, which, in the turmoil of the 1930s, induced him to seek a sure point of reference in the period of the Popular Front. Léon Blum's experiment in government seemed to Lefebvre the real moment in which France finally returned to establish a direct (and accurate) link with revolutionary history. This is the context for his political commitment and his willingness to combat the rise of Fascism, which led him, from his arrival in Paris, to collaborate with the *Comité de vigilance des intellectuels antifascistes*[42] and to create, at the Sorbonne, a *Cercle Descartes*, where national sentiment was regarded in patriotic terms and seen as something very different from chauvinism.[43]

However, his political commitment found full realization with the birth of the *Institut d'Histoire de la Révolution française*. This did not come out of nowhere: there had been a *Centre d'études de la Révolution française* since 1932 at the Sorbonne, promoted by Sagnac and a law historian, the Russian refugee Boris Mirkin-Gecevič, thanks to the support of the rector (and historian of the revolution in Lyon) Sébastien Charléty. The Popular Front's victory allowed Lefebvre, who had just succeeded Sagnac, to request the aggregation of the *Centre* to the Faculty of Arts and to obtain from the Minister of Education, Jean Zay, the founding decree of a new institute which, in fact, excluded those who in previous years had represented the tradition of revolutionary studies at the Sorbonne. The consequent exclusion of Mirkin-Gecevič, too anti-communist to remain associated with Lefebvre, placed the *Institut d'Histoire de la Révolution française* under the banner of the Popular Front and demonstrated the rapprochement between the *Société des études robespierristes* and the Sorbonne to the scientific community.

This was a fundamental step: the Sorbonne, which, after the creation of the Chair of History of the French Revolution, was a Dantonian, and soon anti-communist, fiefdom, passed to another political and cultural sphere. However, it did not appear to be an irreversible change: Sagnac, now professor emeritus, obtained the presidency of the *Institut international d'histoire de la Révolution française*, created in 1936 to organize the events planned for the now imminent 150th anniversary, biding his time until Lefebvre's retirement in 1939 made way once more for Mirkin-Guetzevich. In the meantime, however, Lefebvre had not been standing around and had agreed with the director of the *Archives nationales*, Pierre Caron, to set up a coordinated management of the celebrations. This allowed him to receive strong financial support from the state, to associate the new institute directly with the University, to ask that the institute promoted by Sagnac no longer appear in student guides, and, exceptionally, to obtain an extension of his tenure.

For the 150th anniversary, Lefebvre organized a series of public events to commemorate the revolution, in which it was difficult to distinguish the scientific aspect from the political. In a conference held on February 22 at the *Cercle Descartes*, at the Sorbonne, he established what would be the cultural line for the celebrations, insisting on the significance of 1789 in 1939. The approach was obviously a political one: Lefebvre related the experience of the revolution to the international situation of the moment and introduced analogies – somewhat reductive, it has to be said – on the one hand between liberal democracies and the work of the Constituent Assembly and, on the other, between dictatorships and Bonapartism. It goes without saying that, by referring to Robespierrist social democracy, Lefebvre intended to underline the Popular Front's only possible predecessor – the Front remaining the only point of reference for those who, faced with the agreements signed in the meantime in Munich, did not intend to bend the knee to National Socialist Germany.

The conclusion clearly showed the militant vision of the revolutionary precedent and predicted what he now perceived as an inevitable choice, which would lead to war:

> throughout history, we find so many peoples who have preferred to obey, which, moreover, has spared them neither hardship nor war. Nothing would expose us to the supreme peril more than to give the impression that we too are resigned. Let those who claim to be partisans of freedom shoulder their responsibilities: freedom is earned, freedom is defended.[44]

These are the same motivations that inspirit his book *Quatre-Vingt-Neuf*, whose conclusions summarize the militant aspect of the work:

> Youth of 1939! The *Déclaration* is also a tradition, and a glorious tradition. Hear, as you read it, the voice of your ancestors speaking to you, those who fought at Valmy, at Jemappes, at Fleurus, to the cry of *Vive la Nation*! They gave you your freedom [. . .]. They tell you that your fate lies in your hands and that the fate of the future city depends on you, and you alone. You see the risk: but since it is something that attracts you, it will not make you back down. Measure the magnitude of the task, but also the dignity which it bestows upon you. Would you renounce this? Your elders place their trust in you; you will soon be the Nation: *Vive la Nation*![45]

These words say a great deal about the great, unresolved contradiction that still, in 1939, accompanied Lefebvre the historian: on the one hand, in his works he had shown the inconsistency in the thesis that there existed a revolutionary bloc in 1789; on the other hand, he had never wanted to draw the consequences from this, remaining within the framework of that socialist and patriotic dimension in which he had grown up and which even his distrust of parliamentary practice had never entirely managed to undermine. Thus he was never able to draw the direct consequences from the breadth of his research, which led him to demolish the – to a great extent 'opportunistic' – political identity of the Third Republic, until the outbreak of hostilities. Indeed, even at the time of the Phoney War, he insisted on the idea of a patriotic war and believed that the example of 1793 would return to rouse the national spirit. He was all the more disillusioned by his country's sudden collapse: hence his revolt against the SFIO, which he held responsible for the parliamentary debacle of 1940. This also gave rise to his profound contempt for the socialist world in general: its hodgepodge of positions during the crisis of 1939 seemed to have led to defeat, to the seizure of power by Pétain and to the excessive collaboration of the French population with the Germans. In the dark years of the German occupation of Paris, Lefebvre, behind the walls of the Sorbonne, where he continued to teach despite his retirement, was called upon to face his most difficult test. His trajectory as a scholar, however, was by no means over. After the war, in fact, his career flourished once again and enjoyed another, and in some ways even more important, chapter.

3. Re-establishing a national order

One of those who, on the eve of the Second World War, could not conceal his intolerance towards the legend of the revolution was Daniel Halévy, an upper middle-class Parisian who had abandoned his initial passion for literature to turn to Proudhonism and had fought in support of Dreyfus. Disappointed by the solution found for the end-of-century crisis, for a long time he was a follower of Charles Peguy, an essayist whose political attitudes combined socialism and nationalism. In the aftermath of the Great War, in which he had participated as an interpreter, his distrust of the French political system increased: he became strongly critical of parliamentary democracy and of the political-cultural values that formed the basis of the Third Republic.[46] In the 1930s, he turned his attention to the study of contemporary France through a series of articles where, on the one hand, he denounced the plutocratic character of the republican system and, on the other, showed keen interest in the peasant world – there, in his view, lay France's deepest values, and it was a world that threatened to soon vanish. In July 1939, at the time of the celebrations of the 150th anniversary of the revolution that the war was about to interrupt, in the context of close criticism of the parliamentary system, Halévy published a small book, which was a disparaging attack on 1789 as the founding myth of modern France: in a few pages, Halévy described how, throughout the nineteenth century, the revolutionary dogma had increased in strength and the extent to which its legend had permeated French society.[47] In his eyes, it was nothing less than true national degeneration: the sensation of the inevitability of 1789 accompanied the rejection of the

French spirit's most profound values, setting aside what had, in a decisive way, and long before the revolution, helped to forge the country's national identity. Responsibility for this rejection of the deepest aspects of French history in order to pay homage to sectarian modernity was, he believed, to be equally shared between the worlds of politics and of academe. The former had swiftly swept away all critical attention towards the Revolution, homogenizing the national discourse in terms of complete respect for the profound values of 1789; the latter had set itself the task of perpetuating, among the younger generations, the false belief that the collapse of the old order was followed by timely progress. It was an easy matter for Halévy to point out that, in the France of the Third Republic, significant figures in the intellectual world had paid the price for this ideological orientation. A veil of academic silence was thus immediately drawn over Renan and Taine, guilty of indicating that the myth of 1789 was a problem for French modernity. For this reason, the 150th anniversary, which claimed to celebrate a long succession of avowed French triumphs, seemed to Halévy to be merely the apotheosis of a national superstition, where, with respect to the equivocation on the issue of popular sovereignty, new ideological fuel was being pumped into the engine of corrupt and inefficient parliamentarism. He thus deployed the observations of those – from Maistre to Proudhon, in his view the greatest thinkers of the nineteenth century – who had emphasized the destructive effects of 1789 on French society. He arrived at a lapidary conclusion: the memory of the revolution and its centrality in the ideological universe of modern France comprised a dramatic problem and only with the removal of that obstacle, which the national political system had based itself around, could France recover an authentic relationship with its own past and therefore equip itself for a more balanced future.

Halévy's approach therefore assigned to the Third Republic a role as the epitome of the process of subversion of France's profound values that began in 1789. In this sense, his political path was not such an original one: it mirrored the fate of other Dreyfusards, disappointed first by the political solution to the affair and then by the outcome of the First World War. For all of them, the events of the Third Republic had become mired in humiliating parliamentarism. However, in Halévy it was also something else: his rediscovery of a France uncontaminated by modernity on the one hand made him a precursor of some of the watchwords of Pétainism and, on the other, a sort of forerunner of the reasons for ecology.

His stance thus, at the end of the 1930s at the latest, ended up intersecting with the claims of those who, between the two world wars, had remained firm in rejecting 1789 to insist on the attractions of traditionalism. Halévy's ideas here were close to those of Charles Maurras's *Action française*, created as has been seen in 1899, in the middle of the Dreyfus affair, but coming into its own especially after the First World War, when it took advantage of the space for manoeuvre that suddenly opened up for the right to launch intense criticism of the values of 1789. However, it would be simplistic to make Halévy a sort of comrade in arms of the *Action française* – a more promising suggestion, perhaps, is that in the climate of difficulty that the republican political system was experiencing, Maurras had no need to err on the side of subtlety in order to enlist in his own movement those who, even with opinions far removed from his own, or that certainly did not coincide with them, were nevertheless useful in throwing down the glove to representative democracy.

The most significant example in this regard is represented precisely by the way in which, in the immediate post-war period, the *Action française* rethought the role of history as an instrument of political struggle.[48] On the eve of 1914, the positions of the Maurras movement did not differ from those of Gustave Gautherot, a professor of the history of the French Revolution at the *Institut catholique de Paris* who presented his own teaching as a counterweight to Aulard's. His works were dominated by an anathema towards 1789, an epochal change soon reduced to a humiliating persecution of the Church, and opinions flew, criticizing the nefarious role of Freemasonry and denouncing parliamentarism, viewed as link in the chain between the revolutionary years and the present moment of the Third Republic. His writings on the revolutionary democracy, which appeared in 1912, summed up this approach well and certainly represented a definite landmark for history writers close to *Action française*.[49]

Pierre de la Gorce, for example, a Catholic magistrate who resigned from office in the aftermath of the Combes law on the separation of State and Church, published that same year (1909) his *Histoire religieuse de la Révolution française*, which was proposed as an accurate survey of the vicissitudes of Catholicism from 1789 until the Napoleonic Concordat.[50] Also on the eve of war, Frantz Funck-Brentano, librarian at the Arsenal Library, took an interest in Maurras's movement. Funck-Brentano was a scholar specializing in the *ancien régime* and, since the end of the nineteenth century, was happy to play a part in the dispute regarding 1789. In his *La Prise de la Bastille*, published with some success,[51] he had already downsized the founding act of the revolution from the dawn of modernity – as suggested at the Sorbonne – to the unfortunately successful criminal action of a violent and delinquent working class.[52]

The Great War, however, changed the way the right wrote the history of the revolution. The patriotic victory gave the *Action française* a lot of rope to play with, even within representative bodies, something previously unimaginable. It immediately took advantage of the situation to make history an important ally in the work of opposing the secularist and republican perspective provided to the general public by university teaching. Thus a plan took shape on the basis of which history had to become narrative, produced by talented writers and brilliant journalists – they alone, with their ability to give elegant form to the debate, could dialogue with the reader. The most significant result in this regard is the *Histoire de France*, published in 1924 by Jacques Bainville,[53] one of the founders of *Action française* in 1899, when he was just twenty. It is a work that inaugurates a narrative model, made up of clarity of presentation and capacity for synthesis, and it would be highly successful in right-wing literature between the two world wars.[54] Bainville's working scheme was deliberately marked by the polemical refusal of official historiography: it rejected scholarship, renounced footnotes, made use of an elegant, involving style and emphasized descriptions of panoramic, epic scenes, as well as employing anecdote and taking refuge in political-diplomatic history. These were ingredients that, with the approval of the big Parisian publishers, made it possible to find broad consensus with a well-read public, whose conservative (and Catholic) tendencies led them to regard political modernity with immense suspicion, the Russian revolution being the most worrying image. The anxiety of an entire social world faced with international events that seemed to threaten its very existence ensured the success of Bainville's work. He died prematurely in 1936, after having delivered a biography of Napoleon to his publisher – a work that would also prove to be highly successful.

His *Histoire de France* had sold almost 180,000 copies by 1939, with another 63,000 added, distributed to French houses only for the years between 1940 and 1942. This editorial triumph should not be underestimated, since it certainly revived the fortunes of the counter-revolutionary cause with the general public. However, the course taken to involve the reader in rejecting 1789 was implicit and certainly did not rely on the trite or commonplace: indeed, in the two chapters of the *Histoire de France* dedicated to the decade following 1789, Bainville went in an opposite direction, overturning the ideas on which counter-revolutionary analysis was based. In his opinion, in fact, a true revolution could only be spoken of as starting from the October Days 1789, when the revolt of Parisian women and La Faÿette's subservience to the mob destroyed the reign of Louis XVI. It was anything but new as a theory, following as it did the lesson of Rivarol and other great counter-revolutionary writers; however, it did start from quite different premises, given that Bainville believed that, since 1774, with the revival of the Parliaments, the monarchy had lost its authority, revealing its fragility as an institution at just the moment when accusations of despotism against the king were flying from all sides. Following this line, Bainville could describe revolutionary events as a progressive weakening of statehood, the lowest point of which was reached in 1792 with the declaration of war. Hence his reading of 1793 as a partially necessary dictatorship, the exercise of which however lost the French any initial advantage, forcing Bonaparte centre stage to finally allow the formation of a precarious equilibrium. Brumaire thus became the dawn of a new era, one that put an end to the weak and despised government that came after the fall of Robespierre. The denunciation of the Directory as a corrupt and divisive regime summed up Bainville's profound hostility towards parliamentarism and the form of representative democracy that the Third Republic saw itself as heir to. In this way, the foundations were laid for the right to have a positive interest in Napoleon, his authoritarianism foreshadowing the reassertion of statehood that the years following 1789 had instead failed to do. The revolutionary decade, on the other hand, signified a degeneration of traditional political life, the lowest point of which was the diminishment of France in a European context and its difficult struggle for survival, the dramatic sequel to a long and unchallenged period of hegemony in continental Europe.

And yet, running parallel to Bainville's success, to consolidate this image of the revolution with a wider public, there was also the posthumous reputation of Augustin Cochin. It has already been mentioned that, in 1922, the latter's memory was hovering over the hall of the Parisian municipal council when, with Aulard now coming to the end of his teaching career, Cochin was evoked by the right to denounce the lack of balance in Aulard's historical analysis. Reference was, for the occasion, to Cochin's recent posthumous publications, promoted by his family. Thanks to the care of his friend and collaborator Charles Charpentier, from 1920 the publication of his writings was set in motion and in the introduction to the first book,[55] it was clarified the theme that would ensure Cochin's success especially in the second half of the twentieth century: the appearance of the *sociétés de pensée*, their purpose to form opinion, their activity to soon become the true collective actor of the revolution. It's a context that also explains the publication, in 1921, of another book that encompasses a wide variety of pieces: on the one hand, a reprinted essay on the elections in 1789 in Burgundy – published in 1904 in the journal of the *Action française*, a fact that curiously goes unmentioned; on the other, the article on Aulard's disagreement with Taine and the reprinting of the introduction, only released the year before, to the previous volume.[56] These works were accompanied by other writings from conferences held in the immediate pre-war period that once again emphasized the role of political associationism as the prime mover of the revolution, as well as a study on the origins of the 1792 war, which reiterated the sectarian nature of those – the Jacobins – who had wanted to initiate hostilities in the name of a democratically defined patriotism.

In its choice of texts, the book seemed to be putting forward Cochin, a national martyr, as the standard-bearer of the anti-revolutionary cause and it goes without saying that in this work of making his writings available, starting from those who wanted his unpublished writings to be printed, there was an attempt to force its meaning in that direction alone. It was an almost inevitable occurrence: in the aftermath of First World War, the political crisis following military victory, the affirmation of Bolshevism, the link soon introduced between Lenin and Robespierre and the aggressive return of right-wing forces to France were all factors designed to favour the reading of 1789 in this particular way.

This explains why, as early as 1924, another collection of Cochin's writings appeared, this time with a preface by Augustin Ackermann, an Alsatian religious figure who had engaged with Cochin in philosophical dialogue.[57] In the introductory pages, Ackermann was quick to suggest the demonic nature of direct democracy's interference with the parliamentary version. The same perspective was put forward in another work of editorship the following year, where it was emphasized how central the Rousseauian discourse on democracy was for Cochin, suitably described as an incubating element of tyranny and terror. On the same occasion, reaching for easy analogy, Ackermann also indicated that Year II alone foreshadowed 1917 and concluded by extolling Cochin as the harbinger of the totalitarian aspect assumed by politics in the aftermath of the First World War.[58]

It was Cochin's old friend Charpentier, at the time still involved in the publication of the last volume of the *Actes*, who unsuccessfully tried to bring some balance to Ackermann's remarks, refusing, despite the protest of Cochin's family, to complete the edition that he had been responsible for. It was, nevertheless, a line of resistance that could not hope to succeed. Indeed, the preference Cochin's parents gave to Ackermann's reading, where the mix of history and sociology was overshadowed by a dogmatic philosophical perspective, encouraged revived interest in the writer from Maurras. In deference to the papal excommunication that had in the meantime arrived for the *Action française*, Cochin's mother repeatedly denied that her son, a good Catholic, had ever had any sympathies for that particular world; but her protests were of no avail. Maurras instead insisted on reiterating that Cochin was a sort of *maître à penser* of his movement, and that he had even helped deepen and clarify its doctrine. All this was enough, thanks to Ackermann's biased interpretations, for Cochin to become a form of epigone of Abbot Barruel, so that his *sociétés de pensée* in the vulgate that soon spread became the equivalent of Masonic lodges and methods of consensus formation were reduced to simplistic ideas of conspiracy. Cochin's family bore a serious responsibility in this regard, given that they had not only preferred Ackermann to Charpentras, but, faced with the latter's refusal to complete his edition of the *Actes*, had even thought of turning to the rising (right-wing) star of French Revolution historiography, Pierre Gaxotte.[59]

Gaxotte, the author, in 1928, of a history of the French Revolution that was highly successful throughout the twentieth century,[60] was a leading figure in Maurras's movement and responsible for defining the interpretation of 1789 for the *Action française*.[61] His work was very much indebted to the model recently proposed by Bainville: political history was once more placed at the centre of the debate with socio-economic elements employed as elements of confirmation, while the reader's attention was attracted by descriptive scenes constructed with great elegance.[62] From a strictly historiographical point of view, a certain refinement was also present: with authors appropriately cited, Gaxotte showed that he knew the tradition of great republican historiography and could refer accurately to the world of academe, with works, however, noted only to the extent that they provided a useful contrast to his own polemical discourse. The result was a work both wide-ranging and extremely ambitious, which aimed to summarize the counter-revolutionary tradition by adapting it to the political framework that had come into being after the war. Hence, in the context of a suitably Maurrassian discourse, the nostalgia for the *ancien régime* – not irremediably lost by any means – and, at the same time, the denunciation of the demonic nature (and precursor of communism) of all the revolutionary radicalism that appeared after 1789. Tocqueville and Taine were Gaxotte's guides, therefore, although in different ways: the first called upon to assist in the many pages dedicated to the old order, even though Gaxotte's treatment loses that sense of moderation in the study of absolutism that was instead the great strength of the *Ancien Régime et la Révolution*; the second, instead, to help navigate through the waves of popular violence – in Gaxotte, the *Origines* is often evoked to recall the horrors and miseries of the revolutionary process, the dissolution and violence of the lower classes and the moral and mental degradation of their improvised leaders.

However, Gaxotte's narrative could not forgo the easy analogy with the present moment, with 1793 Paris constantly linked to 1917 Moscow, the Terror a foreshadowing of Bolshevism and the revolutionary violence of Year II the example that had always fascinated Lenin. The unified nature of the first revolutionary years thus triumphed, once again, over the period that followed Thermidor: the Directory was dismissed in a few pages as the anticipation of that parliamentary system that the entire *Action française* was determined to reject. However, in the discussion of the early years, the figure of Augustin Cochin stood out, duly cited when it came to introducing the mechanism of revolutionary conspiracy as an instrument for accelerating the direction of the political process. The reading of the *sociétés de pensée* as so many Masonic lodges, pulling the strings of the revolutionary process from within their enclosured intolerance, was extremely prominent in Gaxotte's work and present at the very origins of 1789, not only on the occasion of the electoral campaign for the Estates General, where Cochin's example was too entrancing to be ignored, but also through extension to the *Grande Peur*, a movement, in Gaxotte's view, too coordinated to lack skilful direction.

Ultimately, Gaxotte's work had little good to say with regard to the cause of the revolution: beyond some moderate reform initiatives and together with a suspicious silence on religious politics (after all, the work came out just after the pope had condemned the *Action française* on its list of prohibited works) there remained just a limited appreciation of the national war effort in 1793 – as if to note the analogy with the much more recent event in 1917 and as a consequence safeguard its favourable acceptance by a public that still regarded participation in the Great War as a clear identitary motif. Overall, therefore, Gaxotte's work provided brilliant evidence of how influential the openly reactionary reading of Cochin's writings had been and constituted a new pillar on which, between the two world wars, to found a reactionary interpretation of 1789. Moreover, it is no coincidence that, in 1930, a *Cercle Augustin Cochin* was formed, where the most prestigious conservative and Catholic intellectuals gathered in good numbers to spread the thinking of their fallen countryman, but even more so to fight openly against socialism, communism and, more generally, against any consequence of democratic political life. In this context, reference to Cochin ended up consolidating around the problem posed by the Masonic world, in France between the two wars perceived as a dark force, the direct heir of the spirit of Jacobinism, alive and strong enough to control and direct the public authorities and to dictate the political line of the Third Republic.[63]

The *Cercle* came to an end in 1933, but the following year the explosion of the Stavisky affair – a swindler of Jewish origin in league with the minister of justice, Albert Dalimier, a well-known Freemason – reinvigorated the anti-Semitic and anti-Masonic protest that accompanied the failed insurrectionary attempt against parliament on 6 February 1934. Just after that dramatic moment, in right-wing circles Cochin's work was joined by that of Bernard Faÿ, *croix de guerre* at Verdun and professor at the *Collège de France*, a specialist in eighteenth-century revolutions who had hitherto built all his academic success on the link between France and the United States. Nothing, apparently, in his work, until the turning point of the mid-1930s, indicated that he would come up with the idea of 1789 as a Masonic conspiracy. In fact, his writings[64] were read with interest in French lodges and his profound knowledge of the American world excluded him from being associated with those who regarded late-eighteenth-century political developments with repulsion. However, shortly thereafter, the experiment of the *Front populaire* seemed to make it clear that France was drifting to the left and the fact that more than a few government members were Freemasons revived, not only in far-right circles, the idea that there existed a direct link between Freemasonry and Bolshevism. This was the climate, in all probability, that inspired Faÿ's sudden move into the reactionary camp,[65] something that became obvious on the occasion of the 150th anniversary, when, determined to oppose socialist reconstructions on cultural grounds, he started a series of works dedicated to the French Revolution.[66] The elite of right-wing historiography were invited on to the editorial board, including Louis Madelin, Marcel Marion and Gaxotte himself. The project was to put forward the theory that 1789, the dawn of diseased French modernity, had originated as a Masonic plot and, needless to say, the figures of Taine and Cochin were brought back to illuminate this act of cultural reactionarism, called upon to oppose the official reconstructions and to denounce the falsity of the republican vulgate.

The war prevented the project from taking off, but France's military and political collapse revived the fortunes of the French right along other lines, as, with the period of collaboration, many of the historians mentioned here were attracted by the actions of Marshal Pétain. Gaxotte was clever: in 1941, he continued to sing the praises of Bainville with a preface to an old piece by the latter that, in Gaxotte's view, prophetically identified the decrepitude of the French political system.[67] However, not long after, he withdrew from public life, preferring an anonymity that saved him from the post-Liberation purge and meant he was able resume work as a journalist in the new France. Madelin also remained on the sidelines during the occupation, thus avoiding the repression that followed the collapse of Vichy, but confirming where his sympathies lay with the 1948 initiative, becoming president of the committee for the liberation of Pétain. Bernard Faÿ, on the other hand, one of the last to join the right, was swift in his support of Vichy and the German occupation. Appointed head of the National Library of Paris in August 1940,[68] he organized exhibitions on Pétain and Freemasonry's (nefarious) role in 1789, participated in the anti-Semitic repression and supplied the Nazis with the names of members of French lodges. Arrested at the moment of the Liberation, he was sentenced to life imprisonment, but managed to escape to Switzerland in 1951. He was officially pardoned in 1959.

As shown by the careers of Gaxotte, Madelin and Faÿ, the right, in various ways and forms, managed to survive the aftermath of the Second World War. In 1947, Gaxotte's *Révolution française* was already back in bookshops in a revised and expanded edition and would continue to enjoy great success more or less until the 1789 bicentenary. The fact that it was this particular general history to do so well in the decades following the war speaks volumes about the persistence of a reactionary element in French society that, throughout the twentieth century, was always capable of opposing revolutionary historiography in the arena of public popularity.

4. Democracy in danger

The post–First World War period also forced Britain to reflect on what was happening in continental Europe, torn apart by the Bolshevik revolution and the civil wars that followed it. The democratization of political life following victory had meant a revival of interest in civil rights, but the political and social transformations aroused deep concern in conservative circles, which denounced the Bolshevik threat and more than once warned of the risk of a rapid contagion from the continent. The spectre of revolution (once 1793, now 1917) returned to haunt their imagination and the fear was spreading that, this time, British exceptionalism and the cultural tradition that sustained it could do little to avoid the threat. In 1919, an English writer with a passion for history, Nesta Helen Webster, led by the events of the war to adopt openly traditionalist positions, published a successful history of the French Revolution, which promised to make political democracy the connecting link between the Terror, Babeuf, socialism, communism and bolshevism.[69] The work was also resolutely counter-revolutionary in its bibliographical references: among contemporary writers, Webster placed emphasis on those who were openly monarchical, while, in the strictly historiographical field, she made much of Taine, but ignored Aulard, preferring Louis Madelin as the historian of the moment.⁷⁰

Her book, which followed traditional chronological lines to end with the Terror, did have, however, a very ambitious purpose, setting out to write a history of the French Revolution in English which, based on an accurate reading of the sources, founded everything on Burke's ideas and had no time for Carlyle. The Scottish writer was in fact criticized for a superficial use of documents, a naïve belief in the patriotic press, a negative bias towards the *ancien régime*, and, above all, a credulous enthusiasm for the autonomous mobilization of the Parisian mobs that had led him to compose a philosophical rhapsody, as evocative as it was groundless, which had won over British public opinion.

Webster, on the other hand, with a huge amount of documentation to hand, proposed a disenchanted reading of the French Revolution, where the intentions of the main figures, almost all secret and unconfessable, dominate the events themselves and inform the significance of that tremendous political and social upheaval. For this reason, the writer emphasized the traditionally accepted revolutionary stages, such as the storming of the Bastille, the march on Versailles, the assault on the Tuileries, the September Massacres, the Terror: those episodes, hitherto an example of the revolutionary will of the Parisians, permeated her reconstruction of the first revolutionary years. They were useful to her to demonstrate that the love of country and the revolutionary spirit of the lower classes, always made much of, were instead false – the mobs were, she believed, citing Gustave Le Bon here, only the manipulated instruments of skilled puppeteers. Playing with the analogy to her own present times, Webster made the revolution the product of a multiplicity of conspiracies: the plot of the Duke of Orleans to replace Louis XVI; an obscure atheist and Masonic sect that wanted to take over the government; the intrigues of the King of Prussia anxious to break the Franco-Austrian agreement; the cabal organized by British revolutionaries keen to export the French model across the Channel – everything came together to represent the revolution as the first successful experiment of an atheist and communist plot to win control over society. This simplistic idea – hardly new, and already proclaimed by Barruel – took advantage of the climate in Europe favorable towards the right and garnered widespread support. Over the following years, Webster deemed it best to continue along the same lines: in 1921, she published another work on revolution, where, starting from the Illuminati sect in Bavaria, she traced the origins and developments of the subversive forces present in post-war Europe.⁷¹ In 1924, another highly successful work came out, to be repeatedly reprinted.⁷² Here, Cochin, read in the meantime thanks to Ackermann's mediation, was indicated as a sophisticated interpreter of Jacobinism. Webster's work, which placed counter-revolutionary discourse at the centre of her own reconstruction of 1789, also received acclaim in Great Britain in the field of historiography: in 1924, Hutchinson Humphrys, publishing a concise history of the French Revolution, paired her with Madelin as the tutelary deities of his own work.⁷³ Humphrys took the narrative as far as Brumaire and, not by chance, put the Convention and the Directory together as examples of despotic assemblies. He nonetheless emphasized the figure of the agitator as the true promoter of the revolutionary process and concluded with an analogy to the Russian revolution which, certainly not coincidentally, placed Kerensky, Lenin and Trotsky on the same level.

It was a flagrantly political perspective that soon withered away as a certain distance was established in relation to these fascisms, towards which Webster herself was very sympathetic for many years.[74] However, in the ideologically heated climate between the two world wars, her ideas regarding the revolution as a gigantic conspiracy greatly weakened Britain's alleged exceptionalism: to classify all contemporary history as governed by the activity, almost inevitably secret, of forces attempting to subvert the social order, meant that the differences between Great Britain and continental Europe were minimal and that the French Revolution was also a phenomenon with a significant influence across the Channel. Faced with this threat, the proposal to reiterate the centrality of Carlyle's work in the British interpretation seemed a weak one and indeed, between the two world wars, her work was mainly useful in terms of emphasizing the Scottish historian's ability to read and understand the particular nature of French society. This was how Hilaire Belloc saw things: an Anglo-French writer of Catholic faith, but in favour of the liberal shift of 1789, he had written his own history of the French Revolution in 1911, which was also reprinted after the war.[75] In 1929, curating an edition of Carlyle's work, Belloc reiterated that Webster criticized the great Scottish writer for what was in fact of authentic value in his work.[76] He commented upon Carlyle's great qualities in his reading of the French masses, the only mobs in all of Europe to organize themselves spontaneously and to march without the need for leaders or instigators. This robust defence of Carlyle's work, in precisely the terms most dear to French historiography, shows Belloc's political and cultural character – born French but becoming a British citizen, and who saw the war as being decisive with regard to bringing the two countries together.[77] However, he was certainly not the only one to believe that military alliance between France and the United Kingdom had led to the rediscovery of a current of ideas and political practices that had long been stifled by the heated rivalry between the two countries. Philip Brown, killed in action near Armentieres, had left his work unpublished, and, when it came out in 1918, as if to mark the victorious end to the war, it certainly promulgated, over the following years, a much more favourable approach by British historiography towards 1789.[78]

In parallel (and as a response) to Webster's ideas, there were works with a positivist bent, which admired Aulard's interpretation, regarding him – thanks also to his steadfast patriotism and the reason for the alliance with the Anglo-American world – as the French historian most worth consulting. The most significant example here is Eliza Dorothy Bradby, one of the first women to have studied at Oxford and who, before the war, published a biography of Barnave still of interest today.[79] In 1926, on the eve of her death, her concise history of the French Revolution was published, which represented a good general summary of the studies conducted on the subject in the aftermath of the First World War.[80] The structure of the work was attentive to the French interpretative model, limiting the revolution to its early years alone and seeing the Directory as the ebbing of the revolutionary tide that had instead rolled relentlessly forwards until the Terror. However, similarities with the work of French democratic historians, duly referenced as among the most useful to consult, did not stop here: the Girondins were outlined in very negative terms, the Hébertists did not come out much better, the various shades of Danton's character were not avoided, while Robespierre, confirming that Mathiez's research had left their mark, while not re-evaluated, nevertheless had his role as a great statesman restored and in this guise dominated a large part of the work. Taken as a whole, the interpretation of revolutionary events followed the same lines as those that had been developed in France: Bradby suggested that a great period of freedom had been succeeded by an authoritarian shift, dictated, however, by the difficulties of the situation. France had managed to save itself, even though the very methods that had made it possible for the country to survive the storm had prevented it from giving stability to the new order and greatly favoured the rise of General Bonaparte.

Bradby's work thus marked a clear watershed in the field of 1789 studies in Britain: the 1920s had fuelled the hope of a firm return to democracy as a true antidote to Bolshevism and led many, even across the English Channel, to cling to the legacy of the French Revolution as a basis of support for the new order emerging from the Great War. It was a fragile equilibrium, however, because the effects of the 1929 crisis were soon felt, in some ways radicalizing the interpretative framework – on the right, with Burke's ideas making a strong return, and on the left to the advantage of Mathiez and his social reading of Robespierrism. James Matthew Thompson followed the latter course: an Anglican religious figure fascinated by modernism, eventually becoming agnostic, in the post-war period at Magdalen College in Oxford he began a long series of studies of the revolution.[81] His first research was published in 1929, when, in a series of biographical sketches, he demonstrated his loyalty to the line laid down by Mathiez, condemning the pointless belligerence of Brissot and the venality of Danton to instead support a revaluation of the figure of Robespierre.[82] However, he was soon attracted by the ideas of Georges Lefebvre and began an exchange of letters with him in 1932 that developed into a real friendship. Their common concern for Europe's authoritarian involution gave rise to Thompson's *Notes on the French revolution*, a small work, historiographical in nature, published in 1934, in which he denounced the popularity of Webster's ideas.[83] Shortly thereafter, always in close contact with Lefebvre in France, Thompson published a biography of Robespierre, which reined in Mathiez's passionate support for the Incorruptible, though without benefitting the latter's many detractors.[84] Finally, during the Second World War, patriotic commitment against the Nazi threat led to the publication of Thompson's history of the French Revolution in 1943, the culmination of an interpretation that took the contemporary French historiographical school very much into account.[85]

The work constituted an authentic turning point with respect to the tradition of British studies: for the first time, it proposed a reconstruction in English in that was accurately modelled on French historiography. Thompson's work, which went through a number of editions after the Second World War, presented the revolution in a reading that hinged on the years 1789–93 and followed the interpretive guidelines laid down by Mathiez and Lefebvre himself. Obviously, in the first edition there was no lack of, often polemical, references to the present moment: thus, in deference to the strict observance of Montagnardism, Thompson could even suggest that the federalist revolt of 1793 foreshadowed the anti-national choice of the Vichy government.

It would be easy to conclude that Thompson was a sort of English ventriloquist of French historiography if not that in his works, since the late 1920s, he had also taken care to put forward the readings of some general studies of the revolution published in the meantime in America. Thompson's focus on 1789 also grew out of his attention to American historiography, which in turn had begun to take Mathiez's work as a point of reference in its own reconstructions.[86] The war had also inspired a new direction there across the Atlantic: previously, Shailer Mathews's history of the French Revolution, published in 1900, had gone through repeated editions, a work that constitutes an anthology of the main works on 1789 published in France and England in the nineteenth century.[87] However, the global conflict, relaunching the historic alliance between the United States and France, was a watershed in this regard, favouring as it did the political mobilization of scholars and prompting a view of the world war that looked back to its late eighteenth-century precedent.

In 1917, Charles Downer Hazen had already published his *French Revolution and Napoleon*, where 1789 was referenced as an example of liberty and patriotism that should still, at that present moment, inspire the two nations.[88] However, the touchstone was still Aulard and, in 1922, Walter Geer published a concise history of 1789 in which he was careful to indicate the latter's pages as his main point of reference.[89] Victory in war, however, also fuelled interest in the Atlantic world as the bearer of the profound values of Western civilization. Of the first great American historians to tackle this theme, there was above all Carl Lotus Becker, a specialist in the American Revolution with a keen interest in the historical links between the two continents who, from the 1920s, promoted the study of the French Revolution. Louis Gottschalk and then Leo Gershoy studied with Becker at Cornell, becoming two of the leading American experts on 1789 between the two world wars. Their works grew out of no specific point of reference – in 1919 Fred Morrow Fling could still write that in the United States there was no original work on the revolution – and their pioneering aspect certainly encouraged attention towards the French school.

However, in their works there was also an echo of James Harvey Robinson's proposal for a 'new history' that would both favour a much broader approach than the mere political-institutional dimension and somehow distance itself from the European positivist model. For Gottschalk and Gershoy, the stimulus in the direction of a new historiographic method took place in the area of political biography, where they looked for the significance and changes that occurred in revolutionary dynamics: Gottschalk studied Marat, for instance, rescuing him from his demonic legend as a maniac, and then turned to look at Lafayette – here was the example, *par excellence*, of a reading of the revolution that dealt with a political figure common to both sides of the Atlantic.[90] Gershoy, on the other hand, dedicated long years to a political biography of Bertrand Barère, which, however, saw the light only after the Second World War.[91] In short, both agreed – and Eloise Ellery's *Brissot*, which appeared as we have seen in 1915, had been a big influence in this respect – that the genre of biography could produce a more accurate understanding of the concrete modalities of the political radicalization of a part of the French elites in 1789. When, however, both scholars tried their hand at general studies of the revolutionary period, the results turned out to be very disappointing. In 1929, Gottschalk, for example, published *The Era of the French Revolution, 1715-1815*, a text book dealing with an arc of time that already seems to indicate the intention to read the revolution on a very broad scale of social, political and economic change.[92] He moves away from the work of previous authors, Stephens and Mathews in particular, citing them mainly in order to reject their ideas, and chooses Mathiez's reading as a guideline, taking from the latter's work his interpretation of the main events. This last point, from the perspective of the present text, encapsulates the particular nature of his reconstruction, which speaks volumes with regard to how, in the 1920s, even overseas, the changing of the guard took place from Aulard to Mathiez. The same approach is seen in Leo Gershoy's *The French Revolution and Napoleon*, New York, F. S. Crofts & Co., 1933, published in 1933, another university text book, which deals with the events of the *ancien régime* and the revolutionary period, with the aim of presenting an up-to-date general overview of the historiographical lines being followed in France.[93]

Far more significant than the works of Gottschalk and Gershoy, however, is that of Crane Brinton, who studied at Harvard with Harold Laski and decided to follow him to Oxford, where he graduated in 1926.[94] After returning to the United States, he soon crossed the Atlantic again with a study grant and lived in France for three years, where he got to know Mathiez and conducted extensive research in the archives. However, when Brinton published his work on the Jacobin party, in 1930, Mathiez's reaction was, as often happened, harsh and he treated the work of the young American scholar as a sociological mess.[95] It was presented, as the title reveals, along the lines of Robinson's ideas in the years immediately before the Second World War. The latter, with reference to 1789, had suggested it was necessary to expand the examination of the revolution from political-military history to socio-economic history, making use of the contribution that new disciplines could provide and he expressed the hope that the new American historiography would go down that particular road. Apart from the protests from Mathiez, now extremely suspicious of any entanglement with sociology, Brinton's work was therefore an important step on the path outlined by Robinson and resulted in the construction of an original political portrait of Jacobinism.

The study of the activity of the clubs scattered throughout France allowed him to take Cochin's work into account but to convincingly dismiss the conspiracy-centred reading revived by Webster, suggesting that the organization was that of a properly established political party and not of a mysterious sect. His reading of Jacobinism thus relied on the networks of relations and the circuits of diffusion of original political messages to suggest, against counter-revolutionary anathema, that those practices belonged entirely to the social world of the time, and even radical circles were a clear expression of this world. At the same time, his decision to emphasize the cultural profile of Jacobinism allowed him to distance himself from Mathiez's interpretation: Brinton tended to a great extent to play down the impact of a specific economic imprint, even on the political line of extremist circles. What prevailed, on the other hand, was the portrait of a party whose originality lay in a series of radical practices intended to transform patriotism into a form of fanaticism, whose ambition to achieve social palingenesis was similar to the approach of a religious order.

As a consequence, the Terror lost all economic and social foundations to become the instrument – an exceptional one, certainly – of a truly political decision, dictated by the certainty that, faced with the dramatic circumstances of Year II, the elimination of impure subjects – incapable, in other words, of achieving the regeneration of society – constituted an obligatory passage for the triumph of the democratic ideal. This was an influential perspective: in 1935, one of Brinton's students, Donald Greer, published a statistical study of the victims of the Terror that led to the same conclusion, indicating that the majority of victims were not in fact aristocrats and excluding socio-economic prejudice as a motive for the repression.[96] In this way, while admitting that the exceptional circumstances of Year II had played some role in the accelerating the move towards totalitarianism, Brinton could at the same time suggest that the Terror was only the operative instrument of a specific political culture, which aimed to establish a new order on the basis of a coercive utopia typical of all religious radicalism. Brinton defined this perspective in 1934, through a general study of the history of the revolution, which offered a broadly different picture from other reconstructions of the time.[97]

His reading of the revolutionary decade in fact broke with the centrality of 1793, commonly accepted by historiography's various fields, to see the experiment of the Terror as one mere episode in the revolutionary narrative. Intelligent use of Cochin's work also allowed him to demolish the counter-revolutionary theses that a conspiracy lay behind the developments that followed 1789. The circles studied by Cochin became, in other words, the wellspring of a first political party which developed and improved thanks to the events that followed 1789 and was decisive in the choice to go to war and then to overthrow the monarchy. From this point of view, the authoritarian acceleration of republican politics was read as the consequence of the inability of the new political class – especially the Girondins, whom Brinton pointed to as the true architects of radical change – to dominate the difficult political situation. In this context, the Terror became the conclusion of a political process that experienced swift disenchantment in relation to the patriotic project of social palingenesis. Faced with the difficulties encountered and a social world that seemed to reject the revolution's redemptive message, it became a time of coercion, of virtue imposed from above, which instead of inspiring a new order was transformed by a small group of extremists into an experiment in government. Thermidor signified the interruption of this downward spiral of revolutionary politics and the attempt to reopen a dialogue with a society seriously prostrated by the grim period of the Terror. Here, above all, Brinton's work went against the current, illustrating how Year II was not the culmination of the revolutionary process but only a moment of transition, a painful parenthesis in the liberalization process of French society. For this reason, the Directory period was largely transformed – no longer a time when corruption silted up and even less an inept experiment in government, but a stabilizing attempt to be regarded with interest. While it lacked social consensus, the new executive had worked well to give France a grounding in parliamentary life.

When his study of revolutionary history came out, however, Brinton had already embarked on another intellectual path, taking a keen interest in the perspective of the physiologist Lawrence Henderson who, on the basis of Pareto's reading, had suggested identifying the contribution of social disciplines to scientific ones. Brinton instead took an opposite line, studying how the scientific world could contribute to the social sciences. In 1939, he published his most well-known work, *Anatomy of Revolution*, a comparative study of the English, American, French and Russian revolutions. In this context, however, attention was drawn in particular to 1789, considered modernity's authentic watershed, from which all other revolutionary movements derived.⁹⁸

The French Revolution, after all, offered the example of a cyclical aspect: it consisted of an initial consensus for change, followed by the ephemeral triumph of the moderates, soon undermined by the radicalization of the political process, which then came to an end in a reaction to the intolerable growth of extremisms – revealing a repetitive mechanism that bore close similarities to the course of an illness. For this reason, Brinton was convinced that every revolution could be subjected to diagnosis. He also suggested that political analysts, on the basis of these analogies, could recognize the features of the phenomena and therefore indicate how to oppose, and even prevent, them. In other words, the work was a reflection of American concern in the face of a Europe shaken by the rising tide of totalitarian revolutions. In light of this, the work enjoyed great success in the post-war period, when it went through a number of reprints and became a point of reference for Hannah Arendt in making comparisons between the revolutions of the modern era. At the same time, it also marked the end of Brinton's specific interest in 1789, a subject he would never return to. His *Decade of Revolution* therefore remained largely unexplored as a study, and was soon forgotten as, in the United States, too, French revolutionary historiography made an energetic comeback.

5. Revolution's imitators?

In 1939, at the same time as *Anatomy of Revolution*, another work related to the drama of the times, *Dictatorship*, came out. Here, a young English scholar, Alfred Cobban, suggested reading the affirmation of dictatorship throughout Europe in a line of continuity with the distant revolutionary past.⁹⁹ The book made clear that, at the basis of what had happened in Russia, then in Italy, then in Germany, lay the Bonapartist precedent, where first uncle, then nephew, in a logic that was always authoritarian, had profited from the Jacobin dogma of popular sovereignty. The figure of one man holding the reins of power, in other words, whether Mussolini, Hitler or Stalin, owed a great deal to the French example, where the rise of the Bonapartes had never failed to pay homage to the general will.

In conservative public opinion, which looked with great suspicion at the democratization that followed the end of the First World War and blamed the rise of dictatorships on the lack of restraint over popular sovereignty, Cobban's perspective must have sounded an extremely attractive one and his ideas continued to circulate after the Second World War. In the early 1950s, in an occupied and divided Germany stunned by defeat and in search of a justification to explain how National Socialism could have come to power, Cobban's denunciation of the perverse intertwining between Jacobinism and totalitarianism came in useful in the attempt to shift responsibility for the horror that had taken place from the spirit of the German nation. With slightly different emphases, Gerhard Ritter and Ludwig Dehio thus tried to suggest that the National Socialists were nothing more than revenant Jacobins – an excrescence on the healthy body of the German nation that shared nothing with nineteenth-century Germany's political-cultural tradition, whose roots lay in the sectarianism of much of French politics between the eighteenth and nineteenth centuries.

Such ideas were not new, however: the link between National Socialism and Jacobinism had been introduced in 1933 by Gerhard Ritter as a response to Goebbels, who had celebrated Hitler's seizure of power by noting that, at that moment, the values of 1914 that the Weimar Republic had neglected were alive once more. This comparison is indicative of how both, albeit from very different positions, agreed to reject the French Revolution in order to lay claim to a Germanic specificity which, in their view, provided an alternative to the values of 1789. The perspective was linked to the cultural framework of Wilhelminian Germany: this was what *Sonderweg* meant and, at the very moment the war broke out, German intellectuals had, not coincidentally, returned to place great emphasis on this. In 1915, *Die Ideen von 1914* was published, written by Rudolf Kjelén, a Swedish political scientist, for whom the hostilities then in progress had far greater significance than mere political conflict.[100] The war that was being fought was instead, in his view, a decisive ideological challenge to replace commercialism and individual selfishness – the triumphant result of the diffusion of 1789's values – with the new morality based on duty, order and justice represented by Germanism. In the same year, Johann Plenge, with a book evocatively intertwining 1789 and 1914, attempted an even more daring operation, claiming that the Germanic model was, in dialectical terms, the complete overwhelming of the cultural significance of the revolution.[101] Against liberalism and the individualism that sustained it, Plenge summoned the developments of Germany's cultural nineteenth century to suggest another trajectory – one that rejected the role of the individual to the advantage of an organicistic structure, at the basis of which the rejection of capitalism involved the creation of a social model where statehood was dominant.

The differences between Kjelén and Plenge were not insignificant: the latter saw 1914 as the conclusion of 1789, recomposing the fragmented society that had emerged from the *ancien régime* in the name of Germanic primacy, while the latter limited himself to opposing two antithetical visions of world in order to announce that the reasons for revolutionary universalism were exhausted. And yet, the fact that, in 1933, Goebbels returned to Kjelén's approach, while Ritter responded to him from a position of conservative dissent, giving historiographical strength to Plenge's perspective, means that both of them, in any case, repudiated the cultural experience of the Weimar Republic, seen as the intolerable abjuration of the German political tradition in order to make way for an unacceptable foreign model.

They were not wrong on this point, either, given that during the 1920s, in an even more decisive way than in Great Britain, the ideological framework of French democracy had also encouraged the wave of cultural renewal in Germany. In other words, the defeat by National Socialism should not overlook the fact that, certainly in parallel with the maintenance of a historiographic tradition which defeat in the Great War had not hindered to any great extent, an attempt was also made to revive the values of 1789 in the now democratic Germany.

Hedwig Guggenheimer, married to Otto Hintze, the historian of institutions, represents the most significant example in this regard: from a wealthy Jewish family, in the aftermath of the First World War, she committed herself to demonstrating that Weimar Germany gave concrete voice for the first time to a national political tradition that during the nineteenth century, and in particular in 1848, had gambled everything on a close, democratic alliance with France.[102] In 1927, when she had already made the decision to devote herself to the study of the French Revolution, she confirmed this political line by publishing some writings by Hugo Preuss, the author of the Weimar constitution, who had died just two years before. This was her tribute to the statesman, who she defended against the accusations that immediately rained down on him from conservative circles of having drawn up a constitutional foreign to German tradition. On the contrary, Hintze suggested that Preuss was in line with a democratic tradition that had shown its worth in the nineteenth century at the time of the national revolution and had always indicated its debt towards the values of 1789. It was a reference that made it possible to grasp the guidelines of Preuss's constitutional decisions: he had done everything he could to build a new Germany, where the new state, unitary and decentralized, sidelined historical Prussia and established legitimacy in a combination of forces that, while heterogeneous, were nevertheless united by the ideal of a social democracy.[103]

Hintze's political ideas say a great deal about the reason for her interest in Alphonse Aulard, and, from 1925, she promoted, the first German translation of his *Histoire politique*.[104] In the introductory pages, she showed that she was very familiar with the debate on the subject in France and took a stand in favour of Mathiez, pointing out Aulard's lack of attention to the socio-economic issue. And yet, apart from this reservation, which reveals that she regarded the *Histoire politique* in critical terms from a properly historiographical point of view, her introduction was a sincere political eulogy of Aulard's work: it demonstrated, in her view, that 1789's values of freedom had become democratic at the time of the republic and had found full realization in that specific institutional framework. The example of 1792 was therefore also a light to the generations of her own time and should lead to what, Hintze believed, Aulard's work already particularly emphasized – the free and peaceful relationship between the democratic states of Europe in the name of the common values inherited from revolutionary France.

Hintze's decision to embrace the political-cultural world of revolutionary France was initially greeted with more than a little perplexity by German historians who were not at all willing to cancel their own tradition for a model which many of them had specifically studied to oppose. However, for Hintze the choice was fundamental in terms of building another tradition, one that rejected *Sonderweg* forever and brought the history of modern Germany back to the values inherited from 1789. Her thesis, discussed in the presence of leading historian Friedrich Meinecke, was dedicated to the historical development of the unitary principle and federalism in the *ancien régime* and revolutionary France. Published in 1928,[105] her work was immediately subject to the scathing comments of Albert Mathiez, for whom any deviation from the interpretative orthodoxy that he believed he had established clearly constituted a crime of historiographic treason.[106] Here, in fact, once more looking at the past to illuminate the present, Hintze touched on a subject that was still taboo for the historiographical doctrine of the Third Republic – specifically how, in revolutionary France, with all the consequences of the old order, the state was able to achieve unity and indivisibility. The hendiadys on which the democratic republic was founded was widely disputed by Hintze: she noted that 1789 was a revolt against centralization and the extent to which, in the early years of the revolution, the federative ideal was at the centre of the political debate within Jacobinism. In this context, Hintze stated her appreciation for the Girondins, noting the properly revolutionary aspect of the faction and suggesting that, when it fell, the democratic revolution fell with it. The theme therefore of unity and indivisibility, far from being innate to French statehood, was the result of a dramatic political involution. This had sacrificed France's revolutionary heritage in favour of an authoritarian solution at the basis of which, despite the attempts set in motion by the Directory, the figure of Bonaparte was already prominent. Needless to say, her ideas were considered largely heretical in France at that time.

The rise of National Socialism then put an end to the possibility of Hintze continuing along these lines and developing an interpretation of the revolution inspired by its European dimension. She was soon forced into exile without her ailing husband, first to France and then to Holland, and after war broke out tried in vain to secure a passage to the United States. Threatened with imminent deportation, she preferred to take her own life. Her tragedy summarizes the immense ease with which National Socialism, developing ideas on the continuity of the German spirit within national borders, was able to overwhelm any dissent inspired by the values of political democracy.

The same thing, a few years earlier, had occurred with Bolshevism, which also took an opposing view in relation to the Jacobin experience – so much so as to continue its tradition, to the point of assuming the role of its direct inheritor and then to conclude, in Stalin's time, with the incomparable superiority of their own Russian model to the precedent of 1789.[107] At first, the Bolsheviks had more than one competitor in this regard, and, from the February insurrection, references to the late-eighteenth-century event were squandered by all the various political parties. Kerensky, for example, had admired the republican position in 1792 and believed he could readily join the Entente in the democratic war on the Central Empires. However, first October, then the dissolution of the newly elected assembly and finally the peace of Brest-Litovsk swiftly confirmed that the Bolsheviks were the direct heirs of the Montagnards, but while, for example, they adopted the internal politics of the Year II government experiment, they rejected the idea of a patriotic war. However, the turn towards authoritarianism was not undisputed even in the field of historical writing: those who had tried their hand at the study of the French Revolution were also ready to underline the disturbing analogies between Bolshevism and the Reign of Terror.

In 1918, Nikolai Kareev, who had dedicated studies to the French countryside at the time of the revolution and was considered the leading Russian historian of 1789, completed a general, liberally inclined overview of the revolution, which condemned the revolutionary direction of Year II and immediately had the appearance of a – not too thinly veiled – critique of the shift towards dictatorship following October.[108] Evgeny Tarle, who before the First World War had written about the French workers in 1789 and during the revolution had sided with the socialists against the Bolsheviks, maintained his opposition stance and between 1918 and 1919 published a work on the Year II revolutionary tribunal which, in turn, sounded like a denunciation of the post-October repression.[109] The fact should also be taken into account that, leading the opposition against Lenin from the left, was Kropotkine, author a few years before of a successful history of the French Revolution that – as has been seen – had been highly popular with anarchist circles throughout Europe. The conclusion must be that, at first, the Bolsheviks did not enjoy a wide consensus in the world of historians and the references to the link between Jacobinism and Leninism were mostly a denunciation of an unacceptable move in the direction of dictatorship. This explains why the regime immediately took action, calling up those loyalists who were prepared to revisit the Russian historiographical tradition on the subject. The choice fell on Nicolai Lukin, a Bolshevik from the beginning, who had been in a tsarist prison in 1907. He left jai the following year and obtained a degree in history in 1910 with a thesis on the fall of the Girondins. At the time of the Russian Revolution, Lukin, who was only a university assistant lecturer, turned to journalism for his party and in Bolshevik-inspired papers emphasized the link between 1793 and 1917. However, the gates of academe would have remained closed to him if, after October, it had not seemed clear to Lenin that the world of education merited careful scrutiny. Lukin's name came up, and in a short time, he had ascended to the heights of Moscow University, while at the same time working on texts aimed at dictating the new regime's line regarding the interpretation of Europe's historical past. In the space of just a few years, he turned out five volumes, all of contemporary European history, including a portrait of the Western world, a more detailed look at Germany, a study of the Paris Commune, a general study of the revolutionary armies throughout the whole of Europe and a biography of Robespierre.[110] Above and beyond the value of all these initiatives, the pages dedicated to the Incorruptible took on the tricky task of confirming Robespierre as a protector and anticipator of Bolshevism and at the same time reaffirming the full originality of the experiment that had taken place in Russia.[111] By the end of the 1920s, difficulties were beginning to surface: Grigori Fridland declared the uselessness of any analogy between 1793 and 1917 – his opinion was that the Robespierrist dictatorship had been a matter of a petty-bourgeois democracy, broken by the aggressive return, in Thermidor, of the true interests of the very class it had hoped to represent.

There returned in these words, albeit skewed to the interests of Soviet primacy, the old argument of the French radical circles against Jacobinism, held responsible for the difficulties undergone by the proletariat and wholehearted participants in the unjust social order that emerged from the revolution. Thermidor had therefore been the highest point of the bourgeois revolution, and it made no sense to indicate it as the forceful revival of a world hostile to 1789. Fridland's perspective met with consensus among a new generation of Russian historians, who, mostly trained under the aegis of Lukin, set themselves the goal of valorizing 1917 by distinguishing it from, and contrasting it with, 1793. In this way, following Stalin's insistence on dictating the cultural line to all the other communist parties, they presumed to establish the new reading of the French Revolution at an international level and entered on a collision course with French historiography itself. Mathiez ended up paying the price for this: his *Reaction thérmidorienne* was harshly contested and when he died, in 1932, the

French Communist Party marked his passing by pointing out the irremediably petty-bourgeois nature of his commitment as a militant historian.[112]

Even more dramatic, however, was the fate of those who, in the Soviet Union, did not completely toe the political-cultural line. Accounts were first settled with what remained of the historiographic school prior to the revolution: Tarle was arrested under the accusation of having plotted a conspiracy, while Kareiev, now very old, died from the stress of psychological pressure. The purge then hit the early Soviet historians, about whom, evidently, the Stalinist regime harboured more than one doubt. Fridland was shot in 1937; Lukin was imprisoned in 1938. Tarle, publicly repenting and pardoned by Stalin, managed to save himself from the maelstrom of repression and undertook to conclude a general study of 1789, inspired by the regime, which Lukin himself had been working on before his fall from grace. The work appeared in 1941, in the midst of the patriotic war against Fascism and was a hodgepodge of positions expressed by the regime. The year 1789 was no longer 'the great revolution' but, more simply, a bourgeois revolution, whose chronological arc, 1789–94, once again emphasized the late-nineteenth-century dispute with regard to the grave responsibilities of Jacobinism for incapacitating the popular will. In this context, the analogy between 1793 and 1917 was duly contested and the discussion of events aimed to illustrate the episode as a necessary preliminary step towards the advent of another, proletarian and socialist, revolution. In this way, in the context of the recognition of the value of popular mobilization, judgement on Jacobinism was wholly directed at illustrating the class aspect of its political decisions: not Year II, but another revolution, in other words, would signify the overcoming of the bourgeois logic in which 1789 was begun and would come to an end.[113]

Events in the Soviet Union, like the parallel circumstances in Nazi Germany, demonstrate the significance of 1789 for totalitarian systems. Both aspired to represent modernity's one true revolution and, in this desire to represent what had never happened before, they were particularly careful to eradicate any historiographical voice that did not wholly take their side. Starting from the 1930s, Italian Fascism also tried to do the same thing, when, faced with National Socialist rivalry in the anti-Bolshevik dispute, it once again put itself forward as the champion of European modernity. Previously, until the advent of National Socialism, things had gone differently and Fascism had never set itself the problem of wide-ranging control over the Italian cultural world – as evidenced by the fact that reference to the values of 1789, whether in a democratic, liberal or strictly conservative context, remained for the most part in circulation.

In the field of political democracy, there was no shortage of interventions from those who continued to support the debt of the Risorgimento towards 1789, but rejected the Robespierrist direction of the revolutionary process. In a more specifically liberal context, the voices were once again raised of those who saw in the events of the French First Republic the sign of a democracy that seemed to them the enraged outcome of the 'vertiginous speed of the revolution'. In Catholic circles, the jeremiads continued against 1789's unnatural destruction of a world held together by the bonds of traditionalism. At first, the regime responded by proposing a national history along liberal lines that kept entirely within the country's own borders and held the example of 1789 at a distance from the process of forming the national spirit. However, during the

1930s, National Socialist rivalry imposed a change of course, and in this particular area it was useful for Mussolini to return to earlier interests, when he had even dedicated a sonnet to Babeuf and shared the beliefs of revolutionary syndicalists, who condemned the Year II government as a plutocratic executive. Under the aegis of the Duce, some of them were, unsurprisingly, asked to teach at universities – Angelo Oliviero Olivetti, Paolo Orano and Roberto Michels, who, influenced by the teaching of Georges Sorel, on that basis soon denounced Bolshevism as a variant of Jacobinism.[114] They all found a place at the fascist Faculty of Political Science in Perugia, established in 1929 with the aim of forming the regime's new ruling class. Here, the idea of Fascism as a vanquishing of 1789 took shape: Mussolini and his party had been able to bring to a conclusion that gigantic process of social and political transformation that the French Revolution had only initiated. Worth reading in this regard is the work of a young teacher, Giuseppe Maranini, published in the Faculty's series of fascist studies and dedicated to the Duce himself.[115] For the occasion, he reread Mathiez's work, which had just been translated into Italian, as concrete proof of the bourgeois and plutocratic dimension of the revolution and likewise underlined that the class struggle had taken shape thanks to the abolition of the guilds. Maranini therefore embraced the official line of the regime – the fascist corporative state had resolved the many contradictions transmitted from 1789 to the nineteenth century – but it was precisely this premise that led him to view the Terror as an instrument of government, which had allowed Robespierre to try, rightly, to interrupt the society-lacerating process in the aftermath of the subversion of the old order. And yet, leafing through Maranini's work, lingering on his sophisticated use of Jaurès and above all of Mathiez, his debt to leftist French historiography is clearly apparent. There was a great deal in those pages – that is to say that, starting from 1789, as a reaction to a liberalism that soon became predominant, the new economic order had begun to be questioned – that he completely agreed with, even if he immediately chose his own path in the matter of solutions: instead of an unacceptable communist perspective, he indicated the way for a renewed agreement between capital and labour under the aegis of the corporative order.

Maranini's work thus translates into historiographical terms the fascist claim to assume leadership in the field of totalitarian systems, crediting it, uniquely and solely, with the merit of having resolved the social question that had troubled European development since the immediate results of 1789. This approach was destined to radicalize the clash with liberal opposition circles, which insisted on the significance of 1789 and 1789 alone in European history, and democrats, who saw the Terror as the true precursor of Napoleonism and the modern dictatorships that came later. Maranini's reading of 1789 was the worrying reflection of a totalitarian approach which ended up further restricting the margins of manoeuvre of its opponents, some of whom had in the meantime been forced to go into exile.

One of these was Guglielmo Ferrero, an early opponent of Fascism, who had already distanced himself from the Terror at the end of the nineteenth century and viewed Bonapartism as the baleful product of the revolution.[116] In Swiss exile, between 1936 and 1942, the year of his death, he worked on a trilogy that focuses on the significance of the French Revolution in modern Europe. The first book is dedicated to the exploits of the young Bonaparte in Italy and suggests how the damaging seeds of authoritarianism were also sown on that side of the Alps.[117] The second one is an examination of how, after the Napoleonic storm, the Congress of Vienna had managed to re-establish stability, when, by analogy, Versailles in 1919 had failed.[118] The third one, *Deux Révolutions*, meanwhile, which appeared posthumously in 1951, contrasts the hopes for freedom raised by 1789 with the descent into the Year II horror of dictatorship.[119] In this work, Ferrero made 1793 the turning point between a revolutionary phase, which had nevertheless tried to create political legitimacy, and a subsequent one, in which the inability to achieve stabilization paved the way for the Terror and totalitarianism. From this point of view, a close analogy was often introduced between the direction taken by 1789 and the consequences of the Great War, which favoured both the Bolshevik revolution and the rise of Fascism. This is certainly an intriguing nexus, which deserves to be carefully circumscribed, since it has to be remembered that Ferrero had long had the Napoleonic issue at the centre of his interests and that this attention was the result of a concern, as it was of the whole Italian democratic camp, which long preceded the world conflict. To neglect this particular aspect would run the risk of losing sight of an important interpretative key to understand the assumptions that lay behind Ferrero's identification of two revolutions in the years following 1789 and why the second, the totalitarian phase, had, in his view, begun only after the fall of the Girondins – in other words, following the days of insurrection of 31 May and 2 June 1793. What has been suggested so far indicates rather that Ferrero's interpretation was not so different from that of nineteenth-century Italian historiography – relocating it, more appropriately, in the wake of the tradition started by Salvemini.

It has already been noted that the latter chose to interrupt his work on the revolution with the fall of the monarchy. Ferrero intended to develop the other's pages, continuing into the agitated initial phase of the Republic, in which optimistic expectations of a democratic life were swallowed up in the vortex of authoritarianism. He thought it possible to explain the impossibility, in such a tormented moment – after 1789, after the First World War – of seeing a *pars construens* succeed the *pars destruens*. The premises all lay in the Italian democratic and radical historiographical tradition which, since the second half of the nineteenth century, had distanced itself from the Terror and which, after the Great War, had felt no need for a reassessment of Robespierre's rule and the Year II revolutionary government. From there, Ferrero went on to indicate the breaking point of the legitimacy of the Convention in the fall of the Girondins, and therefore in the violence perpetrated by the Parisian sections against national representation. Acceptance of the coup, in other words, ensured Robespierre's definitive rise and the Committee of Public Safety's seizure of control, prepared to launch an illiberal power system that Bonaparte would merely continue and develop. But it is also true that writing these ideas in the midst of the Second World War, from his secluded exile in Geneva, meant both sounding the alarm for the destinies of European civilization and making a desperate profession of faith in parliamentary democracy, the only remedy capable of fighting the totalitarianisms that had taken shape after the First World War.

6

Revolutionary orthodoxy and historians' heresies, 1946–89

The victory over Nazi-Fascism marked a political and cultural turning point which had significant repercussions also on historiography. The delegitimization of conservative and reactionary views fostered the creation of an interpretative orthodoxy – also thanks to its proximity to the Communist movement then reaching its acme – whose interpretative parameters were being established through the works of the by now aged Lefebvre, as much in France as all over Europe. The challenge laid by Guérin, who tended to criticize the central role played by Robespierrism, seen as the forerunner of Stalinism, ended with a clear victory for the historiography of Lefebvre and his disciples, Soboul, Rudé and Cobb, leading to the deification of the Marxist interpretation of the Revolution.

Such hegemonic dominance, based on noteworthy studies of labour in urban contexts and of the peasant world, was, however, called into question both in the English-speaking area, by Cobban, and, in France, in the late 1970s, by Furet. Arriving at it from different perspectives, both disputed once again the teleological interpretation of the Revolution as the affirmation of the middle classes, favouring instead an approach privileging the content of political and intellectual debates. This view was strongly disputed as 'revisionist', though it gradually gained ground during the 1980s thanks to works by English-speaking historians demolishing the monolithic interpretation of earlier years. Such a plurality of views – new for the times – invited once again to turn to an Atlantic interpretation of the revolutionary events, which had already been given full treatment in the 1950s by Palmer and Godechot, who had insisted on the importance of the circulation of ideas and people within the Atlantic space, seen as the matrix of democratic modernity.

1. War on Guérin

The period after the Second World War opened up a new scientific life for Georges Lefebvre, which continued until his death in 1959. However, the drama, on a personal level as well, following the defeat of 1940, left a vivid mark on his figure as a scholar. Nor could it be otherwise: at the beginning of the hostilities he had resolutely sided with French military intervention and, even after the defeat, he had no intention of giving up. In April 1940, in a letter to his British colleague Thompson, he wrote that 'the majority of the people have realized, as have you over there, what is at stake and now that the Allies seem ready for action and are indeed acting, it seems to me that, in some respects, the most difficult times have passed.'[1] But times remained difficult, and Lefebvre, despite his retirement, spent the years of German occupation behind the walls of the *Institut d'histoire de la Révolution français*,[2] where he avoided the worst of the situation probably thanks to the protection ensured by certain members of the *Société des études robespierristes*, such as Georges Michon, its vice-president, and Paul Vaillandet, who had both in the meantime gone over to the side of the occupiers. Not long afterwards, in those terrible years, his brother Théodore, who had worked for the Resistance, was killed by the Gestapo.

These facts are sufficient to explain why, during the war, Lefebvre's political positions hardened, leading him to openly take a stance against the Socialist Party, which, in his opinion, had brought the country to defeat and was guilty, among other things, of serious responsibility for the parliamentary collapse of 1940 that would pave the way for Marshal Pétain. Hence his closeness, immediately after the liberation, to the Communist Party, in his eyes now the only openly revolutionary political formation. It was a decision that would also dictate a new cultural line in his studies of the revolution. He clearly justified this new orientation in an edition of the *Annales historiques de la Révolution française* in 1947, in which there was a communication, where Lefebvre responded directly to the accusations that Daniel Guérin had addressed to him from the left, in a work just published.[3]

In a few pages, the famous *Pro domo*, which constitute a kind of cultural autobiography,[4] Lefebvre defined himself as a student (albeit indirect) of Jaurès, moved away from Mathiez and spoke up for methodological rigour and respect for the scientific aspect of his discipline. Here, he above all reaffirmed his own consistency, noting that he had supported the same positions in his speech in 1933 in Arras, during the inauguration of a monument to Robespierre. His words then had provoked resentment within the *Société des études robespierristes*, because he had presented the Incorruptible as sincerely in favour of a defensive war, and because he had mentioned the threat of Hitler, to the perplexity of pacifists and conscientious objectors. There was, however, another reason why Lefebvre, now in the post-war period, referred back to his speech in 1933: in that circumstance, he had noted that Robespierre was hostile to the choice of appointing Briez to the Committee of Public Safety, since he had not prevented the city of Valenciennes from surrendering to Prussian troops. Here the analogy with the pacifists of the war years was obvious and aimed to remove any right of revolutionary citizenship from those who, rejecting the patriotic war or, worse, collaborating with the Germans, did not, once the national sacrifice was over, deserve to remain with the left. In other words, *Pro domo* foreshadowed a purge within the *Société des Études robespierristes*, from which Vaillandet was expelled. Michon himself, who, in Paris in 1941, published a volume of Robespierre's correspondence, dedicated to Lefebvre, for the *Société des Études robespierristes*,[5] was going to be removed, had he not, perhaps providentially, died in 1945. Experience of war and occupation therefore radicalized Lefebvre's political positions, pushing him to settle accounts with a left that had never accepted the patriotic direction that Jaurès had taken and that still, in 1939, refused to make 1793 the paradigm of French social democracy.

Daniel Guérin, with whom Lefebvre decided to cross swords while reviewing his *Lutte des classes* in 1947, represented that world, pacifist and libertarian, which the elderly follower of Jaurès wholly distrusted. Guérin, in fact, unlike Lefebvre, was not an academic but a militant politician who, first with similar views to the revolutionary syndicalist Pierre Monatte, had then followed him in his move towards the Communist Party. However, prevailing party dogmatism and the 1925 purges against the left wing had disillusioned him and convinced him, for lack of anything else, to join the Socialist Party in the early 1930s, occupying a place in the left-wing group led by Marceau Pivert. The Popular Front period saw him defend the demands of the workers, challenging the left-wing executive. His Trotskyite sympathies date back to this period, as well as his first analyses of fascism, an enemy to be fought at the same time as any political alliance with bourgeois forces was rejected. He became a convinced pacifist, while denouncing the unacceptable collusion between social-patriotism on the one hand and national-communism on the other, all to the benefit of the capitalist system.[6]

It was in these years, as the spectre of war came closer, that Guérin began to take an interest in the events of the French Revolution. Proof of this was his initial belief in Robespierre's pacifism, as indicated by the Georges Michon's research – Michon being Mathiez's pupil, later to fall under the influence of the German occupier.[7] There was also his intellectual and political proximity with Maurice Dommanget, who was passionately interested in the figure of Babeuf,[8] and with whom, in 1938, he organized some pacifist meetings. In the same period, Guérin joined the *Société des études robespierristes*, and he was still a member in 1946, confirming that he considered it to be a society that was certainly not devoted to proposing an image of Robespierre as a patriotic warrior. When war broke out, Guérin, true to his pacifist beliefs, decided to take refuge in Norway, where he arrived in September 1939 thanks to the support of *Nansenhjelpen*, an organization that assisted persecuted Jews. In Oslo, he began to publish a monthly bulletin directed at members of the International Workers' Front, a short-lived, pacifist-inspired, left-wing political group. In April 1940, shortly after the invasion of Norway, Guérin was arrested by the Gestapo and transferred to Germany as a civil internee. Not long after, at the end of December, he was released and returned to Norway, designated a 'pacifist refugee'.

Here – there is only his own testimony for this – he was forced by necessity to carry out various manual jobs: however, according to information from the Norwegian emigration office, during all of 1941, before returning to his homeland in 1942, he was 'employed by the German public authorities'. In any case, again according to his reconstruction of those times, it was at that moment that he decided to write a work on the great revolution. The research began in Norwegian libraries, continued in Paris during the German occupation, while he worked for a publishing house, and was on the library shelves soon after the Liberation.[9]

The *Luttes des classes* therefore grew out of the context of the dissent manifested by its author towards the politics of the French left. Since the experiment of the *Front Populaire*, which seemed to him to have artificially kept alive, with the assistance of the workers, the bourgeois democracy which he had always fought against, Guérin was quick to challenge the left-wing parties, considering them co-responsible for the crisis of the Third Republic and the disaster that followed with the war against Nazi Germany. For this reason, he had become passionately interested in the events of the First Republic and in relation to this, on the eve of the war, the 150th-anniversary celebrations certainly played an important role. For the occasion, 1793 was presented by all the left-wing parties, communists included, as a fundamental point of reference in terms of fostering the relationship between the masses and patriotism. But Guérin regarded the nationalist exaltation of Robespierre and the unanimistic interpretation of Year II as a plethora of lies, which professional historians had been happy to go along with. It was time, he thought, to reveal and report these lies once and for all. It was necessary, he believed, to turn the picture upside down and speak out: Year II was not the culmination of social democracy at all, but rather the highest point of a clash between the bourgeoisie and the popular masses, which had given rise to the modern class society.

In other words, the revolutionary government was not a socialist (or communist) epiphany but the instrument that had made bourgeoisie violence possible against the workers and its complete triumph on the social scene of modern France. Guérin made no bones about speaking as a revolutionary here and not at all as a scholar. In his book, he went back to the analysis of revolutionary dynamics deployed by Trotsky in the name of permanent revolution, as well as his admiration for Rosa Luxemburg's reading of mass spontaneity. However, while Guérin repeatedly expressed his modesty with regard to his work as a historian and proposed himself as a mere amateur in the world of historical studies, the truth is that his actual intention was to provide a new interpretation of the events. He therefore felt it was absolutely essential to clear the ground from the historiographical readings that had accompanied and endorsed the political myth of 1793. Thus, while he claimed the perfect right of politics to take precedence over scholarship, the work presented a number of in-depth interpretations with the aim of rereading all of them in an original way – an approach that led to a direct confrontation with Jaurès, another politician who had given himself over to history. Needless to say, Guérin was opposed to the founder of the SFIO, but at the same time he intended to emulate him: his goal was to write a new history of the French Revolution, one that dismissed the democratic tradition aggrandized by Jaurès to replace it with an openly class reading which, strongly influenced by 1917 Russia, would substitute the *Histoire socialiste* on the French left. It was an enormous undertaking: to put an end to Michelet's captivating myth, as well as to Jaurès's political example, in order to identify another way of making 1793 the starting date of modernity. It did not, however, come out of nowhere: since the origins of the Third Republic, many ex-Communards had contested the Great Revolution that was the political model of reference for their adversaries. In other words, Guérin had Gustave Tridon and the legacy of Blanquism on his side, together with Georges Sorel, the resolute enemy of all parliamentarism, as well as those who, at the beginning of the twentieth century, had opposed the favourable acceptance of Jaurès's representative democracy. Guérin was also careful to look beyond French borders: he therefore had Kautsky's Marxist reading as a point of reference, as well as Kropotkine's libertarian interpretation. While his attention to all the above was acknowledged, Guérin nevertheless believed that he could now supersede them: the example of Russia and the epochal developments that had followed had, in the meantime, thanks to the mediation of Lenin and of Trotsky, made it possible for him to reread the social conflict that had inspired the revolutionary decade in a much deeper way.[10]

Hence his decision – a wholly political one, once again – to emphasize only the republican period of the French Revolution, making the analogy between past and present even clearer; hence his decision to limit the discussion of events to the phase which began with spring 1793 and ended with the death of Babeuf in 1796, but dedicating almost all his numerous pages to the period running from the fall of the Girondins to Robespierre's final moments. In that short span of time, in his view, the dramatic contest was played out between the revolutionary bourgeoisie and the indistinct world of the working class – which Guérin, following Michelet, defines as *bras nus* ('bare arms') and says was not a proletariat in the modern sense of the term. And it was this social war, this class conflict that had always remained concealed beneath the reassuring cloak of the entire nation's revolutionary effort, that Guérin intended, once and for all, to reveal. In this regard, the procedure was all too linear, almost schematic and laid itself open to the easy charge of brutally dividing the revolutionary camp along social lines that were those of the twentieth century but not yet of the late 1700s. However, it was a risk that Guérin deliberately took upon himself – indeed, claimed openly, when he took the analogy between past and present as the guiding star of his venture.

Not surprisingly, playing with mirror images, he begins by denouncing the war of freedom initiated by the Girondins, blaming it on a conflict for commercial supremacy against the British, but making it clear that the conflict, the idea of the bourgeoisie and accompanying its rise, lay at the origins of those that would come after it and continue into the twentieth century. European war – not by chance the incubator for Russia's 1917 – was always, in Guérin's eyes, the decisive passage for the creation, at the time of the First Republic, of the class conflict that he intended to uncover. The cost of the war begun by the bourgeoisie was, however, through the choice of paper money inflation, to be paid by others: the 1793 price increases caused serious discontent among the working classes of the urban centres and favoured the rise of the *Enragés*. Marx had already indicated the latter as the true representatives of the revolutionary movement, and it is an idea Guérin follows, even when he notes the contradiction of their anti-capitalist and anti-bourgeois proposals, aimed only at regulating the traditional economic order through price controls and the forced distribution of products.

And yet, having made all this clear, Guérin nonetheless sees the *bras nus* as the true revolutionary element present on the scene, praises Roux and Varlet, but also (with a clear reference to Monatte) the unknown typographer Tiger. They all tried to overturn the representative framework of the revolution to put forward forms of direct democracy and even seemed, with the days of insurrection against the Convention of 31 May and 2 June 1793, to anticipate the modern dictatorship of the proletariat. But it was all in vain: Robespierre, by managing to have the assembly itself expel the Girondins, prevented the triumph of direct democracy, all to the advantage of the centrality of a Convention now dominated by his own party. These days, in Guérin's view, were the real turning point of the French Revolution: contesting Jaurès's reconstruction, who had defended the legal forms maintained by the Convention, he described a now irreconcilable clash between Montagnards and *bras nus*, which would give rise to a class conflict from which the bourgeoisie would emerge triumphant only through the violent repression of the popular movement.

And yet, again according to Guérin, although the defeat of the *Enragés* was inevitable, the clash lasted for months and in that period of time the revolutionary movement struck more than one blow in terms of both the practice of direct democracy (in the sections and the Commune, as well as in the surveillance committees and the revolutionary armies) and economic controls. It is true that the Montagnards, their victory complete, then went on to the physical elimination of the *Enragés*, but their place was soon taken by the Hébertistes. Guérin was quick to describe the latter as unscrupulous but, in accordance with Trotskyist theories regarding the need for popular movements to have political leadership, he praised them, too – in particular because they launched the initiative of the de-Christianizing campaign, certainly only to obtain the support of the popular masses, but soon triumphant thanks to the enthusiastic consent it received. The cult of the goddess Reason, with the ceremony at Notre Dame in November 1793, constituted for Guérin the peak of revolutionary momentum and, not surprisingly, in his view, it seemed to the bourgeoisie that a non-negotiable limit had been passed, forcing them to definitively settle accounts with the popular movement.

The Committee of Public Safety took charge of the matter, establishing a dictatorial system –bourgeois, authoritarian and centralizing – on behalf of the Montagnards, certainly aimed against the aristocrats, but equally against the popular movement, the Paris Commune, the capital's sections and all the militants who thronged therein. With the decree of 14 Frimaire, Year II (4 December 1793), the new regime gave the decisive push towards the creation of a modern, bourgeois and authoritarian statehood, foreshadowing what Napoleonism would only come to perfect during the nineteenth century, eliminating revolutionary spontaneity and the many self-managed powers in the country with a government staff loyal to the central power.

This was the context for Guérin's attack on Robespierre, regarded as the deceiver of the popular masses, the figure chosen by the Montagnards to mediate with the people, in the interests of the bourgeoisie. The author meticulously noted where the Incorruptible's exegetes, Mathiez especially, had allowed themselves to be dazzled by the imaginary figure of the champion of social democracy: in reality, Robespierre was the same as Danton, horrified by the revolutionary spontaneity of the masses. With all his might, he opposed the sections and the Commune, fought de-Christianization as much as ever and, always in the name of class interests, provided an example for Bonaparte. The reluctant concessions to the demands of the *bras nus*, the praise of the good people of the revolution, the decrees that apparently met the needs of the more radical circles were only so many defensive manoeuvres while waiting to strike the decisive blow against the working classes, at which point they would all be withdrawn. Evidence for this, in Guérin's view, lay in that only Mathiez's imagination could see, in the decrees of Ventôse, an attempt to redistribute property, the sacredness of which the Incorruptible never called into question. Rather, under the protection of Robespierre's popularity, technocrats went to work within the Committee of Public Safety: they soon developed an economic policy aimed at favouring bourgeois groups and decided to rid themselves of their ambassador to the people when he insisted on adopting a form of religion that had nothing to do with Catholicism and continued to show doubts about the wars of annexation. Hence, Thermidor and the true face of the bourgeois revolution that followed.

The popular movement certainly tried to resist against the economic disaster following the liberalization of prices wanted by the Convention, now that the Robespierrists were gone. The last gasp of the practice of direct democracy came first in Germinal and then, above all, in Prairial, Year III, halted by the last Montagnards – aggrandized by democratic historiography, but in reality, and once more, among the most ferocious opponents of the revolutionary momentum of the population. On the other hand, the defeated of Prairial were, in Guérin's view, the forerunners of those who would later rise up, first in 1848 and then in 1871: they therefore had to be rightly classified as the first combatants in a truly proletarian revolution. It is no coincidence that their sacrifice made the recovery of Babeuf a tempting gesture: private property would have been brought to an end for him, eliminating parliamentary democracy to the advantage of an insurrectionary body called upon to assume dictatorship in the name of the general interest. Hence, Guérin's recognition that the project of Babeuf clearly embodied a communal direct democracy that only the Soviets would later be able to realize.

Unfortunately, the sacrifice of Gracchus was made much of by Philippe Buonarroti, who communicated it to the nineteenth-century socialists, noting that, for the conspirators, the figure of Robespierre was the only reference point. The result was the birth of the legend of Year II on the French left and the triumph of the lie that the French Revolution was a decisive step in the struggle for the emancipation of the proletariat. Hence Guérin's conclusion that, in the study of 1789, the page should be definitively turned – it had to be said that the event was a damaging moment for the proletariat, given that the class domination of the bourgeoisie actually began with the government of Year II.

The ambitions of the *Lutte des classes* were therefore great, since the radical historiographical revision of Year II underpinned the intention to rebuild the entire French left. In the aftermath of the war, Guérin believed there was room for a new libertarian and pacifist communist left to put an end to the national patriotism that socialists such as the PCF still demonstrated. The point is decisive, and speaks volumes with regard to Guérin's desire to put an end to the political experiment started by Jaurès, fighting his decision in favour of representative democracy through the revival of direct democracy. In his opinion, the time was ripe for the French left, strengthened by what had happened in Russia in 1917 together with the Soviet Union's political experience between the two wars, to try to bring Marxism and anarchism closer together to struggle against bureaucratic and centralist statehood in the name of a revolutionary politic

In the aftermath of the Second World War, however, it was a project soon destined to dash itself against the wall quickly erected by the PCF. The latter, combining patriotism with devotion to the Soviet Union, managed to win over the left and establish itself as a definite point of reference for the majority of intellectuals attempting to reposition themselves in a Fourth Republic that found the path it was on made more than a little rocky by the first signs of the Cold War. In addition, Guérin's belonging to a left marked by syndicalism and Sorelian origins worked against him and his ideas – a left, too, which, shortly after 1940, had, in some cases, made its peace with the German occupier.

It is no coincidence that the demonization of the bourgeois dictatorship in the years of the revolution had informed the political discourse of Georges Albertini, a former socialist with ideas similar to those of the *Confédération générale du Travail* (CGT), but creator with Marcel Déat of the *Rassemblement National Populaire* (RNP), a new collaborationist party and, still in 1942, pronouncing very laudatory remarks with regard to the alleged pacifist and anti-bourgeois Robespierrism extolled by Georges Michon.[11] The latter, after all, in addition to continuing to write against Girondin belligerence in occupied Paris, suggested to Léon Émery, a former trade unionist-turned-collaborationist, to work on a general study of the French Revolution, concluded in 1944 but only published in 1955.[12] Here, equality is opposed to freedom, and it is noted that, in 1793, the civil war in the departments gave the revolution the look of a class struggle. The Terror is stigmatized, transformed first into the political vacuum of Thermidor and then of the Directory – into, in other words, a conservative and oligarchic republic dominated by plutocracy and arms.

The conclusion is clear: although Guérin claimed to interpret the very significance of the French Revolution in a completely new way, in reality his *Lutte des classes* was already outdated by 1946, trapped as it was between the ideological tensions of the immediate aftermath of the First World War and the new political context of France as it emerged from a second global conflict. And yet, he never gave up and in the following years, every time the political scenario seemed to reshuffle the left's cards, he repeatedly went back to the work, invariably re-presenting it as an infallible instrument for the correct analysis of the first modern revolution. It is no coincidence that in the following years, parallel to de-Stalinization, Guérin resumed intervening in the historiographical debate to respond to his numerous detractors. He confirmed his theories point by point and proposed a new unified period for the left, in which, to smooth over differences and affinities, the origin of all possible revolutions, present and future, could be recognized in 1793. That is why, immediately after 1968, he decided to publish a new edition of *Lutte des classes*, in which the Parisian May was interpreted as the continuation of the 1871 Commune and the Soviets of 1905 and 1917.[13] The work thus found a second life and accompanied the new left criticism of the centralism and authoritarianism that, undaunted, the Communist Party continued to demonstrate in France until 1989. And yet, the fact that the *Lutte de classes* became the reference text for a left that wanted to renew itself and for which the institutions of direct democracy were opposed to those of Soviet-style bureaucracy cannot conceal that Guérin's work had been produced in an outdated historical-political context – something that, despite new additions and claims of adaptation, would always leave its mark.

2. Père Lefebvre

In 1946, when *Lutte des classes* was published, Daniel Guérin had presented Georges Lefebvre as a 'disciple and continuator' of Albert Mathiez, pointing out how a certain 'shyness' had prevented him from moving away from the Robespierrism of his predecessor and above all from leaving behind the framework of bourgeois democracy. He even went as far as to express regret for the huge advance that historiography might have made if only Lefebvre had had the courage to distance himself from the environment in which he had been trained.

The comments on Lefebvre were not perhaps as harsh as they first looked, reflecting as they did the hope that the new interpretative line laid out in *Lutte des classes* would be able to find an echo in academic circles. Instead, the opposite happened: the work immediately received very negative criticism and in the following years Lefebvre and his school never missed an opportunity to underline the contradictions inherent in Guérin's ideas. Thus, in 1969, at the time of the publication of the second, revised and expanded, edition, of *Lutte des classes*, he felt forced to confirm all the criticisms of Lefebvre made in the previous version. Commenting on the career trajectory of the great father of revolutionary historiography, he added that, in his latter years, he had adopted a rigid Robespierrist conformism that his first writings had certainly never suggested.

By the 1970s, therefore, Guérin was making interesting distinctions in Lefebvre's historical work, identifying his post-war period as much less interesting than his previous phase, in which the master had shown himself intolerant in the face of any heterodox interpretation of the French Revolution and had become the scientific guarantor of a Robespierrism that reflected the authoritarian and statist dimension of the French Communist Party. All in all, even more than a judgement on Lefebvre himself, this idea represented an indictment of the French left after the Second World War – a left that had not known how, had not wanted, to recover the vitality and plurality that first the disaster of 1940 and then the hegemony at the time of the resistance had erased. Lefebvre's political biography, moving from his commitment to the Socialist Party at the time of the Popular Front to his sympathies for the Communist Party immediately after the war, seemed, as Guérin saw it, to wholly confirm this direction. He was not wrong, generally speaking – as we have seen, the war and the drama of German occupation had left their mark on Lefebvre, bringing a certain rigidity to his somewhat dogmatic reading of the revolution.

This decline can be followed starting with the handouts for the courses held at the Sorbonne under the German occupation: although retired, taking advantage of some funds made available to the rectorate, he continued as a lecturer. The chosen topics seem to testify to the will of the elderly historian to keep the political tradition of revolutionary France high on the agenda and, faced with a moment of enormous difficulty, not to give in.[14] With the Liberation, Lefebvre's retirement became official and, although he was unable to nominate his successor – in this case, Marcel Dunan, a colourless scholar of the Napoleonic period – he did manage, instead, to hang on to the direction, for life, of the *Institut d'histoire de la Révolution française*. Immediately resuming meetings of the *Société des études robespierristes*, of which he was still the president, Lefebvre believed the time had come to settle accounts with those who, in his view, bore responsibility for the terrible events undergone by the French nation.

He certainly blamed the entire Third Republic ruling class, which had betrayed its mandate by handing the country over to Pétain, but his contempt was particularly directed at the old *compagnons de route* – the fellow travellers within the socialist world that gave their consensus to the Vichy regime and support to Germany's National Socialist model, both gestures often fuelled by a pacifism which in 1939, in Lefebvre's view, had compromised France's ability to face up to the enemy challenge. His move in the direction of the PCF was therefore understandable, given that, since the times of the Popular Front, that political party had adopted the revolutionary myth as its own, defending the Stalinist purges of 1936 in the name of a new (and equally necessary) Soviet-style Terror. In the following years, the PCF chose to openly situate his historical-political point of reference in Year II.

Still in 1939, on the occasion of the 150th anniversary, some Communist historians, such as a very young Albert Soboul, who later became Lefebvre's favourite pupil, had adopted the political line that informed the demonstrations promoted by the government authorities. Lefebvre, in particular, in the aftermath of the conflict, in a France that had emerged from the Resistance, firmly maintained the revolutionary war of Year II as an example that the PCF had taken as a guideline in the course of its fight against the occupier.

It was natural, therefore, for Lefebvre, just after the war, to leave the socialist camp – which in the following years went on to disappoint him even further – to move to the PCF, the only political party he saw, in the name of the patriotic tradition of Year II, as having never succumbed to National Socialism. On the basis of this decision, demonstrated from 1946 on by his diligent collaboration with *Pensée*,[15] the PCF journal that played host to the intellectual world, Lefebvre returned to galvanize the organization of revolutionary studies. While the PCF's exclusion from government in 1947 and then France's membership of NATO in 1949 soon confirmed Lefebvre in the correctness of his move, his historiographical approach suffered greatly. The, by now elderly, historian soon displayed a sincere (and declared) adherence to Marxism, which, though it was something his new party very much wished to see, he had never supported before the war. His meeting with Ernest Labrousse became a reflection and support of this choice, the latter also a member of the PCF. This meant a decisive return of Lefebvre's interest in the quantitative model, though it was a perspective that lacked the plurality of intersections which, before the war, had gone into the building of his own historiographical originality. The most significant legacy of this last historiographical period are thus the *Etudes orléanaises*, which appeared posthumously between 1962 and 1963: here, the plurality of interests in his pre-war historiographical method seems to have been sacrificed to the advantage of a return to the quantitative method, in which economic history, based on a statistical approach, predominated over the study of mentalities.[16] This was the framework in which, in agreement with Labrousse, Lefebvre could relaunch his Marxist reading of the revolution, which seemed much more schematic than the one that had made it possible for him to publish his most significant works in the pre-war period. A pivotal point in this regard, and a decisive moment therefore in initiating Lefebvre's final historiographical phase, was his decision to return to the general study of the revolution's history that, in 1930, he had worked on together with Sagnac and Guyot.

With Guyot dead, Lefebvre easily obtained permission from Sagnac to go back to their work, combining it with his other writings that continued on from Mathiez's study to thus cover the entire revolutionary decade. The book came out in 1951 and went through multiple reprints and translations, consecrating Lefebvre's historiographical reputation with regard to the French Revolution.[17] It would be wrong, however, to see it as a collage of previous works: in the meantime, the new political framework and his use of the quantitative method had impelled its author to reread the events in a way that was certainly not foreshadowed in his pre-war works, even though they formed the basis of his writings.

The *French Revolution*, which followed the evolution of late-eighteenth-century events closely, constituted a sort of balance sheet of the studies carried out until then, in which politics, economics and social structures represented the narrative backbone. The year 1789 appeared as an irremediable rift between the *ancien régime*, a corporatist system with foundations in privilege and birth, and the period that followed the revolutionary watershed, marked instead by the advent of individualism. The bourgeoisie thus became a class fully aware of its potential and, thanks to 1789, would take part in the construction of the new civil order, becoming, through its own liberal decisions, the new centre of gravity. The struggle against the privileges of the Church and the aristocracy was also a necessary stage in the construction of a capitalist society, in which private property represented the basis of a new political system. The book, which paid great attention to the works of Ernest Labrousse, emphasized the interweaving of economic and social factors in order to identify the political perspectives opened up by the revolutionary struggle. In this context, the Terror, albeit determined by the need to defend France, constituted a useful element in terms of interpreting the changing power relations between the revolutionary political class and the popular movements in the cities and countryside. On the other hand, the rupture between Robespierre's government and the sans-culottes had played a key role: Thermidor and the end of the planned economy had represented the subsequent stages in the separation of two worlds that only necessity had briefly brought together. Babeuf's vain rebellion and Bonaparte's seizure of power, ratifying the triumph of a primordial form of capitalism in the French economic system, formed other points of reference underlining the importance of 1789 in the construction of modernity in both a liberal and a socialist perspective.

Considering the fact that this version constitutes Lefebvre's final word in revolutionary matters, the text on which any confrontation was based with those who were not in agreement with his ideas, it is inevitable to conclude that the destiny of the twentieth century's greatest historian of the revolution was a rather bitter one, given that there is no doubt that the period of his best work ended up being sacrificed to a moment far less significant. And all this took place precisely because Lefebvre's decisions after the Second World War became the polemical target of the many disputes that arose from the 1950s on, including those in response to his study. The consequence was that the interpretative approach of Lefebvre's latter years, especially after his death, and thanks to the personal attention of his followers, formed the ramparts where a resistance could establish itself – a resistance that historical-political developments made less and less defensible. And yet, it would not do justice to the complexity of things were it not mentioned that Lefebvre was also largely responsible for encouraging disputes against himself: after the controversy with Guérin, which marks the starting point of his warfare against any reconstruction that deviated from his own, he showed great determination in presenting his position as a hegemonic one, including through meticulous control over revolutionary studies inside and outside France.

In this context, scientific and political at the same time, the interest of a generation of European historians in his teaching developed a mirror-like form. There were many who looked with admiration at his work, with its increasingly evident dogmatic features: East German scholar Walter Markov, who started studying Jacques Roux, the *enragé* who had so fascinated Guérin;[18] the Italians Alessandro Galante Garrone and Armando Saitta, who dedicated their work to the Robespierrist figure of Philippe Buonarroti;[19] from England, the aforementioned J. M. Thompson, and from Switzerland, Alfred Rufer,[20] continued to acknowledge his teaching as undisputed. All were in agreement on his work and deferential towards his figure. The reasons for this admiration obviously varied. For historians from what was now Europe on the other side of the Iron Curtain, reference to Lefebvre was also an opportunity to try to escape the strict rules that communist countries imposed even on historiographical reconstruction (Markov's difficulties are there to testify how compromising it was to try to find a balance in research between political faith and impartiality).[21] For historians in Western Europe, the Italians above all, what was important was the image of a scholar who saw 1793 as the starting date of a social democracy that was even capable of assimilating 1917 without being sucked in by it – that succeeded in retaining primacy in the political civilization of continental Europe with respect to the threat arriving there from the Anglo-American world. Exemplary, in this regard, is the work that Franco Venturi dedicated to Jaures and other historians of the French Revolution in 1948, which emphasized Lefebvre's exceptional importance. Venturi compared him to Jaurès, preferring him to Mathiez, but he was silent with regard to his post-war ideas, praising only the first period of his research.[22]

This fascination, its deep roots lying certainly in Lefebvre's figure as a militant historian in the 1930s, remained powerful until his death, and throughout the 1950s, in the concrete field of research, it overcame his own political ideas, which were not always completely shared by those who explicitly continued to refer to his teaching. The most significant example is offered by the studies of those who, attracted by Lefebvre's diatribe with Guérin just after the Second World War, set about renewing the study of popular movement in urban centres. Reference is obligatory here to Albert Soboul, who studied the Year II sans-culottes with a monumental thesis published in 1958,[23] and to the English historians George Rudé and Richard Cobb, who, roughly around the same time, published two important works dedicated respectively to the protests of the urban working classes and the organization of the Year II revolutionary armies.[24] The Norwegian Kåre Dorenfeldt Tønnesson should also be mentioned, who tackled the final phase of popular movement with an extensive monograph on the failed uprisings of Year III.[25]

For all of them, Lefebvre's masterful work in the *Grande Peur* was a constant reference point for their studies of the political mentality of the working classes in a properly urban context. Furthermore, they all dealt with the issue with the Lefebvre-Guérin dispute in mind and, certainly not coincidentally, were critical of Guérin's central ideas in the many articles they produced in preparation for their works. And yet, their work, which involved massive amounts of archival investigation, did not manage to erase what Guérin had succeeded in putting forward with just the help of printed sources. It was even possible for Guérin, in 1965, to indicate Soboul and Cobb's work as following on from his own – though the latter never mentioned him, they came to conclusions quite similar to those he had already reached some time before.[26] There was more than a little truth in Guérin's comments. Soboul's work placed at its centre the relationship between *sans-culotterie* and the revolutionary government, highlighting more than once that the Committee of Public Safety bore clear responsibility first for its containment and then its elimination, something that greatly advantaged a bourgeois continuation of the revolutionary course. At the same time, Cobb's work exalted the popular dimension of the revolutionary armies and pointed the finger against Robespierrism, charging it with direct responsibility in the work of devitalizing the popular movement.

Guérin, with right on his side, found it an easy matter to overturn the accusations against him, pointing out the particular positions (Lefebvre's teaching, in other words) that inspired this criticism of his past work. In this, he could count on the solidarity of a British scholar from a very different ideological background, Alfred Cobban – of whom more later – who, in the mid-1960s, was able to conclude that the dispute was mainly a matter of Guérin's Trotskyist reputation rather than a question of two different versions of the revolution.[27] In his opinion, not a mistaken one, all historians in France, from Lefebvre to Guérin, saw the French Revolution as the fundamental political point of transition in the birth of the capitalist and bourgeois system. And yet, when Cobban came to this conclusion, the period of study that provoked his remarks was long over.

George Rudé, whose communist sympathies resulted in his making a career in Australia, soon moved away from the study of the French Revolution to address popular protests in a broader geographical and chronological framework.[28] In later life, in 1988, on the eve of the bicentenary, he produced a general study (that dutifully follows the line laid out long before by Lefebvre).[29] While Tønnesson actually vanished from the annals of historical research, Cobb, who was never a Marxist, continued his research on the revolution, retaining Lefebvre's interest in the revolutionary mentality, but in the end rejecting his overall reading of the event and indeed – coming round to Guérin's way of thinking albeit from the opposite side – developing an increasingly caustic anti-Robespierrism.[30]

This only left Albert Soboul to take charge of Lefebvre's legacy, inheriting the directorship of the *Annales historiques de la Révolution française* and also editing the *Etudes orléanaises* for posthumous publication. A few years later, in 1967, Soboul managed to take over the direction of the *Institut d'histoire de la Révolution française* from Marcel Reinhard, who had replaced Dunan in 1955. His arrival in Paris after a few years of university teaching in Clermont-Ferrand marked the apogee of his career as a scholar and seemed to restore full university dominion to the historiographical tradition which, through Mathiez and Lefebvre, acknowledged its ancestry in the work of Jaurès. Soboul came to his new position with a reputation boosted by a general study of the revolution that he hoped would dictate the line to be followed in the years to come.[31] This was not a new piece of work: the first version was published in 1939 for the 150th anniversary,[32] to be followed by a second version, *La Révolution française 1789-1799*, shortly after the war.[33] Then, some years later, after his enormous work on the sans-culottes, came another version, this time entitled *Précis d'histoire de la révolution française*. Published in 1962, he intended it to gather together and sum up Lefebvre's historical inheritance.[34]

However, the initiative was not as fortunate as was hoped: in those same years, first in Britain and the United States and then in France, too, the interpretative model that supported the structure of the work was openly questioned. The *Précis*, in its established form after going through a number of different editions, was extremely vulnerable to criticism, laying firm claim to the interpretative legacy of Lefebvre's later work while greatly tightening up the guidelines in this regard. Previously, however, Soboul's interpretation of the revolutionary decade had been much more flexible than the latest version of his study suggested – a flexibility that leads to the conclusion of the previous versions' analysis, where the Jacobins are presented as the force closest to the popular movement: capable, in other words, of establishing a political alliance to the advantage of the Convention. Soboul, however, preferred to emphasize the political spontaneity that inspired the action of the sans-culottes, for whom he felt genuine empathy.[35]

Compared to this line of interpretation, the 1962 version instead constitutes a schematic reproposition of the reading of 1789 as a bourgeois-capitalist revolution, with every nuance and distinction stifled in the dogmaticism of its approach. The revolutionary decade thus becomes an exceptional period in which anti-feudal struggle overlaps with the advent of the bourgeoisie as well as the birth of capitalism in the name of a promise of liberty, but also of equality, that is soon capable of involving the entire French nation. Hence the revolutionary event, with its democratic inspiration finding its apex in Year II, when the period of the Terror seemed a turning point in the emancipation process of the lowest classes and therefore a decisive step in the liberation process of the oppressed – foreshadowing, in its universalistic significance, the Russian Revolution of 1917 itself.

In the following years, this reading became even more inflexible as an entirely defensive response to the demolition work carried out on his ideas by the new interpretations of 1789. Soboul saw in this flood of criticism a sort of unacceptable challenge to the universe of values which he had believed in since the 1930s. He thought – wrongly, even if the error was more than understandable given his personal history – that the new reading of the Revolution were undermining the founding values of the French left's political identity: patriotism, Marxism (in its Leninist form) and respect for the political experiment that the Soviet Union had launched with such immense difficulty. Soboul thus rose to be the high pontiff of a historiographical orthodoxy which, rejecting the idea of any dialogue with the other party, he ended up – vainly – fighting against until the last day of his life. At the time of his death in 1982, however, the line was already certainly drawn. He fought against revisionist readings to the bitter end, seeing in them a barely disguised way of attacking the revolution's leftist identity, but, the wind in their sails, they sailed forward to their appointment with the bicentenary. Even though, after 1968, exorcising the dissent of a Maoism-fascinated left, it seemed a definitive interpretation of the revolution and therefore an authentic centre around which, thanks to the Marxist analysis of 1789, the progressive destinies of humanity could be mapped, this was soon revealed as simply a sensational illusion. With its failure, it was destined to create a void that today, even more so than in the recent past, seems too difficult to fill.

3. Conflict across the Channel

Soboul's adventure at the Sorbonne did not begin well: while he successfully managed to cope with student protest, which had rediscovered Guérin's reading, he soon ran into difficulty with regard to revisionist interpretations, which contested the reconstruction of 1789 in a Marxist-Leninist context and expressed disagreement with Lefebvre's school of historiography. The result was that, for the duration of his time in Paris, Soboul had to fight a rearguard action in order to protect the sacredness of an interpretation of the revolution that he defined as classic. He lost twice over in the confrontation, however, soft-pedalling the innovative system of his research, but, despite this sacrifice, not managing to avoid defeat.

In his partial defence, the fact is that he inherited a situation already largely compromised: criticism of the reading that, from Jaurès onwards, was based around the centrality of Year II, dated back to before the 1960s and in particular to the immediate post-war period, when it was closely intertwined with Cold War developments. Rebuke began as a response to the interpretation that identified (and at the same time claimed) a direct bloodline between 1917 and 1793: the link between the two revolutions – sustained by the Soviet Union itself, with Stalin represented as a new Robespierre – soon prompted the opposing camp to take it up again with a contrary perspective, the radiant future of socialism replaced by the descent into hell of totalitarianism. In this context, there is no doubt that counter-revolutionary writers – think of the success of Gaxotte's *Révolution française*, which, undaunted, went through various reprintings after the war – soon joined forces with their liberal colleagues, very concerned about the triumph, in Western Europe, of an interpretation that went along very much with Moscow's wishes.

One work opposing the rise of communism, and with the idea of historicizing Soviet despotism by linking it back to the Terror, was Jacob Talmon's *The Origins of Totalitarian Democracy*. Talmon was a Polish Jew who had found refuge in England during the war and then moved to Israel. In the overheated ideological climate following 1945, it described the birth, thanks to Rousseau's success during the French Revolution, of a totalitarian democracy that would assert itself and attempt to overwhelm its liberal rival. This totalitarian aspect would take shape at the time of Year II, return in the Babouvist utopia and then become highly successful, first in France's political nineteenth century and then, thanks to the Bolshevik revolution, throughout Europe.[36]

Talmon's work, a staunch liberal's indictment of Year II, would go completely unnoticed in France. Things went differently in Britain: his work came out in the context of renewed interest in French history, with Alfred Cobban leading the way – he was thanked by Talmon for having followed him in his research. Cobban, as seen earlier, had already dealt with the concept of dictatorship; he had also studied Burke and Rousseau,[37] among other things, and then moved on to study 1789 following the confrontation in Great Britain between those who tried to provide a Marxist interpretation of the English revolution of 1640 and those who instead peremptorily rejected the idea. With this debate in progress, Cobban thought of looking again at the bourgeois aspect of the French Revolution and he was soon pointing his finger at those who, in his view, neglected the concrete mechanics of the historical process to the advantage of a determinism that suggested that a new class would inevitably rise triumphantly from the ruins of the *ancien régime*.

He lit the fuse to his 'revisionism' with a brief public speech, given in 1954, the title of which, *The Myth of the French Revolution*, is self-explanatory.[38] Cobban challenged the capitalist and bourgeois aspects of the revolution by noting that the year 1789 had not replaced the *ancien régime* with a new social order and had, even less so, favoured the development of capitalism in France In his view, feudalism was no longer present in eighteenth-century France and the ancient rights of the aristocracy were rightly classified under that heading. For Cobban, the bourgeoisie itself – if that term was meant to encompass capitalist groups – was an invention of the historiographic determinism of France: the revolution was not their work; indeed, its aim was to combat developments of this kind in the economic system. Cobban went on to emphasize this particular line over the following years. In 1958, in another work,[39] he took twentieth-century French historiography as a point of departure. No one was spared: not Jaurès, crushed by the idea that history originated with economic interests; not Mathiez, with his unacceptable dogmatism in the materialistic conception of history; not Labrousse, too entangled in the economicist schematism of bourgeois triumph; and not Lefebvre, castigated for a Marxist direction that to a great extent ended up invalidating the originality of his research.

A few years later, when the works of Rudé and Soboul had relaunched that same interpretation, Cobban felt that the time had come to renew his own challenge, even if it was no longer Marxism to be targeted, but its Leninist drift. It seemed to him that most recent French historiography warped the study of economic development and social structures simply to suit a reading dominated by the struggle for power. In other words, in the name of Marxism-Leninism, French historiography had gone back to an old approach that accentuated the reading of 1789 in a wholly political light that neglected the specifically social dimension. In 1964, publishing his interpretation of the French Revolution, Cobban clearly had Soboul's *Précis* in his sights. It seemed to him to sum up that new direction: wrong to believe that a bourgeois and capitalist revolution had overthrown an ancient feudal order; wrong to treat *sans-culotterie* as an anticipation of the working class, which nevertheless would always remain within the framework of the bourgeois revolution; wrong to transform peasant revolts into a phenomenon subverting the feudal system of production and therefore glorify them in a movement that would inevitably be subsumed within the properly bourgeois uprising; wrong to see in the party struggle within patriotism the reflection of bourgeois groups that would soon be in conflict with each other.[40]

Cobban, on the other hand, rejected the idea of a revolutionary bourgeoisie: 1789 had been the work of a mix of middle classes that regarded innovation with extreme suspicion – so much so that it found support in the countryside especially, where the end of aristocratic rights, benefitting a wholly traditional system of production, meant they could not be classified in terms of a revolution of modernity.

Likewise, in urban centres, *sans-culotterie* was simply a political phenomenon, with nothing especially social about it, the section militants made up of a host of different elements held together only by a mistrust of economic liberalism, which seemed to them damaging to the relatively advantageous positions of the traditional guild system. Cobban's conclusions were lapidary: it was not a growing bourgeoisie that had brought about the revolution, but a middle class that had been on the defensive for some time, incited by an economic vision of the old order, composed of landowners, rentiers and public officials. For all these figures, the watershed of 1789 meant their role being reproposed in a social structure that seemed instead to call it into question.[41]

It was no coincidence that the revolution, triggered by aristocratic protest, had found its most fervent supporters in the officials who had obtained the abolition with compensation of the venal offices they had until then occupied and had profited from the subversion of feudalism. In short, their revolutionary action rose out of a sense of frustration with regard to the impossibility of ascending a social ladder still dominated by an aristocracy that induced them to radicalize the conflict in order to carve out a space for themselves they had never previously envisaged as property owners and rentiers. These figures, whose ideological universe had no room for the abolition of feudalism, knew only how to take advantage of the favourable moment and turn those peasant revolts to their own use, as rebellion led to the abolition of aristocratic rights and to lands otherwise reserved only to the nobility becoming available on the market.

In Cobban's view, there was therefore no anti-feudal front consisting of a close alliance between the bourgeois and peasant world, but a widespread intolerance towards the aristocracy's ability to become bourgeois itself, through participation in the business world and its willingness to include a moderate inclusion of *roturiers* (commoners) in its own ranks. In this way, in the countryside, Cobban believed, the revolt was against this new form of lordly power, which in some cases had also taken on a capitalist aspect that the rural masses had been quick to reject. The revolution in the countryside, in other words, seemed an opportunity for a bourgeois class on the fringes of social ascent to break the power hold of aristocratic dominance and acquire the prospect of a career in civil and military administration which had previously always been denied to them. For this reason, the revolution was as much opposed to the aristocracy as it was to the affirmation of capitalism: it was a class of firmly conservative property owners, in both countryside and city, who stood to benefit, their distrust of modernity in the production sector stretching across the whole nineteenth century.

Cobban's view, then, was that there had never been a revolution in 1789, but rather a plurality of revolutions: while they had very little in common with one another, they had, with difficulty, in that particular year, found a common goal in the fight against aristocratic privilege. The revolutionary events thus lost all sense of consequentiality, their origins lying in the fortuitous intersection of a variety of unpredictable circumstances. Hence Cobban's proposal for an empirical approach to the subject, one that acknowledged that the revolution could only be evaluated over a long arc of time and that its meaning could not be based on an analysis limited only to its own specific period.

This explains why Cobban never wrote a history of the French Revolution himself: in his opinion, those years were not the watershed between the old order and the modern world, something only Tocqueville and Taine had previously dared to suggest. In the context of French history, the revolution was only a period of great importance, where a governing class shaped by anti-aristocratic sentiment took over the leadership of the nation, never to leave. Its main accomplishment, however, was that of maintaining, through the Napoleonic experiment, a clear line of continuity with its *ancien régime* past.

Needless to say, Cobban's ideas were largely ignored in France. Lefebvre himself dismissed his 1954 lecture,[42] while his *Social Interpretation* was reviewed by Jacques Godechot with equal severity.[43] But there was also no lack of criticism from English-speaking historians: Norman Hampson in Britain and Crane Brinton in the United States protested firmly against an interpretation that seemed to them much ado about nothing.[44] Apart from the specific merit, their comments speak volumes about the extent to which Cobban actually called into question not only the French canon of interpretation but also the very approach that had been successful between the two wars on both sides of the Atlantic Ocean. In Britain, his reinterpretation of 1789 clashed head-on with the reading, favourable to the revolution, that appeared following the First World War and, after 1945, maintained its presence in Albert Goodwin's own work. The latter – a lecturer in Manchester, but trained in Oxford under Thompson's guidance – had published a history of the French Revolution in 1953, its third and last edition in 1965.[45] Here, he presented the story of the early years of the Revolution, 1789–94, in the light of an irreducible conflict between aristocracy and democracy, suggesting that the clash arose from the Crown's aggressive reaction towards every possibility of transformation, even after the turning point of 1789. From this point of view, Goodwin read the declaration of war – something he was ultimately in favour of, since it made it possible to reveal Louis XVI's treachery – and the insurrection of August 10, which seemed to him only the consequence of the counter-revolutionary threat, as well as the days of 31 May and 2 June 1793, as in turn dictated by the panic that galvanized the Paris sections in the face of military reversals. It was a short step from here to greatly limiting the differences within the democratic movement: Jacobins and Girondins, in his opinion, were not so unalike and only the dramatic events of revolutionary politics following the beheading of the king caused division between them. Robespierre's own political actions demonstrated this: the execution of the Hébertists and then of the Dantonists was not preordained, reflecting rather the Incorruptible's need to remain with his own group at the centre of the political process – only from that position was it possible for him to contain the subversive forces arising from popular protest. Hence the decision to control the economy, as well as the political developments and religious decisions of the Terror – all responses in some ways improvised, and above all endured, with respect to the demand for social palingenesis, and for protection against the aristocratic enemy, that came from the Parisian sections. Goodwin could thus conclude, especially in relation to Talmon, that it was wrong to compare 1793 to 1917 in Russia: the period of the Terror, precisely because of this direct connection with the political situation of the moment, could in no way be ascribed to a system and as a consequence could not be accused of having given rise to twentieth-century totalitarianism. The revolution remained the dawn of democracy, where the theme of popular sovereignty had found its first, profound application in the field of politics: Bonaparte's overcoming of the Directory could not conceal the fact that the period of the Year III constitution, despite succumbing to the Napoleonic sword, had marked an important stage in this regard. The conclusion was to revive the truly European nature of 1789, something Goodwin would always firmly support, emphasizing in the following years the role of the French Jacobins in the construction of British democratism.[46] It was a reading that chimed with Brinton's, who believed that Cobban simply wanted to make a space for himself in the historiographical debate by raising the stakes against a historiographical tradition that was far from static. Indeed, thanks to its fortunate involvement with other disciplines in the early twentieth century – particularly sociology, which Cobban heartily disliked – it had developed its own originality.

However, as interpretations, their fate was sealed. In the field of empirical research, Cobban's theses greatly encouraged the study of multiple themes and subjects in revolutionary history in territorial contexts that were often never investigated: the result was a wealth of works that differed fairly emphatically from Lefebvre's ideas with regard to the origins of 1789. This is clearly reflected in the various studies that came out in those years, even though they remained within the traditional chronological parameters of 1789–94. In 1963 Norman Hampson, who also studied in Oxford with Thompson, agreed that bourgeois dissension in relation to the old order was not only economic in nature.[47] Shortly thereafter, in 1965, one of Cobban's own students, Michael Sydenham, ventured to produce a general study along purely political lines, which highlighted the substantial social homogeneity of the revolutionary parties that had fought each other so bitterly.[48]

However, criticism of Lefebvre's reading accelerated during the 1960s with the work of a student of the French historian Richard Cobb, who, starting out alongside Soboul and Rudé, soon moved away from them. Teaching at Oxford, he increasingly distanced himself from his old teacher through a social reading of the revolution that aimed to emphasize the concrete impact of 1789 on ordinary people. His discovery of a prosopographic method and the attention he increasingly gave to the years where documentation was better (especially those following the Terror) favoured consideration of the Directory period among his students. From this particular chronological context, where ideological fury (of the events, but above all, perhaps, of its interpreters) seemed largely to have faded, there originated a crop of studies that accompanied the critique of the significance of the revolutionary decade's epochal transformation. Examination of the concrete impact of the revolution on the daily life of single individuals or small, specific groups in the wider context of the French provinces thus ended up prompting reconsideration of the main historiographical categories still in use at the beginning of the 1970s.[49]

Curiously, the perspectives of Cobban and Cobb, so different from one another, helped their students to distance themselves from the political-ideological cornerstones across the Channel, to the advantage of an empirical approach to the history of the Revolution. The rejection of Marxist categories was accompanied by great indifference towards theories and led to a very critical historical judgement of 1789. In 1978, John Morris Roberts, a specialist in contemporary history very close to Cobb, gave a measured account of these developments.[50] Here, political events were profoundly influenced by war, first at the frontiers and then within France itself, which determined the dramatic stages of the revolutionary process. Yet, in Roberts's view, there is such a tangle of continuity and discontinuity in the events that discrimination and contrast are made difficult: on the one hand, modernity is confirmed by the profound transformations in the world of politics, where revolutionary action is informed by a new language, and which overshadow the fact that there were no great, immediate changes in the specifically socio-economic area; on the other, the element of continuity returns repeatedly in his pages to indicate that the transformations announced with 1789 struggled to make their way into French society and appeared there in times and ways that would only be defined by the full extent of the nineteenth century.

Meanwhile, still in 1978, the publication of François Furet's *Penser l'histoire de la révolution française* also opened a new phase of study in the English-speaking world – a world that felt very comforted in its revisionism by the fact that, by now, even in France, Lefebvre's reading was being openly questioned.[51] At the same time, there was a new international political climate tending towards a revival throughout the West of a liberalism often inflected with strongly conservative features, as well as the imminent bicentennial, which scholars expected would inevitably establish the terms for reading 1789. In the English-speaking world, all this favoured an explicit relaunch of Cobban's ideas, as is clear from the principal histories of the revolution that appeared in English in the 1980s. The most significant of these included Donald Sutherland's history of the French Revolution (and Counter-revolution) in 1986 – he was a student of Cobban's at the time;[52] and in 1988, another former student, John Bosher, published a *French Revolution* to sit alongside William Doyle's *The Oxford History of the French Revolution*.[53] Finally, in 1989, Simon Schama, who had studied with Cobb but admired Cobban, published a chronicle of the French Revolution, which, in publishing terms, enjoyed the greatest success.[54]

These works, although different sensibilities are at work in each, have certain distinctive traits in common: they all make use of an empirical approach, one that ends up rejecting the classic social interpretation of the revolution in favour of a political reading in which chance and unpredictability are predominant; judgement of the revolutionary outcome, meanwhile, is mainly critical. But there are remarkable differences between the four texts, nevertheless, and these, albeit with varying levels of intensity, sum up the work on 1789 that had been carried out in the meantime. Doyle's study in particular shows to what extent the interpretation of the origins of the French Revolution had moved away from Lefebvre's model: here, the revolution begins with an elite where aristocrats and middle class mix together, galvanized by the intention of obtaining a few political concessions – the lower classes joining in the fray only at the last moment. It was a belated and precarious conjunction, a sore weight on the work of the Constituent Assembly, which, with its often authoritarian measures, was portrayed as bearing the real responsibility for the radicalization that took place over the following years. According to Doyle, at the end of 1791, the Legislative Assembly inherited a situation that had already deteriorated terribly, riven by political conflict within the social groups. The disastrous consequence of this was the decision to go to war in an attempt to rally the revolutionary front. With the outbreak of hostilities, the infighting actually increased, dictating the various political phases, from the fall of the Girondins to the Terror to Thermidor. Given that Doyle adopts the traditional reading of the Directory, its unpopularity explaining Bonaparte's rise, the inevitable conclusion must be that his work illustrates the sensational failure of revolutionary politics, which dragged into the nineteenth century all the problems it had raised but been unable to solve.

Sutherland's reading of a few years before presents notable similarities, though here it is counter-revolution rather than war that is placed at the centre of the vertiginous process experienced by the new order. If it is true that resistance to change determined the revolutionary momentum, the opposite is also true: the decisions of the Constituent Assembly froze those who remained in an attitude of prudent expectation of change. Sutherland's reading of the revolutionary (and Napoleonic) period thus appears to show instability marked by an ever-diminishing consensus in relation to the new order, which ends up setting not only revolution and counter-revolution, but also the revolutionaries themselves, against each other. Hence, the birth of the republic, the clash between the democrats, the intervention of the *sanculotterie* and, ultimately, the Terror as an instrument of government centralization designed to stabilize, albeit artificially, a regime that increasingly seems to lack social consensus. Sutherland also sees Thermidor as the closure of an authoritarian parenthesis: however, due to the violence and opposition that had gone before, it leaves a dramatic backwash on the Republic's course – thus, the failure of the Directory's liberal experiment and the rise of Bonaparte, restoring a state power that seems to link back to the monarchy of the *Grand Siècle*.

If Tocqueville informs Sutherland's conclusive judgement, in Bosher's work, and especially in Schama's, there seem to be other, far more conservative, tutelary gods. Bosher shows a poignant nostalgia for the *ancien régime*, revealing great faith in its capacity for reform – so much so, that he believes that 1789 was a movement for liberty, promoted by an elite that grew within it, a mix of aristocracy and commoners. It was a political turnaround that could have (and for Bosher should have) exhausted its function with the construction of a liberal monarchy, which placed equality before the law at the centre of its identity. He blames the move towards radical change on the manoeuvres of a Jacobin elite, who did not hesitate to unleash popular protest as a means of subverting the monarchy. The rallying cry of the *sans-culotterie* thus brought the revolution to the Republic and the Terror, causing it to deviate from its own liberal path. This might still have been recovered had the Directory period – he places great emphasis on its conservative aspects – not been overwhelmed by Bonaparte, once more portrayed as an unscrupulous revolutionary. In line with this interpretation, where conservative features are highlighted and the ideas disseminated by British nineteenth-century historiography make a vigorous comeback, Schama's work constitutes, if possible, a further revival.

In his reconstruction, criticism of the monarchy was aimed at a limited liberal revision of the state structure, not at equality – this was suddenly put forward only by a tiny section of the elite in order to win over the support of the lower classes. The result was social catastrophe: violence and anarchy soon prevailed and in 1789, with the collapse of all law and order, the Terror was already apparent. Violence, in other words, spread across the whole revolution and if Thermidor was responsible for putting an end to this macabre popular protagonism, all that remained was rubble. With Robespierre's fall, Schama's lengthy work – a good half of it dedicated to the *ancien régime* – finds its conclusion. The decision to carry the narrative no further says a great deal about his intentions: to demonstrate the close continuity between 1789 and 1793 in terms of an operation to destroy the old order, constructed through the rhetorical artifice of a revolutionary language that put an end to the best of eighteenth-century France's political tradition through the deliberate recourse to plebeian violence.

In this way, things come full circle, with Schama condemning the revolution as a whole. His attention to individuals, it has been said, echoes the example of Carlyle, but there is also the clear influence of other writers: one is Burke and his praise of British order contrasted with the destructive anarchy of France; another, Taine, better able than any other to depict the feral nature of the Parisian lower classes and whose descriptive capacity Schama brilliantly evokes, the basis for his work's publishing success. And yet, in the end, following the trajectory of British historiography in the second half of the twentieth century, the conclusion would have to be that the mountain gave birth to a mouse. Cobban's criticisms, and Cobb's, of the traditional reading of the revolution soon spilled over from the arena of social interpretation to that of general surveys marked by widespread suspicion of the revolution itself – which some saved in parts, but others rejected as a whole.

The result, seen from its conclusion, would suggest that historiography on the other side of the Channel, from Burke through Carlyle, underwent few major changes: 1789 continued to be regarded with a deep-rooted suspicion. But this line of continuity is an illusory one, and what looks like the outcome of a specific political tradition actually frames an even more complex discourse where, as we shall see, a significant role was played by Furet's reception in Britain.

4. The politics of the revolution

The four general studies in English released close to the bicentenary still, as mentioned, bear the strong imprint of Cobban. However, they also take into account the developments of revolutionary historiography, which in the 1970s and 1980s experienced a sudden surge. There is thus an echo in their works of the new ways of looking at the relationship between religion and revolution (the line here laid down in the works of Dale van Kley and Timothy Tackett),[55] as well as the intellectual characteristics (given fresh impetus by Robert Darnton).[56] The specific nature of politics in the French provinces was considered anew, with Cobb as the main inspiration, his pupils William Scott, Alan Forrest, Colin Lucas, Gwynne Lewis and Martyn Lyons shedding light on the richness of the political process.[57] There was a turning point, too, in the United States, in the study of the language and rhetoric of the revolution, especially in the works of Keith Baker and Lynn Hunt.[58]

It is difficult to say how much the English works written on the occasion of the bicentenary directly owed to François Furet, who, in the 1970s and 1980s, came to refute Marxist historiography of the revolution across the board and soon dominated the scene internationally.[59] Not a great deal, it would be tempting to say, given that British historiography, with its robust empirical approach, looked a little askance at the ideological shadings that Furet brought to his own (re)reading of 1789. But he spoke with admiration of Cobban, and, although he never made direct reference to him in his harsh confrontation with the French historiographic tradition, he certainly had his works in mind. It is certainly no coincidence that Furet's first work dedicated to 1789 – written together with Denis Richet between 1965 and 1966[60] – came out on the heels of Cobban's *Social Interpretation* and with an approach that reflected its leading lines, but placing them within the framework of a narrative that the English historian would never have proposed.

In some way it could be said that Furet and Richet's *Révolution française* constitutes a translation, in narrative terms, of what, following Cobban's criticism, was happening at an international level in relation to the historiographical interpretation then dominant in France. The work, in fact, was certainly not just one more study of revolutionary history, never concealing its ambition to place the events within the structure of a strong and original interpretation. It went against the current, in other words, from its elegant position with the publisher Hachette: the latter had the idea of a prestigious edition to be produced by two authors who were not specialists in the subject, but whose journalism (both worked for the *Nouvel Observateur*) might arouse the interest of a cultured and select public – as the high cost of the book would suggest.

An ambitious historiographical operation, in other words, took shape in the guise of a prestigious gift, which, by transferring to French soil some of the criticism originating in Britain, should have made it possible to turn the page with respect to Lefebvre's traditional reading. This was suggested by the fact that the two authors certainly dealt with the entire decade, though focusing on the initial years on the one hand and the final years on the other, with Year II – until then the fulcrum of every revolutionary reconstruction – being given little importance in the overall balance of their narration. Their version, in fact, was dominated by the idea that the French Revolution was the result of a phenomenon both bourgeois and aristocratic, which, inspired by Enlightenment culture, had unified the best part of three classes within the framework of a sincere conviction in the values of liberalism. Popular intervention, however, was soon grafted onto this political process, with the result that the year 1789 was the outcome of various distinct movements, where confrontation prevailed over debate and cast a sinister shadow over the revolutionary bloc that Lefebvre, in his time, had once described.

The autonomy of the popular forces, instead of an extraordinary push forward, thus became an element of subversive importance. The juxtaposition of the revolution of the lower classes with that of the Enlightenment soon caused problems for the liberal and bourgeois course of 1789. The result was an acceleration in the revolutionary process, compounded by the choice to issue assignats and inflation on the one hand and the unexpected flight of the king and the decision to go to war on the other. At the time of the Legislative Assembly, there was thus a sudden *dérapage* in the revolutionary process, which veered away from the path to constitutional monarchy on which it had been set towards a republican democracy with anti-parliamentary tendencies. There was no desecrating intent in the minds of the two authors by the use of a term such as *dérapage* (skid), unusual in the historiographical language of the time (and which attracted the ironic condescension of Richard Cobb).[61] Rather, they wanted to offer a powerful image to show that republic and democracy were not preordained by 1789 and were instead the unexpected result of a political drama. The deviation was brought about, Furet and Richet believed, however, not only by the political protagonism of the sans-culottes – which led them to lay down the line to the Convention itself – but, perhaps even more so, by the deputies themselves, unable to cope with the serious task of tackling the dramatic situation that the war had created. (skip

In other words, if the Legislative Assembly had derailed the revolutionary process, the Convention was unable to return it to the right tracks: it was equivalent to saying that the terrible circumstances of 1792–3 did not bear the responsibility for having torn the revolutionary process from its course, given that, even before, the inadequacies of political representation had dragged democracy into the abyss of the Terror. For this reason, the two authors made no distinction between Girondins and Montagnards, who appeared to them to be an expression of the same social forces. The diminishment, meanwhile, of the *sans-culotterie* to the rank of a pastist force, utterly useless to a future order, led them to greatly minimize the political tradition of the Robespierrist party, which had instead based its own interpretation on the relationship between the Montagnards and the popular movement. Thus, the insurrection of May 31 was, along the lines of Michelet, only a severe blow to the parliamentary system and the Terror the government's response to the factional struggles that divided the republicans and risked bringing down the new order. Thermidor, meanwhile, was presented as a form of shortcut: victory at the frontiers gave rise to an expansionist peace and the Year III constitution planned, after having done away with the popular movement, a return to origins – something that proved impossible.

It was a trenchant reading, which tended to link the last revolutionary period to the early years and which made the rise of the *sans-culotterie* a parenthesis destined to make impossible any attempt to bring the revolution to a positive conclusion. Faced with this perspective, the question also arose of how it had been possible to build a myth around Year II – the revolutionary period where stabilization of the new order was prevented by the return of pastist forces, which shared nothing with the spirit of the Enlightenment and the expectations of late-eighteenth-century elites. The question had a sinister sound to it, because it indicated that a profound distrust of a system of liberty prevailed in the national political culture: hence the denunciation of anti-parliamentarism as a constant in French public life, which since the times of the revolution had, in reading the country's historical events, led to the favouring of revolutionary spontaneity rather than the difficult exercise of representative institutions. For Furet and Richet, it was precisely the historiographical misfortunes of the Directory – never studied in depth, squeezed as it was between the greatness of Year II and the splendours of Bonaparte – that confirmed this worrying trend. And yet, according to the two authors, that particular system of government, founded on the normal functioning of representative institutions, was the expression of a constitution that retrieved all the eighteenth-century values and enjoyed the support of a bourgeois world that, with agreement between landowners, thought it would close the circle of the revolutionary experiment.

The two writers, in other words, believed that the new France could have been founded on the constitution of the Year III , if only the new regime had not been delegitimized at birth by the Two-Thirds Decree, which confirmed the same political class in government, exposed it to the joint challenge of monarchist right and Jacobin left and meant it had no other means of survival than brutal intervention on the, not surprisingly unfavourable, electoral results. For this reason, the Directory was threatened by protest that once more came from outside, no longer brandished on the pikes of the sans-culottes, as on 31 May 1793, but on the bayonet tips of Bonaparte's soldiers on the occasion of Brumaire. And with the rise of the First Consul, for Furet and Richet the French Revolution was well and truly over: the sick roots of government authoritarianism and the rejection of representative institutions were destined to flourish abundantly in France's political nineteenth century.

What has been said so far perhaps conveys, albeit briefly, how the work of Furet and Richet, while adopting an informative slant, constituted an authentic historiographical challenge, demolishing as it did the main assumptions on which the traditional interpretation of the revolution was based. This explains why the work immediately met with violent criticism from those who still acknowledged themselves as followers of Georges Lefebvre's interpretative line. The reservations were also certainly exacerbated by the political history of the two authors, both ex-Communists, but in 1960 founder-members of the Parti socialiste Unifié (PSU), a party that aimed to overcome the impasse in which the entire French left found itself. As if that were not enough, at the time of the publication of the work, the *Nouvel Observateur*, with a laudatory review by Gilles Martinet, partly designed to boost Hachette's sales, revealed how both authors had worked for the journal for a long period under a nom de plume.[62] At that point, among those who regarded the publishing operation with great suspicion, everything seemed to fall into place and Furet and Richet's rereading of 1789 went hand in hand with their journalistic stances in favour of a renewal of the French left – something foreshadowed, to the detriment of the PCF, by François Mitterrand's excellent results in the 1965 presidential elections.

All this was enough for Furet and Richet to pass as renegades in the eyes of Communist historians, their move across to the opposing camp requiring the destruction of the founding myth of the French left as a sort of entrance fee. Among specialists in revolutionary history, the two also sinned in other ways: they had never dealt with the subject before, both worked in the VI section of the *Ecole pratique des Hautes Etudes* and were accused of having benefitted from easier access to academic life. Furet, meanwhile, who had not even completed his *thèse d'état*, was also known, at the time of his militancy in the PCF, to have supported Jean Poperen in denouncing the heterodoxy of certain historiographical views held by Soboul.

Claude Mazauric was the first to intervene,[63] noting that the revolution was, in 1789, a single *bloc*, given that it could only take shape thanks to the fact that the bourgeoisie had accepted and interpreted the demands of the people. This already indicated, in Mazauric's view, that there was no liberal project in the origins of the revolution and that the *dérapage* was therefore an invention, the result of wishful thinking that 1789 could be seen as the dawn of a world that instead was soon contested in the very same bourgeois circles. When Mazauric wanted to republish his article in a collection of essays, Soboul himself, now director of the *Institut d'histoire de la Révolution française*, decided to write the preface, and was unsparing in his remarks with regard to the political past and scientific correctness of Furet and Richet's *Révolution française*.[64] Not by chance, at the same time, Michel Vovelle, a historian of the *ancien régime* mentality who moved on to study 1789, started his own work on the first years of the revolution, published in 1972 under the title *La chute de la monarchie, 1787-1792*. He took Furet and Richet's work as a polemical point of reference, dismantling the idea of *dérapage* and criticizing the negative slant given to the direction of the revolutionary process, as if their book lent support to those who criticized the people's assertiveness in terms of an impossible bourgeois, moderate stabilization of 1789.[65]

In the meantime, Furet and Richet had not remained silent, though their reactions were different: the latter had a vitriolic exchange with Soboul, the former's interests instead seemed to turn elsewhere, continuing his journalism and, in the aftermath of the student protests of May 1968, collaborating in the reform of the university system pushed for by Minister Faure. This was not a popular choice for the left, which suggested that behind the support for the abolition of teaching posts lay the bitterness of someone who had never completed his *thèse d'état*. But the temptation of a political life was short-lived: as early as 1969, Pompidou's election to the presidency of the Republic paved the way for Furet's return to the groves of academe and led to long periods of study in the United States. In Princeton, he found himself regarding 1789 from a different perspective, taking an interest in the work of Tocqueville and dedicating an article to his nature as a historian of the French Revolution that appeared in the *Annales* in 1970.[66] It was a decisive step in taking his dispute with the Marxist school in other directions: when, in 1971, again in the *Annales*, he published a long article entitled *Le catéchisme révolutionnaire*, little remained of the Furet that the world of traditional historiography still had in its sights.[67] He no longer spoke of the work written with Richet – in fact, tended to distance himself from it, declaring that, if the opportunity came up again, he would write it in a very different way. Freed from the restrictions his opponents had tried to bind him in, Furet was thus able to seize the opportunity to classify them as outdated followers of a world that identified with Montagnard rhetoric and that, in the name of interpretative orthodoxy, silenced any spirit of criticism in the reconstruction of revolutionary events. In other words, twentieth-century French historiography was accused of maintaining a Lenino-populist vulgate in circulation, still insisting on a collision between 1789 and October. This also imposed the concept of class struggle on the late eighteenth century, yoking together conflicts that were very different from one another, such as that – still to be demonstrated – between bourgeoisie and aristocracy or, the result of the dramatic political situation, that between Girondins and Montagnards.

In relation to this procedure, which ended up modelling 1789 according to the criteria dictated by the Soviet 1917, it was an easy matter for Furet to note that most recent lines of research indicated that the origins of the revolution were far more complex: its bourgeois dimension could not be accepted without its various aspects – social, economic, political and ideological – first being broken down and the concrete impact that each of them had on the development of events being measured. Curiously, while his criticism of the traditional reading was severe, Furet no longer spoke of *dérapage*, as if he had in turn repudiated a reading that his opponents had rebuked him for. This forgetfulness arose from a wise polemical calculation: by giving up any defence of his previous ideas, he could throw himself headlong into the dispute triggered by the attacks of Mazauric and Soboul, which offered him the opportunity to counterattack and target the entire Marxist reading of the revolution. In other words, sacrificing the work he had carried out with Richet made it possible for him to challenge his opponents on their own ground, illustrating all their weaknesses and subjecting them to ruthless criticism.

It was a first, decisive step on the way to a new reading of the revolution, and was helped along, in the years immediately following, by the riptide nature of French politics. In 1972, the *Union de la gauche* signalled the convergence between communists and socialists in the electoral field, but this alliance between rivals did not spark Furet's interest – it did not seem to solve any of the left-wing dilemmas that had prompted his departure from the PCF. After becoming president of the *Ecole des Hautes Etudes en Sciences Sociales* and promoter of a revival of interest in liberal thought, he instead looked carefully at the debate on Soviet totalitarianism that had opened up on the left: he himself recalled how these criticisms were decisive in freeing the study of the revolution from the straitjacket that Marxist historiography had placed it in. This resolutely countercurrent decision resulted in the publication, in 1978, of his *Penser la Révolution française*, which constitutes the point of arrival for the reflections that began with the publication of *Catechisme révolutionnaire*. This explains the curious structure of the work, which consists of two parts: in the first, with the caustic title of *La Révolution est terminée*, Furet described his interpretation of 1789; in the second he explained how he had arrived at those conclusions, reconstructing his own intellectual path through three essays, two of which – the *Catechisme révolutionnaire* and the essay on Tocqueville – had already been available for some time.

On the whole, therefore, the new research that brought him to produce a fresh reading of 1789 was in the last essay alone, which praises the work of Augustin Cochin, an author forgotten – as has been seen – in France after the Second World War and who Furet himself admitted to having discovered in 1971 on the library shelves of the University of Michigan. That discovery made it possible for him to put forward a reading of the origins of democratic politics destined to intersect with Tocqueville's teaching on the link between the Revolution and the birth of an even stronger centralized state. The result took the form of a highly original piece of historiography and as a cultural operation it was as brilliant as it was devastating. *Penser la Révolution française* represented the demolition of the Marxist-Leninist vulgate which, according to Furet, the reading of the revolution had become entangled around during the course of the twentieth century. There was thus no hesitation in describing the Lefebvre brand of historiography as a doctrinal school by now played out, its equivalences between the French Revolution and the bourgeois revolution confirming a militant approach to the event, which ended up assuming the point of view of the revolutionaries of the time – 1789 as a total break with the past – as justification of any future progress.

The result was that Marxist historiography had ended up transforming an item of study into an object of veneration, where the image that the revolutionaries themselves had given of the event prevailed. It was an easy matter for Furet to argue that the revolution had long since ended and the men of the Third Republic, combining secularism and liberal democracy, had brought it to a positive conclusion. This meant that only a commemorative logic, dictated by the belief that the revolution was a model for every future, allowed it to remain a myth to which France's political destiny could be anchored. Hence the move away from Michelet to emphasize Tocqueville, who had the merit of indicating that the revolution began within the framework of government centralization, fed on the conflict between the *ancien régime* elites and became radicalized thanks to the triumph of the political notion of equality. The discovery of Cochin also took place in this context, with Furet acknowledging the former's reflection on the role of democratic ideology, a decisive step in his view in terms of interpreting the revolutionary developments that followed 1789. Because if the Marxists believed the French Revolution had meant the advent of a bourgeois society, for Furet it had marked the birth of a democratic society. The *dérapage* was thus rejected in order to underline that this had been the general direction since 1789, and the Terror itself, rather than an easy quest for absolution in dramatic circumstances, was innate to the very origins of the revolution, fuelled by the anti-aristocratic and egalitarian impulse that found confirmation in the popular pamphlet by Abbé Sieyès. In this way, Furet brought the political-ideological identity of the revolution to the centre of attention, carefully, and with magisterial skill, deploying traditional chronological demarcations in order to better oppose the Marxist reading on its own terms.[68]

It was a well-calculated risk, making it possible to demonstrate his adversaries' inconsistencies and weaknesses in a decisive manner; on the other hand, it involved sacrificing his previous reading of the revolutionary decade. The Directory period, following the lines of traditional reconstructions, lost the importance that Furet had accorded it in 1965 and was recompartmentalized within its moment of impossible parliamentary stabilization, given that French society remained at the mercy of the myth of popular sovereignty. No coincidence, therefore, that it would choose a plebiscite as a solution, through which Bonaparte confirmed the primacy of equality over freedom that had been the fulcrum for the whole revolution. Thus, in the contradiction between the appeal to popular sovereignty and the quest for a representative political model, the revolution was able to win out even over the years of Empire and spread throughout a large part of the nineteenth century, finally finding an arduously achieved structure in the years of the Third Republic in terms of a stabilization accepted by the social body. For this reason, Furet recommended a long-arc reading of the French Revolution, from the crisis of the *ancien régime* with its various projects of reform until the 1870s. Finally, on the ashes of the Second Empire and the dramatic civil war following the uprising of the Commune, a republican and democratic political class was, albeit with difficulty, able to find a point of equilibrium in which the great majority of French could recognize themselves.

The choice to adopt a cooler perspective towards the French Revolution, making it a subject of study immune from the passions and ideologies that had thronged around it up to then, was not, however, without approval from undesirable quarters. Furet remained a man of the left, intending to put forward a democratic solution to the political dilemma of a France over-polluted by an easy enthusiasm for revolution; but his campaign against the Leninist reading made him vulnerable to a robust comeback from the counter-revolutionary right, given that the proposal to link the Terror to 1789 provided confirmation of the whole revolution's irremediably subversive nature.

For this reason, worried that his historiographical operation might end up supporting the traditional lamentations of right-wing nostalgia for the splendours of the old order, he constantly rejected the idea that his work should be read along these lines, a viewpoint he went on to corroborate through numerous articles during the 1980s.

His frenetic pace of work showed that he was preparing for the decisive appointment with 1989: on the one hand, he continued his dispute with Marxist historiography through the reading of how 1789 was regarded across the nineteenth century; on the other, he developed an international network, which made it possible for him to guide the historiographic renewal that built on his ideas. This was reflected in the three volumes published between 1987 and 1989 in tandem with Keith Baker, Colin Lucas and Mona Ozouf.[69] Meanwhile, again together with Ozouf, he published a dictionary of the French Revolution,[70] as well as a general overview, where he explained his overall interpretation of the meaning of 1789 in the modernity of France.[71] In this last work, he fixed the coordinates of France's long revolutionary history, which began with the crisis of absolutism following the reform proposals of the Enlightenment and ended in decline in the nineteenth century with stable republican institutions and the full acceptance of universal male suffrage.

In its pages, over the course of those hundred years or so, the history of France became the first experience of democracy and, through many setbacks and dramatic contortions, thus took upon itself an assumption of universalistic significance. Overall, it was a reading that confirmed what his 1978 book had already suggested: the Third Republic returned to the example of the Constituent Assembly, an authentically strong subject, believed Furet, in the field of revolutionary assemblies, and the Constituent Assembly's project of freedom and modernity was the inspiration behind the Third Republic's ultimately successful actions. The entire revolutionary decade thus became the terrain where the contradictions persisting in democratic ideology had led political practice to repeatedly short-circuit, preventing any form of parliamentary stabilization. It had also, in the name of popular sovereignty, favoured an authoritarian structure which French society was forced to struggle to extricate itself from. In this context, it could be said that the mountain of Furet's huge historiographical efforts had given birth to the mouse of a neo-liberal reading of the revolution.

In reality – if it is true that the strictly *construens* phase in his work does not stand comparison with the *destruens* part – it remains indubitable that *Penser la Révolution française* constitutes a point of no return in the long history of revolutionary narratives: for the first time there was a move away from the event that had so constantly accompanied French politics. In his work, Furet offered a never-before-tested interpretation to reread the past of a nation that had established a huge part of its own identity around the iconic significance of 1789. In this work of truth-telling, which meant making a clean sweep of stylistic elements and clichés that were deeply imbedded within the collective imagination, Furet found himself involved in violent clashes and diatribes. Atoning for his communist past, he treated former fellow travellers in sarcastic terms to ease the discomfort he had felt for such a long time, constantly clashing with an adversary always ready to launch insinuations, never lacking the courage to make the difficult choice. There is no shortage of those who, in deference to a well-cushioned idea of what it means to be a historian, suggest some sort of political one-upmanship in his interpretation, or even dispute its qualities, noting that he had renounced the tools of the trade too quickly in preference for a career as a polemicist. But what remains incontrovertible is that only thanks to Furet did the historiography of the French Revolution divest itself of a messianic character that had dogged it for so long and that after his intervention nothing, in the field of revolutionary studies, would be the same as it was before.

5. An Atlantic history

Revisionism had many victims. The first was certainly the Marxist reading that Albert Soboul, with a hint of nostalgia for a time he felt was fading away, found a way to define as classic. But the work of Cobban, giving back to British historiography a markedly conservative slant on the French Revolution, like that of Furet, making the French identity of 1789 the basis for his arguments against the Lenin-Marxist vulgate, were similarly decisive in terms of sweeping away what remained of a democratic tradition which, after the First World War and following the advent of totalitarianism in Europe, had found its last outpost in America. Aulard's last followers had found refuge in New York, especially in the aftermath of the fall of the Third Republic. These included Boris Mirkine-Guetzevich, a Russian juif exile who, in Paris, during the 1930s, with the support of Philippe Sagnac's professorship, had done much to relaunch the study of 1789 from a truly democratic perspective. The United States was, moreover, the ideal place, also from a strictly historiographical point of view, to sustain the idea of a republicanism, which rose out of the democratic revolutions of the late eighteenth century.[72]

Between the two wars, historians across the Atlantic had regarded French historiography with great warmth and the Second World War, with the United States once again giving a helping hand to the old continent, had reinforced the link between the French and American revolutions – a link that had already experienced a certain amount of rapid, if apparently ephemeral, success during the First World War. In the aftermath of 1945, although the political climate of the Cold War greatly encouraged a conservative shift among American historians, insistence on the political link with France had not been completely exhausted, had indeed been strengthened by the prospect of re-establishing democracy as the necessary point of contact with what in the meantime had become Western Europe. Robert Roswell Palmer was one of the most committed to this, first by writing about the Terror, then by pointing out the importance of French historiography in the American academic world and, later, through his long work on the age of democratic revolutions. Here, the late-eighteenth-century revolutions formed the spearhead for a gigantic democratization, destined to change the world in the name of a total war on privilege.[73]

The work reflected a move away from a political line that the Cold War had for too long closed within the constraints of conservative exceptionalism, but there is no doubt that it was at the same time the point of arrival for a first phase of American historiography on 1789, whose roots lay entirely between the two wars. Palmer was also a scholar who had taken his first professional steps during the 1930s and whose interest in the French Revolution dated back to those years, when he had started his own academic career with the subject of the link with 1776.[74]

A pupil in Chicago of Louis Gottschalk, instrumental, as seen earlier, in introducing the United States to the work of Mathiez, Palmer, at his suggestion, then went to Cornell, where he completed his doctorate under the guidance of Carl Lotus Becker, Gottschalk's former teacher. Here, in 1934, Palmer discussed a thesis which reflected the interest of his entire future life as a scholar, its theme concerning the way in which the events of 1776 had been regarded at the time of 1789.[75] Becker's influence was clear in the centrality of the American Revolution with respect to the last twenty-five years of the eighteenth century. And yet, there was also a reference to the originality of the revolutionary experiment in France, which made it impossible to conclude that there had been a direct transmission of the ideals of liberty from the new world to the old: the two events, instead, had to be considered as different products of the same political earthquake destined to change the history of the world.

In the following years, having in the meantime embarked on an academic career at Princeton, Palmer repeatedly found a way to reflect worriedly on the relationship between the revolutions: the crisis of representative democracies in the old continent, coupled with a clearly conservative challenge within the American academic world, seemed to indicate that the late eighteenth-century's battle for freedom, having inspired democratic politics until the First World War, was now coming to an end. The protests in Europe against the democratic system, from both right and left, seemed to him the proof, and not the cause, of a decline exemplified by French democracy. This is what the crisis of the Third Republic, which fascism accused of being a mere plutocracy and communism dismissed as a decrepit bourgeois statehood, seemed to indicate and in the United States that acknowledgement suggested renewed enclosure within the reassuring shell of the spirit of 1776. Palmer, who had spent time in France for his studies, believed that the task of American historians was instead to keep their guard up against the challenge to liberty that seemed to be convulsing the whole of Europe.

For this reason, after having published a work on Catholicism and free thought in eighteenth-century France,[76] at the same time as the collapse of the Third Republic, he began working a history of the Committee of Public Safety, which came out just a few weeks before the Japanese attack on Pearl Harbour.[77] This work, like others dedicated to revolutionary France in the same years,[78] arose out of a profound interest in French democracy, which Palmer did not believe should be confused with the often authoritarian and violent logic of Year II. His study of the revolutionary government grew out of an intention to demonstrate that, in addition to the atrocities of which it was guilty, the Terror remained part of a revolutionary experience that had ensured profound civil change and favoured an equally significant work of political as well as social democratization. His reconstruction of government action in Year II allowed Palmer to underline that the revolutionary event was a different and more complex thing, in which neither the Terror nor Napoleonic triumph could be dealt with as consequences that were equally inevitable.

This perspective, which ended up restoring a democratic identity to the revolutionary decade that concrete analysis of Year II confirmed rather than contested, constituted a precise choice of subject area: the aim was not only to reaffirm, through reference to the present moment, the need for an American commitment to Europe at war; rather, and more profoundly, Palmer also intended to challenge Crane Brinton's line of interpretation, whose equation of the revolutionary fact with a social pathology seemed to him to have opened the way to the demonization of any political and social upheaval. The dispute between the two, a courteous one, went on throughout the years of the conflict, coming to the fore again in the immediate post-war period, when Palmer decided to promote a more precise awareness of French historiography in the United States in order to put forward another interpretation with respect to Brinton's prevailing view, which, not surprisingly, was very popular with conservative circles. Palmer thus translated Georges Lefebvre's *Quatre-Vingt-Neuf* into English in 1947, a work that in his opinion had the merit of maintaining a balance between social and political history and which brought out all the breadth and depth of the revolutionary character of 1789.[79] Thanks to his acquaintance with France's high priest of revolutionary studies, who even helped him with the translation, Palmer also came into contact with Jacques Godechot, a former student of Mathiez's, who in 1947 had published a study on the Atlantic, where there was already a clear reference to the particular civilization of that area.[80] The work, which defined the coordinates of a cultural space destined to embrace the two continents, had a profound impact on Palmer, who in the meantime, had written a successful text book on the modern world where Western civilization was placed centre stage at the expense of reconstruction at a national level.[81] Godechot's perspective seemed to him to bring the old and the new world together in the context of modernity, and constitute, in a truly American context, a possible antidote to American exceptionalism, which was benefitting greatly from the developments of the Cold War.

For this reason, again thanks to Lefebvre, Palmer invited Godechot to Princeton, where they prepared an essay together entitled *Le problème de l'Atlantique du XVIIIe au XXe siècle*, which they then presented in Rome, in 1955, at the 10th International Congress of Historical Sciences.[82] At the heart of the speech was the idea of an Atlantic civilization, which the two authors said had taken shape, during the eighteenth century, between Anglo-French colonial America, Europe and the Spanish Empire. The close connection between Europe and America had then been lost over the course of the nineteenth century, something revolutionary events had played a decisive role in: their assumptions had indeed been common, but their consequences had instead determined different developments on either side of the Atlantic. Not everyone was happy with the essay, many seeing it as a sort of historical justification for NATO, and Godechot soon established a certain distance between himself and Palmer, emphasizing that both had somehow been deceived by the organizers.

A few years later, when he had taken a different historiographical path and returned to the reassuring embrace of national tradition, Godechot felt obliged to justify his decision to write the essay with Palmer. He noted that one member of the American contingent was Donald Cope McKay, a specialist in nineteenth-century France with a conservative perspective on the revolution, who, Godechot reported, had urged that a marked political emphasis be given to American participation. Palmer, in reality, had gone to Rome with clear ideas that he had no intention of giving up: he remained convinced, following on from Gottschalk and Becker, that the American and French revolutions were much more similar than their respective national historiographies gave them credit for. He felt it was clear that the Atlantic panorama of the late eighteenth century was far more integrated and cohesive than subsequent events would suggest. The existence of a common Atlantic civilization, from which the late-eighteenth-century revolutions originated, had above all the merit of denying not only that they were different, but also that they were in opposition to one another, because it confirmed that effect had for too long been confused with cause.

In other words, suggesting the existence of a geographical area – the Atlantic world – that cohered around the same model of civilization meant that an end could be put to all exceptionalism – in both the United States and France – and made it possible at the same time for the origins of modernity to be reread in a transnational framework. This gave rise to *The Age of Democratic Revolution*, which appeared in two volumes that came out five years apart. In the first, *The Challenge*, published in 1959, the focus was almost exclusively on the American Revolution; the second, *The Struggle*, published in 1964, dealt with 1789 and all the revolutions that domino-like took place as European countries were invaded by the troops of republican France.[83] The common thread was the idea that the birth of modern democracy was due to these late-eighteenth-century revolutions: the advent of the United States, the collapse of the French monarchy, the revolutions that convulsed the old continent from Holland to Italy to Poland. Despite having different causes and above all different outcomes, they shared a unitary nature based on similar objectives and principles, everywhere calling into question the legitimacy of the powers of the *ancien régime*.

This crisis, which swept across the entire Western world, from one side of the Atlantic to the other, was the consequence of different factors – the outcome of the Seven Years' War, the fiscal crisis of absolute monarchies, economic tensions throughout the vast Atlantic world, the aggressive return of traditional power groups. But the result took the form of a mighty challenge to privilege, to all those elites who made income from positions guaranteed by privilege into an instrument of domination. These power groups, which only schematically corresponded to the aristocracy, had begun to face opposition from a composite social universe, where the excluded mixed with those who claimed greater recognition. This clash produced the first generic protests against injustices, soon transformed, through resistance and the resultant conflict, into an affirmation of equality, the results of which would take the form of political democracy.

As the first volume of the work illustrated in detail, the United States was the place where it all began: the war of independence was in reality a war of democracy, originating from the intention to found a new order, designed to give juridical form to secession from the mother country, on popular sovereignty. In this way, Palmer had resolutely in his sights an American historiographical tradition, the prevailing one at that time, which denied the very existence of a revolution on American soil and proposed that the Declaration of Independence had only sanctioned the return of the colonists to their original freedoms, which King George III's unfortunate policies had dared to question. In Palmer's opinion, however, the turning point of 1776 was correlated to the constitutional watershed of the following years and the link was the revolutionary war itself: it had not only set the colonists against British troops, but had also triggered an internal conflict with the loyalists, whose political elimination was a necessary premise for the birth of a new political society founded on the will of the people. On this basis, in his second volume, Palmer suggested looking for analogies with what would happen in Europe shortly thereafter. Revolutionary France seemed to him to follow the same model as revolutionary America: after 1789, the centre of its political activity was the construction of a constituent power based on popular sovereignty. Subsequent developments, marked by the outbreak of hostilities with the powers of the old order, seemed to him to echo the American war of independence and to guarantee an equally democratic character to the revolutionary process not only in France but also in a Europe soon traversed by the armies of the Republic. All this did not mean making the French Revolution a mere continuation of the American one: Palmer was careful to indicate the particular traits of 1789, but he did not intend to give up his central idea of the late eighteenth century, on both sides of the Atlantic, as the breeding ground for an impulse towards equality and democracy that, over the long course of the nineteenth century, only the different outcomes of the revolutionary movement would end up concealing.

It was no coincidence that his work suggested that, even at the start of the nineteenth century, the paths of the United States and France were similar and comparable: on the one hand, first Brumaire, and then victory at Marengo immediately afterwards, had ensured the triumph of forces in favour of the equality that Jefferson's electoral victory in America soon confirmed. In this way, in Palmer's reconstruction, everything could, after all, work out: but the nineteenth century tasked itself with erasing the traces of modernity's common genesis in the Atlantic world and that (re)discovery served to ensure a different way of looking at the origins of the political traditions of both countries.

Reception of the work varied: the first volume was a success and in the midst of the transforming moment of the Kennedy presidency was awarded the Bancroft prize for the best book of history in the United States. It rejected the widely shared conservative nature of American independence in order to give 1776 a properly revolutionary dimension – in other words, it seemed to be of great advantage to an American model of democracy, which, from its very origins, connoted its international presence in terms of a policy of freedom. A few years later, when it came to dealing with the effects of the same crisis in Europe with the second volume, the result was instead very different and criticism rained down on both sides of the Atlantic. In America, the wind of American exceptionalism was blowing strong once again, partly thanks to the success of Hannah Arendt, whose essay *On Revolution* (1961) established a clear contrast between the American revolution, which began, and remained, liberal, and its French cousin, which degenerated swiftly into the totalitarianism of the Terror: Palmer's pairing of the two events therefore came across as unacceptable. It is no coincidence that the third reprint of Crane Brinton's *Anatomy of Revolution* took place in 1965, a work that implicitly confirmed that 1776 could in no way be seen as a subversive phenomenon and even less could it have inspired the politics of a France which, breaking away from the old order, would soon be enveloped in violence. In Europe, above all in France, the reception was if possible even worse, although there were some similarities with the many American reservations, albeit from an opposite perspective.

In this case, too, another successful work helped undermine any possible success Palmer's might have had: this was *The Age of Revolution: Europe, 1789-1848*, by Eric Hobsbawm, which appeared in 1962.[84] As is known, here, the Marxist scholar indicated two specific places as the origins of modernity: France, with the political transformations that followed 1789, and England, whose industrial revolution had forever changed economic structure. There was no trace of 1776 in Hobsbawm's pages – American independence had nothing in common with a revolutionary moment that remained a European prerogative alone. French Marxist historians, needless to say, were happy to agree with this approach, which confirmed the political centrality of 1789 and rejected as groundless Palmer's claim to trace it back to 1776 and to subordinate it, at least in their eyes, to what had happened in America. All French historiography felt hurt in its pride, as did its American counterpart, by a work that moved away from the reassuring shell of national tradition to face the open seas of wider geo-political spaces. It was this, really, the insurmountable obstacle that Palmer's work had to face. It had grown out of a refusal to reconstruct the revolutionary period by restricting itself to national borders, assuming a cosmopolitan perspective in order to move away from the impact of national historiographical traditions and, in this context, at that time in the 1960s, it could not win.

In France, in the silence that greeted his work, there was not only diffidence towards the coupling of 1789 and 1776 (something that even Lefebvre in his latter years had indicated), but above all the rejection of the concrete reconstruction that he had carried out on the revolutionary decade. In dealing with the events that followed on from 1789, Palmer's interest focused immediately on the republican moment, given that the 1792 watershed clearly prevailed over 1789 in terms of the drive towards democratization. However, in the reading of the events that immediately follow, the Year II period seemed to be sacrificed to a large extent compared to the subsequent phase, with the result that, for Palmer, it was the Directory above all that constituted the authentic point of reference for making an assessment of the French Revolution. In his opinion, the real republican moment of the revolutionary events, where attempts at democratization tried to find form and stability in a constitutional framework, lay in the Directory period, when the Year III constitution seemed to ensure a point of balance for the revolutionary impulse of previous years. French democracy, again according to Palmer, was therefore not born in the aftermath of 1789, with the collapse of the *ancien régime*, and not even during 1793, when the mobilization of patriotic forces transformed the revolution into an act of religious faith and, under the aegis of the Year II government, brought about the loss of freedom. No, democracy in France had arisen, rather, in the aftermath of Thermidor, when, resisting a host of challenges, it found a balance in freedom. This was also a model it believed could be reproposed, in the guise of the Year III constitution, in the countries its troops were one by one bringing liberty to. In rehabilitating the Directory, Palmer could count on brilliant precedents, starting with the *Grande Nation* that Jacques Godechot developed during his stay at Princeton and published in 1956, where attention to revolutionary expansion in Europe prompted a renewal of interest in the years that the Year III constitution was exercised.[85] Also in 1956, another French scholar, who had just become director of the *Institut d'histoire de la Révolution française*, Marcel Reinhard, had found a way, in his courses at the Sorbonne, to reopen the dust-covered dossier of the Directory. He noted that the most important work dedicated to that particular period up to then, by Ludovic Sciout, while endowed with an apparatus of highly respectable erudition, had a *maurrassien* slant which had ended up distorting the meaning of the Directory, dismissed as a corrupt and incapable regime.[86] In France, however, things went no further, partly because, after 1956, with the repression of the revolution in Budapest, the PCF cracked down on the university world – Soboul himself, as previously mentioned, paying the price.

Palmer, however, who certainly knew those works, followed other coordinates in his reconstruction: his point of reference was Crane Brinton's *Decade of Revolution*, which, as seen earlier, had begun revaluation of the Directory in 1931 and, in contrast, greatly restricted the significance of Year II in the French democratization process. The cultural coordinates underlying Palmer's entire work were based on this decision, which, in hindsight, constitutes the arrival point of a historiographical tradition which, although extremely lively between the two wars, was soon muted by the developments of international politics following the Second World War. In other words, in its rediscovery of the Atlantic world, in its attention to the link between 1776 and 1789, in its interest in the gigantic democratic wave that had swept across a large part of the world at the end of the eighteenth century, it was the intelligent reinterpretation of a line of research that had established itself after the First World War, especially on the other side of the Atlantic. In the transformational 1960s, with the relaunch of a policy of democratic ideals and the triumphs of 'Western Civilization', it seemed to come into favour once again.

However, it soon turned out to be an Indian summer for the revival of attention in the Atlantic origins of democracy: in the United States, the conservative reading of 1776 held its place at the centre of historiographical interests, while the challenge of youthful protest, sparked by the Vietnam War, made no difference to the unshakable rejection of those who seemed to occupy positions of privilege within the academic world. Palmer's successful textbook on the modern world, which continued to be updated and reprinted, was harshly depicted as an instrument designed to indoctrinate new generations into the WASP traditions of their past; while his *Age of the Democratic Revolution*, in appearance a sort of monument to the radiant destinies of the West, was something to keep at a distance. In 1970, Palmer was elected to the presidency of the American Historical Association, but without the votes of its most radical members, who complained that the decision represented the convergence of a number of academic conservatisms and preferred the pacifist Staughton Lynd.

Contested and criticized in its native land, the second volume of Palmer's work was greeted with even greater coolness in Europe. In Great Britain, where Cobban's revisionism was preeminent, the tradition of studies that Palmer represented had long been set aside and was not about to be revived. In France, the Marxist reading was still dominant, and this would never accept the idea of subordinating 1789 to 1776: Godechot's prompt realignment with respect to the centrality of the French events in international destinies, as well as, shortly thereafter, youthful protest with characteristics that soon took on a pastist aspect – to the point of rediscovering (and reprinting) the work of Daniel Guérin – all provided evidence that, in France, Palmer's work was largely swimming against the tide. This is shown by the abridged version of his lengthy work, written in 1967 for a French audience.[87] It seemed to take note of the difficulties his ideas had encountered and restore centrality to the French Revolution in the democratic wave that swept over the two continents. The mutual interdependence of the two great late-eighteenth-century revolutions was thus largely sidelined, to the advantage of 1789 – something that indicates the insurmountable difficulties his work had met with.

The first to recognize this was Palmer himself. He was blessed with a long life, long enough for him to see the collapse of the communism which – not wholly incorrectly – his work was said to be set against. In the 1980s, as the bicentenary approached, going back to his beloved studies of French history, he was the first to admit that his attempt of many years before to place 1789 in the framework of a wider revolutionary space had failed. However, after 1989, with the Berlin Wall fallen, in Italy, Franco Venturi, the great historian of the Enlightenment, wanted to bestow on Palmer a recognition of his achievement, and, on this occasion, the American historian, going back somehow to his original point, expressed hope that the other Europe, finally restored to freedom, might be able to resume a path only hinted at so long ago.[88] The turning point of 1989, in other words, seemed to him to suggest a renewed Western interpretation of Atlantic history and to once again put forward, in the name of the values of 1789, the theme of democracy as the engine of modernity. It was a wish that fell on deaf ears, rejected by Great Britain and America's historiographical exceptionalism, as well as by France's retention of the identitary theme in the cultural debate on the evolution. So, as was noted at the beginning of this book, only the cynical and deceptive irony of historiographical tendencies has ensured that his work – much cited, certainly not much read – has been able to experience unpredictable and renewed popularity, thanks to the success of a new Atlantic history in search of progenitors. It is, nonetheless, in many ways a largely predatory operation: *The Age of the Democratic Revolution* is not the dawn of a new historiographical approach but rather the sunset of the idea that 1789 was the forge of modernity.[89]

Conclusion

The ashes of the revolution?

The Bicentenary of 1989 – carefully staged by the authorities – represented the last great opportunity for visibility for the French school of historiography. The success that such celebrations enjoyed could not conceal either Furet's or Vovelle's helplessness in their attempts to impose, or even draw, a furrow within which new researchers might find a role, thus proving that the revolution had lost not just its central role as a collective field of expectations, but also its attractiveness for French academia. Whereas research worksites were multiplying, focusing on novel themes, from the counter-revolution in the Vendée to the Directoire Republic, new interpretations of the meaning as a whole of the Great Revolution were conspicuous by their absence. Indeed, while the *global turn* had made new interpretations of 1789 possible by unleashing them from the parochial limits of domestic studies – see, for example, Annie Jourdan's brilliant work – there is no question that what was definitely in dispute at the end of this path was the very idea of the French Revolution as the foundational moment of the modern world. Bayly's works, as well as those by Armitage and Subrahmanyam, encouraged such a perspective, which was not just the result of a different configuration of fields of study as a mutation on a political level, calling into question the ideological moment as an instrument for transforming the world.

François Furet had started preparing for the bicentennial anniversary well in advance. Since 1983, he had laid his cards on the table, declaring his concern that in a few years the occasion would be turned into a display of patriotic love destined to strengthen the traditional cult of French statehood.[1] The 1981 presidential victory of François Mitterrand, with the Communist Party playing a role in his government that was by no means negligible, threw him on the defensive against the commemorations, which he imagined would be dominated by a Marxist left with whom he no longer had anything in common. And yet, the frenetic pace of French politics, with first the crisis on the left between socialists and communists and then an aggressive comeback from the right, ready to force President Mitterrand to work together with Jacques Chirac as prime minister, offered him a certain reassurance. The bicentenary, which took place when Mitterrand had in the meantime been re-elected, had been organized beforehand and seemed, in terms of how this had been done, to be seeking to find a difficult balance between the parties, both historiographical and political, who were at that time in open conflict. Furet prepared for the clash by publishing together with Mona Ozouf a dictionary of the French Revolution, where the dominating concept was the intention to set aside all the social readings of 1789 and instead emphasize the impact of the democratic idea in French society of the time. It seemed important to the editors to once more underline the illiberal dimension of 1789: above and beyond the slogans on human rights, it had in fact greatly favoured the aggressive return of an absolute power that was swift to override individual liberty and then spill over into the Terror. Furet and Ozouf mixed reflection on political categories with the study of revolutionary figures, to conclude with the birth of a popular sovereignty that retained a number of the old order's characteristics. The success of the work meant they were able to restrict their opponents' field of manoeuvre, despite the fact that Michel Vovelle – who in the previous years had replaced Soboul, had become director of the *Institut d'histoire de la Révolution française* and of the *Annales historiques de la Révolution française* and he was president of the *Société des études robespierristes*, had been appointed responsible for the historical supervision of the many commemorations scheduled.

So the result of 1989, as an occasion, was apparently a draw – something duly symbolized by the honours that Mitterrand was keen to offer even-handedly to both Vovelle and Ozouf during the celebrations. The idea was to clasp the classical and revisionist interpretations together in the embrace of the Republic, placing them both under the aegis of a French exceptionality destined to illuminate Europe and all other continents. The image of revolutionary France in the world, with freedom and human rights preeminent, was also the theme of the conference organized in Paris under the auspices of the Mitterrand presidency. The subject suggested a patriotic assemblage, something designed to appeal to Vovelle's sensibility and to which Furet could not greatly object. The common thread of the conference was thus the passionate way in which the Revolution was regarded outside France, and how its example soon became a point of reference for other countries on making their entrance into political modernity.[2]

At first, it was a perspective that really seemed capable of healing the dramatic fracture that occurred following the affirmation of revisionism: in the end, moving the meaning of the revolution outside the Hexagon meant returning to France a political and cultural particularity in relation to the entire world – one that, as long as there was not too much hair-splitting with regard to the model of inheritance left to others, everyone could, in principle, agree upon. Michel Vovelle insisted vociferously on this point, transforming himself, in a gruelling tour de force, into a sort of permanent ambassador of the French Revolution abroad. By emphasizing the overall value of the revolutionary decade, he found a way to retain reference to Year II and contain the accusations of totalitarianism that opponents constantly directed at the period of the Terror.

The results were fairly satisfactory: the bicentenary seemed to justify, at an international level, those who saw 1789 as modernity's universal event and effectively opposed the counter-revolutionary discourse that in previous years had charged down Furet's revisionism, transforming the traditional nostalgia for Vendée martyrdom into grounds on which to denounce the application of a French genocide.[3] Meanwhile, it was the moment of the other Eighty-nine, which, in just a short time, put an end to the division of Europe inherited from the Second World War. The democratic revolutions in the communist world seemed to condemn without appeal the October 1917 connection that had long dominated twentieth-century revolutionary historiography, sanctioning Furet's definitive triumph as one who had never ceased to denounce the profound authoritarian nature of that particular link. However, the collapse of communism did not exclude – in fact, apparently even reinvigorated – the image of 1789 that the bicentenary had intended to promote: the huge political turnaround following the collapse of the Berlin Wall encouraged a rereading of the history of Europe in a unitary perspective. This made it possible to read the events of the old continent in terms of a path with many features in common and, in the name of the values of 1789, to relaunch those ideals of liberty and equality around which the French Revolution had built its own success.

Furet himself seemed to take the opportunity to reread the history of Europe in terms of a political democracy that now, in his view, appeared irreversible. In a speech given in the Chamber of Deputies in Rome at the end of 1991, shortly after the collapse of the Soviet Union, he even prophesied a future for Europe where civil rights, ennobled by a revolution that had in its time been overwhelmed by the Terror, could return to guide the old continent's democratic politics. His words almost seemed to indicate that his reading of the revolution, from its beginning the incubator of future totalitarianism, had given way to a much more measured approach, where 'the principles of 1789, socialised within free institutions, and drawn closer by experience of American tradition' formed the boundaries of a new policy within which the whole of Europe might be restructured.[4]

Furet, however, never followed up on those words, which risked, in referring to the values of a finally achieved representative democracy, to undermine his entire previous reconstruction of the revolution. He preferred to focus on the theme around which he had built his dissent from twentieth-century historiography, swiftly moving on to write a sort of epitaph for the communist utopia, where he seems to bid an emotional farewell to something that had formed a large part of his own existence.[5]

However, what Furet had restricted himself to giving voice to was a shared sentiment that others would try to develop. It is true that the history of the French Revolution, after 1989, suffered in some way from the many insights produced by the bicentenary-inspired examination of its many stages, until it now seems an impossible subject to reduce to any kind of synthesis. Nonetheless, even in the context of an expansion of interests and fields of study, which seemed to act as a sort of bulwark with respect to a renewed, unified reading of the revolutionary decade, political history was once again on the move and encouraging the opening up of new and fascinating areas of investigation.[6] The study of the Vendée, above all, dragged out from the nostalgic, pastist framework in which Catholic memory had placed it, proved to be highly useful in terms of measuring, in an original way, the impact made by the sudden modernity of politics on a society that was still a very traditional one. Jean-Clément Martin – who deserves credit for having brought resistance to the values of 1789 back to the attention of revolutionary historiography – thus made the study of the Vendée an opportunity to read and assess the excessive number of difficulties which, in the end, the revolutionary decade lost its way within. In this regard, his *Contre-révolution, Révolution et Nation*, published in 1998, constitutes a decisive change of pace with respect to the uncertainties following the bicentenary: for the first time an overall reading of the revolutionary decade was attempted that made good use of long-past historiographical diatribes while at the same time keeping them at a distance. Soboul's work, and Furet's, were both dealt with by Martin, who, however, had the shrewdness to oppose, and indeed quash, them. He argued that the former had demonized the counter-revolution without ever studying it, while it had been easy for the latter, thanks to a void in historiography, to ignore any concrete threats that had helped produce the mechanics of the Terror. Martin identifies the multiple resistances to the revolution in 1789 itself, going on to meticulously track their developments, and also, thanks to the fierce internal struggle that soon took place, the predatory use that the various contending parties made of the accusation of being enemies of the revolution. All this provided an opportunity to write, from yet another angle, a history of the political decade that had begun in 1789. The common thread was the multiple conflicts between the parties involved, which the author followed up to Brumaire and which, in his view, Bonaparte's experiment in governance set aside but did not solve. In this whirlwind process of the opposition and fragmentation of the various alignments, in the revolutionary camp as well as in its opponent's, it was, however, the progressive nature of events that was (almost immediately) abandoned to the advantage of a more balanced reading of the revolutionary period. The achievements did not exceed the failures and they worked together to give a more precise image of the many contradictions that dominated the reality of modern France.[7]

It goes without saying that the work was the result of reflection on what new research, thanks partly to the French Revolution bicentennial, had meanwhile brought to the subject.[8] The many merits of the book – which in 2000 would lead Martin to the direction of the *Institut d'histoire de la Révolution française* – included the emphasis placed on the Directory period, long neglected by classical historiography and never supportive of Furet's revisionism. Martin was careful to place there, in that particular arc of time, the development of the significance that still connotes today the political category of the counter-revolution. The clarification also arose from a sudden surge of interest in the Directory: in France, scholars trained in the world of classical historiography, such as Bernard Gainot and Pierre Serna, had meanwhile exonerated the period from the accusation of being the antechamber to Brumaire. In their monographic works, the years after Robespierre's fall, marked by the exercise of the Year III constitution, were once again the moment when democracy set out on its arduous path: the repeated recourse to electoral mechanisms had opened up spaces of freedom in the revolution's political process that had previously barely been glimpsed. It was a line of research that crossed over with other areas of study that ran in parallel in other national historiographies traditionally interested in what had occurred in France. The result was to strengthen the reasons for an approach to the origins of democracy that extended from the traditional (and at the same time restrictive) French national dimension to a wider European framework.[9]

The perspective was benefitted by the transforming wave of the present political moment: the return of freedom throughout Europe made it possible to go back to look at the revolution in a different way. The Terror was once more a mere deviation into authoritarianism – a dramatic parenthesis, in other words, on the path to representative democracy, something for which there had been no lack of witnesses since 1789. In this way, it became possible to reread the overall meaning of the revolutionary events on the basis of a close intertwining between France and Europe: throughout the entire old continent, it was finally possible to introduce a strict equivalence between revolution and representative democracy, between a European past and a present governed by the hendiadys of liberty and equality.

A transnational reading of the revolution took shape along these lines, which found its most original synthesis in Annie Jourdan's essay, *La Révolution, une exception française?* Published in 2004, it put forward a rereading of 1789 which eschewed the commonplace of a revolution that, thanks to a uniqueness which soon became universal, had become a crucible of modernity.[10] In contrast, it suggested returning to accommodate the American Revolution alongside the other movements that in Europe, even before 1789, had indicated that the *ancien régime* had come to the end of its centuries-old course. In this reconstruction, while the Revolution remained decisive in establishing modern French identity, the exaggerated attention that patriotic nationalism had bestowed upon it constituted an obstacle that had for too long been insurmountable on the path to a broader reading – a reading that would indicate that, at the end of the eighteenth century, the entire Atlantic world, from one side of the ocean to the other, was in the throes of profound social upheaval. The French 1789 thus became a transitional moment – an important one, certainly, and, thanks to the war, with almost immediate and devastating consequences – in an even longer journey, which began in the colonies of North America, and then in the United Provinces and ended, as it spread from France, in the experiment of the Sisters republics. Needless to say, this perspective echoed Palmer's pioneering work to a great extent, corroborating it with specific attention to the European framework. In this framework, the idea was the differences in a democratic political culture – which had its birthplace in many places and not only in France in 1789 – could be more clearly and more extensively measured.[11]

This interpretation, however, was open to various criticisms, different in nature but sharing the same scepticism towards the Western world making a united claim, some arguing for the reaffirmation of the French standpoint, others the denial of a properly Western identity. The former was put forward by Patrice Gueniffey, Furet's favourite pupil: he would always remain loyal to Furet's ideas, drawing from him the universal value of the revolutionary experiment that took place in France as a non-negotiable guideline. He had begun to deal with 1789 through the study of electoral phenomena in a work, where, in addition to the methods, he above all emphasized the limits of the practices of political legitimation introduced in revolutionary France, concluding with the ability of small circles of militants to profoundly alter the vote.[12] The dyscrasia between a population still uncertain about the new rules and a revolutionary minority whose civilizing pretensions would soon lead to violence committed upon the will of the majority indicated the serious contradiction in a political process that arose in the name of the general will but was soon forced to face a plurality of dissensions and open challenges. From here, Gueniffey chose to return to the question of Terror, which in his opinion offered a dramatic synthesis of the hiatus between revolutionary hope and the state of society, between the demand for everything to change and the obstacles that stood in the way of the new. Published in 2000, his work was a substantially successful attempt to restore the phenomenon of political exceptionality par excellence – the Terror itself – to the normality of a government practice marked, from its first developments, by the desire to make the break with the past irreversible, come what may.[13] In this way, the Terror was not identified with a precise moment of the revolution, when only circumstances forced those responsible for national politics to go beyond the framework of rules that they had set for themselves and to which they would have liked to remain faithful. Instead, it was the product of a conscious political line, built around a discourse of radical subversion and a moral rhetoric, which aimed to deploy violence in the service of a collective project whose full legitimacy and insuppressible necessity could not be contested. It is true that the revolution was threatened and that the war and multiple conspiracies indicated a dramatic situation of conflict both within and outside the country: the Terror did not, however, grow out of a reaction to the state of siege in which the democratization process was taking place, so much as the attempt to impose a legal framework from above which, even through violent coercion, was still recognized from below. Discourse on the Terror, therefore, always ready to justify excess and discrimination, was nothing more than a wholly political tool – one to move through in order to conquer power and then defend it in the face of the inevitable challenges launched at the group only temporarily in control. For this reason, violence surged forward from the very origins of the revolution and accompanied (and conditioned) its tumultuous and unpredictable course.

Faced with the enormous void left by the collapse of traditional sovereignty and the impossibility of filling it through shared forms of consent, the use of terror as a practice became a necessary instrument of government well before Year II. Extremism, never the prerogative of only one party and resorted to by all the groups who succeeded each other at the helm of the political process, thus became an integral part of the revolutionary dynamic. Apparent from the summer of 1789, violence would never fail to be a presence, not after the fall of Robespierre, not even after the attempt to establish the Republic with the Constitution of Year III – so much so, that Gueniffey concluded that the category of the Terror, closely intertwined with that of revolution, ensured a paradigmatic, if not universal, value for the French experience. The reaffirmed centrality of 1789 in the study of revolutions of the modern age, as Gueniffey proposed, was not, however, the only obstacle to a reading that intended to embrace all of the late eighteenth century's political upheavals, on both sides of the Atlantic.

As Annie Jourdan completed her work, establishing the irreversibility of a new Europe federated around values that were not indebted to the French example alone, historical research into the age of revolutions received another, significantly different, contribution. In 2004, Christopher Bayly's book set itself on a collision course with all the ideas of the old continent's centrality in the construction of new interpretative models in relation to modernity.[14] While the work highlighted the revolutionary period, it suggested a global, rather than a European, nature: the transcending of national histories – identified as the result of old continent historicism – appeared to be the ineliminable prerequisite for a reading of politico-social changes on an international scale. The so-called age of revolutions was for Bayly a period of extraordinary political developments not only in the old continent, but also in Asia and Africa, all related to themes of interdependence and interconnection. The basis of such a perspective was thus another history of the modern world, one that played down the centrality of the revolutionary phenomenon which post–Second World War historiography had instead taken great care to place at the very heart of its reconstruction.

Testifying to this is the successful work by David Armitage and Sanjay Subrahmanyam that appeared in 2010.[15] Here, again in a global interpretation, the 1776–89 connection is declared to be exhausted, the two events being so distant and different from one another that only a generic concept of revolution could encompass both. In place of this obsolete link, the two, underlining the Eurocentric direction of Palmer's work long before, instead emphasize the existence of a plurality of crises in the late-eighteenth-century world, each of them in direct correlation with the others, which deny 1789's claim to be the leading revolutionary event destined to change the entire planet in the early nineteenth century.[16]

Faced with the challenge launched by the global perspective, revolutionary historiography responded by accepting, to a certain extent, the wager of involving 1789 in the broader framework of a global process. Pierre Serna, above all, who succeeded Martin as director of the *Institut d'histoire de la Révolution française* in 2008, committed himself to this direction. He set himself the task of moving past the otherwise unamalgamable aporia – one always inherent in French political discourse – between the language of liberty and equality and the practices inspired by colonialism. Serna had a great interest in transnational history, which had led him first to look at the relationship between France and the Sister republics and then at the truly Atlantic dimension of 1789. Impressed by what he saw happening in the Arab Spring, he put forward the proposal to change the significance of the French Revolution, making it the conclusive act of the many resistances to colonial power that had taken place throughout the whole modern age. The year 1789 thus became a war of liberation and a work of decolonization with respect to the violently abusive manoeuvres that had been implemented by the monarchy.[17] It was an original and innovative idea, which ended up bringing the revolution back to the very centre of a global process that otherwise would have greatly reduced its importance. Making 1789 the final act of a war of independence of colonized subjects against a Crown that behaved in the same way towards its own metropolitan territory as towards the colonies also made it possible to resolve the contradiction of a French Revolution anticipating colonialism.

The example of Saint-Domingue, where the Republic had intervened to declare the enfranchisement and extension of citizenship to all regardless of skin colour, made it possible to charge another period (see the Napoleonic years) with responsibility for what colonial France would then put into practice. It also continued, in the context of an Atlantic world at boiling point, to guarantee an otherwise easily contested political and civil primacy to 1789. In other words, for Serna, a French Revolution read as a war of independence from colonialism was the only way to escape the grip of global history without losing out in terms of the event's positioning on the value scale of the political phenomena of the time.[18]

Specialist historians of the French Revolution across the Atlantic were quick to pick up on his ideas, soon reclaiming them in the context of a global reading of the events. In 2013, for example, a collection of essays came out, edited by Lynn Hunt, Suzanne Desan and William Max Nelson, which aimed to bring a renewed line of research to studies on the French Revolution. The premise was the global impact of 1789, which permeated not only the Atlantic world but also a great part of the African and Asian continents, taking advantage of the crisis of the imperial systems which occurred at the end of the eighteenth century. The perspective suggested by the three editors invited us to read the French Revolution as the consequence of the profound renewal taking place in the world at that time, deeply imprinted by the centrality that colonization, the dizzying rhythm of circulating ideas and the global economy had assumed in the context of international politics. All this, according to the three scholars, also helped to mould 1789, which then in turn ensured a decisive push to the elements that shaped it, given that the revolution's message of liberation accompanied the critique of colonial practices on an international scale.[19] This renewed attention to the extra-European aspect of the French Revolution, its scope taking it far beyond the Atlantic context to involve the entire colonial world wherever it formed, made it possible for the editors to put forward the idea that the diatribes in recent decades between those who supported the social nature of the revolution and those who saw it as essentially ideological could be considered closed. In their opinion, the two lines – political culture on the one hand, economic frameworks on the other – deserved to be encompassed within the form of a global approach. This, bringing together the impact of trade, financial speculation and debt manoeuvres in the context of the mercantile war with Britain for the control of international markets, influenced the developments of French statehood and the choices of fiscal policy that ended up – also in terms of a violent response – intertwining with the revolutionary dynamics.

From this point of view, Pierre Serna's ideas, included at the end of the collective volume as a conclusion indicating further study,[20] were confirmation of the consensus his words had found from many historians: his proposal to see the revolutions as a number of wars of independence from central authorities encouraged renewed attention to eighteenth-century colonial identity and made 1789 a turning point in a centuries-old process that began with the resistance of the United Provinces to the Spain of Philip II and extended far beyond the revolutionary decade, even up to the Arab Spring of the early twenty-first century. The conclusion, which the editors of the volume agreed with, was therefore a rereading of the Revolution, where French exceptionalism was entirely set aside in order to restore the phenomenon to a global dimension.

And yet, even without resorting to easy hindsight in relation to the so-called Arab Spring, it is hard to imagine that Serna's brilliant manoeuvre can restore to 1789 that centrality in the international political and cultural debate which, in company with the category of modernity, it possessed for so long. Nevertheless, it seems that this downgrading depends only in part on the political framework of the world at the beginning of the twenty-first century. The decline of the European project seems more significant in this regard, giving way as it has to the 'imperial' specificity of the British world – a world that, even when the wind blew strong in favour of the unity of the old continent, never renounced its own particularity. Therefore, one should not see as a coincidence the fact that Steven Pincus recently declared the English Revolution of 1688, the Glorious Revolution, to be the first authentic contemporary revolution, a kind of pivotal event in English, European and world history.[21] Needless to say, these words reflect the desire to replace 1789 with 1688 and, to the detriment of the French model, make the English event the central junction on the road to liberty, re-establishing a political and cultural primacy that would find its axis along Anglo-American coordinates.[22]

It is this perspective, which encompasses world history itself, that constitutes the real threat to the meaning of 1789 in the twenty-first century. With a forcefulness heretofore never possessed, the English-speaking world has returned to meticulously point out that European civilization is a plurality of histories, each very different from one another, and in no way ascribable to a common narrative thread – something that British particularity provides the best example of in terms of an international perspective.

Faced with this challenge, scholars more particularly attentive to 1789's centrality in the construction of modernity responded by resorting both to traditional interpretative lines and to those instead that took into account the demands imposed by the expansion of the geographical and chronological framework of revolutionary time. Those that chose the former route, within the framework of a history of ideas invited to explain the extraordinary change that took place following 1789, but also the various prospects and digressions it would quickly initiate, include Jonathan Israel's great attempt to take a resolutely democratic approach towards the first revolutionary years, distinguishing the legacy of the radical Enlightenment from the authoritarian directions that soon followed.[23] Not surprisingly, it was a venture that aroused strident lamentation from those who accused him of simplistic recourse to anachronism in order to legitimize a pre-established thesis with no solid documentary basis. In reality, there was a simple and linear aspect to his work: going back to the old idea – one that ensured so much success for counter-revolutionary readings – of a direct connection between the Enlightenment and the Revolution, Israel suggested a detailed redevelopment of that traditional link, indicating that only radical philosophy, derived from the thinking of Diderot, D'Holbach and Hélvetius, lay at the origins of the democratic and republican revolution. From this angle, returning to an Atlantic history of the circulation of ideas, it was a simple matter for Israel to identify the instrument of acceleration of a political practice – a practice ready to assume, thanks to 1789, the complete form of a democratic politics – in the construction of libertarian, atheistic and radical thought that, traceable to its root in Spinoza, was quick to whirl giddily from one side of the ocean to the other.

Obviously, to demonstrate the enormous renewal that occurred at the time, Israel had no problem suggesting that the revolution that he explored with such deep interest was certainly not the only one going on. In parallel – this time in the footsteps of Montesquieu – there had developed a monarchical and constitutional revolution, and another, with authoritarian and extremist traits – its origins all to be found in the thinking of Rousseau and Mably – would soon be added. However, while the parliamentary and liberal revolution was short-lived, overwhelmed by the radical initiative, the substantially authoritarian and fiercely populist movement had the strength to oppose and crush it, derailing the democratic process into totalitarian catastrophe. This leads to Israel reaching a conclusion which then galvanizes his whole reconstruction of the revolutionary narrative: progress was the result of only one particular philosophy, because only this philosophy would inform the most ideal development of the political process that followed on from 1789.

The democratic and republican revolution, essentially represented by the Girondins – a political party which Israel regards with poignant admiration – was therefore the best thing to come out of 1789: tolerance and freedom of opinion, and equal rights for all, including religious minorities and women, constitute the authentic and redemptive outcome. This reading by juxtaposition of the revolutionary political process, with the Girondins, supporters of human rights, set against the Montagnards, who saw a period of republican freedom to its grave, informs his entire reconstruction of events, where a moral and political judgement, passed down from the heights of hindsight, far from hidden, is proudly declared. It has been pointed out that his work is not so much a historical operation as a philosophical one: over its great length, Israel never shies away from putting forward his own point of view and all his comments, designed to orientate the reader, are aimed at distinguishing those who might have been benefactors of humanity from those who, while speaking in its name, simply threw open a Pandora's box of dark and disturbing modernity.

This explains why his work was greeted with great hostility: he was accused of wanting to track down, teleologically, the iniquities of the twentieth century to the revolutionary past, as if, coming to the revolution through a procedure in reverse, the way he found to illustrate the positions of the various groups was far too schematic, distinguishing the bringers of progress from the forerunners of the evil growth of authoritarianism and the precursors of an overbearing, populist radicalism.

However, rather than insisting on the strictly historical weakness of his ideas, it would more be appropriate, perhaps, to look at Israel's work from another angle, situating it in the context of a present time that the author deliberately has no intention of ignoring and around which he constructs his entire, positive, reading of the French Revolution. His insistence on the nature of a democratic and republican movement inspired by the profound values of tolerance and political radicalism constitutes the reflection of a reaction to present times darkened by religious and political fanaticism. The Western world, in Israel's view, has to face up to such extremism by rediscovering its history of freedom and progress. From this point of view, while underlining how populism, intolerance, fascism and communism find more than one illuminating antecedent in the revolutionary events themselves, for Israel the point lies elsewhere – in particular, in the need to unite, through militant intervention, over the profound values of a Western world that multiculturalism and globalization have, where their responsibilities are concerned, too often set aside when faced with the great number of dramatic twentieth-century situations.

From this point of view, his words are only in appearance light years away from other historiographical reconstructions essentially favourable towards Year II and which we have seen bear the brunt of François Furet's attack. In fact, all of them maintain a firm belief in the exceptional nature of 1789 as the date of the founding of modernity, untempted by the idea of diluting the revolution within a wider political and geographical context. An example is offered by Peter McPhee's 2017 history of the French Revolution.[24] The Australian historian had already tried his hand at a general study in 2002,[25] his historiographical background centred around the return of attention to the provincial political dynamics that English-language historiography had started to focus on in the 1970s. His recent work, at least at first glance, seems to follow traditional lines, its pages characterized by a temporal arc limited to the revolutionary decade, its spatiality remaining within the borders of the Hexagon. His studies regarding the French provincial world, however, prompt him to emphasize the crisis of consensus that the new public authorities underwent over the course of the decade.

Thus, if on the one hand his preference for Year II remains clear, seen as the moment where the foundations are laid for a socio-economic regeneration from the ashes of the *ancien régime*, he does not, on the other, hide the many, perhaps too many, difficulties that the revolutionary process had to undergo on its whirlwind path. In this way, if the circumstances remain an instrument of measurement of the excessive violence and the many authoritarian deviations that characterized the developments of 1789, there is no doubt that the author does not even try to conceal that all this constituted a serious obstacle to the stabilization of the revolutionary process in the context of a new order that was more just, not only in a legal sense but also in political and social terms. Overall, it is a work that, while a long way from Israel's work, has in common with it the idea of the revolution's primacy. Refusing to dialogue with the global direction present in the panorama of French Revolution research, McPhee's study shows just how, and to what extent, despite globality's challenge, for many the revolution remains an essentially European matter, its originality and values elements that the identity of the old continent should continue to remain committed to.

Notwithstanding these positions, which say so much with regard to how consolidated historiographical tradition stays firmly bound to the centrality of the old continent, the fact remains that the challenge of globalization constitutes a strong cause for concern for many European historians, sensing as they do the idea of definitively setting aside the cumbersome legacy of national historiographies. In a specifically French context, perhaps the most ambitious operation is Annie Jourdan's, who we have already seen contesting French exceptionalism at the beginning of the century with brilliant results. In 2018, she returned to national historiography and to the serious responsibilities that, in her opinion, this still had with regard to the idea of a revolution of solidarity, supported, at least at the beginning, by the overwhelming majority of the French. She was careful, with her new work, to suggest yet another interpretative path, where unanimity is replaced by division and the impulse of solidarity by partisan opposition.[26] The revolution no longer involved the sudden appearance of a unanimous dream of freedom, but rather the dramatic collision course of divergent positions, which soon faced off against one another through the armed violence that would lead to civil war.

In this particular context, it was an easy matter for Jourdan to backdate the clash between revolutionaries and counter-revolutionaries to 1789 itself, underlining, through meticulous investigation into the sources, the repeated attempts of the revolution's opponents to overturn to their own benefit the political equilibrium that emerged from the Estates General. Hence the idea that civil war was not only an instrument of acceleration for the revolutionary event, but, if not above all, the factor that would make it possible to read the many elements of revolutionary violence in a more restrained light. In the author's view, the long-standing idea that the ideological (and authoritarian) nature of the revolution was due to the obligation to foster liberty was contradicted by the fact that revolutionary violence was above all the consequence of a power vacuum and not at all an instrument of government – in other words, the sign of a sudden, and, to a certain extent, unpredictable collapse of the political framework rather than the result of an ideology with strict rules.

Hence the approach to the Terror as a consequence of the inability of the revolutionary government to move away from a dead-end situation, where the counter-revolutionary challenge seemed to overwhelm everything: the collapse of the old order in the summer of 1789 cleared the field for political recriminations and punitive impulses, destined to reach an intensity that could no longer be controlled. From this point of view, too, the revolutionary government was not therefore a dramatic parenthesis, the sudden *dérapage* of a political process that had, with enormous difficulty, to found an institutional equilibrium in the context of a republican democracy. The execution of Robespierre, rather than opening a new phase, in some ways actually prolonged that particular period, which in theory was declared closed forever: the Directory years to some extent continued the work of stabilizing the republic on a legal basis, but establishing this legality was undermined by the tensions of a civil war that never seemed to end. From this point of view, Jourdan's book, which makes no concessions to the Consulate period, provides a traditional chronological arc, with Bonaparte bringing (negative) closure to the time of civil wars. The work returns to dialogue with other contemporary revolutions: not so much those following the advance of French troops through Europe, as those overseas, especially the American Revolution, assigned here a sort of primacy in terms of coercive government practices. Taking up an interpretative line that circulated widely in the 1940s in the United States, distancing herself from Hannah Arendt's successful reading which that tradition, after the Second World War, had then set aside, Jourdan goes back to pointing out that the American Revolution, too, was an arduous and painful civil war. At a territorial level, colonial society split into a host of internal conflicts, to be followed by repressive measures against native inhabitants, slaves and the most fragile groups in society at that time – all not infrequently drawn towards a loyalist line. Rather than opening a dark period of violence, rather than being the result of ideological invention, this was, perhaps more simply, the outcome of a long-shared social past.

Jourdan's work marks, precisely in terms of what has been said so far, an important, and in some ways decisive, step in moving away from a historiographical rhetoric that had, through reference to national identity, built its strength on French exceptionalism and patriotism. The success of a globalized world, but also a nationalism ready to rediscover an original form, has certainly been the driving force for a less unilateral approach – one in which it was possible to leave behind the contrast between economic moment and ideological aspect through a resurgence of political practices designed to produce an onerous emancipation from an order of values still strongly permeated by the weight of tradition. Hence, within the framework of Annie Jourdan's unconcealed interest in the Atlantic revolutionary world, the keen attention to the American precedent – its identification as an ante-litteram laboratory of political practices, later destined to be applied only to France's Year II – constitutes a high-impact acquisition to more appropriately circumscribe the revolutionary events of the late eighteenth century. This was a plural phenomenon, marked on both sides of the ocean by the attempt to build, with all the difficulties of oppressive tradition, a more just order. This was not entirely successful on either side of the Atlantic, precisely because of the impediments that the traditional world would again and then again be able to put in its way.

And yet, the work today that reflects even more clearly the new political-cultural sensibility regarding the revolution is Jeremy Popkin's very recent history of the French Revolution.[27] This is perhaps the most ambitious attempt to bring together the history of 1789 with the developments that research has latterly produced in relation to certain, hitherto very neglected, aspects. Popkin's own intellectual biography follows the route, fraught with contrasts and sudden slips, which, especially since 1989, has been a feature of the revolutionary field. His interest in 1789 actually goes even further back in time, to the 1970s, when, as a young university student, he came to the study of the revolution in the wake of the protest movements. There is no doubt, however, that his contributions to the subject are almost all ascribable to the period following the collapse of the Berlin Wall and have been deeply marked by Furet's challenge to the interpretative orthodoxy of the revolution. Popkin had previously dedicated a work to the revolutionary decade's conservative and reactionary press, which already signalled the heterodoxy of his interests.[28] While this was later followed, at the beginning of 1990s, by a more wide-ranging work dealing with the press in the revolutionary years,[29] he also managed to produce a brief, stock-taking general study in 1995, which to date has gone through seven editions.[30] Here, Popkin's attention to the new historiographical acquisitions that have taken place over the last quarter of a century is clearly visible. In the meantime, his interest shifted to the French Revolution outside the Hexagon, with particular regard to events in Saint-Domingue, to which he dedicated a number of studies, above all a general overview where events are carefully related to, and intertwined with, those of the mother country.[31]

It is in this context that his desire to return to the revolutionary history of France must be read, with a work rich in new perspectives: on the role of women in revolution, on the importance of the political-cultural debate about race and slavery, on the historical significance of the decree of abolition and on the difficulties involved in building a complete democratic political practice. Overall, his history of the French Revolution constitutes the most determined and accurate response to those who tend to divest 1789 of its profound stimulus to the birth of democracy. In this particular frame of reference, where surveying the French Revolution once again is an opportunity to read the difficulties and developments of democratic political practice, it should not be surprising that Popkin's work stands out as a concrete answer to a trend that in the last two decades has invariably been on the defensive with regard to referencing 1789. Curiously, the answer comes – once more, it could be said – from a European outside Europe: in the old continent, the questioning of national historiographies, in some respects well merited, has left a worrying void, unable as it has been to formulate a proposition effective enough to balance the successful reading of modernity along an Anglo-American axis.

After all, given the fact that the strength of some often depends on the weakness of others, all this depends on the lack of a political project in the European world, where cultural choices have too often been questionable. Its decisions have turned out to be suicidal: on the one hand, public discourse on the unity of the old continent was decisive in indicating national historiographies as vestiges of a past time – an obstacle, therefore, on the way to the common history to be set in place as the foundation of the new political construction; on the other, the desire to bypass the national element in order to rush through the construction of a European identity imposed from above has ended up provoking expressions of rejection – while, in the area of historiography itself, it has not provided a single tool able to stand comparison with the new gospel of globalization.

There should be little surprise, therefore, that reference to 1789 has found itself in free fall, the event increasingly considered as one with roots set in a vast global framework – the result being the erasure of the very premise of revolutionary ideology. Yet it was proposed, it is worth remembering, from the very beginning, as an exceptional event – one without comparison, one intended to create that new world whose values, even today, the old continent should continue to cherish, in order to find, within the global framework, its own legitimacy, its own ascendancy and, ultimately, its own strength.

Notes

Introduction

1 Ch. Walton, 'French Revolutionary Studies: Challenges and Potential Ways Forward', in *New Perspectives on the French Revolution*, ed. A. Fairfax-Cholmeley and C. Jones, vol. 4 (e-France, 2013), 6–15.
2 V. Titone, *Introduzione alla rivoluzione francese* (Milan: il Milione, 1966), 5.
3 P. Viola, *L'Europa moderna. Storia di un'identità* (Turin: Einaudi, 2004).
4 Here I am drawing on numerous works concerning the historiography of the French Revolution. Among the most important are P. Geyl, 'French Historians for and against the Revolution', in *Encounters in History*, ed. P. Geyl (New York: Meridian Books, 1961); A. Gérard, *La Révolution française. Mythes et interprétations* (Paris: Flammarion, 1970); J. Godechot, *Un jury pour la Révolution* (Paris: Laffont, 1974) and E. Schmitt, *Einführung in die Geschichte der Französischen Revolution* (München: Beck, 1976). The Bicentenary offered then a great opportunity for revisiting 1789: see notably O. Bétourné-I. Hartig, *Penser l'histoire de la Révolution: deux siècles de passion française* (Paris: La Découverte, 1989); B. Bongiovanni and L. Guerci, *L'albero della Rivoluzione. Le interpretazioni della rivoluzione francese* (Turin: Einaudi, 1989); E. Hobsbawm, *Echoes of the Marseillaise: Two Centuries Look Back on the French Revolution* (London; New York: Verso, 1990); A. Saitta, ed., *La storia della storiografia europea sulla Rivoluzione francese*, 3 vol. (Rome: Istituto storico italiano per l'età moderna, 1990-1991); A. Faure, ed., *Le XIXème siècle et la Révolution française* (Paris: Créaphis, 1992) and S. L. Kaplan, *Farewell, Revolution. 1. Disputed Legacies, France, 1789-1989* and S. L. Kaplan, *The historians' feud: France, 1789-1989* (Ithaca, NY: Cornell University Press, 1995). See also, J. Solé, 'The Historiography of the French Revolution', in *A Companion to Historiography*, ed. M. Bentley (London: Routledge, 1997), 509–25; Antoine de Baecque, *Pour ou contre la Révolution* (Paris: Bayard, 2002); E. Pelzer, ed., *Revolution und Klio. Die Hauptwerke der Französischen Revolution* (Gottingen: Vandenhoeck & Ruprecht, 2003); P. Serna, 'Révolution française. Historiographie au XIXe siècle', in *Historiographies. Concepts et débats*, ed. C. Delacroix (Paris: Gallimard, 2010), 2: 1186–99; C. Mazauric, 'Retour sur 200 ans d'histoire et de révolution', in *La Révolution française. Une histoire toujours vivante*, ed. M. Biard (Paris: Tallandier, 2009), 421–3; J.-N. Ducange, *La Révolution française et l'histoire du monde. Deux siècles de débats historiques et politiques, 1815–1991* (Paris: Colin, 2014); P. McPhee, ed., *A Companion to the French Revolution* (Chichester: Wiley-Blackwell, 2013) and A. Forrest and M. Middell, eds, *The Routledge Companion to the French Revolution in World History* (London; New York: Routledge, 2016).

Chapter 1: The rules of all revolutionary history, 1789–1815

1. Among the numerous works on Condorcet, see especially K. M. Baker, *Condorcet: From Natural Philosophy to Social Mathematics* (Chicago: University of Chicago Press, 1975); E. and R. Badinter, *Condorcet, 1743–1794: un intellectuel en politique* (Paris: Fayard, 1988) and D. Williams, *Condorcet and Modernity* (Cambridge: Cambridge University Press, 2008).
2. J.-A. de Caritat de Condorcet, *Esquisse d'un tableau historique des progrès de l'esprit humain* (Paris: Agasse, an III) [Engl. transl. *Outlines of an Historical View of the Human Mind being a Posthumous Work of the Late M. de Condorcet* (London: J. Johnson, 1795)]. On the *Esquisse* see namely B. Binoche, ed., *Nouvelles lectures du "Tableau historique" de Condorcet* (Paris: Hermann, 2013).
3. In my understanding of the first historians of the French Revolution I rely above all on A. Aulard, *Études et leçons sur la Révolution française* (6e série, Paris: Alcan, 1910), M. Ozouf, 'De Thermidor a Brumaire: le discours de la révolution sur elle-même', *Revue Historique* 243 (1970): 31–66 and J.-R. Suratteau, 'L'histoire de la Revolution par elle-même', in *La storia della storiografia europea*, vol. 2, 7–16. Two more recent important works are Ph. Bourdin, ed., *La Révolution, 1789–1871: écriture d'une histoire immédiate* (Clermont; Ferrand: Presses de l'Université Blaise-Pascal, 2008) and L. Chavanette and F. Dendena, eds, 'L'historien vivant, 1789–1830', *La Révolution Française* 5 (2016): n. 10. For a renewed interpretation of the political uses of the past during the revolutionary decade, see notably F. Dendena, *Nella breccia del tempo. Scrittura e uso politico della storia in Rivoluzione* (Milan: Bruno Mondadori, 2017).
4. L.-M. Prudhomme, *Histoire générale et impartiale des erreurs, des fautes et des crimes commis pendant la Révolution française* (Paris: rue des Marais, an V).
5. On Prudhomme, see J. Zizek, '"Plume de fer": Louis-Marie Prudhomme writes the French Revolution', *French Historical Studies* 26 (2003): 619–60 and A. Duprat, *Louis-Marie Prudhomme et l'*Histoire générale et impartiale des erreurs et des crimes commis pendant la Révolution française *(1797). Les réflexions d'un républicain sur la Terreur*, in Bourdin *La Révolution, 1789–1871*, 111–27.
6. J.-P. Rabaut Saint-Étienne, *Précis historique de la Révolution fran- çaise* (Paris; Strasbourg: Onfroy et Treuttel, 1792); Engl. transl. *The History of the Revolution of France* (London: Debrett, 1792) and (Dublin: Wogan et al., 1792).
7. G. P. Rabaut, *Compendio storico della rivoluzione francese, seguito dall'atto costituzionale della Francia* (Nice, Alpi Marittime: s.n.t. anno IV).
8. On the political life of Rabaut de Saint-Etienne, see especially C. Borello, 'Les sources d'une altérité religieuse en révolution: Rabaut Saint-Étienne ou la radicalisation des représentations protestantes', *Annales historiques de la Révolution française* 378 (2014): 29–49.
9. A.-E. Fantin-Desodoards, *Histoire philosophique de la Révolution de France, depuis la convocation des notables, par Louis XVI, jusqu'à la séparation de la Convention nationale* (Paris: Imprimerie de l'Union, an IV); F. Pagès, *Histoire secrète de la Révolution française, depuis la convocation des notables jusqu'à ce jour, 1er novembre, 1796, v. st.* (Paris: Jansen, an V) [Engl. transl. *Secret History of the French Revolution, from the Convocation of the Notables in 1787 to the First of November 1796* (London: T.N. Longman, 1797). On both see namely J.-L. Chappey, *L'*Histoire philosophique de la révolution de France *de Fantin Desodoards. Dynamiques croisées entre statut d'historien et identité politique*, in Bourdin *La Révolution, 1789–1871*, 129–58 and

C. Hould, Les « Discours » des Tableaux de la Révolution française. Écriture d'une histoire immédiate et passions contemporaines, 1789-1817, 180-97.
10 Ch. De Lacretelle, Précis historique de la Révolution française (Paris: Treuttel & Würtz and Onfroy an IX [1801]).
11 F.-E. de Toulongeon, Histoire de France, depuis la révo-lution de 1789, écrite d'après les mémoires et manuscrits recueillis dans les dépôts civils et militaires (Paris: Treuttel & Würtz, an IX [1801]-1810).
12 A. F. Bertrand de Molleville, Histoire de la Révolution de France (Paris: Giguet, an IX-XI [1801-1803]).
13 On Toulongeon, see O. Ritz, 'L'an IX ou l'historiographie de la Révolution en débat', in L'historien vivant, and his 'L'historien dans la tempête: images de l'écriture de l'histoire chez les premiers historiens de la révolution, 1789-1815', in Entre deux eaux. Les secondes Lumières et leurs ambiguïtés, 1789-1815, ed. A. Vasak (Paris: Editions le Manuscrit, 2012), 309-28.
14 On Lacretelle, see E. Barrault, 'Lacretelle et son Précis historique de la Révolution de France. Quand un publiciste se transforme en historien de la Révolution', in La Révolution, 1789-1871, ed. Bourdin, 157-70.
15 P. Paganel, Essai historique et critique sur la Révolution française (Paris: Plassan, 1810).
16 See J. Jefferson Looney, ed., The Papers of Thomas Jefferson, Retirement Series, 12 August 1810 to 17 June 1811 (Princeton: Princeton University Press, 2006), 3: 219-21.
17 C.-A- de Calonne, Lettre adressée au roi, le 9 février 1789 (Londres: T. Spilsbury, 1789) and Lettre à l'Assemblée nationale (Paris: Laporte, 1789). On the rejection of the Revolution and the first emigration – with a peculiar attention to Calonne – see K. Carpenter, Refugees of the French Revolution. Emigrés in London, 1789-1802 (London: Palgrave, 1999).
18 A. de Rivarol, Journal politique-national des États-Généraux et de la Révolution de 1789, n. 17 (1789), 2-3.
19 On Rivarol, I still rely on B. Faÿ, Rivarol et la Révolution (Paris: Perrin, 1978). See also P. Matyaszewski, La pensée politique d'Antoine de Rivarol (Lublin: Katolickiego Uniwersytetu Lubelskiego, 1997) and more recently V. Baranger, Rivarol face à la Révolution française (Paris: Éditions de Paris, 2007).
20 On the Monarchiens R. H. Griffiths, Le Centre perdu: Malouet et les"monarchiens" dans la Révolution française (Grenoble: Presses universitaires de Grenoble, 1988).
21 On Edmund Burke's polemical attitude towards the French Revolution, I rely on A. Goodwin, The Political Genesis of Edmund Burke's Reflections on the Revolution in France (Manchester: Manchester University Press, 1968) and J. C. Whale, ed., Edmund Burke's Reflections on the Revolution in France: New Interdisciplinary Essays (Manchester: Manchester University Press, 2000).
22 E. Burke, Reflections on the Revolution in France and on the Proceedings in Certain Societies in London Relative to that Event in a Letter Intended to have been Sent to a Gentleman in Paris (London; J. Dodsley, 1790). See also the first French translation: Réflexions sur la Révolution de France, et sur les procédés de certaines sociétés à Londres, relatifs à cet événement (Paris; Londres: Laurent fils & Edward, 1790).
23 R. Bourke, Empire & Revolution: The Political Life of Edmund Burke (Princeton: Princeton University Press, 2015).
24 E. Jones, Edmund Burke and the Invention of Modern Conservatism, 1830-1914: An Intellectual History (Oxford; New York: Oxford University Press, 2017).

25 The crucial works here are J. Godechot, *The Counterrevolution: Doctrine and Action, 1789-1804* (London: Routledge, 1972) and G. Gengembre, *La contre-révolution ou l'histoire désespérante* (Paris: Imago, 1989).
26 F.-R. de de Chateaubriand, *Essai historique, politique et moral sur les révolutions anciennes et modernes, considérées dans leurs rapports avec la Révolution française* (Londres; Hambourg; Paris: J. Deboffe, J. F. Fauche & Le Mière, 1797). English transl. of the abridgment of 1815, *Historical, Political, and Moral Essay on Revolutions, Ancient and Modern* (London: H. Colburn, 1815).
27 J. Mallet du Pan, *Les Considérations sur la nature de la Révolution de France* (Londres; Bruxelles: Flon, 1793). English transl. *Considerations on the Nature of the French Revolution and on the Causes which prolong its Duration* (London: J. Owen, 1793).
28 J. De Maistre, *Considérations sur la France* (Londres: s.n.t. 1797). Engl. transl. *Considerations on France* (Montreal: McGill-Queens University Press, 1974).
29 On Mallet, see namely N. Matteucci, *Jacques Mallet du Pan* (Bologna: il Mulino, 1967) and F. Acomb, Frances Acomb, *Mallet du Pan, 1749-1800: A Career in Political Journalism* (Durham, NC: Duke University Press, 1973).
30 A. Barruel, *Mémoires pour servir à l'histoire du jacobinisme* (Ham bourg: P. Fauche, 1798-1799). Engl. transl. *Memoirs, Illustrating the History of Jacobinism* (London: T. Burton & Co., 1798).
31 See M. Riquet, *Augustin de Barruel: un jésuite face aux jacobins franc-maçons, 1741-1820* (Paris: Beauchesne, 1989).
32 See especially R. A. Lebrun, ed., *Joseph de Maistre's Life, Thought and Influence. Selected Studies* (Montreal: McGill-Queen's University Press, 2001).
33 See namely P. Gueniffey, 'Joseph de Maistre, la Révolution et la France', in *Christianisme et Vendée. La création au XIXe siècle d'un foyer de catholicisme*, ed. A. Gerard (La Roche-sur-Yon: Centre Vendéen de recherches historiques, 2000), 73–116 and C. Armenteros, *The French Idea of History. Joseph de Maistre and his Heirs, 1794-1854* (Ithaca: Cornell University Press, 2011).
34 For a summary of Maistre's reception see especially C. Armenteros and R. A. Lebrun, eds, *Joseph de Maistre and his European Readers: From Friedrich von Gentz to Isaiah Berlin* (Leiden: Brill, 2016).
35 Among the books that directly focus on the impact of revolutionary ideas in Germany, see G. P. Gooch, *Germany and the French Revolution* (London: Longmans, 1920) and M. Boucher, *La Révolution de 1789 vue par les écrivains allemands, ses contemporains, Klopstock, Wieland, Herder, Schiller, Kant, Fichte, Goethe* (Paris: Didier, 1954).
36 F. Schulz, *Geschichte der Grossen Revolution in Frankreich* (Berlin: F. Vieweg der Ältere, 1790).
37 E. Brandes, *Politische Betrachtungen über die Französische Revolution* (Jena: J. M. Mauke, 1790). French transl. *Considérations politiques sur la Révolution de France* (Paris: Laurent fils, 1791).
38 J. Möser, 'Der Arme Freie. Eine Erzählung', *Berlinische Monatschrift* 20 (1792): 113–41.
39 A. W. Rehberg, *Untersuchungen über die Französische Revolution* (Hannover; Osnabrück: C. Ritscher, 1793).
40 See U. Vogel, *Konservative Kritik an der bürgerlichen Revolution: August Wilhelm Rehberg* (Darmstadt: Hermann Luchterhand Verlag, 1972) and E. Pelzer, *Die Wiederkehr des girondistischen Helden: deutsche intellektuelle als kulturelle mittler zwischen Deutschland und Frankreich während der Französischen Revolution* (Bonn: Bouvier, 1998).

41 U. M. A. Bond, 'The Political Conversion of Friedrich Gentz', *European History Quarterly* 3 (1973): 1–12.
42 W. Von Humboldt, 'Ideen über Staatverfassung, durch die Neue Französische Konstituzion veranlasst', *Berlinische Monatschrift* 19 (1792): 84–97.
43 F. von Gentz, *Betrachtungen über die Französische Revolution, nach dem Englischen des Herrn Burke neu Bearbeitet* (Berlin: F. Vieweg, 1793–1794).
44 F. von Gentz, *Mallet du Pan über die Französische Revolution und die Ursachen ihrer Dauer* (Berlin: F. Vieweg, 1794).
45 On the impact of the French Revolution on Italy, see A. De Francesco, *L'Italia di Bonaparte. Politica, statualità e nazione nella penisola italiana tra due rivoluzioni, 1796–1821* (Turin: Utet, 2011). On the adventurous life of Saverio Scrofani, see namely R. Zapperi, 'La fortuna di un avventuriero: Saverio Scrofani e i suoi biografi', *Rassegna storica del Risorgimento* 49 (1962): 447–84.
46 S. Scrofani, *Tutti han torto ossia Lettera a mio zio sulla rivoluzione di Francia* (Italia: s.n.t. 1791). On Scrofani's *Tutti han torto*, see namely R. Tufano, 'Una reazione italiana alle idee rivoluzionarie francesi. Il *Tutti han torto (1791) di Saverio Scrofani*', *Triennio* 18 (1991): 41–60.
47 Ch. M. Wieland, *Aufsätze über die Französische Revolution und Wieland's Stellung zu derselben* (Berlin: Helben, 1879), 151.
48 F. G. Klopstock, *Oden und Epigramme* (Leipzig: Reclam, 1803).
49 See namely T. C. W. Blanning, *The French revolution and the Modernization of Germany* (Cambridge: Cambridge University Press, 1989). See also A. J. La Vopa, 'The Revelatory Moment: Fichte and the French Revolution', *Central European History* 22 (1989): 130–59.
50 See namely R. Comay, *Mourning Sickness: Hegel and the French Revolution* (Stanford, CA: Stanford University Press, 2011).
51 V. Cuoco, *Saggio storico sulla rivoluzione di Napoli* (Milan: Tipografia Milanese anno IX, [1801]). Engl. transl. *Historical Essay on the Neapolitan Revolution of 1799* (Toronto: Toronto University Press, 2014).
52 On Cuoco's political theories concerning revolution, see A. De Francesco, *Vincenzo Cuoco. Una vita politica* (Rome; Bari: Laterza, 1997).
53 Quoted in C. D. Hazen, *Contemporary American Opinion of the French Revolution* (Baltimore: John Hopkins University Press, 1897, 1897), 142.
54 R. Price, *A Discourse on the Love of our Country, Delivered on Nov. 4, 1789, at the Meeting-House in the Old Jewry, to the Society for Commemorating the Revolution in Great Britain* (London: Cadell, 1790).
55 Among the numerous works concerning the impact of 1789 on the British political debate, I rely namely on A. Goodwin, *The Friends of Liberty. The English Democratic Movement in the Age of the French Revolution* (Cambridge, MA: Harvard University Press, 1979) and more recently P. O'Brien, *Debate Aborted 1789-91: Priestley, Paine, Burke and the Revolution in France* (Edinburgh: Pentland Press, 1996); I. Hampsher-Monk, ed., *The Impact of the French Revolution: Texts from Britain in the 1790s* (Cambridge: Cambridge University Press, 2005); G. Claeys, *The French Revolution Debate in Britain* (London: Palgrave, 2007); W. Verhoeven, *Americomania and the French Revolution Debate in Britain, 1789–1802* (Cambridge: Cambridge University Press, 2013).
56 M. Wollstonecraft, *A Vindication of the Rights of Men in a Letter to the Right Honourable Edmund Burke, Occasioned by his Reflections on the Revolution in France* (London: J. Johnson, 1790).

57 C. Macaulay, *Observations on the Reflections of the Rt. Hon. Edmund Burke, on the Revolution in France* (London: J. Owen & J. Debrett, 1790).
58 For the most recent studies on the democratic movement in Great Britain, see namely. S. Blakemore, *Crisis in Representation. Thomas Paine, Mary Wollstonecraft, Helen Maria Williams and the Rewriting of the French Revolution* (London: Associated University Press, 1997) and *Intertextual War: Edmund Burke and the French Revolution in the writings of Mary Wollstonecraft, Thomas Paine, and James Mackintosh* (Cranbury, NJ: Associated University Press, 1997); Adriana Craciun, *British Women Writers and the French Revolution: Citizens of the World* (London: Palgrave, 2005) and J. Hodson, *Language and Revolution in Burke, Wollstonecraft, Paine, and Godwin* (London: Routledge, 2017).
59 G. Rous, *A Letter to the Right Honourable Edmund Burke* (London: J. Debrett, 1791).
60 B. Boothby, *A Letter to the Right Honourable Edmund Burke* (London: J. Debrett, 1791).
61 Ch. Pigott, *A Political Dictionary, Explaining The True Meaning of Words, Illustrated and Exemplified in the Lives, Morals, Character and Conduct of most Illustrious Personages* (London: D. I. Eaton, 1795).
62 J. Priestley, *Letters to the Right Honourable Edmund Burke Occasioned by his 'Reflections on the Revolution in France'* (London: J. Johnson, 1791).
63 J. Mackintosh, *Vindiciae Gallicae. Defence of the French Revolution and its English Admirers, against the Accusations of the Rght Hon. Edmund Burke, Including some Stricturs on the Late Production of mons. de Calonne* (London: J. Robinson, 1791).
64 Th. Paine, *Rights of Man, being an Answer to Mr Burke's Attack on the French Revolution* (London: J. S. Jordan, 1791).
65 Th. Paine, *Rights of Man, being an Answer to Mr Burke's Attack on the French Revolution. Part the second: combining Principles and Practice* (London: J. S. Jordan, 1792).
66 *An Impartial History of the Late Revolution in France, from Its Commencement to the Death of the Queen, and the Execution of the Deputies of The Gironde Party* (London: printed for the authors, 1794).
67 *Biographical Anecdotes of the Founders of the French Republic* (London: R. Phillips, 1797–1798).
68 On the importance of Paine in British democratic political culture at the end of the eighteenth century, I still rely on E. P. Thompson, *The Making of the English Working Class* (London: Gollancz, 1963).
69 S. Perry, *An Historical Sketch of the French Revolution* (London: Symons, 1796).
70 W. Playfair, *The History of Jacobinism: Its Crimes, Cruelties and Perfidies: Comprising an Inquiry Into the Manner of Disseminating, Under the Appearance of Philosophy and Virtue, Principles which are Equally Subversive of Order, Virtue, Religion, Liberty and Happiness* (Philadelphia: William Cobbett, 1796).
71 J. Moore, *A View of the Causes and Progress of the French Revolution* (London: J. Robinson, 1795).
72 See F. P. Lock, *Edmund Burke* (Oxford: Clarendon Press, 2006), 2:560.
73 For a summary of the American conservative positions, S. Elkins and E. McKitrick, *The Age of Federalism. The Early American Republic, 1788–1800* (Oxford; New York: Oxford University Press, 1993), 303–73 and especially on William Cobbett D. A. Wilson, ed., *Peter Porcupine in America: Pamphlets on Republicanism and Revolution* (Ithaca, NY: Cornell University Press, 1994).
74 P. Porcupine [W. Cobbett], *History of the American Jacobins, Commonly Denominated Democrats* (Philadelphia: printed for William Cobbett, 1796).

75 Th. Paine, *Dissertation on First Principles of Government* (Paris; London: V. Griffiths, 1795).
76 *An Impartial and Concise History of the French Revolution: From Its First Causes and Commencement in 1789 to the Conclusion, and Coronation of Bonaparte, Emperor of the French, on the 2d Dec. 1804* (New York: E. Low, 1810), iv.
77 J. Adolphus, *The History of France from the Year 1790 to the Peace Concluded at Amiens in 1802* (London: George Kearsley, 1803).
78 G. de Staël-Holstein, *Considérations sur les principaux événements de la Révolution française* (Paris: Delaunay, 1818).
79 Among the numerous works devoted to Madame de Staël and the origins of liberalism in France, I have relied namely on M. Winock, *Madame de Staël* (Paris: Fayard, 2010) and B. M. Fontana, *Germaine de Staël: A Political Portrait* (Princeton: Princeton University Press, 2016). See also M. Berlinger and A. Hofmann, eds, *Le Groupe de Coppet et l'histoire* (Genève: Droz, 2007); K. Steven Vincent, *Benjamin Constant and the Birth of French Liberalism* (London: Palgrave, 2011) and A. Craiutu, *A Virtue for Courageous Minds: Moderation in French Political Thought, 1748-1830* (Princeton: Princeton University Press, 2012).
80 On the political action of Madame de Staël, I rely on K. Szmurlo, ed., *Germaine de Staël: Forging a Politics of Mediation* (Oxford: Voltaire Foundation, 2011).
81 J. Necker, *De la Révolution française* (Paris: Maret, 1797).
82 On Benjamin Constant, see namely D. Verrey and A.-L. Delacrétaz, eds, *Benjamin Constant et la Révolution française, 1789-1799* (Genève: Droz, 1989).
83 Here I take issue with A. Omodeo, *La cultura francese nell'età della Restaurazione* (Milan: Mondadori, 1946).
84 D. Klinck, *The French Counterrevolutionary Theorist, Louis de Bonald, 1754-1840* (Berlin: Peter Lang, 1996).
85 J.-Ch. Bailleul, *Examen critique de l'ouvrage posthume de Mme la B^{nne} de Staël, ayant pour titre: «Considérations sur les principaux événements de la Révolution française »* (Paris: A. Bailleul, 1818).

Chapter 2: Confronting France's revolutionary past, 1815–47

1 For a general overview on the French Restoration, see especially E. de Waresquiel and B. Yvert, *Histoire de la Restauration, 1814-1830. Naissance de la France moderne* (Paris: Perrin, 1996).
2 On the legacy of the Revolution in the aftermath of 1815, see F. Furet, ed., *Héritages de la Révolution française* (Paris: Hachette, 1989). See also E. Fureix, 'Une transmission discontinue. Présences sensibles de la Révolution française de la Restauration aux années Trente', in *Histoire d'un trésor perdu. La transmission de l'évènement révolutionnaire, 1789-2012*, ed. Sophie Wahnich (Paris: Les prairies ordinaires, 2012), 149–94.
3 F.-R. de Chateaubriand, *Essai historique, politique et moral sur les révolutions anciennes et modernes, considérées dans leurs rapports avec la Révolution française* (Londres; Hambourg; Paris: Deboffe, Fauche, Le Mière, 1797). Engl. transl. *An Historical, Political and Moral Essay on Revolutions, Ancient and Modern* (London: H. Colburn, 1815).
4 See on this subject F. Hartog, *Regimes of Historicity, Presentism and Experiences of Time* (New York: Columbia University Press, 2015) and I. Rosi and J.-M. Roulin, eds,

Chateaubriand, penser et écrire l'histoire (Saint; Étienne: Université de Saint-Étienne, 2009). For a general oveview on Chateaubriand interpreting the revolution, see instead B. Aureau, *Chateaubriand penseur de la Révolution* (Paris: Honoré Champion, 2001), J.-P. Clément, 'Chateaubriand prophète du romantisme face à la Révolution', in *Romantisme et révolution(s)*, ed. D. Couty and R. Kopp (Paris: Gallimard, 2008), 1: 175–96 and B. Didier and J Neefs, eds, *Sortir de la Révolution: Casanova, Chénier, Staël, Constant, Chateaubriand* (Saint-Denis: Presses Universitaires de Vincennes, 1994).

5   E. Rebardy, 'La Révolution contraire. Chateaubriand et Le génie du christianisme, 1802. Genèse d'une pensée réactionnaire', *Annales historiques de la Révolution française* 309 (1997): 492–501.

6   On the political career of Chateaubriand after 1815, see Benoit Yvert, *La Restauration, Les idées et les hommes* (Paris: CNRS, 2013).

7   On the political uses of history in the French Restoration, see G. Bertier de Sauvigny, 'L'historiographie de la Révolution française de 1814 à 1830', *Revue de la société d'histoire de la Restauration et de la monarchie constitutionnelle* 4 (1990): 63–77. On the discovery of history as a tool of political struggle, see instead, S. Mellon, *The Political Uses of History. A Study of Historians in the French Restoration* (Stanford: Stanford University Press, 1958); R. Alexander, *Re-Writing the French Revolutionary Tradition: Liberal Opposition and the Fall of the Bourbon Monarchy* (Cambridge: Cambridge University Press, 2003); S. Aprile, *La Révolution inachevée* (Paris: Belin, 2010) and V. Robert, *Le temps des banquets. Politique et symbolique d'une génération, 1818–1848* (Paris: Publications de la Sorbonne, 2010).

8   V. Cousin, *Leçons d'histoire de la philosophie à la Sorbonne* (Paris: Marmet, 1828).

9   A. Thierry, *Lettres sur l'histoire de France pour servir d'introduction à l'étude de cette histoire* (Paris: Sautelet, 1827). On this aspect, see A. Denieul Cormier, *Augustin Thierry. L'histoire autrement* (Paris: Éditions Publisud, 1996).

10 On Thierry's interpretation of history, see L. Rignol, 'Augustin Thierry et la politique de l'histoire. Genèse et principes d'un système de pensée', *Revue d'histoire du XIXe siècle* 25 (2002): 87–100; C. Crossley, 'Augustin Thierry (1795–1856) and the Project of National History', in *French Historians and Romanticism* (London: Routledge, 1983), 45–70; S. M. Gruner, 'Political Historiography in Restoration France', *History and Theory* 8 (1969): 346–65; P. Petitier, 'La découverte du passé chez Augustin Thierry et Michelet', in *La Découverte et ses récits en sciences humaines*, ed. J. Carroy and N. Richard (Paris: L'Harmattan, 1998), 195–210; J.-N. Ducange, 'Marx, le marxisme et le « père de la lutte des classes », Augustin Thierry', *Actuel Marx* 58 (2015): n. 2, 12–27.

11 A. Thierry, *Histoire de la conquête de l'Angleterre par les Normands* (Paris: Firmin-Didot père et fils, 1825). Engl. transl. *History of the Conquest of England by the Normans with its Causes and Consequences to the Present Time* (London: Whittaker & Co., 1841).

12 On this subject, see notably M. D'Auria, 'From Royal to Bourgeois: Augustin Thierry's National Narrative', in *Historicising the French Revolution*, ed. C. Armenteros et al. (Cambridge: Cambridge Scholar Publishing, 2008), 64–78; A. Aramini, 'A Linguistic Archeology of Power and the People by Augustin Thierry', *Revue d'histoire du XIXe siècle* 2 (2014): 179–93.

13 Dietrich Gerhard, 'Guizot, Augustin Thierry und die Rolle des Tiers État in der französischen Geschichte', *Historische Zeitschrift* 190 (1960): 290–310.

14 F. Guizot, *Du gouvernement de la France depuis la Restauration. Des conspirations et de la justice politique* (Paris: Ladvocat, 1820).

15　C. Crossley, 'François Guizot (1787–1874) and Liberal History: The Concept of Civilisation', in *French Historians*, 71–104 and P. Rosanvallon, *Le moment Guizot* (Paris: Gallimard, 1985).
16　D. Hoeges, *François Guizot und die Franzosische Revolution* (Berlin: Peter Lang, 1981).
17　See on this subject K. Bigane, 'French Historiography of the English Revolution Under the Restoration: A National or Cross-Channel Dialogue?', *European Journal of English Studies* 14 (2010): 249–61.
18　P. L. B., *De la restauration, considérée comme le terme et non le triomphe de la révolution, et de l'abus des doctrines politiques; en réponse à l'ouvrage de M. F. Guizot, intitulé: 'Du gouvernement de la France depuis la restauration, et du ministère actuel'* (Paris: Le Normant, 1820).
19　Ch. de Lacretelle, *Histoire de la Révolution française* (Paris: Treuttel et Würtz, 1821–1826).
20　Ch. de Lacretelle, *Histoire du Consulat et de l'Empire* (Paris: Amyot, 1846).
21　J.-D. Lanjuinais, *Mémoire justificatif pour le Cte Lanjuinais, Pair de France, dénoncé par quatre de ses collègues pour avoir publié son opinion sur le projet de la loi nouvelle concernant des mesures de sûreté générale* (Paris: Delaunay, 1815).
22　On the political and cultural positions of Lanjuinais, see J.-P. Clément, 'Lanjuinais lecteur de Madame de Staël à propos des «Considérations sur les principaux événements de la Révolution Française (1818)', *Cahiers staëliens* 45 (1993–94): 91–107.
23　On the *Mémoires* published during the 1820s, see Jean-Luc Chappey, 'La Révolution française dans l'ère du soupçon. L'enjeu des mémoires révolutionnaires', *Cahiers d'histoire* 65 (1996): 43–57 and more recently A. Karla, *Revolution als Zeitgeschichte. Memoires der Französischen Revolution in der Restaurationzeit* (Göttingen; Zürich: Vandenhoeck & Ruprecht, 2014).
24　J.-S. Bailly, *Mémoires. Avec une notice sur sa vie, des notes et des éclaircissements historiques* (Paris: Baudouin frères, 1821–1822).
25　J.-B. Louvet de Couvray, *Mémoires de Louvet de Couvray, avec une notice sur sa vie, des notes et des éclaircissements historiques* (Paris: Baudouin frères, 1823).
26　A. Thiers, *Histoire de la Révolution française* (Paris: Lecointe et Durey, 1823–1830). Engl. transl. *The History of the French Revolution* (London: R. bentley, 1838).
27　F. A. Mignet, *Histoire de la Révo- lution française depuis 1789 jusqu'en 1814* (Paris: F. Didot père et fils, 1824). Engl. transl. *History of the French Revolution, from 1789 to 1814* (London: David Bogue, 1846).
28　On the origins of the liberal historiography of the Revolution, see namely J. Walch, *Les maîtres de l'histoire: 1815–1850: Augustin Thierry, Mignet, Guizot, Thiers, Michelet, Edgard Quinet* (Genève: Slatkine, 1986).
29　J.-C. Bailleul, *Examen critique des Considérations de Mme. la baronne de Staël, sur les principaux événemens de la Révolution française, avec des observations sur les Dix ans d'exil, du même auteur, et sur Napoléon Bonaparte* (Paris: Renard et Delaunay, 1822).
30　On this subject, S. Luzzatto, *Il Terrore ricordato* (Genoa: Marietti, 1988) transl. In French as *Mémoire de la Terreur* (Lyon: PUL, 1991).
31　F. A. Mignet, *De la Féodalité, des institutions de St Louis, et de l'influence de la législation de ce prince* (Paris: L'Huillier, 1822).
32　See Y. Knibiehler, *Naissance des sciences humaines: Mignet et l'histoire philosophique au XIXe siècle* (Paris: Flammarion, 1975) and 'Une révolution « nécessaire »: Thiers, Mignet et l'école fataliste', *Romantisme* 10 (1980): 279–88.
33　On Thiers, see namely R. Tombs and J. Bury, *Thiers 1797–1877: A Political Life* (London: Allen & Unwin, 1986) and G. Valance, *Thiers bourgeois et révolutionnaire*

(Paris: Flammarion, 2007). See also R. Tombs, 'Making the Revolution History: Adolphe Thiers, 1823–1873', in *Historicising the French Revolution*, ed. Armenteros et al., 79–95. At any rate it is still worth of drawing on the portrait of Theirs outlined by A. Aulard, 'Thiers. Historien de la Revolution Francaise', *La Revolution Francaise* 66 (1914): 492–520.

34 A. Thiers, *Histoire du Consulat et de l'Empire faisant suite à l'Histoire de la Révolution française* (Paris: Paulin, Lheureux et C.ie, 1845–1869). Engl. transl. *The History of the Consulate and the Empire of Napoleon, forming a Sequel to the History of the French Revolution* (London: H. Colburn, 1845–1862).

35 On the Republican and socialist Left during the Monarchy of July see S. Hazareesingh and K. Nabulsi, 'Entre Robespierre et Napoléon: les paradoxes de la mémoire républicaine sous la monarchie de Juillet', *Annales. Histoire, Sciences Sociales* 65 (2010): 1225–47. For a general overview it is worth of referring to T. Judt, *Marxism and the French Left: Studies on Labour and Politics in France, 1830–1981* (New York: New York University Press, 2011).

36 J.-A. Dulaure, *Esquisses historiques des principaux événemens de la Révolution française, depuis la convocation des États-Généraux jusqu'au rétablissement de la maison de Bourbon* (Paris: Delongchamps, 1825).

37 Ph. Buonarroti, *Conspiration pour l'égalité, dite de Babeuf suivie du procès auquel elle donna lieu et des pièces justificatives* (Bruxelles: Librairie romantique, 1828). Engl. transl. *Buonarroti's History of Babeuf's Conspiracy for Equality: With the Author's Reflections on the Causes & Character of the French Revolution, and His Estimate of the Leading Men and Events of That Epoch: Also, His Views of Democratic Government, Community of Property, and Political and Social Equality* (London: Hetherington, 1836).

38 On Buonarroti and his work, see A. Saitta, *Ricerche storiografiche su Buonarroti e Babeuf* (Rome: Istituto storico italiano per l'età moderna e contemporanea, 1986) and more recently A. Galante Garrone and F. Venturi, *Vivere eguali. Dialoghi inediti intorno a Filippo Buonarroti* (Bologna: Diabasis, 2009).

39 A. Laponneraye, *Cours public d'histoire de France, depuis 1789 jusqu'en 1830* (Paris: David, 1831).

40 Emmanuel Fureix, 'L'histoire comme subversion: le cas de Laponneraye au début de la monarchie de Juillet', in *L'historiographie romantique*, ed. Francis Claudon et al. (Pompignac: Editions Bière, 2007), 129–38; Ph. Darriulat, 'Morales révolutionnaires et prophètes néojacobins de la Monarchie de Juillet', in *Morales en révolutions: France, 1789–1940*, ed. S. Hallade (Rennes: Presses Universitaires de Rennes, 2015), 65–76.

41 A. Laponneraye, *Histoire de la Révolution française, depuis 1789 jusqu'en 1814* (Paris: chez l'auteur, 1838), 101.

42 Ibid., 106.

43 Ph. Buchez and P.-C. Roux, *Histoire parlementaire de la Révo- lution française, ou Journal des assemblées nationales depuis 1789 jusqu'en 1815: contenant la narration des événements précédée d'une introduction sur l'histoire de France jusqu'à la convocation des États-Généraux* (Paris: Paulin, 1834–1838).

44 See namely M. Albertone, '*Pensare la Rivoluzione*: Buchez et la Histoire de la Révolution française', in *Pensiero cristiano, questione sociale e liberalismo in Francia nel XIX secolo*, ed. C. Giurintano (Palermo: DEMS, 2015), 58–86; see also Jean-Baptiste Duroselle, 'Buchez et la Révolution Française', *Annales historiques de la Révolution française* 183 (1966): 77–107 and E. Guccione, *Philippe Buchez e la rivoluzione francese: pensiero politico e storiografia* (Palermo: Palma, 1993).

45 É. Cabet, *Histoire populaire de la Révolution française, de 1789 à 1830, précédée d'un Précis de l'histoire des Français depuis leur origine* (Paris: au bureau du *Populaire*, 1845–1847).
46 R. Tumminelli, *Etienne Cabet: critica della società e alternativa di Icaria* (Milan: Giuffré, 1981).
47 A. Esquiros, *Histoire des Montagnards* (Paris: V. Lecou, 1847).
48 See A. Zielonka, *Alphonse Esquiros (1812–1876)* (Genève: Slatkine, 1985).
49 Moses Myer, ed., *Full Annals of the Revolution in France, 1830. To Which is Added a Full Account of the Celebration of the Revolution in France in the City of New York on the 25th November, 1830: Being the Fourth-Seventh Anniversary of an Event that restored our Citizens to Their Homes and to the Enjoyment of their Rights and Liberties* (New York: Tarper, 1830).
50 William C. Rives, *Discourse on the Uses and Importance of History, Illustrated by a Comparison of the American and French Revolutions* (Richmond, VA: Shepherd and Collins, 1847).
51 For a general overview of Republicanism in nineteenth-century France, see especially P. Nord, *The Republican Moment. Struggles for Democracy in Nineteenth-Century France* (Cambridge, MA: Harvard University Press, 1995) and J. Gilmore, *La République clandestine (1818–1848)* (Paris: Aubier, 1997).
52 L. Gallois, *Histoire pittoresque de la Révolution française, mise à la portée de tout le monde* (Paris: Audin, 1830).
53 See M. Harder, 'Ex-conventionnels Versus Historians of the French Revolution', in *Historicising the French Revolution*, ed. C. Armenteros et al. (Cambridge: Cambridge University Press, 2008), 300.
54 J.-A. Dulaure, *Histoire de la Révolution française depuis 1814 jusqu'à 1830 et années suivantes* (Paris: Librairie historique, 1834), 1: vi.
55 A. Marrast, *Fastes de la Révolution française, revue chronologique de l'histoire de France, depuis 1787 jusqu'en 1835* (Paris: Guillaumin, 1836). On Armand Marrast, see namely J.-M. Ambert, *Portraits républicains* (Paris: Librairie international, 1870), 157–213.
56 L. Gallois, *Histoire de la Convention nationale d'après elle-même, précédée d'un tableau de la France monarchique avant la Révolution et d'un précis de notre histoire nationale pendant la session de l'Assemblée constituante et celle de l'Assemblée législative* (Paris: A. Mie (et Dutertre), 1834–1848).
57 C. Crossley, *Edgar Quinet, 1803–1875. A Study in Romantic Thought* (Lexington, KY: French Forum, 1983), 48.
58 A. de Lamartine, *Histoire des Girondins* (Paris: Furne & Coquebert. 1847). Engl. transl. *History of the Girondists* (London: Bohn, 1847–48).
59 J. Michelet, *Histoire de la Révolution française* (Paris: Chamerot, 1847–1853). Engl. transl. *History of the French Revolution* (London: Bohn, 1847).
60 L. Blanc, *Histoire de la Révolution française* (Paris: Langlois et Leclercq, 1847–1862). Engl. transl. *History of the French Revolution* (Philadelphia: Lea & Blanchard, 1848).
61 On Lamartine and the French Revolution, see namely A. Rigney, *The Rhetoric of Historical Representation. Three Narrative Histories of the French Revolution* (Cambridge: Cambridge University Press, 1990). See also W. Fortescue, 'Poetry, Politics and Publicity, and the Writing of History: Lamartine's Histoire des Girondins (1847)', *European History Quarterly* 17 (1987): 259–84; S. Bernard-Griffiths and Ch. Croisille, *Relire Lamartine aujourd'hui* (Paris: Nizet, 1993); A. Court, *L'Auteur des "Girondins" ou les Cent vingt jours de Lamartine* (Saint-Etienne: Université de Saint-Etienne, 1988).

62 On Tocqueville's political positions, see F. Furet, 'Tocqueville est-il un historien de la Révolution française?, *Annales. Économies, Sociétés, Civilisations* 25 (1970): 434–51 (English transl. *Interpreting the French revolution*) (Cambridge: Cambridge University Press, 1981) and F. Mélonio, *Tocqueville et les Français* (Paris: Aubier, 1993).
63 A. de Tocqueville, *De la démocratie en Amérique* (Paris: Gosselin, 1835–1840). English transl. *Democracy in America* (London: Saunders & Otley, 1835–1840).
64 C. Desmarais, *Histoire des histoires de la révolution française, pour servir de complément à tous les écrits sur la même époque* (Paris: P. Méquignon, 1834).
65 E. Labaume, *Histoire monarchique et constitutionnelle de la révolution française, composée sur un plan nouveau et d'après des documents inédits, précédée d'une introduction et d'un tableau du règne de Louis XVI, jusqu'à l'ouverture des États généraux* (Paris: Anselin, 1834–1839).
66 P. Manzi, *Istoria della Rivoluzione di Francia dalla convocazione degli Stati Generali fino allo stabilimento della monarchia costituzionale* (Florence: L. Pezzati, 1826).
67 For a general overview of nineteenth-century Italian historians of the French Revolution, see F. Diaz, *L'incomprensione italiana della Rivoluzione francese: dagli inizi ai primi del Novecento* (Turin: Bollati Boringhieri, 1989).
68 J. S. Mill, 'Scott's Life of Napoleon', *Westminster Review* 9 (1828): 251–313.
69 J. S. Mill, 'Modern French Historical Studies', in *Essays on French History & Historians*, ed. J. S. Mill (Toronto: University of Toronto Press, 1985), 15–52.
70 J. Coleman, 'John Stuart Mill on the French Revolution', *History of Political Thought* 4 (1983): 89–110.
71 A. Alison, *History of Europe during the French Revolution* (Edinburgh; London: Blackwood & Cadell, 1833–1842).
72 J. S. Mill, 'Alison's History of the French Revolution', *Monthly Repository* 7 (1833): 507–16.
73 B. Morawe, *Faszinosum Saint-Just: Zur programmatischen Bedeutung der Konventsrede in 'Danton's Tod' von Georg Büchner* (Bielefeld: Aisthesis Verlag, 2012).
74 L. Papi, *Commentarii della rivoluzione francese, dalla morte di Luigi XVI fino al ristabilimento de Borboni sul trono di Francia* (Leighorn: Giusti, 1830–1831).
75 L. Papi, *Commentarii della rivoluzione francese* (Turin: Ferrero & Franco, 1853), iii.
76 W. Smyth, *Lectures on the History of the French Revolution* (Cambridge: Deighton, 1840).
77 For William Smyth see H. Ben-Israel, *English Historians on the French Revolution* (Cambridge: Cambridge University Press, 1968).
78 F. Fysh, *History of the French Revolution, with Special Reference to the Fulfilment of Prophecy. With a Treatise on the Approaching Fall of the Mohammedan and Papal Power, and the Cleansing of the Jewish Sanctuary* (London: Nisbet and Co., 1842).
79 Ch. MacFarlane, *The French Revolution* (London: Knight, 1844).
80 F. Rowan, *History of the French Revolution: Its Causes and Consequences* (London: J. W. Parker, 1844).
81 Th. Carlyle, *The French Revolution: A History* (London: James Fraser, 1837).
82 On Carlyle and the impact of his interpretation of the French Revolution on the British political culture, see H. M. Leicester, 'The Dialectic of Romantic Historiography: Prospect and Retrospect in" The French Revolution"', *Victorian Studies* 15 (1971): 5–17; W. Britton, 'Carlyle, Clemens, and Dickens: Mark Twain's Francophobia, the French Revolution, and Determinism', *Studies in American Fiction* 20 (1992): 197–204; R. Stott, 'Thomas Carlyle and the Crowd: Revolution, Geology and the Convulsive 'Nature' of Time', *Journal of Victorian Culture* 4 (1999): 1–24; G.

Stedman Jones, 'The Redemptive Power of Violence? Carlyle, Marx and Dickens', *History Workshop Journal* 65 (2008): 1–22; D. R. Sorensen, '"The Unseen Heart of the Whole": Carlyle, Dickens, and the Sources of The French Revolution in A Tale of Two Cities', *Dickens Quarterly* 30 (2013): 5–26. See also, for Carlyle's role in the British conceptual universe of the French Revolution, S. Prickett, *England and the French Revolution* (London: Macmillan, 1989) and G. Varouxakis, *Victorian Political Thought on France and the French* (London: Palgrave, 2002).

Chapter 3: From national myth to the myth of nations, 1848–75

1. For the political engagement of Lamartine, see F. L'Huillier, *Lamartine en politique* (Strasbourg: Presses Universitaires de Strasbourg, 1993).
2. A. de Lamartine, *Critique de l'Histoire des Girondins par l'auteur des Girondins lui-même* (Paris: chez l'auteur, 1861).
3. On Lamartine as historian, see A. Court, 'Les Girondins de Lamartine. Un incendie. Un feu de paille', *Cahiers de l'Association internationale des études francaises* 47 (1995): 305–21.
4. J. Michelet, *Histoire de France* (Paris: L. Hachette, 1833–1841). Engl. transl. *History of France* (New York: Appleton, 1847).
5. The role of Michelet's work in the historiography of the French Revolution is doubtless and it represented a step onward to the national narrative, even though its legacy is increasingly being questioned. In this regard, it remains fundamental R. Barthes, *Michelet* (Paris: Seuil, 1954). See also, in addition to the aforementioned work by Ann Rigney, L. Orr, *Jules Michelet: Nature, History and Language* (Ithaca, NY: Cornell University Press, 1976); P. Viallaneix, ed., *Michelet écrit L'Histoire de la Révolution* (Paris: Les Belles Lettres, 1993); P. Petitier, *Jules Michelet: l'homme histoire* (Paris: Grasset, 2006). See also Rigney, *The Rhetoric of Historical Representation*.
6. Aurélien Aramini, *Michelet, à la recherche de l'identité de la France. De la fusion nationale au conflit des traditions* (Besançon: Presses Universitaires de Franche-Comté, 2013); Arthur Mitzman, *Michelet, Historian: Rebirth and Romanticism in Nineteenth-Century France* (New Haven, CT: Yale University Press, 1990).
7. J. Michelet and E. Quinet, *Des jésuites* (Paris: Hachette et Paulin, 1843). J. Michelet, *Du Prêtre, de la femme, de la famille* (Paris: Hachette, 1845). Engl. transl. *Priests, Women and Family* (London: Whitaker, 1845).
8. J. Michelet, *Le Peuple* (Paris: Hachette et Paulin, 1846). Engl. transl. *The People* (London: Whitaker, 1846).
9. See D. Johnson, *Michelet and the French Revolution* (Oxford: Clarendon Press, 1990).
10. Michelet's *Histoire de France* is discussed in Ch. Delacroix et al., *Les courants historiques en France* (Paris: Gallimard, 2007), 59–74.
11. J. Michelet, *Histoire de France. Tome XVII: Louis XV et Louis XVI* (Paris: Chamerot et Lauwereyns, 1867).
12. J. Michelet, *Histoire de la Révolution française* (Paris: Lacroix, 1868–1869).
13. E. Hamel, *Histoire de Robespierre d'après des papiers de famille, les sources originales et des documents entièrement inédits* (Paris: A. Lacroix, Verboeckhoven & Cie, 1865–1867).
14. On the political life of Louis Blanc, see Jean Vidalenc, *Louis Blanc* (Paris: Presses Universitaires de France, 1948) and L. A. Loubère, *Louis Blanc, his Life and his*

Contribution to the Rise of French Jacobin-Socialism (Evanston, IL: Northwestern University Press, 1961) and F. Bracco, *Louis Blanc dalla democrazia politica alla democrazia sociale, 1830–1840* (Florence: Centro editoriale toscano, 1983). See also J. G. Amuchastegui, *Louis Blanc y los origenes del socialismo democrático* (Madrid: Centro de investigaciones sociológicas, 1989). On his political role, see namely F. Démier, ed., *Louis Blanc, un socialiste en république* (Paris: Créaphis, 2006).

15 Louis Blanc, *Histoire de dix ans, 1830–1840* (Paris: Pagnerre, 1842–1844) and *Organisation du travail* (Paris: Cauville frères, 1845).

16 About his interpretation of the Revolution, in addition to Rigney's work, see instead W. H. Sewell, 'Beyond 1793: Babeuf, Louis Blanc and the Genealogy of Social Revolution', in *The French Revolution and the Creation of Modern Political Culture* 3: 509–26 and J.-F. Jacouty, 'Robespierre selon Louis Blanc. Le prophète christique de la Révolution française' *Annales historiques de la Révolution française* 331 (2003): 103–25.

17 On the impact of Louis Blanc's work on the French political culture see F. Furet, ed., *La gauche et la Révolution française au milieu du 19. siècle: Edgar Quinet et la question du jacobinisme: 1865–1870* (Paris: Hachette, 1986).

18 G. Tridon, *Les Hébertistes, plainte contre une calomnie de l'histoire* (Paris: l'auteur, 1864).

19 On Blanquism in French Republican political life, see M. Dommanget, *Blanqui et l'opposition révolutionnaire à la fin du Second Empire* (Paris: Colin, 1960); J.-J. Barthélemy, *L'héritage hébertiste dans le blanquisme, 1864–1881* (Lyon: Faculté de Lettres, 1967) and namely P. H. Hutton, *The Cult of the Revolutionary Tradition: The Blanquists in French Politics, 1864–1893* (Stanford: University of California Press, 1981).

20 M. Riberioux, 'Lectures socialistes de la Révolution française, de Louis Blanc à Jaurès', in *Jaurès historien de la Révolution Française*, ed. M. Dommanget et al. (Castres: Centre National et Musée Jean Jaurès, 1989) and J. El Gammal, 'La mémoire de la Révolution au XIXe siècle', in *Histoire des gauches en France, vol. I: L'héritage du 19ᵉ siècle*, ed. J.-J.Becker and G. Candar (Paris: La Découverte, 2004), 135–49.

21 G. de Beaumont, ed., *Œuvres et correspondance inédites d'Alexis de Tocqueville* (Paris: Michel-Lévy frères, 1861).

22 For a biography of Tocqueville, see Andre Jardin, *Alexis de Tocqueville* (Paris: Hachette, 1984) and H. Brogan, *Alexis de Tocqueville. A Life* (New Haven, CT: Yale University Press, 2007).

23 See also note 33 of previous chapter.

24 On Tocqueville as a politician of the Second Republic, see especially S. B. Watkins, *Alexis de Tocqueville and the Second Republic, 1848–1852: A Study in Political Practice and Principles* (Lanham, MD: University Press of America, 2003).

25 An excellent starting point in the literature concerning Tocqueville's role in the historiography of the Revolution is Furet, *Tocqueville et le problème de la révolution française*, which broke new ground in rereading the events of 1789. See also P. Manent, *Tocqueville and the Nature of Democracy* (Lanham, MD: Rowman & Littlefield, 1996); N. Capdevila, *Tocqueville et les frontières de la démocratie* (Paris: Presses Universitaires de France, 2007) and L. Jaume, *Tocqueville: the Aristocratic Sources of Liberty* (Princeton: Princeton University Press, 2013). In Italian, see V. De Caprariis, *Profilo di Tocqueville* (Naples: ESI, 1962) and N. Matteucci, *Alexis de Tocqueville. Tre esercizi di lettura* (Bologna: il Mulino, 1990).

26 A. Denis, *Amable-Guillaume-Prosper Brugière, baron de Barante (1782–1866): homme politique, diplomate et historien* (Paris: Champion, 2000).
27 P. Brugière de Barante, *Histoire de la Convention nationale* (Paris: aux bureaux de la Revue contemporaine, 1853).
28 A.Thierry,, *Lettres sur l'histoire de France. Dix ans d'études historiques* (Paris: Furne, 1853).
29 L. Mortimer-Ternaux, *Histoire de la Terreur, 1792–1794: d'après des documents authentiques et inédits* (Paris: C. Lévy, 1862–1881).
30 On this peculiar point, see M. Zetterbaum, *Tocqueville and the Problem of Democracy* (Stanford: Stanford University Press, 1967) and R. Boesche, *The Strange Liberalism of Alexis de Tocqueville* (Ithaca, NY: Cornell University Press, 1987).
31 A. C. Thibaudeau, *Mémoires sur la Convention et le Directoire* (Paris: Ponthieu, 1827).
32 A. de Tocqueville, *L'Ancien Régime et la Révolution* (Paris: Michel Lévy frères, 1856).
33 V. Chauffour- Kestner, *Monsieur Thiers, historien: notes sur l'histoire du consulat et de l'empire* (Paris: Lacroix, 1863).
34 J. Barni, *Napoléon et son historien M. Thiers* (Geneva: les principaux libriers, 1865).
35 Edgar Quinet, *Histoire de la campagne de 1815* (Paris: C Lévy, 1862): 5.
36 Edgar Quinet's work was rediscovered by François Furet in *La gauche et la Révolution française au milieu du 19. Siècle*. See also W. Aeschimann, *La pensée d'Edgar Quinet* (Genève: Anthropos & Georg, 1986) and S. Bernard-Griffiths, 'Rupture entre Michelet et Quinet', *Romantisme* 5 (1975): 145–65.
37 E. Quinet, *La Révolution* (Paris: Lacroix, 1865).
38 S. Bernard-Griffiths, 'Autour de la Révolution (1865) d'Edgar Quinet. Les enjeux du débat Religion-Révolution dans l'historiographie d'un républicain désenchanté', *Archives de sciences sociales des religions* 66 (1988): 53–64. See also A. Almeida da Silva, 'Edgar Quinet e a filosofia da Revolução Francesa', *Revista de História* 146 (2002): 223–66.
39 E. Quinet, *Le Christianisme et la Révolution française* (Paris: Wouters, 1845).
40 E. Quinet, *Les Révolutions d'Italie* (Paris: Chamerot, 1851–1852).
41 Simone Bernard-Griffiths, 'Histoire et histoire(s) dans l'autobiographie d'Edgar Quinet', in *A la croisée de deux cultures. Etudes en mémoire de Tivadar Gorilovics, 1933-2014*, ed. F. Skutta and G. Tegyey (Debrecen: Kossuth Egyetemi Kiadó, 2016), 137–54.
42 Vladimir López Alcañiz, 'Magnifique désolation. Edgar Quinet entre la Republique et la Terreur', *Trienio: Ilustración y liberalismo* 67 (2016): 153–63.
43 G. Ferrari, *L'Italia dopo il colpo di stato del 2 dicembre 1851* (Capolago: Tipografia elvetica, 1852), 29. On the impact beyond France of the return of the revolution in France in 1848 and of the rise to power of another Bonaparte, see, from the Italian point of view, A. De Francesco, 'Pour une histoire du mouvement républicain dans l'Italie du XIXe siècle', *Revue française d'histoire des idées politiques* 29–30 (2009): 231–51.
44 G. Mazzini, *Scritti editi e inediti. Tomo XLVII* (Imola: Galeati, 1927), 184.
45 See now C. A. Bayly and E. F. Biagini, eds., *Giuseppe Mazzini and the Globalisation of Democratic Nationalism, 1830–1920* (Oxford: Oxford University Press, 2008).
46 On Marx's approach to the French Revolution: François Furet, *Marx et la Révolution française* (Paris: Flammarion, 1986) and from another point of view C. Mazauric, *L'histoire de la Révolution française et la pensée marxiste* (Paris: Presses Universitaires de France, 2009).

47 P.-J. Proudhon, *Du principe fédératif et de la nécéssité de reconstituer le parti de la révolution* (Paris: Dentu, 1863).
48 G. Mazzini, *Il comune e l'assemblea di Francia nel 1871* (Roma: Commissione editrice degli scritti di Giuseppe Mazzini, 1887).
49 [K. Marx], *The General Council of the International Workingmen's Association on the War* (London: E. truelove, 1870): 8.
50 P. Lanfrey, *Essai sur la Révolution française* (Paris: Chamerot, 1858):5.
51 E. Renan, *Essais de morale et de critique* (Paris: Michel-Lévy Frères, 1859), xi.
52 V. Gioberti-G. Pallavicino, *Il Piemonte nel 1850-51-52* (Milan: Rechiedei, 1875), 185.
53 A. Manzoni, *La rivoluzione francese del 1789 e la rivoluzione italiana del 1859* (Milan: Rechiedei, 1889).
54 C. F. E. Ludwig, *Geschichte der Letzten fünfzig Jahre* (Altona: Kammerich, 1834).
55 W. Wachsmuth, *Geschichte Frankreichs im Revolutionszeitalter* (Hamburg: F. Perthes, 1840-1844).
56 *Historisch-Politische Zeitschrift*, herausgegeben von leopold Ranke (Hamburg: F: Verthes, 1832).
57 A. Jansson, 'Building or Destroying Community: The Concept of Sittlichkeit in the Political Thought of Vormärz Germany', *Global Intellectual History* 5 (2020): 86–103.
58 F. C. Dahlmann, *Geschichte der Französischen Revolution bis auf die Stiftung der Republik* (Leipzig: Weidmann, 1845).
59 B. E. Vick, *Defining Germany: The 1848 Frankfurt Parlamentarians and National Identity* (Cambridge, MA: Harvard University Press, 2002).
60 H. von Sybel, *Geschichte der Revolutionszeit von 1789 bis 1795* (Düsseldorf: J. Buddeus, 1853-1870).
61 On Heinrich von Sybel, it remains useful A. Guilland, *L'Allemagne nouvelle et ses historiens: Niebuhr, Ranke, Mommsen, Sybel, Treitschke* (Paris: Félix Alcan, 1899). See namely H. Flaig, 'The Historian as Pedagogue of the Nation', *History* 59 (1974): 18–32; W. Grab, 'Französische Revolution und die deutsche Geschichtswissenschaft', *Jahrbuch des Instituts für deutsche Geschichte* 3 (1974): 11–43; K. Malettke, 'Heinrich von Sybel et son « Histoire de l'Europe pendant la Révolution Française »', *Storia della storiografia europea sulla rivoluzione* 1: 83–120.
62 H. von Sybel, *Histoire de l'Europe pendant la Révolution française* (Paris; Londres; New York: Baillière, 1869-1888); *History of the French Revolution* (London: Murray, 1867-1869).

Chapter 4: A republican history?, 1875–1914

1 H. Dippel, '1871 versus 1789 German Historians and the Ideological Foundations of the Deutsche Reich', *History of European Ideas* 15 (1992): 829–37.
2 H. von Sybel, 'Edmund Burke ünd die französische Revolution', *Allgemeine Zeitschrift für Geschichte* 7 (1847): 1–53 and 'Graf J. De Maistre', *Historische Zeitschrift* 1 (1859): 153-98.
3 A. de Tocqueville, *L'Ancien Régime et la Révolution* (Paris: Levy frères, 1877 and Paris: Calmann Levy, 1887).
4 H. Taine, *Les Origines de la France contemporaine* (Paris: Hachette, 1876-1901). English transl. of the first two volumes, *The Ancient Régime* (London: Daldy Isbister, 1876). For an abridged translation of hi sentire work, see also *The Origins of Contemporary France* (Chicago: Chicago University Press, 1974).

5   H. Taine, *Histoire de la littérature anglaise* (Paris: Hachette, 1863). English transl. *History of English Literature* (London: Chatto & Windus, 1871).
6   On the political positions held by Taine, see namely J.-P. Cointet, *Hippolyte Taine. Un regard sur la France* (Paris: Perrin, 2013) and É. Gasparini, 'Hippolyte Taine', *Revue française d'histoire des idées politiques* 2 (2014): 229–42.
7   Among the numerous works on Hyppolite Taine, see J.-T. Nordmann, *Taine et la critique scientifique* (Paris: Presses Universitaires de France, 1992); S. Michaud and M. Le Pavéc, eds, *Taine au carrefour des cultures du XIXe siècle* (Paris: Bibliothèque Nationale de France, 1993); F. Leger, *Monsieur Taine* (Paris: Criterion, 1993) and N. Richard, *Hippolyte Taine: histoire, psychologie, littérature* (Paris: Garnier, 2013). An important work on Taine and his role in the French political culture is R. Pozzi, *Hippolyte Taine. Scienze umane e politica nell'Ottocento* (Venice: Marsilio, 1993).
8   On this peculiar aspect, see especially P. Seys, *Hippolyte Taine et l'avènement du naturalisme: un intellectuel sous le Second Empire* (Paris: l'Harmattan, 1999).
9   H. von Sybel, 'The Ancien Régime and the Revolution in France', *The Contemporary Review* 36 (1879): 432–50.
10 A. Sorel, *L'Europe et la Révolution française* (Paris: Plon-Nourrit et C., 1885–1904). English transl. *Europe and the French Revolution. The political Traditions of the Old Regime* (London: Collins, 1969).
11 On Albert Sorel, see especially B. Gödde-Baumanns, *Deutsche Geschichte in französischer Sicht. Die französische historiographie von 1871 bis 1918 über die Geschichte Deutschlands und der deutsch-französischen Beziehungen in der Neuzeit* (Wesbaden: Steiner, 1971) and her 'Etude comparée de la vision de la Révolution française chez Heinrich von Sybel et Albert Sorel', *La storia della storiografia europea sulla rivoluzione francese* 1: 121–35.
12 L. Madelin, *La Révolution* (Paris: Hachette, 1911), iv. English transl. *The French Revolution* (London: Heinemann, 1916).
13 É. Boutmy, *Taine, Scherer, Laboulaye* (Paris: Colin, 1901).
14 J.-J. F. Poujoulat, *Histoire de la Révolution française* (Tours: A. Mame, 1848).
15 Sylvain Venayre, *Les origines de la France. Quand les historiens racontaient la nation* (Paris: Seuil, 2013) is an excellent contribution to the uses of the past in nineteenth-century France. In making an argument about how the historical writing sustained the emergence of nationalism in France I am drawing namely on S. Berger and Chris Lorenz, eds, *Nationalizing the Past: Historians as Nation Builders in Modern Europe* (London: Palgrave Macmillan, 2010); M. Samuels, *The Spectacular Past: Popular History and the Novel in Nineteenth-Century France* (Ithaca, NY: Cornell University Press, 2004). On the beginnings of historical science in France, see also Ch. Delacroix et al., *Les courants historiques en France* (Paris: Gallimard, 2007), 93–154 and O. Dumoulin, 'Histoire et historiens de droite', in *Histoire des droites en France*, ed. Jean-François Sirinelli (Paris: Gallimard, 1992), 2: 327–99.
16 See namely A. De Francesco, 'Plumas contrarrevolucionaria en Francia durante la III Republica: el ejemplo de la coleccion Brochures populaires sur la révolution française', in *El desafío de la revolucion: reaccionarios, antiliberales y contrarevolucionarios, siglo XVII y XIX*, ed. P. Rujula and F. Ramon Solans (Madrid: Editorial Comares, 2017), 265–79.
17 See M. de la Rocheterie, *Marie Antoinette* (Paris: Librairie de la Société bibliographique, 1877). On right-wing historians and their battle against turning the memory of 1789 into one of the founding moments of contemporary France, see namely M. Simpson, 'Taming the Revolution? Legitimists and the Centenary

of 1789', *The English Historical Review* 120 (2005): 340-64 and S. D. Kale, 'The Countercentenary of 1889, Counterrevolution and the Revolutionary Tradition', *Historical Reflections/ Réflexions Historiques* 23 (1997): 1-28.

18 On the celebrations (and counter-celebrations) of 1889, see P. Ory, 'Le centenaire de la Révolution française', in *Les lieux de mémoire. La République*, ed. P. Nora (Paris: Gallimard, 1984): 523-60 and on the attitude of the Catholics B. Peschot, 'Le contre-anniversaire de 1789 à travers la littérature populaire catholique de la fin du XIXe siècle', *Annales de Bretagne et des pays de l'Ouest* 91 (1984): 269-78.

19 Ch.-È Freppel, *La Révolution française, à propos du centenaire de 1789* (Paris: A. Roger et F. Chernoviz, 1889).

20 On Monseigneur Freppel, who is an excellent example of a traditionalist interpretation of the French Revolution, see J.-Cl. Martin, 'Monseigneur Freppel et la Révolution française', *Annales de Bretagne et Pays de l'Ouest* 102 (1995): 75-88 and B. Plongeron, ed., *Catholiques entre monarchie et république. Monseigneur Freppel en son temps* (Paris: Letouzey et Ané, 1995).

21 G. Feugère, *La Révolution française et la critique contemporaine* (Paris: V. Lecoffre, 1889).

22 P. Baudry, *Révolution française* (Rouen: impr. de E. Cagniard, 1890).

23 G. Romain, *La Révolution et son œuvre, à propos du centenaire de 1789* (Paris: Bloud et Barral, 1889).

24 On this topic see W. R. Keylor, *Academy and Profession: The Foundation of the French Historical Profession* (Cambridge, MA: Harvard University Press, 1975) and especially P. den Boer, *History as a Profession. The Study of History in France, 1818-1914* (Princeton: Princeton University Press, 1998).

25 See for example V. Pierre, *L'École sous la Révolution française, d'après des documents inédits* (Paris: Tardieu, 1881) and *Quelques déportés de fructidor, d'après leurs lettres intimes inédites* (Angers: germain et Grassier, 1882).

26 L. Sciout, *Histoire de la constitution civile du clergé, 1790-1801* (Paris: Firmin-Didot, 1872-1881).

27 L. Sciout, *La chute des Girondins* (Paris: Librairie de la Société bibliographique, 1877).

28 L. Sciout, *Decadi* (Paris: Librairie de la Société bibliographique, 1882).

29 L. Sciout, *Le Directoire* (Paris: Firmin-Didot, 1895-1897).

30 See F. Huguenin, *L'Action française: une histoire intellectuelle* (Paris: Perrin, 2011) and namely on the attention reserved for the Revolution Ph. Boutry, 'L'Action Française, la Révolution et la Restauration', in *L'Action Française. Culture, société, politique*, ed. J. Prévotat and M. Leymarie (Lille: Presses Universitaires du Septentrione, 2009), 1:25-59.

31 Cochin's most important biography is F. Schrader, *Augustin Cochin et la République française* (Paris: Seuil, 1992), but - as it is well known - François Furet (*Interpreting the French revolution*) rediscovered and reinterpreted his works. Following this latter's perspective, see also Jean Baechler's preface in A. Cochin, *L'esprit du jacobinisme* (Paris: Presses Universitaires de France, 1979).

32 A. Cochin and Ch. Charpentier, *La campagne électorale en 1789 en Bourgogne* (Paris: H. Champion, 1904).

33 A. Cochin and Ch. Charpentier, *La crise de l'histoire révolutionnaire: Taine et M. Aulard* (Paris: H. Champion, 1909).

34 Ibid., 64.

35 G. Le Bon, *La Révolution française et la psychologie des révolutions* (Paris: E. Flammarion, 1912). On Gustave Le Bon, I am drawing namely on B. Marpeau,

Gustave le Bon. Parcours d'un intellectuel. 1841-1931 (Paris: CNRS, 2000); R. Nye, *The Origins of Crowd Psychology. Gustave Le Bon and the Crisis of Mass Democracy in the Third Republic* (London: Sage, 1975); S. Barrows, *Distorting Mirrors. Visions of the Crowd in Late 19th Century France* (New Haven, CT: Yale University Press, 1981) and O. Bosc, *La foule criminelle. Politique et criminalité dans l'Europe du tournant du XIXᵉ siècle* (Paris: Fayard, 2007).

36 A precise biography of Alphonse Aulard is still missing. I am drawing on G. Belloni, *Aulard historien de la Révolution française* (Paris: Presses Universitaires de France, 1949).

37 F.-A. Aulard, *Les orateurs de l'Assemblée constituante: l'éloquence parlementaire pendant la Révolution française* (Paris: Hachette, 1882).

38 F.-A. Aulard, *Les Orateurs de la Législative et de la Convention. L'éloquence parlementaire pendant la Révolution française* (Paris: Hachette, 1885-1886).

39 F.-A. Aulard, *Danton* (Paris: Librairie Picard-Bernheim & cie, 1884).

40 The origins of an academic historiography on the French Revolution are well outlined by C. Wolikow, 'Centenaire dans le bicentenaire: 1891-1991. Aulard et la transformation du cours en chaire d'histoire de la révolution française à la Sorbonne', *Annales historiques de la Révolution Française* 63 (1991): 431-58.

41 See on this subject J. Friguglietti, 'Alphonse Aulard and the Politics of History', *Proceedings of the Western Society for French History* 15 (1988): 379-87. For a new approach to Aulard's work, see now J. Tendler, 'Alphonse Aulard Revisited', *European Review of History: Revue européenne d'histoire* 20 (2013): 649-69.

42 See also Ch.-O. Carbonell, *Histoire et historiens. Une mutation idéologique des historiens français, 1865-1885* (Paris: Institut d'Etudes Politiques, 1976).

43 F.-A. Aulard, *Histoire politique de la Révolution française, origines et développement de la démocratie et de la République, 1789-1804* (Paris: A. Colin, 1901).

44 F.-A. Aulard, *Taine historien de la révolution* (Paris: A. Colin, 1907).

45 On the attempts to create a radical interpretation of the Revolution throughout the early decades of the Third Republic, see J. Stone, *Sons of the Revolution. Radical democrats in France, 1862-1914* (Baton Rouge, LA: Louisiana State University Press, 1996).

46 H. Carnot, *La Révolution française. Résumé historique* (Paris: impr. de Dubuisson et Pagnerre, 1867-1872).

47 E. Hamel, *Précis de l'histoire de la Révolution française* (Paris: Pagnerre, 1870).

48 E. Hamel, *Histoire de la République française sous le Directoire et sous le Consulat* (Paris: Pagnerre, 1872).

49 J.-G. Courcelle-Seneuil, *L'Héritage de la révolution. Questions constitutionnelles* (Paris: Guillaumin, 1872).

50 L. Combes, *Histoire populaire des révolutions françaises et des insur-rections et complots, depuis 1789 jusqu'à nos jours* (Paris: impr. E. Blot, 1872) and E. Duvergier de Hauranne, *Histoire populaire de la Révolution française* (Paris: G. Baillière, 1879).

51 P. Laffitte, *La Révolution française, 1789-1815* (Paris: E. Leroux, 1880) and A. Rambaud, *Histoire de la Révolution française, 1789-1799* (Paris: Hachette, 1883).

52 E. Guillon, *Histoire de la Révolution et de l'Empire* (Paris: Charavay, 1892).

53 P. Janet, *Centenaire de 1789. Histoire de la Révolution française* (Paris: C. Delagrave, 1889).

54 See especially P. Serna, 'La République et le coup d'État. Les crises de la IIIe République et la hantise du 18 Brumaire', *Politix* 39 (1997): 131-54.

55 A. Aulard, *La société des Jacobins. Recueil de documents pour l'histoire du club des Jacobins de Paris* (Paris: Jouaust et Noblet, 1889–1897) and *Recueil des actes du Comité de salut public avec la correspondance officielle des représentants en mission et le registre du Conseil exécutif provisoire* (Paris: Imprimerie Nationale, 1891).
56 See among the numerous contributions J. Claretie, *Camille Desmoulins, Lucille Desmoulins. Étude sur les dantonistes* (Paris: Plon, 1875). English transl. *Camille Desmoulins and his Wife. Passages from the History of the Dantonists* (London: Smith, Elder & Co., 1876). See also J.-F. Robinet, *Condorcet, sa vie et son oeuvre, 1743–1794* (Paris: Quantin, 1893).
57 F.-A. Aulard, 'La Révolution française 1789–1799', in *Histoire générale du Ive siècle à nos jours*, ed. E. Lavisse and A. Rambaud (Paris: A. Colin, 1896).
58 On the heritage of the Revolution on the French socialist movement, see namely J.-N. Ducange, ed., *Le socialisme et la Révolution française* (Paris: Editions Demopolis, 2010).
59 G. Sorel, *Les Girondins du Roussillon* (Perpignan: Charles Latrobe, 1889).
60 I am drawing namely on V. Duclert, *Jean Jaurès* (Paris: Fayard, 2014).
61 On Jean Jaurès historian of the French Revolution see G. Candar, 'L'accueil de l'Histoire socialiste de la Révolution française', *Bulletin de la Société d'études jaurésiennes* 122 (1991): 81–97. See also V. Lecoulant, *Jaurès, historien de la Révolution française* (Montreuil: Musés de l'histoire vivante, 1993) and Ch. Peyrard and M. Vovelle, *Héritages de la Révolution française à la lumière de Jaurès* (Aix-en-Provence: Publications de l'Université de Provence, 2002).
62 J. Jaurès, *Histoire socialiste de la Révolution française* (Paris: Jules Rouff, 1901-1904). English transl. *A Socialist History of the French Revolution* (London: Pluto Press, 2015).
63 See namely F. Venturi, *Jean Jaurès e altri storici della rivoluzione francese* (Turin: Einaudi, 1948). See also M. Rébérioux, 'Jaurès historien de la Révolution française', *Annales historiques de la Révolution française* 184 (1966): 171–95 and M. Dommanget et al., *Jaurès historien de la Révolution française* (Paris: Centre national et Musée Jean Jaurès, 1989).
64 A. Mathiez, *Les Origines des cultes révolutionnaires (1789–1792)* (Paris: Société nouvelle de librairie et d'édition, 1904). On this early moment of Albert Mathiez's academic work, see the introduction by Javier Ramón Solans and the prologue by Pierre Serna to the Spanish translation of his work on revolutionary cults (Albert Mathiez, *Los orígenes de los cultos revolucionarios, 1789–1792* (Zaragoza: Prensas de la Universidad, 2012, IX–LXXI).
65 J.-N. Ducange, *Jules Guesde, l'anti-Jaurès?* (Paris: Colin, 2017).
66 P. A. Kropotkin, *La grande Révolution, 1789–1793* (Paris: Stock, 1909). English transl. *The Great French Revolution, 1789–1793* (London: Heinemann, 1909).
67 For a discussion of Kropotkin's historical works, see C. A. McKinley, *Illegitimate Children of the Enlightenment. Anarchists and the French Revolution, 1880–1914* (New York: P. Lang, 2008): esp. 48–82.
68 Georges Sorel, *Réflexions sur la violence* (Paris: Librairie de *Pages libres*, 1908): 73. English transl. *Reflections on Violence* (London: Allen & Unwin, 1908).
69 On Sorel and the French Revolution, see M. Charzat, *Georges Sorel et la révolution au XXe siècle* (Paris: Hachette, 1977); R. Vernon, *Commitment and Change: Georges Sorel and the Idea of Revolution* (Toronto: University of Toronto Press, 1978) and J. Julliard, 'Rousseau, Sorel et la Révolution française', *Cahiers Georges Sorel* 3 (1985): 5–15.

70 A. Scheibe, *Die Französische Revolution* (Gotha: F. A. Perthes, 1909).
71 F. Zach, *Die Französische Revolution, 1789–1795* (Klagenfurt: Verlag der St. Josef-Bücherbruderschaft, 1914).
72 K. Kautsky, 'Die Klassengegensätze von 1789 zur hundertjährigen Gedenkfeier der großen Revolution', *Die Neue Zeit* 7 (1889): 97–108.
73 Karl Kautsky, *La lutte des classes en France en 1789* (Paris: Jacques, 1901).
74 Karl Kautsky's writings on the French Revolution were crucial to the construction of Marxism as a systematic theory based on historical studies. See J.-N. Ducange, *The French Revolution and Social Democracy. The Transmission of History and its Political Uses in Germany and Austria, 1889–1934* (Leiden: Brill, 2019). See also B. Nygaard, 'Constructing Marxism. Kark Kautsky and the French Revolution', *History of European Ideas* 35 (2009): 450–64.
75 K. Kautsky, *Terrorismus und Kommunismus. Ein Beitrag zur Naturgeschichte der Revolution* (Berlin: Verlag Neues Vaterland, 1919). English transl. *Terrorism and Communism: A Contribution to the Natural History of Revolution* (London: National Labour Press, 1920).
76 W. Blos, *Die Französische Revolution, volksthümliche Darstellung der Ereignisse und Zustände in Frankreich von 1789 bis 1804* (Stuttgart: J. H. W. Dietz, 1889).
77 Ph. Buonarroti, *Babeuf und die Verschwörung für die gleichheit, mit dem durch sie veranlassten prozess und den belgstücken* (Stuttgart: Dietz, 1909).
78 Ducange, 32–49.
79 D. Shlapentokh, 'Forgotten Predecessors: The Russian Conservative Historians of the French Revolution', *International Journal of Politics, Culture and Society* 9 (1995): 57–85.
80 Their works are cited in L. Knowles, 'New Light on the Economic Causes of the French Revolution', *The Economic Journal* 29 (1919): 1–24.
81 On Karejev see now T. Goncharova, 'Trois historiens de la Révolution française à Saint-Petersbourg: Kareiev, Tarlé, Revunenkov', *Dix-huitième siècle* 1 (2018): 597–613.
82 J. Jaurès, *Storia socialista della rivoluzione francese*, (Rome: Mongini, 1902).
83 E. Ricotti, *La rivoluzione francese dell'anno 1789. Discorsi storici* (Turin: Unione TipograficoEditrice, 1888).
84 F. Montefredini, *La Rivoluzione francese: reazione socialista* (Rome: Loescher, 1889).
85 C. Tivaroni, *Storia critica della Rivoluzione francese* (Rome: L. Roux, 1881).
86 On the impact of the French Revolution on nineteenth-century Italian political culture, see A. De Francesco, *Mito e storiografia della «grande rivoluzione». La Rivoluzione francesce nella cultura politica italiana del '900* (Naples: Guida, 2004).
87 G. Salvemini, *La rivoluzione francese* (Milan: L. F. Pallestrini & C., 1905). English transl. *The French Revolution, 1788–1792* (London: Jonathan Cape, 1954).
88 E. Belfort Bax, *The Story of the French Revolution* (London: S. Sonnenschein, 1890).
89 H. Morse Stephens, *A History of the French Revolution* (London: Rivingtons, 1886–1891).
90 H. Morse Stephens, *A History of the French Revolution* (New York: Scribner, 1886–1891).
91 L. Hunt, 'Forgetting and Remembering: The French Revolution Then and Now', *American Historical Review* 100 (1995): 1119–35.
92 On the origins of the historiography of the French Revolution in the United States, see K. M. Baker and J. Zizek, 'The American Historiography of the French

Revolution', in *Imagined Histories. American Historians interpret the Past*, ed. A. Molho and G. S. Wood (Princeton: Princeton University Press, 1988), 349–91.
93   J. S. C. Abbott, *The French Revolution of 1789 as Viewed in the Light of Republican Institutions* (New York: Harrap, 1858).
94   W. O'Connor Morris, *The French Revolution and First Empire. An Historical Sketch* (New York: Scribner, 1875).
95   J. H. Robinson, 'Aulard's Political History of the French Revolution', *Political Science Quarterly* 26 (1911): 133–41.
96   L. B. Pfeiffer, *The Uprising of June 20, 1792* (Lincoln: University of Nebraska, 1912) and E. Ellery, *Brissot de Warville. A Study in the History of the French Revolution* (Boston; New York: Houghton Mifflin Company, 1915).
97   R. M. Johnston, *The French Revolution. A short History* (London: Macmillan, 1909).
98   A. Aulard, *The French Revolution. A Political History, 1789-1804* (New York; London: Scribner's Sons & Fisher and Unwin, 1910).
99   J. E. E. Dalberg Acton, *Lectures on the French Revolution* (London: Macmillan, 1910).
100 Ch. E. Mallet, *The French Revolution* (London: J. Murray, 1893).
101 On Acton political attitude, see namely See Th. Lang, 'Lord Acton and the « Insanity of Nationality', *Journal of the History of Ideas* 63 (2002): 19–49.

Chapter 5: The revolutionary use of history, 1914–45

1   On the analogy between 1793 and 1917 in the aftermath of the Russian revolution, see F. Furet, *Le passé d'une illusion. Essai sur l'idée communiste au 20e siècle* (Paris: Laffont, 1995). English transl. *The Passing of an Illusion. The Idea of Communism in the Twentieth Century* (Chicago: University of Chicago Press).
2   With regard to the positions taken by the historians of the French Revolution vis-à-vis the Soviet revolution, in particular Aulard and Mathiez, reference should be made to S. Luzzatto, *La Marsigliese stonata. La sinistra francese e il problema storico della guerra giusta, 1848–1948* (Bari: Dedalo, 1992). French transl. *L'impôt du sang. La gauche française à l'épreuve de la guerre mondiale, 1900–1945* (Lyon: Presses Universitaires de Lyon, 1996).
3   See A. De Francesco, 'D'une révolution à l'autre: Alphonse Aulard face aux événements russes de 1917', *La Révolution française* 5 (2013): online.
4   See his letter published on the newspaper *L'Humanité*, 26 October 1919.
5   An excellent analysis of Albert Mathiez's work is found in J. Friguglietti, *Albert Mathiez, historien révolutionnaire, 1874–1932* (Paris: Société des études Robespierristes, 1974), to which reference is made with regard to all the foregoing bibliography. For more recent work, reference should be made to F. Gauthier, 'Albert Mathiez, historien de la Révolution Française', *Annales historiques de la Révolution française* 353 (2008): 95–112.
6   A. Mathiez, *La Corruption parlementaire sous la Terreur* (Paris: E. Leroux, 1912).
7   A. Mathiez, *La victoire en l'an II. Esquisses historiques sur la défense nationale* (Paris: F. Alcan, 1916).
8   A. Mathiez, *Sur la formation de la légende dantonienne* (Paris: Impr. de Daupeley-Gouverneur, 1916).
9   A. Mathiez, *Etudes robespierristes* (Paris: A. Colin, 1917).

10 A. Mathiez, *La Révolution et les étrangers. Cosmopolitisme et défense nationale* (Paris: La Renaissance du Livre, 1918).
11 See on all these aspects A. Mathiez, *Révolution russe et révolution française*, présentation de Y. Bosc et F. gauthier (Paris: Editions critiques, 2017).
12 J. Jaurès, *Histoire socialiste de la Révolution française*, édition revue par A. Mathiez (Paris: Librairie de L'Humanité, 1922–1924).
13 A. Mathiez, *La Politique de Robespierre et le 9 Thermidor expliqués par Buonarroti* (Le Puy: Rouchon et Gamon, 1910).
14 A. Mathiez, *Le Bolchevisme et le Jacobinisme* (Paris: Librairie du Parti socialiste et de L'Humanité, 1920). English transl. 'Bolshevism and Jacobinism', *Dissent* 2 (1955): 1–76.
15 A. Mathiez, *La Vie chère et le mouvement social sous la Terreur* (Paris: Payot, 1927).
16 A. Mathiez, *La Révolution française* (Paris: A. Colin, 1922–1927).
17 A. Mathiez, *La Réaction thermidorienne* (Paris: A. Colin, 1929).
18 A. Mathiez, *Le Directoire. Du 11 brumaire an IV au 18 fructidor an V*, publié, d'après les manuscrits de l'auteur, par Jacques Godechot (Paris: A. Colin, 1934).
19 On Ernest Lavisse's work, see P. Nora, *Realms of Memory* (New York: Columbia University Press, 1996–1998), 1: 317–75 and on Philippe Sagnac's involvement, reference should be made to A. Gerard, 'Philippe Sagnac revu et corrigé par Ernest Lavisse: un modèle de censure discrète', *Revue d'histoire moderne et contemporaine* 4 (2001): 123–60.
20 Ph. Sagnac, *La Révolution (1789–1792)*, t. I de l'*Histoire de France contemporaine, depuis la Révolution jusqu'à la paix de 1919*, sous la direction d'Ernest Lavisse (Paris: Hachette, 1920).
21 G. Pariset, *La Révolution (1792–1799)*, t. II de l'*Histoire de France contemporaine, depuis la Révolution jusqu'à la paix de 1919*, sous la direction d'Ernest Lavisse (Paris: Hachette, 1920).
22 We have two convincing examples of this perspective in his *Girondins et Montagnards* (Paris: Firmin-Didot, 1930) and *Journée du 10 août* (Paris: Hachette, 1931).
23 A. Mathiez, *La chute de la royauté* (Paris: A. Colin, 1922).
24 A. Mathiez, *La Gironde et la Montagne* (Paris: A. Colin, 1924).
25 A. Mathiez, *La Terreur* (Paris: A. Colin, 1927).
26 L. Lévy-Schneider, *Le Conventionnel Jeanbon St André, membre du Comité de salut public, organisateur de la marine de la Terreur, 1749–1813* (Paris: F. Alcan, 1901).
27 'La chaire de M. Aulard et le Conseil Municipal', *La revolution française* 75 (1922): 346–7.
28 'Leçon d'ouverture de M. Sagnac à la Sorbonne', *La Révolution Française* 76 (1923): 364.
29 See on Sagnac's contribution to the collection 'Peuples et civilisations', L. Gottschalk, 'Philippe Sagnac and the Causes of the French Revolution', *The Journal of Modern History* 20 (1948): 137–48.
30 G. Lefebvre- R. Guyot and Ph. Sagnac, 'La Révolution française', in *Peuples et civilisations. Histoire générale*, ed. L. Halphen and Ph. Sagnac (Paris: F. Alcan, 1930).
31 G. Lefebvre and R. Guyot and Ph. Sagnac, *La Révolution française* (Paris: F. Alcan, 1930).
32 P. Viola, 'La storiografia francese sulla rivoluzione da Albert Mathiez a Georges Lefebvre', *La storia della storiografia europea sulla rivoluzione* 2: 143–59.
33 G. Lefebvre, *Les Paysans du Nord pendant la Révolution française* (Lille: O. Marquant, 1924). On this aspect, see namely J.-P. Jessenne, 'Des paysans du Nord à la France

directoriale. Georges Lefebvre et l'histoire sociale de la Révolution entre œuvre fondatrice et dépassement', *Révolution Française* 2 (2010): online.
34 O. Dumoulin, 'Georges Lefebvre et les premières Annales', *La Révolution française* 2 (2010): online.
35 On Lefebvre as a social historian, see namely A. Soboul, *Georges Lefebvre, historien de la Révolution française, 1874–1959, in Hommage à Georges Lefebvre (Nancy: Société des études robespierristes), 1960*, 1–20; C. Mazauric, *L'histoire de la Révolution française et la pensée marxiste* (Paris: Presses Universitaires de France, 2009) and S. Buzzi, 'Georges Lefebvre (1874-1959) ou, une histoire sociale possible', *Mouvement Social* 200 (2002): 177–95.
36 See R. Cobb, *A Second Identity. Essays on France and the French History* (Oxford: Oxford University Press, 1969), 84–100 and P. M. Jones, 'Georges Lefebvre and the peasant revolution. Fifty Years On', *French Historical Studies* 16 (1989–90): 645–63. See also D. Roche, *Georges Lefebvre tra storia scientifica e storia socialista*, preface to the Italian translation G. Lefebvre, *La rivoluzione francese* (Turin: Einaudi, 1987).
37 Georges Lefebvre, *La Grande Peur de 1789* (Paris: A. Colin, 1932).
38 Georges Lefebvre, *Quatre-ving-neuf* (Paris: Maison du Livre français, 1939).
39 On Lefebvre's role as a political activist, see L. Davis, 'Georges Lefebvre, Historian and Public Intellectuel, 1928–1959', PhD dissertation, University of Connecticut, 2001.
40 L. Davis, *Les Thermidoriens* (Paris, A. Colin, 1937).
41 L. Davis, *Napoléon* (Paris: F. Alcan, 1935). English transl. *Napoleon* (New York: Columbia University Press, 1936).
42 See N. Racine-Furlaud, 'Le Comité De Vigilance Des Intellectuels Antifascistes (1934–1939). AntiFascisme et Pacifisme', *Le Mouvement Social* 101 (1977): 87–113.
43 See Lefebvre's words at the opening session of the Cercle in *Cahiers du Cercle Descartes* 1 (1936): 26–7.
44 G. Lefebvre, 'Les principes de 1789 en 1939', *Cahiers du Cercle Descartes* 9 (1939): 20.
45 G. Lefebvre, *Quatre-Vingt-Neuf* (Paris: La Maison du livre français, 1939): 246–7. English transl. *The Coming of the French Revolution: 1789* (Princeton: Princeton University Press, 1947).
46 On Halévy, see namely S. Laurent and Daniel Halévy, *Du libéralisme au traditionnalisme* (Paris: Grasset, 2001). See also on his role in the public debate at the beginning of the twentieth century J. Wright, 'After the Affair: The Congrès de la Jeunesse and Intellectual Reconciliation in 1900', *French History* 23 (2009): 491–516.
47 D. Halévy, *Histoire d'une histoire esquissée pour le troisième cinquantenaire de la Révolution française* (Paris: B. Grasset, 1939).
48 On the French Right during the years of the Third Republic, see namely R. R. Locke, *French Legitimists and the Politics of Moral Order in the Early Third Republic* (Princeton: Princeton University Press, 1974); L. Joly, *Naissance de l'Action française. Maurice Barrès, Charles Maurras et l'extrême droite nationaliste au tournant du XXe siècle* (Paris: Grasset, 2015) and F. Huguenin, *L'Action Française. Une histoire intellectuelle* (Paris: Perrin, 2011), S. Giocanti, *Charles Maurras. Le chaos et l'ordre* (Paris: Flammarion, 2008). On the French Right and the French Revolution,, see M. Weyembergh, *Charles Maurras et la Révolution française* (Paris: Vrin, 2000) and Z. Sternhell, *Neither Right nor Left. Fascist Ideology in France* (Princeton: Princeton University Press, 1996).
49 G. Gautherot, *La Démocratie révolutionnaire. De la Constituante à la Convention* (Paris: Beauchesne, 1912). On Gustave Gautherot, see namely R. Kingston, 'The

French Revolution and the Materiality of the Modern Archive', *Libraries & the Cultural Record* 46 (2011): 1–25.
50 See A. de la Gorce, *Une vocation d'historien: Pierre de La Gorce* (Paris: Plon, 1948).
51 F. Funck-Brentano, *La Prise de la Bastille: 1789, 14 juillet* (Paris: Fontemoing, 1899).
52 R. Barroux, 'Frantz Funck-Brentano', *Bibliothèque de l'École des chartes* 107 (1948): 174–7.
53 J. Bainville, *Histoire de France* (Paris: Fayard, 1924).
54 W. R. Keylor, *Jacques Bainville and the Renaissance of Royalist History in Twentieth-Century France* (Baton Rouge, LA: Louisiana State University Press, 1979) and O. Dard and M. Grunewald, eds, *Jacques Bainville entre histoire et journalisme* (Berlin: Peter Lang, 2010).
55 A. Cochin, *Les actes du gouvernement révolutionnaire (23 août 1793–27 juillet 1794). Recueil de documents* (Paris: A. Picard et fils, 1920).
56 A. Cochin, *Les Sociétés de pensée et la démocratie. Etudes d'histoire révolutionnaire* (Paris: Plon-Nourrit et Cie, 1921). English transl. *Organizing the Revolution. Selections from Augustin Cochin* (Rockford, IL: Chronicle Press, 2007).
57 A. Cochin, *La Révolution et la libre pensée. La Socialisation de la pensée (1750–1789). La Socialisation de la personne (1789–1792). La Socialisation des biens (1793–1794)* (Paris: Plon-Nourrit et Cie, 1924).
58 A. Cochin, *Les sociétés de pensée et la Révolution en Bretagne* (Paris: Champion, 1925).
59 On all these aspects, see now Denis Sureau's introduction to A. Cochin, *La machine révolutionnaire* (Paris: tallandier, 2018).
60 P. Gaxotte,*La Révolution française* (Paris: Fayard, 1928). English transl. *The French Revolution* (New York: Scribner's Sons, 1932).
61 On this aspect, P. Gaxotte, 'Préface', in, *Mes idées politiques*, ed. Ch. Maurras (Lausanne: l'Âge d'homme, 2002).
62 E. Ahounou-Thiriot, *Pierre Gaxotte. Un itinéraire de Candide à l'Académie Française* (Paris: Publibook, 2006), esp. 32–5.
63 See Boutry, *L'Action française*: 50. On the inclusion of Augustin Cochin's work in the Golden Book of the French Right, see Meaux, *Augustin Cochin et la genèse de la Révolution* (Paris: Plon, 1928) and G. Goyau, 'Une belle vie d'historien, Augustin Cochin', *Revue des deux mondes* (1926): 621–53. In the wake of the posthumous publication of his works, both confirm the reactionary perspective of his researches.
64 See namely B. Faÿ, *L'Esprit révolutionnaire en France et aux États-Unis à la fin du XVIIIe siècle* (Paris: E. Champion, 1925). English transl. *The Revolutionary Spirit in France and America; a Study of Moral and Intellectual Relations between France and the United States at the End of the Eighteenth Century* (New York: Harcourt, 1927) and B. Faÿ, *La Franc-Maçonnerie et la révolution intellectuelle du XVIIIème siècle* (Paris, Éditions de Cluny, 1935). English transl. *Revolution and Freemasonry, 1680–1800* (Boston, Little, Brown & Co., 1935).
65 On Faÿ's change of political attitude, reference should be made to A. Compagnon, *Le cas de Bernard Faÿ. Du College de France à l'indignite national* (Paris: Gallimard, 2009).
66 B. Will, *Unlikely collaboration. Gertrude Stein, Bernard Faÿ, and the Vichy dilemma* (New York: Columbia University Press, 2011): 77–9.
67 J. Bainville, Refléxions sur la politique (Paris: Plon, 1941).
68 B. Faÿ, *Le fonctionnement et la réorganisation de la Réunion des Bibliothèques nationales de Paris: 15 juin 1940–31 décembre 1942, rapport présenté à M. le Maréchal de France, chef de l'État* (Paris: Bibliothèque Nationale, 1943).

69 N. H. Webster, *The French Revolution. A Study in Democracy* (London: Constable & Co., 1919). Her work was praised by Winston Churchill himself: see his 'Zionism versus Bolshevism', *Illustrated Sunday Herald*, 8 re 1920: 5.
70 Nesta H. Webster, see M. F. Lee, 'Nesta Webster: The Voice of Conspiracy', *Journal of Women's History* 17 (2005): 81–104.
71 N. H. Webster, *World Revolution. The Plot Against Civilization* (London: Constable & Co., 1921).
72 N. H. Webster, *Secret Societies and Subversive Movements* (London: Boswell, 1924).
73 H. Humphrys, *Short History of the French Revolution* (London: Sidgwick & Jackson, 1924).
74 See J. W. Gottlieb, *Feminine Fascism. Women in Britain's Fascist Movement, 1923–1945* (London: Bloomsbury, 2000): 31–41.
75 H. Belloc, *The French Revolution* (London: Williams and Norgate, 1911 and then 1925).
76 Th. Carlyle, *The French Revolution* (London: J. M. Dent & Sons, 1929).
77 J. Pearce, *Old Thunder. A Life of Hilaire Belloc* (London: Harper Collins, 2002).
78 Ph. Brown, *French Revolution in English History*, Londres, Crosby Lockwood & Son, 1918.
79 E. D. Bradby, *The Life of Barnave* (Oxford: Clarendon Press, 1915).
80 E. D. Bradby, *A Short History of the French Revolution, 1789–1795* (Oxford: The Clarendon Press, 1926).
81 As Bradby, James Matthew Thompson, who was the first to introduce Mathiez and Lefebvre to Britain has not received any attention.
82 J. M. Thompson, *Leaders of the French Revolution* (Oxford: Blackwell, 1929).
83 J. M. Thompson, *Notes on the French Revolution as a Special Subject in the Honour School of Modern History* (Oxford: Blackwell, 1934).
84 J. M. Thompson, *Robespierre* (Oxford: Blackwell, 1935).
85 J. M. Thompson, *The French Revolution* (Oxford: Blackwell, 1943).
86 For other American historians of the period, the only reference available is P. Novick, *That Noble Dream: The "Objectivity Question" and the American Historical Profession* (Cambridge: Cambridge University Press, 1988).
87 S. Mathews, *The French Revolution: A Sketch* (New York: The Chautauqua Press, 1900).
88 C. D. Hazen, *The French Revolution and Napoleon* (New York: Holt, 1917).
89 W. Geer, *The French Revolution. A Historical sketch* (New York: Brentano's, 1922).
90 L. R. Gottschalk, *Jean Paul Marat: A Study in Radicalism* (London: Allen & Unwin, 1927); L. R. Gottschalk, *Lafayette Comes to America* (Chicago: University of Chicago Press, 1935); L. R. Gottschalk, *Lafayette joins the American Army* (Chicago: University of Chicago Press, 1937) and L. R. Gottschalk, *Lafayette and the Close of the American Revolution* (Chicago, University of Chicago Press, 1942).
91 L. Gershoy, *Bertrand Barère, a Reluctant Terrorist* (Princeton: Princeton University Press, 1962).
92 L. R. Gottschalk, *The Era of the French Revolution, 1715–1815* (Boston: Houghton Mifflin Co., 1929).
93 L. Gershoy, *The French Revolution and Napoleon* (New York: F. S. Crofts & Co., 1933).
94 See J. Friguglietti, 'Remembering Crane Brinton: American Historian of France (1898–1968)', *Proceedings of the Western Society for French History* 26 (2000): 275–82.

95 C. Brinton, *The Jacobins. An Essay in the New History* (New York: Macmillan, 1930).
96 D. Greer, *The Incidence of the Terror during the French Revolution: A Statistical Interpretation* (Cambridge, MA: Harvard University Press, 1935).
97 C. Brinton, *A Decade of Revolution, 1789-1799* (New York: Harper & Brothers, 1934).
98 C. Brinton., *The Anatomy of Revolution* (London: Allen & Unwin, 1939).
99 A. Cobban, *Dictatorship. Its History and Theory* (London: J. Cape, 1939).
100 R. Kjellén, *Die Ideen von 1914: eine Weltgeschichtliche Perspektive* (Leipzig: S. Hirzel, 1915).
101 J. Plenge, *1789 und 1914. Die Symbolischen Jahre in der Geschichte des Politischen Geistes* (Berlin: Springer, 1916).
102 On this, see Brigitta Oestreich, 'Hedwig und Otto Hintze. Eine Biographische Skizze', *Geschichte und Gesellschaft* 11 (1985): 397–419; B. Faulenbach, 'Hedwig Hintze-Guggenheimer (1884–1942): Historikerin der Französischen Revolution und republikanische Publizistin', in *Frauen in den Kulturwissenschaften*, ed. B. Hahn (München: Beck, 1994), 136–51; R. Jütte, 'Hedwig Hintze (1884–1942): Die Herausforderung der traditionellen Geschichtsschreibung durch eine linksliberale jüdische Historikerin', *Jahrbuch des Instituts für deutsche Geschichte* 14 (1985): 249–79.
103 H. Preuß, *Verfassungspolitische Entwicklungen in Deutschland und Westeuropa. Historische Grundlegung zu einem Staatsrecht der Deutschen Republik*, hrsg. u. eingel. von Hedwig Hintze (Berlin: Heymanns, 1927).
104 On Germany between the two world wars, the most notable reference is Hedwig Hintze.
105 H. Hintze, *Staatseinheit und Föderalismus im alten Frankreich und in der Revolution* (Stuttgart: Deutsche Verlags-Anstalt, 1928).
106 See the review by Mathiez in *Annales historiques de la Révolution française* 5 (1928): 577–86.
107 On communist Russia, reference should be made instead to D. Shlapentokh, *The French Revolution in Russian Intellectual Life: 1865–1905* (Westport, CT: Praeger, 1996); A. Narochnitski, ed., *La Révolution française et la Russie* (Moscow: Editions du Progrès, 1989); T. Kondratieva, *Bolcheviks et Jacobins. Itinéraire des analogies* (Paris: Payot, 1989); A. Tchoudinov, 'La Révolution française. De l'historiographie soviétique à l'historiographie russe. Changements de jalons', in *Les historiens russes et la Révolution française après le communisme*, ed. V. Smirnov (Paris: Société des études robespierristes, 2003), 43–56 and now J. Bergman, *The French Revolutionary Tradition in Russian and Soviet Politics, Political Thought, and Culture* (Oxford: Oxford University Press, 2019).
108 N. I. Kareiev, *Velikaya frantsuzskaya revolyutsiya* (Petrograd: Izd. Marks, 1918).
109 E. V. Tarle, *Revolyutsionnyy tribunal v epokhu velikoy Frantsuzskoy revolyutsii; vospominaniya sovremennikov i dokumenty* (Petrograd: Izd-vo "Byloe", 1918–19).
110 A. Tchoudinov, 'La révolution française dans le discours politique des bolcheviks: le cas de Nicolai Lukin', *Annales historiques de la Révolution française* 387 (2017): 9–30.
111 See N. M. Lukin, *Maksimilian Robespe r [Robespierre]* (Moscou: Gosizdat, 1919).
112 V Poghosyan, 'Sur la polemique entre Albert Mathiez et les historiens soviétiques', *Annales historiques de la Révolution française* 387 (2017): 31–54.
113 *Francuzskaja burzuaznaja revolucija 1789–1794* pod redakciej V. P. Volgina i E. V. Tarle (Moscow: Izdatel'stvo Akademii Nauk SSSR, 1941).

114 On Italy between the two World Wars, see A. De Francesco, *Mito e storiografia della "Grande Rivoluzione". La Rivoluzione francese nella cultura politica italiana del '900* (Naples: Guida, 2006).
115 G. Maranini, *Classe e Stato nella rivoluzione francese* (Perouse: Sansoni, 1935).
116 See for example G. Ferrero, *Il militarismo* (Milan: Treves, 1898). On Ferrero's political thought and his anti-Napoleonism, A. De Francesco, 'Discorsi interrotti. Guglielmo Ferrreo, Corrado Barbagallo e la critica della rivoluzione francese', *Nuova rivista storica* 88 (2004): 147–82.
117 G. Ferrero, *Aventure. Bonaparte en Italie, 1796–1797* (Paris: Plon, 1936). English transl. *The Gamble. Bonaparte in Italy, 1796–1797* (London: G. Bell and Sons, 1939).
118 G. Ferrero, *Reconstruction, Talleyrand à Vienne, 1814–1815* (Paris: Plon, 1940). English transl. *The Reconstruction of Europe. Talleyrand and the Congress of Vienna, 1814–1815* (New York: G. P. Putnam's Sons, 1941).
119 G. Ferrero, *Les Deux Révolutions françaises, 1789–1796* (Neuchâtel: La Baconnière, 1951).

Chapter 6: Revolutionary othodoxy and historians' heresies, 1946–89

1 'Georges Lefebvre. Correspondance avec J. M. Thompson', *Annales historiques de la Révolution française* 321 (2000): 116.
2 C. Mazauric, 'Les chaussées sont désertes, plus de passants sur les chemins » (Esaïe 33.8). La SER dans la tourmente: 1940–1945', *Annales historiques de la Révolution française* 353 (2008): 169–207.
3 D. Guérin, *La Lutte des classes sous la Première République, bourgeois et « bras nus », 1793–1797* (Paris: Gallimard, 1946). English transl. *Class Struggle in the First French Republic. Bourgeois and Bras Nus, 1793–1795* (London: Pluto, 1977).
4 G. Lefebvre, 'Pro domo', *Annales historiques de la Révolution française* 106 (1947): 188–9.
5 See *Correspondance de Maximilien et Augustin Robespierre*, recueillie et publiée par G. Michon (Paris: Librairie Nizet et Bastard, 1941).
6 For a more direct take on Guérin's political personality, see D. Berry, 'Metamorphosis: The Making of Daniel Guérin, 1904–1930', *Modern & Contemporary France* 22 (2014): 321–42 and his 'The Search for a Libertarian Communism: Daniel Guérin and the 'Synthesis of Marxism and Anarchism', in *Libertarian Socialism. Politics in Black and Red*, ed. A. Prichard et al. (London: Palgrave, 2012), 187–209. On Guérin's political positions in the aftermath of the Second World War, see also, D. Berry, 'Daniel Guérin à la Libération. De l'historien de la Révolution au militant révolutionnaire: un tournant idéologique', *Agone* 29/30 (2003): 257–73. On the changes made in 1968 to the first edition of Lutte des classes, see N. Carlin, 'Daniel Guérin and the Working Class in the French Revolution', *International Socialism* 47 (1990): 197–223.
7 G. Michon, *Robespierre et la guerre révolutionnaire, 1791–1792* (Paris: Rivière, 1937).
8 See for example *Pages choisies de Babeuf*, recueillies, commentées par Maurice Dommanget etpréface de Georges Lefebvre (Paris: A. Colin, 1935).
9 See A. De Francesco, 'Daniel Guérin et Georges Lefebvre, une rencontre improbable', *La Révolution française. Cahiers de l'Institut d'histoire de la Révolution française* 2 (2010): online.

10 See D. Berry et al., *Daniel Guérin: révolutionnaire en mouvement(s)* (Paris: L'Harmattan, 2007).
11 G. Albertini, *Le parti de la guerre depuis 1789* (Paris: Éditions du RNP, 1944).
12 L. Émery, *La Révolution française* (Lyon: Les Cahiers libres, 1955).
13 D. Guérin, *La Lutte de classes sous la Première République, 1793–1797* (Paris: Gallimard, 1968).
14 See G. Lefebvre, *La chute du roi* (Paris: Centre de Documentation Universitaire, 1940); *Napoléon*, 2nd edn. revue et corrigée (Paris: Presses Universitaires de France, 1941); *La révolution aristocratique* (Paris: Centre de Documentation Universitaire, 1942); *La Révolution de 1789* (Paris: Tournier et Constans, 1942); *Le Directoire* (Paris: Centre de Documentation Universitaire, 1943).
15 See namely P. Serna, 'Lefebvre au travail, le travail de Georges Lefebvre: un océan d'érudition sans continent Liberté ?', *Révolution française* 2 (2010): online.
16 G. Lefebvre, *Études orléanaises* (Paris: Bibliothèque nationale, 1962-1963).
17 G. Lefebvre, *La Révolution française* (Paris: Presses Universitaires de France, 1951). English transl. *The French Revolution* (London: Routledge; New York: Columbia University Press, 1962).
18 M. Middell, 'Walter Markov', *Annales historiques de la Révolution française* 298 (1994): 763-6.
19 See namely A. M. Rao, 'Alessandro Galante Garrone, historien de la révolution française', *Annales historiques de la Révolution française* 344 (2006): 219-37.
20 See 'Georges Lefebvre. Lettres à Alfred Rufer', in *Annales historiques de la Révolution française* 242 (1980): 615-20.
21 S. Heitkamp, 'Walter Markov. Ein Leipziger DDR-Historiker zwischen Parteilichkeit und Professionalität', *Die Hochschule: Journal für Wissenschaft und Bildung* 11 (2002): 148-58.
22 Venturi, *Jean Jaures*, 101-7. See also his considerations on Lefebvre's political ideas in Galante Garrone -Venturi, *Vivere eguali*, 160.
23 A. Soboul, *Les Sans-culottes parisiens en l'an II. Mouvement populaire et gouvernement révolutionnaire (1793-1794)* (Paris: Clavreuil, 1958). An abridged English transl. *The Parisian sans-culottes and the French Revolution, 1793-4* (Oxford: Clarendon Press, 1964).
24 G. Rudé, *The Crowd in the French Revolution* (Oxford: Calrendon Press, 1958) and R. C. Cobb, *Les armées révolutionnaires. Instrument de la Terreur dans les départements. Avril 1793–Floréal An II* (Paris: La Haye: Mouton and Co, 1961–1963). On Lefebvre's disciples – Soboul, Cobb and Rudé, otherwise known as « the three musketeers» – See C. Mazauric, *Albert Soboul (1914-1982). Un historien en son temps: essai de biographie intellectuelle et morale* (Paris: Albret, 2004).
25 K. Tønnesson, *La defaite des sans-culottes. Mouvement populaire et réaction bourgeoise en l'an III* (Paris: Clavreuil, 1959).
26 See L. Guerci, 'Daniel Guérin', *Belfagor* 32 (1977): 167-8.
27 A. Cobban, *The Social Interpretation of the French Revolution* (Cambridge: Cambridge University Press, 1964), 120-2.
28 With regard to Rudé's life and work, see namely D. Munro, 'The Strange Career of George Rudé, Marxist Historian', *Journal of Historical Biography* 16 (2014): 118-69; see also James Friguglietti, 'The Making of an Historian: The Parentage and Politics of George Rudé', in *Revolution, Nation and Memory: Papers from the George Rudé Seminar in French History*, ed. Greg Burgess (Hobart: University of Tasmania, 2004), 17-9; F. Krantz, '*Sans érudition, pas d'histoire*': The Work of George Rudé, and H.

Stretton, 'George Rudé', in *History from Below: Studies in Popular Protest and Popular Ideology in Honour of George Rudé*, ed. F. Krantz (Montreal: Concordia University, 1985), 3-33 and 43-54 and G. M. Betros, 'Introduction', *French History and Civilization: Papers from the George Rudé Seminar* 3 (2009): 1-6.

29 G. Rudé, *The French Revolution* (London: Weidenfeld and Nicolson, 1988).
30 M. Lyons, 'Cobb and the Historians', in *Beyond the Terror. Essays in French Regional and Social History, 1794-1815*, ed. G. Lewis and C. Lucas (Cambridge: Cambridge University Press, 1983), 15.
31 See C. Mazauric, *Albert Soboul, un historien en son temps* (Aubenas: Éditions d'Albret, 2003). See also M. Vovelle, 'Albert Soboul, historien de la société', *Annales historiques de la Révolution française* 250 (1982): 547-53; J. Louvrier, 'Albert Soboul et la Société des études robespierristes', *Annales historiques de la Révolution française* 353 (2008): 209-34; R. Pozzi, 'Albert Soboul: spunti per un ripensamento critico', *Società e storia* 105 (2004): 629-36; M. Di Maggio, 'Tradizione storiografica e innovazione metodologica: rivoluzione contadina e "vie di transizione" nell'opera di Albert Soboul', *Dimensioni e problemi della ricerca storica* 23 (2010): 221-37 and A. Guerra, 'La rivoluzione fra le lettere. Il carteggio fra Albert Soboul e Armando Saitta', *Nuova Rivista Storica* 101 (2017): 103-36.
32 A. Soboul, *1789, L'an I de la Liberté* (Paris: Éditions sociales internationales, 1939).
33 A. Soboul, *La Révolution française, 1789-1799* (Paris: Éditions sociales, 1948). English transl. *A Short History of the French Revolution, 1789-1799* (Berkeley: University of Carolina Press, 1977).
34 A. Soboul, *Précis d'histoire de la Révolution française* (Paris: Éditions sociales, 1962). English transl. *The French Revolution, 1787-1799* (London: NLB, 1974).
35 See for example A. Soboul, *Les sans-culottes parisiens en l'an II* (Paris: Seuil, 1968). English transl. *The Parisian Sanc-culottes and the French Revolution, 1793-1794* (Oxford: Clarendon Press, 1964).
36 J. L. Talmon, *The Origins of Totalitarian Democracy* (London: Secker and Warburg, 1952).
37 A. Cobban, *Edmund Burke and the revolt against the eighteenth century. A study of the political and social thinking of Burke, Wordsworth, Coleridge, and Southey* (London: George Allen & Unwin, 1929). A. Cobban, *Rousseau and the Modern State* (London: George Allen & Unwin, 1934).
38 A. Cobban, *The Myth of the French Revolution; an inaugural lecture delivered at University College, London, 6 May 1954* (London: Lewis, 1955).
39 A. Cobban, *Historiansand the Causes of the French Revolution* (London: Routledge, 1958).
40 A. Cobban, *The Social Interpretation of the French Revolution* (Cambridge: Cambridge University Press, 1964).
41 With regard to Alfred Cobban and his revisionism, reference should be made to G. J. Cavenaugh, 'The Present State of French Revolutionary Historiography: Alfred Cobban and beyond', *French Historical Studies* 7 (1971): 587-606; G. Lewis, *The French Revolution: Rethinking the Debate* (London: Routledge, 1993); G. Kates, ed., *The French Revolution. Recent Debates and New Controversies* (London: Routledge, 1998); G. Lewis, Introduction to Alfred Cobban, *The Social Interpretation of the French Revolution* (Cambridge: Cambridge University Press, 1999), XIII-XLIX.
42 G. Lefebvre, 'Le mythe de la Révolution française', *Annales historiques de la Révolution française* 145(1956): 337-45.
43 See Godechot's review in *Revue historique* 235 (1966): 205-9.

44 See Hampson's remarks in *Irish Hisorical Studies* 14 (1964): 191–2 and Brinton's review in *History and Theory* 5 (1966): 315–20.
45 A. Goodwin, *The French Revolution* (London: Hutchinson's University Library, 1953).
46 A. Goodwin, *The Friends of Liberty. The English Democratic Movement in the Age of the French Revolution* (London: Hutchinson, 1970).
47 N. Hampson, *A Social History of the French Revolution* (London: Routledge, 1964).
48 M. J. Sydenham, *The French Revolution* (London: B.T. Batsford, 1965).
49 See namely C. Cuttica, 'Anti-Methodology Par Excellence: Richard Cobb (1917–96) and History-Writing', *European Review of History: Revue européenne d'histoire* 21 (2014): 91–110.
50 J. M. Roberts, *The French Revolution* (Oxford; New York: Oxford University Press, 1978).
51 See Furet's English translation *Interpreting the French Revolution* (Cambridge: Cambridge University Press, 1981).
52 D. Sutherland, *France. 1789–1815. Revolution and Counter-Revolution* (London: Fontana, 1985).
53 J. F. Bosher, *The French Revolution* (New York: Norton, 1988) and W. Doyle, *The Oxford History of the French Revolution* (Oxford: Clarendon Press, 1989).
54 S. Schama, *Citizens: A Chronicle of the French Revolution* (New York: A. A. Knopf, 1989).
55 D. K. Van Kley, *The Religious Origins of the French Revolution. From Calvin to the Civil Constitution: 1560–1791* (New Haven; London: Yale University Press, 1996 and T. Tackett), *Religion, Revolution, and Regional Culture in Eighteenth-Century France* (Princeton: Princeton University Press, 1986.
56 R. Darnton, *The Literary Underground of the Old Regime* (Cambridge: Harvard University Press, 1982).
57 A. Forrest, *Society and Politics in Revolutionary Bordeaux* (Oxford: Oxford University Press, 1975); C. Lucas, *The Structure of the Terror. The Example of Javogues and the Loire* (Oxford: Oxford University Press, 1973); G. Lewis, *The Second Vendée. The Continuity of Counter-Revolution in the Department of the Gard, 1789–1815* (Oxford: Clarendon Press, 1978); M. Lyons, *Revolution in Toulouse. An Essay on Provincial Terrorism* (Bern-Frankfurt: P. Lang, 1978).
58 K. M. Baker, *Inventing the French Revolution. Essays on French Political Culture in the Eighteenth Century* (Cambridge: Cambridge University Press, 1990) and L. A. Hunt, *Politics, Culture, and Class in the French Revolution* (Berkeley; Los Angeles; London: University of California Press, 1984).
59 On François Furet, it is worth to refer to the latest works concerning him: see M. S. Christofferson, *French Intellectuals Against the Left: The Antitotalitarian Moment of the 1970's* (New; York; Oxford: Berghahn, 2004); R. Halévi, *L'experience du passé. François Furet dans l'atelier de l'histoire* (Paris: Gallimard, 2007) and Ch Prochasson, *François Furet. Les chémins de la mélancolie* (Paris: Stock, 2013). See also E. Chabal, *A Divided Republic. Nation, State and Citizenship in Contemporary France* (Cambridge: Cambridge University Press, 2015), 158–85.
60 F.Furet-D. Richet, *La Révolution* (Paris: Hachette, 1965–1966). English transl. *French Revolution* (London: Weidenfeld & Nicolson, 1970).
61 J. Louvrier, 'Penser la controverse: la réception du livre de François Furet et Denis Richet', La Révolution française in *Annales historiques de la Révolution française* 351 (2008): 160–1.

62 M. S. Christofferson, 'François Furet between history and journalism, 1958–1965', *French History* 15 (2001): 421–47.
63 See his remarks in *Annales historiques de la Révolution française* 189 (1967): 339–68.
64 C. Mazauric, *Sur la Révolution française* (Paris: Éditions Sociales, 1970).
65 M. Vovelle, *La chute de la monarchie, 1787–1792* (Paris: Seuil, 1972). English transl. *The Fall of the French Monarchy, 1787–1792* (Cambridge: Cambridge, University Press, 1989).
66 M. S. Christofferson, '"The Best Help I Could Find to Understand Our Present": François Furet's Antirevolutionary Reading of Tocqueville's Democracy in America', in *In Search of the Liberal Moment. Democracy, Anti-totalitarianism and Intellectual Politics in France since 1950*, ed. S. W. Sawyer and I. Stewart (London: Palgrave, 2016), 85–110.
67 F. Furet, 'Le catéchisme révolutionnaire', *Annales. Éco-nomies, Sociétés, Civilisations* 26 (1971): 255–289.
68 D. Poitras, *Expérience du temps et historiographie au XXe siècle: Michel de Certeau, François Furet et Fernand Dumont* (Montreal: Les Presses de l'Université de Montréal, 2018).
69 *The French Revolution and the Creation of Modern Political Culture*: vol. 1: K. Baker, ed., *The Political Culture of the Old Regime* (Oxford: Pergamon Press, 1987); vol. 2: C. Lucas, ed., *The Political Culture of the French Revolution* (Oxford: Pergamon Press, 1988); vol. 3: F. Furet-M. Ozouf, eds, *The Transformation of Political Culture, 1789–1848* (Oxford: Pergamon Press, 1988); vol. 4: K. Baker, ed., *The Terror* (Oxford: Pergamon Press, 1994).
70 F. Furet and M. Ozouf, eds, *Dictionnaire critique de la Révolution française* (Paris: Flammarion, 1988). English transl. *A Critical Dictionary of the French Revolution* (Cambridge, MA: Harvard University Press, 1989).
71 F. Furet, *La Révolution. De Turgot à Jules Ferry 1770–1880* (Paris: Hachette, 1988). English transl. *The French Revolution, 1770–1814* (Oxford: Blackwell, 1992).
72 On this topic see D. Kévonian, 'Les juristes juifs russes en France et l'action internationale dans les années Vingt', *Archives juives* 34 (2001): 72–94 and now T. Stammers, 'La mondialisation de la révolution française (vers 1930–1960): origines et eclypse d'un paradigme historiographique', *Annales HSC* 74 (2019): 297–335.
73 L. Kramer, 'Robert R. Palmer and the History of Big Questions', *Historical Reflections/ Réflexions historiques* 37 (2011): 101–22.
74 On the pioneering work by Robert Roswell Palmer, reference should be made, among more recent works, to W. O'Reilly, 'Genealogies of Atlantic History', *Atlantic Studies* 1 (2004): 66–84; E. Tortarolo, 'Eighteenth-century Atlantic History Old and New', *History of European Ideas* 34 (2008): 369–74. See also *L'era delle rivoluzioni democratiche di Robert R. Palmer*, a special issue of *Contemporanea. Rivista di Storia dell '800 e del '900* 10 (2007): 125–67 with contributions, among others, by Annie Jourdan and Peter Onuf.
75 R. R. Palmer, 'The French Idea of American Independence on the Eve of the French Revolution', unpubl. PhD thesis.
76 R. R. Palmer, *Catholics and Unbelievers in 18th century France* (Princeton: Princeton University Press, 1939).
77 R. R. Palmer, *Twelve who Ruled. The Committee of Public Safety during the Terror* (Princeton: Princeton University Press, 1941).
78 See for example J. B. Sirich, *The Revolutionary Committees in the Departments of France, 1793–1794* (Cambridge, MA: Harvard University Press, 1943).

79 G. Lefebvre, *The Coming of the French Revolution* (Princeton: Princeton University Press, 1947). See now the 2015 edition with an introduction by Timothy Tackett.
80 J. Godechot, *Histoire de l'Atlantique* (Paris: Bordas, 1947).
81 R. R. Palmer, *A History of the Modern World* (New York: Knopf, 1950).
82 J. Godechot – R. R. Palmer, 'Le Problème de l'Atlantique du XvIIIe au XXe siècle', in *X Congresso internazionale di scienze storiche* (Florence: Sansoni, 1955), V: *Storia contemporanea*, 175–239.
83 R. R. Palmer, *The Age of the Democratic Revolution: A Political History of Europe and America, 1760–1800* (Princeton: Princeton University Press, 1959–1964).
84 E. J. Hobsbawm, *The Age of Revolution: Europe 1789–1848* (London: Abacus, 1962).
85 J. Godechot, *La Grande Nation. L'expansion révolutionnaire de la France dans le monde. 1789–1799* (Paris: Éditions Montaigne, 1956).
86 M. Reinhard, *La France du Directoire* (Paris: Centre de documentation universitaire, 1956), 5.
87 R. R. Palmer, *1789. Les Révolutions de la liberté et de l'égalité* (Paris: Calmann-Lévy, 1968).
88 Tortarolo, *Eighteenth-century Atlantic history*, 372–3.
89 For a reinterpretation of Palmer's work, see the special issue of *Historical Reflections/Reflexions Historiques* 37, no. 3 (2011), entirely devoted to his works. Among others, J. L. Harvey, *Robert Roswell Palmer: A Transatlantic Journey of American Liberalism*, 1–17, M. R. Cox, *Palmer and Furet: A Reassessment of The Age of the Democratic Revolution*, 70–85.

Conclusion: The ashes of the revolution?

1 See M. Ozouf, 'Peut-on commemorer la Révolution française?', *Le Débat* 26 (1983): 161–72 and F. Furet, *La Révolution dans l'imaginaire politique français*, 173–81.
2 With regard to the Bicentenary, see Kaplan, *Farewell Revolution* and P. Garcia, *Le Bicentenaire de la Révolution française: pratiques sociales d'une commemoration* (Paris: CNRS, 2000) should be added to the reference works previously cited.
3 R. Secher, *Le génocide franco-français: la Vendée-vengé* (Paris: Presses Universitaires de France, 1986).
4 F. Furet, *L'Europe et la démocratie, 1789–1989* (Rome: Camera dei Deputati, 1992).
5 F. Furet, *Le passé d'une illusion. Essai sur l'idée communiste au XXe siècle* (Paris: Laffont, 1995). English transl. *The Passing of an Illusion. The Idea of Communism in the Twentieth Century* (Chicago: University of Chicago Press, 1999).
6 With regard to novel approaches to the historiography of the Revolution after the Bicentenary and the end of the Cold War, see J.-Cl. Martin, *Révolution et contre-révolution. Les rouages de l'histoire* (Rennes: Presses Universitaires de Rennes, 1996), which sums up a novel reading of the Vendée events first broached in his *La Vendée et la France* (Paris: Seuil, 1987).
7 J.-Cl. Martin, *Contre-Révolution, Révolution et Nation en France, 1789–1799* (Paris: Seuil, 1998).
8 See P. Serna and J.-C. Martin, 'Contre-Révolution, Révolution et Nation en France, 1789–1799', *Politix* 12 (1999): 167–73.
9 P. Serna, *Antonelle: aristocrate révolutionnaire, 1747–1817* (Paris: Editions du Félin, 1997) and B. Gainot, *1799, un nouveau Jacobinisme?: la démocratie représentative,*

une alternative à brumaire (Paris: CTHS, 2001). This aspect is also touched upon by Ph. Bourdin and B. Gainot, ed., *La République directoriale* (Paris: Société des études robespierristes, 1998), 2 vol. and by J.-Cl. Martin, ed., *La Révolution à l'œuvre. Perspectives actuelles dans l'histoire de la Révolution* (Rennes: Presses Universitaires de Rennes, 2005). On this topic, see also C. Hesse, 'The New Jacobins', *French Historical Studies* 32 (2009): 663–70.

10 The opening of an international perspective, well presented by Annie Jourdan's work cited in the text, may be followed in J. Klaits and M. G. Haltzel, eds, *The Global Ramifications of the French Revolution* (Cambridge: Cambridge University Press, 1994). On this point, see also A. Jourdan, *La révolution batave entre la France et l'Amérique, 1795–1806* (Rennes: Presses Universitaires de Rennes, 2008); P. Serna, ed., *Républiques sœurs. Le Directoire et la Révolution atlantique* (Rennes: Presses Universitaires de Rennes, 2009) and M. Albertone and A. De Francesco, eds, *Rethinking the Atlantic World. Europe and America in the Age of Democratic Revolutions* (London: Palgrave, 2009). See also S. Desan, 'Internationalizing the French Revolution', *French Politics, Culture & Society* 29 (2011): 137–60. With regard to stances opposing the idea of a convergence between the revolutions of the late Eighteenth century, reference should be made to M. Hulliung, *Citizens and Citoyens. Republicans and Liberals in America and France* (Cambridge, MA: Harvard University Press, 2002) and to W. Klooster, *Revolutions in the Atlantic World. A Comparative History* (New York: New York University Press, 2010).

11 A. Jourdan, *La Révolution, une exception française?* (Paris: Flammarion, 2004).

12 P. Gueniffey, *Le nombre et la raison. La Révolution française et les elections* (Paris: EHESS, 1993).

13 P. Gueniffey, *La Politique de la Terreur. Essai sur la violence révo- lutionnaire, 1789–1794* (Paris: Gallimard, 2003).

14 C. A. Bayly, *The Birth of the Modern World, 1780–1914* (Malden, MA: Blackwell Publishing, 2004).

15 D. Armitage and S. Subrahmanyam, eds, *The Age of Revolutions in Global Context, c. 1760–1840* (London: Palgrave, 2010).

16 The same holds true for the Atlantic world, increasingly dominated by an approach tending to underestimate continental Europe: see, among many other works, K. O. Kupperman, *The Atlantic in World History* (Oxford: Oxford University Press, 2012) and J. K. Thornton, *A Cultural History of the Atlantic World, 1250–1820* (Cambridge: Cambridge University Press, 2012). With regard to this perspective, the Haitian revolution has become the linchpin of any research on revolutions in the Atlantic: as an example of a line of research leading to dozens of contributions over the past few years, see Jeremy Popkin, *A Concise History of the Haitian revolution* (Malden: Wiley-Blackwell, 2012) and A. J. Sepinwall, *Haitian History. New Perspectives* (London: Routledge, 2012). For a comparative study of revolutions in the modern age, see now K. M. Baker and D. Edelstein, eds, *Scripting Revolution. A Historical Approach to the Comparative Study of Revolutions* (Stanford: Stanford University Press, 2015).

17 J.-L. Chappey et al., *Pourquoi faire la Révolution ?* (Marseille: Agone, 2012).

18 See for example P. Serna, 'Que s'est-il dit à la Convention les 15, 16 et 17 pluviôse an II ? Ou lorsque la naissance de la citoyenneté universelle provoque l'invention du « crime de lèse-humanité', *La Révolution française* 7 (2014): online.

19 S. Desan, L. Hunt and W. M. Nelson, eds, *The French Revolution in Global Perspective* (Ithaca, NY: Cornell University Press, 2013).

20 P. Serna, 'Every Revolution is a War of Independence', *The French Revolution in Global Perspective* 165–81.
21 S. Pincus, *1688: The First Modern Revolution* (New Haven, CT: Yale University Press, 2014), 486.
22 See among others T. Harris and S. Taylor, *The final crisis of the Stuart Monarchy: The Revolutions of 1688–91 in their British, Atlantic and European Contexts* (London: Boydell Press, 2013).
23 J. Israel, *Revolutionary Ideas: An Intellectual History of the French revolution from the Rights of Man to Robespierre* (Princeton: Princeton University Press, 2014).
24 Peter McPhee, *Liberty or Death: The French Revolution* (New Haven, CT: Yale University Press, 2017).
25 Peter McPhee, *The French Revolution, 1789–1799* (Oxford: Oxford University Press, 2002).
26 A. Jourdan, *Nouvelle histoire de la Révolution* (Paris: Flammarion, 2018).
27 J. Popkin, *A New World begins; the History of the French Revolution* (New York: Basic Books, 2019).
28 J. Popkin, *The Right Wing Press in France, 1792–1800* (Chapel Hill, NC: University of North Carolina Press, 1980).
29 J. Popkin, *Revolutionary News. The Press in France: 1789–1799* (Durham, NC: Duke University Press, 1990).
30 J. Popkin, *A Short History of the French Revolution* (Englewood Cliffs, NJ: Prentice Hall, 1995).
31 J. Popkin, *A Concise History of the Haitian Revolution* (Oxford: Wiley-Blackwell, 2012).

Index

Abbott, John   177
Académie française   46, 116, 295 n.62
Ackermann, Augustin   201–2, 205
Action française   139, 152–3, 198–9, 201–3
Acton, John Emerich Edward Dalberg, baron of   178–9
Adams, John   36
Adolphus, John   37
Albert, *see* Martin, Alexandre Albert
Albertini, Georges   226
Alcan, Félix   190
Alison, Archibald   84
Allemane, Jean   164
American Federalists and the French Revolution   31, 35–6
American historians of the French Revolution   73, 176–8, 208–11, 236–40, 248–55, 263, 269
American Historical Association   254
American Revolution   25, 30, 32
  and French Revolution   2, 10, 249, 251, 261
anarchism   165, 169, 225
  and Blanquist tradition   170
Annales historiques de la Révolution française   168, 190–1, 220, 231, 258
Annales révolutionnaires   190
Arab Spring   263–4
Arendt, Hannah   211, 252, 268
Armitage, David   257, 263
Assignat   19, 241
August 4, 1789 decrees   24
  Blanc on   106
  Michelet on   100, 107
August 10, 1792 insurrection   8, 12, 33, 67, 74, 77, 183, 236
  Aulard on   161
  CMignet on   62
  Dulaure on   74
  and Genet mission   35

Lamartine on   95–6
Mallet du Pan on   21
Michelet on   96, 101
Perry on   34
Quinet on   126
Thiers on   60
Aulard, Alphonse   155, 162, 164, 166–7, 170, 171, 174, 177, 181–2, 185–7, 189–92, 194, 199–201, 205–6, 208, 209, 213, 248
  critic of Taine   152–3, 163, 168
  and First World War   90, 178, 181
  his Dantonism   156, 160–1, 184
  his democraticism   139, 161
  professor at Sorbonne   156–7, 183
  and Russian Revolution   181–3

Babeuf, François-Noël (Gracchus)   71, 151, 170, 173, 188, 204, 223, 229
  Buonarroti on   64, 65, 68
  Guérin on   221, 225
  Kautsky on   173–4
  Laponneraye on   68
  Mathiez on   186, 189
  Mussolini on   217
  Salvemini on   176
  Webster on   204
Bailleul, Jacques-Charles   43–4, 55–6, 64
Bailly, Jean Sylvain   55
Bainville, Jacques   181, 199, 200, 202, 204
Baker, Keith Michael   240, 247
Barante, Prosper de   113–14, 119, 150
Barère de Vieuzac, Bertrand   74, 76, 208
Barnave, Antoine-Pierre-Joseph Marie   166, 206
Barni, Jules Romain   121
Barrot, Camille-Hyacinthe-Odilon   115
Barruel, Augustin   7, 21–2, 201, 205
Bastille, storming of   15, 18, 20–1, 24, 59, 89, 100, 118, 199
  Carlyle on   89
  Lacretelle on   15

Maistre on 20
Mallet du Pan on 21
Michelet on 125
Mignet on 57
Price on 31
Quinet on 125
Webster on 205
Baudry, Paul 149
Bavarian illuminati 22, 205
Bax, Ernest Belfort 176
Bayly, Christopher Alan 257, 262
Beaucourt, Gaston du Fresne marquis of 147
Beaumont, Gustave de 116, 120
Becker, Carl Lotus 208, 249–50
Belloc, Hilaire 206
Berth, Édouard 172
Bertier de Sauvigny, Louis Bénigne 100
Bibliothèque Nationale de France, see National Library of France
Bicentenary of the French Revolution 1, 204, 231–2, 240, 255, 257–60
Bismarck-Schönhausen, Otto prince of 62, 93, 138
Blanc, Louis 27, 48, 74, 78, 93–5, 104, 107, 108, 128–9, 152, 157–8, 167, 186
   critic of Lamartine 109–11
   critic of Michelet 109–11
   critic of Thiers 121–2
   his jacobinism 110–11
   his socialism 106
   political career 105
Blanqui, Auguste 111, 164, 167, 222
Blanquist tradition 170
Bloch, Marc 193
Blos, Wilhelm 173–4
Blum, Léon 195
Bonald, Louis-Gabriel-Ambroise, viscount of 20, 43, 48, 53, 55
Bonaparte, Napoléon 4, 7, 13–6, 23, 27–30, 36–7, 46, 60, 64, 102–3, 109, 113–16, 119, 121, 127–8, 131–3, 140, 148, 158, 161, 173, 176, 182, 188, 200, 211, 214, 217–18, 224, 229, 236, 239, 246, 260, 268
   Aulard on 162
   Blanc on 129
   Furet on 242–3

Lefebvre on 195
Mathiez on 188
Quinet on 93, 124–5, 129
Staël on 7, 40–2
Taine on 144
Bonaparte Louis-Napoléon, see Napoleon III
Bonapartism 61, 69, 115, 117, 120–1, 129, 133–4, 138, 196, 217
   opponents of 54, 81, 95, 115, 140, 159, 175
Boothby, Brooke 32
Bosher, John 238–9
Bossuet, Jacques-Bénigne 23
Boston Gazette 30
Boulainvilliers, Henri count of 51
Boulanger, Georges-Ernest-Jean-Marie 140, 163
Bourbon Restoration 4, 7, 10, 13, 38, 40, 42–3, 45–7, 50–7, 62–76, 90, 98, 113–15, 119–20, 133–5, 147–9
Boutmy, Émile 147
Boutroux, Étienne-Émile-Marc 153
Bradby, Eliza Dorothy 206–7
Brandes, Ernst 25
Briez, Philippe Constant Joseph 220
Brinton, Clarence Crane 211, 236, 250
   interpreting Jacobinism 209, 237
   and the New History 209–10
   and sociology 209
Brissot, Jacques-Pierre 69, 79, 110, 124, 170, 178, 207–8
British historians of the French Revolution 3, 7, 18–37, 45, 70, 84–91, 136–45, 154, 172–9, 204–9, 219–20, 230–41, 247, 253, 257, 262
Broglie, Victor de 38
Brousse, Paul Louis Marie 164, 228–9, 234
Brown, Philip Anthony 206
Brumaire 18, year VIII (1799), coup of 15–7, 23, 27, 36–7, 41–2, 46, 95, 133, 151, 187, 205, 252, 260
   Aulard on 162
   Bainville on 200
   Constant on 39
   Courcelle-Seneuil on 159
   Cuoco on 28–9
   Fantin-Desodoards on 13–4

Furet-Richet on 243
Paganel on 16
Pariset on 187
Quinet on 125, 127–9
Salvemini on 175–6
Sciout on 151
Tivaroni on 175
Tocqueville on 116
Toulongeon on 14
Bryce, James 154
Buchez, Philippe Joseph Benjamin 70, 90, 101, 104, 124, 131
   Robespierrism of 45, 69
   and Saint-Simon 68
Büchner, Georg 85, 135
Buonarroti, Philippe 68, 70, 170, 173, 188
   as Babouvist 64–5
   and Cabet 71
   his Robespierrism 45, 65–7
   and Laponneraye 45, 66
   and Mathiez 186–7
Burke, Edmund 7, 22–3, 31–3, 83–4, 87, 89, 179, 240
   critic of 1789 18–9, 35–7
   reception and legacy of 25–6, 31–3, 140, 205, 207

Cabet, Étienne 70–1, 131
Calonne, Charles-Alexandre 17, 19
Canut revolts 1831 65
Carlyle, Thomas 45, 84, 88, 90–1, 141, 172, 205
   and Burke 89
   reception and legacy of 206, 240
Carnot, Hippolyte 158
Carnot, Lazare 158
Caron, Pierre 196
Cavaignac, Eugène 101, 114–15, 124
Centenary of the French Revolution 1889 148–9, 156, 159–61, 164–5, 171–7
Chambord, Henri-Charles-Ferdinand d'Artois, count of 147
Champ de Mars, shooting on 130, 204, 220
   Lamartine on 96
   Michelet on 101–2
   Mignet on 57
   and Paine 32
   Quinet on 126
   Thiers on 59
Charles X of France 61, 73, 82–3, 113
Charléty, Sébastien 195
Charpentier, Charles 200–1
Charte of 1814 *see* Constitution of 1814
Chateaubriand, François-René viscount of 46–8, 62
Chauffour-Kestner, Victor 121
Chaumette, Pierre Gaspard 111
Chirac, Jacques 257
Civil Constitution of the Clergy 1791 21, 80, 125, 150
Claretie, Jules 156, 160
Clemenceau, Georges 156, 175, 183
Cobb, Richard Charles 219, 230–1, 237–8, 240–1
Cobban, Alfred 231, 235–8, 240
   critic of Marxist interpretations 219
   on dictatorship 211, 233
   reception and legacy of 241, 248, 254
   social interpretation of 234
Cobbett, William 36
Cochin, Augustin Denis Marie 139, 153–7, 168, 190, 200–5, 209–10, 245–6
Cochin, Denys 153
Colin, Armand 161, 187, 194, 240, 247
Collège de France 51, 77–8, 96, 105, 123–5
Collot d'Herbois, Jean-Marie 167
Combes, Louis 189, 199
Committee of Public Safety 145, 220, 231, 249
   Aulard on 160
   Ferrero on 218
   Guérin on 224
   Lefebvre on 191, 195
   Palmer on 249
   Thiers on 60
Comte, Auguste 160
Concordat of 1801 23
Condorcet, Marie-Jean-Antoine Nicolas Caritat, marquis of 7–9, 27, 56
Constant, Benjamin 39–40, 42, 116, 119
Constituent Assembly, *see* National Assembly
Constitution of 1791, 41, 80

Acton on   178
Aulard on   178
Carlyle on   89
Doyle on   238
Furet-Richet on   242
Jaurès on   165
Lamartine on   80
Laponneraye on   67
La Rocheterie on   148
Lefebvre on   195
Necker on   40–1
Staël on   38–9
Sybel on   137
Constitution of 1793   8–9, 95
Constitution of 1795   9–11, 14, 16, 42, 44, 137, 149–51, 237, 253
   Aulard on   161
   Constant on   42
   Fichte on   27
   Furet-Richet on   242, 260
   Gallois on   77
   Goodwin on   237
   Gueniffey on   262
   Janet on   159
   Mathiez on   187–8
   Palmer on   253
   Pariset on   187
   Perry on   34
   Sciout on   149–50
   Serna on   260
   Staël on   41–3
   Sybel on   137
   Toulongeon   14
Constitution of 1799   41
Constitution of 1814   51
Convention, *see* National Convention
Corday, Charlotte   79
Cornell University   177, 208, 249
Courcelle-Seneuil, Jean-Gustave   159
Cousin, Victor   48, 123
Croker, John Wilson   86–7
Cuoco, Vincenzo   28–30

Dahlmann, Friedrich Christoph   135–6
Dalimier, Albert   203
Danton, Georges Jacques   124, 156, 195, 206–7, 224, 236
   accused of September Massacres   60, 79–80, 90, 110, 171

   Aulard on   156, 160–2, 167–8, 184, 186, 191
   Blanc on   105, 109–10
   Buchez-Roux on   69
   Buchner on   85
   critic of Robespierre   66, 69, 71, 80, 109–11, 167–8, 170–1
   Gallois on   75–6
   Lamartine on   79–80, 105
   Marrast on   75
   Mathiez on   168, 184
   Michelet on   102–3
   Taine on   144
   Thiers on   60, 71
Darnton, Robert   240
Darwin, Charles   152
Déat, Marcel   226
Declaration of Rights, 1789   107
Declaration of war, April 1792   200, 236
Dehio, Ludwig   211
De Man, Henri   182
Desan, Suzanne   263
Desmoulins, Camille   100, 171
Deville, Gabriel   165
Dommanget, Maurice   221
Doyle, William   238
Dreyfus affair   4, 150, 152, 157, 163, 165, 171, 174, 197–8
Droysen, Johann Gustav   136
Ducruix, François   165
Dulaure, Jacques-Antoine   64, 74, 84
Dumouriez, Charles-François   185
Dunan, Marcel   227, 231
Duncker, Maximilian   136
Durkheim, Émile   152–4, 168
Duvergier de Hauranne, Ernest   159

École des Hautes Études en Sciences Sociales   243, 245
École Pratique des Hautes Études   243
Ellery, Eloise   178, 208
Émery, Léon   226
émigrés   18, 33, 39, 46, 57, 60, 151
Enghien, Louis-Antoine-Henry Bourbon-Condé, duke of   46
Enragés   169, 223–4
Esquiros, Henri-François-Alphonse   71–2, 104

Estates General   10, 15, 17–8, 21, 39, 42, 57, 83, 90, 100, 119, 125, 147, 173, 175–6, 202, 267

Fantin Desodoards, Antoine-Étienne-Nicolas   11–14
fascism   183, 195, 206, 216, 219, 221, 249, 266
   critic of the French Revolution   181, 217–18
Faure, Edgar   244
Faÿ, Bernard   181, 203–4
February Revolution, 1848   95, 108–9, 112, 116, 130–1
Febvre, Lucien   193
federalist revolt, 1793   8, 50, 76, 189, 207
Ferrari, Giuseppe   130
Ferrero, Guglielmo   175, 217–18
Ferry, Jules   128, 159
Feugère, Gaston   149
Feuillants   21, 35, 46, 194
Fichte, Johann Gottlieb   27–8, 30
Fleurus, battle of   196
Fling, Fred Morrow   177, 208
Forrest, Alan   240
Forster, Georg   27
Forti, Francesco   83
Foulon de Doué, Joseph   100
Fouquier-Tinville, Antoine-Quentin   60
Frederick William II of Prussia   205
Freemasonry   199, 203–4
French Collaborationism   226
French colonies   167, 263
French Communist Party (PCF)   185–6, 216, 220–1, 225–8, 243, 245, 254, 257
French Empire, First, 1804–1815   13, 16, 28, 30, 46, 116–17, 193
French Empire, Second, 1852–1870   4, 62–4, 69, 94, 96, 103, 111, 120–1, 129, 132–4, 136, 142, 159
French-Prussian War, 1870–1871   133, 141, 158, 160, 220
French Republic, First, 1792–1804   8, 35, 36
French Republic, Second, 1848–1852   81, 96, 102, 108, 114–6, 119–30, 147
French Republic, Third, 1870–1940   62, 120, 146–54, 157, 160–5, 168, 176, 183, 194–200, 203, 214, 222, 227, 245–9
French Resistance, 1940–1944   220, 227
French Section of the Workers' International (SFIO)   169, 194, 197, 222
French Workers' Party (POF)   164
Freppel, Charles-Émile, bishop of Angers   148–9
Fridland, Grigory   215–16
Fructidor 18, year V (1797), coup of   60
Funck-Brentano, Frantz   199
Furet, François   5, 129, 242, 244, 247, 261, 266, 269
   and Bicentenary   238, 240, 257–60
   and Cobban   238, 240–1
   and Cochin   245–6
   critic of Marxist interpretation   219, 244–6, 248, 257
   and *dérapage*   241–3
Fysh, Frederick   88

Gainot, Bernard   260
Galante Garrone, Alessandro   230
Gallois, Léonard   73–7
Gautherot, Gustave   199
Gaxotte, Pierre   181, 202–4, 233
Geer, Walter   208
Genêt, Edmond-Charles   35
Gentz, Friedrich von   25
George III of the United Kingdom   34, 251
Gere, Vladimir   174
German historians of the French Revolution   24–30, 135–9, 169–76, 211–14, 222, 230
Germinal 12–13 year III (1795), demonstration   225
Gershoy, Leo   208–9
Gervinus, Georg Gottfried   136
Gioberti, Vincenzo   134
Girondins   8–9, 12, 14, 21, 34, 44, 60, 69, 71, 76, 80–1, 84–5, 94–6, 103, 105, 109–10, 124, 129, 148, 150, 159, 170, 173, 182, 184, 206, 214–15, 223, 237–8, 242, 266
   Aulard on   160–2, 167
   Brinton on   210
   Buonarroti on   65–7
   Ferrero on   218

Furet-Richet on 244
Goodwin on 236
Guérin on 223
Hintze on 214
Jaurès on 167, 171
Lamartine on 78–9
Lefebvre on 194
Mathiez on 188–9
Michelet on 101–2
Michon on 226
Pariset on 187
Quinet on 126–7
Soboul on 244
Glorious Revolution of 1688 19, 31, 38, 264
Godechot, Jacques 187, 219, 236, 250, 253–4
Goebbels, Paul Joseph 212
Goodwin, Albert 236–7
Gottschalk, Louis Reichenthal 208–9, 249–50
Gouverneur, Samuel Laurence 73
Granger, Ernest 164
Greer, Donald 210
Gueniffey, Patrice 261–2
Guérin, Daniel 219–25, 229–31, 233, 254
  anti-Robespierrism 226–7
  and Blanquism 222
  critic of Jaurès and Mathiez 220–1
  and pacifism 221
Guesde, Jules 164–6, 169, 194
Guiguet et Michaud, publishers 14
Guillon, Édouard louis Maxime 159
Guizot, François 45, 51–3, 62–3, 81–2, 97
Guyot, Raymond 190–1, 228

Halévy, Daniel 197–8
Halphen, Louis 190
Hamel, Ernest 93, 104, 129, 158, 186
Hamilton, Alexander 31, 35
Hampson, Norman 236–7
Häusser, Ludwig 136
Haym, Rudolf 136
Hazen, Charles Downer 208
Hébert, Jacques-René 69, 76
Hebertists 76, 109, 111, 158, 167, 169, 206, 224, 236
Hegel, Georg Wilhelm Friedrich 27–8

Henderson, Lawrence Joseph 210
Henry IV of France 107, 145
Herder, Johann Gottfried 123
Hintze, Hedwig 213–14
Hobsbawm, Eric 253
Hohenlinden, battle of 158
Hölderlin, Friedrich 27, 29
Humboldt, FriedrichWilhelm Christian von 25, 27
Humphrys, Hutchinson 205
Hunt, Lynn Avery 240, 263

illuminati, *see* Bavarian illuminati
Institut catholique, Paris 199
Institut d'histoire de la Révolution française, *see* Sorbonne
Institut international d'histoire de la Révolution française, *see* Sorbonne
Institut national 11
Italian historians of the French Revolution 3–4, 26–30, 83–6, 130–9, 174–6, 217–18, 230, 255, 282–6

Jacobinism 12–3, 22, 34–7, 39, 46, 61, 68, 70, 96, 105, 107, 132, 137, 143–5, 154–5, 164–5, 167, 169, 173, 185, 201, 203, 205, 212, 214, 216, 236–7, 239
  Aulard on 160, 183
  Brinton on 209, 211
  Buonarroti on 65–6
  Ferrero on 175
  Furet-Richet on 243, 284
  Goodwin on 236–7
  Hintze on 214
  Jaurès on 185
  Lamartine on 110–11
  Lefebvre on 232
  Mathiez on 209, 215, 217
  Michelet on 103
  Pariset on 187
  Quinet on 124
  Soboul on 232
  Vovelle on 258
James II of England 19, 31
Janet, Paul 159
January 21, 1793, execution of Louis XVI 9, 20–1, 28, 33, 56, 63, 90, 126

Jaurès, Jean   139, 163, 184–7, 189, 192–4, 217, 220–1, 230, 233–4
　economic interpretation   164, 166, 168
　political career   164–5
　reception and legacy of   170–2, 174, 184–7, 189, 192–4, 222–3, 225, 231
　Robespierrism   167
　socialism of   164–9
Jean-bon André, called Jeanbon Saint-André   189
Jefferson, Thomas   16, 36–7, 252
Jemappes, battle of   196
Johnston, Robert Matteson   178
Jourdan, Annie   257, 261–2, 267–8
July Monarchy, 1830–1848   50, 62, 65, 68, 70, 72–4, 78, 82–4, 86, 96, 112–13, 115, 122–3, 133–5, 141
July Revolution, 1830   50, 66, 68
June   20, 1792, march against royal vetos   126, 178

Kant, Immanuel   27
Kareev, Nikolai   174, 214
Kautsky, Karl   139, 169, 172–4, 176, 222
Kennedy, John Fitzgerald   252
Kerensky, Aleksander   185, 191, 205, 214
Kergorlay, Louis-Gabriel-César, viscount of   116
Kjelén, Rudolf   212
Klopstock, Friedrich Gottlieb   27
Kovalevsky, Maksim   174
Kropotkin, Piotr   169, 170, 215, 222

Labrousse, Ernest   228, 229, 234
Labry, Raoul   182
Lacretelle, Charles   7, 14–5, 53
La Fayette, Marie-Joseph-Paul Yves Roch Gilbert du Motier, marquis of   17, 32, 37, 52, 61, 72–3, 79, 101, 208
　Bainville on   200
　Gottschalk on   208
　Michelet on   101
　Thiers on   61
Laffitte, Pierre   159
Lagardelle, Hubert   165
La Gorce, Pierre François Gustave de   199
La Justice   156

Lamartine, Alphonse Marie Louis de Prat de   94, 96, 104, 110–11, 133
　critic of Blanc   105–6
　critic of socialism   105–6
　critic of the Terror   80, 82–3, 95
　political engagement in 1848   81
　republicanism of   45, 78–9, 82
Lamennais, Félicité Robert de   67, 77
Lanfrey, Pierre   133
Lanjuinais, Jean-Denis   54
Laponneraye, Albert   45, 66–8, 71
La Révolution française   156, 168
La Rocheterie, Maxime de   148
Laski, Harold   209
Lavisse, Ernest   161, 187, 190
Le Bon, Gustave   155, 193, 205
Ledru-Rollin, Alexandre   131
Lefebvre, Georges   1, 181, 196–7, 207, 219, 226–7, 250, 253
　antifascism of   195
　and Bloch   193
　communism of   220
　and Jaurès   192–4, 220–1
　and Labrousse   228–9
　and peasant revolution   190–3
　political engagement in the 1930's   191, 193, 195
　professor at Sorbonne   1, 191–2
　reception and legacy of   230–8, 241, 243, 245
Lefebvre, Théodore   220
Legislative Assembly, 1791–1792   8, 16, 24–5, 39, 60, 126, 133, 141, 188, 238, 241–2
　Aulard on   194
　Bertrand de Molleville on   15
　Doyle on   238
　Furet-Richet on   241–2
　Lacretelle on   14
　Lefebvre on   194
　Mathiez on   188
　Sciout on   149
Legislative Assembly, 1849–1851   115, 128, 133, 141
Lenin, Vladimir Ilyich Ulyanov   182–3, 185, 201–2, 205, 215, 223, 232–4, 244–6, 248
Leopardi, Giacomo   156
Leroux, Pierre   66, 105, 131

Lévy Schneider, Léon   189
Lewis, Gwynne   240
Liubimov, Nikolai   174
Lombroso, Cesare   152, 175
Louis XIV of France   145, 147
Louis XVI of France   9–10, 14, 18, 20–1, 28, 33, 39, 56, 63, 79, 88–90, 126, 150, 178, 200, 205, 236
Louis Philippe, duke of Orléans   10, 17, 37, 83, 205
Louis Philippe of France   45, 52, 61–2, 65–82, 85–6, 91–9, 101, 106, 108, 111, 113, 114, 122–3, 131, 186
Louverture, Toussaint   36
Louvet, Jean-Baptiste   39, 55
Lucas, Colin   240, 247
Luchitsky, Ivan   174
Ludwig, Carl Friedrich Ernst   135
Lukin, Nikolai   215–16
Luxemburg, Rosa   222
Lynd, Staughton   254
Lyons, Martyn   65, 240

Macaulay, Catherine   31
Macaulay, Thomas Babington   86–7
Macfarlane, Charles   88
McKay, Donald Cope   250
Mackintosh, James   32, 35
McPhee, Peter   266–7
Madelin, Louis   146, 203–5
Madison, James   36–7, 73
Maistre, Joseph-Marie de   7, 20, 43, 48, 53, 61, 140, 149, 198
    critic of the Enlightenment   53
    critic of the French Revolution   22–3
    reception and legacy of   140, 149, 198
Mallet, Charles Edward   178
Mallet du Pan, Jacques   20, 21, 26, 149
Manzi, Pietro   83
Manzoni, Alessandro   134–5
Maranini, Giuseppe   217
Marat, Jean-Paul   61, 79, 80, 83, 144, 208
Marengo, battle of   158, 252
Marie Antoinette of Habsburg-Lorraine, queen of France   148
Marion, Marcel   203
Markov, Walter   230
Marrast, Armand   74–5

Martin, Alexandre Albert   94
Martin, Jean-Clément   1, 259, 260, 263
Martinet, Gilles   243
Marx, Karl   93, 130–3, 135, 139, 166, 223
Marxism   225, 228, 232, 234
Mathews, Shailer   208–9
Mathiez, Albert   169, 181, 184, 188–90, 193–4, 207–9, 213, 215, 217, 220–1, 224, 226, 230–1, 234
    critic of Aulard   168, 191–2
    and First World War   184, 187–8
    and Jaurès   168, 185–7
    political engagement in 1920's   186–7
    reception and legacy of   228, 249–50
    Robespierrism of   168, 186, 189
    and Russian Revolution   185
Maurras, Charles   152–3, 198–9, 201–2, 254
May 31–June 2 1793, insurrection   8–9, 74, 102
    Aulard on   162, 167, 183
    Ferrero on   218
    Furet-Richet on   242–3
    Goodwin on   236
    Guérin on   223
    Jaurès on   167
    Lamartine on   95
    Lefebvre on   194
    Michelet on   102
    Pariset on   187
    Quinet on   126
Mazauric, Claude   243, 245
Mazzini, Giuseppe   93, 130–4, 285–6
Meinecke, Friedrich   213
Mercier, Louis-Sébastien   11–12
Metternich-Winneburg, Klemens Wenzel Lothar, prince of   26
Miall, Bernard   178
Michaud, Louis-Gabriel   14–5
Michelet, Jules   78, 89, 103, 105, 107, 109–11, 118, 121, 246
    critic of socialism   104, 106
    historian of the French nation   93, 95–8
    opposition to Napoleon III   103
    reception and legacy of   123, 125, 128, 155, 157, 166, 170, 173, 222–3, 242
    republicanism of   93, 96, 99–100

writing of revolution in 1848   95–7, 101–2
Michels, Roberto   217
Michon, Georges   220–1, 226
Mignet, François-Auguste-Marie   45, 58, 61–3, 70, 76, 82–6, 88, 90, 91, 113, 119, 127, 131, 137
   his distrust of February Revolution   62
   his judgenment on inevitability of 1789   57
   his liberalism   55, 57
   re-evaluating Terror   56
   Supporting July Revolution   66
Miliukov, Pavel   191
Mill, John Stuart   85, 89
Millerand, Alexandre   156–7, 165, 183
Mirabeau, Honoré-Gabriel Riqueti, count of   10, 17, 37, 44, 79, 90, 100, 126, 135, 177
Mirkin-Guetzevich, Boris   195–6, 248
Mitterand, François   243
Molleville, Antoine François Bertrand count of   14–5
Mommsen, Theodor   136
Monatte, Pierre   221–3
Monroe, James   36–7, 72–3
Montagnards, see Jacobinism
Montagnards, 1848–1851   95
Montefredini, Francesco Saverio   174
Montesquieu, Charles-Louis de Secondat, baron of   18, 26, 265
Moore, John   35
Mortimer-Ternaux, Louis   113–14, 119, 143
Möser, Justus   25
Mounier, Jean-Joseph   22
Mussolini, Benito   211, 217

Napoleon I, see Bonaparte, Napoléon
Napoleon III   112, 114–15, 122, 124, 130–4, 136, 138, 141, 159
   coup d'état in 1851   95, 113
   defeat at Sedan   62
   elected president in 1848   115
   re-establishing the French Empire   130, 133
Narbonne-Lara, Louis-Marie-Jacques Almaric, count of   39

National Assembly, 1789–1791   51, 59
   Blanc on   106–7
   Bonald on   20
   Buchez-Roux on   69
   Calonne on   17
   Furet on   242, 247
   G. Sorel on   145
   Jaurès on   165
   Kropotkin on   170
   Lacretelle on   14–5
   Lefebvre on   194
   Mackintosh on   32
   Mathiez on   188
   Mignet on   57
   Quinet on   124–5
   Rivarol on   18–20
   Schulz on   24
   Sciout on   149
   Staël on   39, 41
   Sybel on   137
National Convention   10, 16, 43, 46, 54–5, 74, 102, 156, 158, 165, 167, 189, 205, 218, 272, 281, 285
   Aulard on   162
   Barante on   113
   Blanc on   108–9
   and Condorcet   8–9
   Dulaure on   64
   Esquiros on   71–2
   Ferrero on   218
   Furet-Richet on   242
   Gallois on   75–7
   and Girondins   8–9, 60, 76, 96, 103, 126–7, 187–8
   Guérin on   223, 225
   Lamartine on   95–6
   Lefebvre on   194
   Madelin on   205
   Mathiez on   184
   Michelet on   107–8
   and Necker   41
   Quinet on   124
   and Rabaut   10
   Soboul on   232
   Thiers on   60–1
National Library of France   204
National Socialism   211–12, 214, 216, 228
National workshops   94, 98

Necker, Jacques   14, 39–41, 43, 52, 59, 83, 125
Nelson, William Max   263

O'Connor Morris, William   177
October Days, 1789   21
   Aulard on   183
   Bainville on   200
   Lefebvre on   193
   Mallet du Pan on   21
   Mathiez on   185
   Michelet on   100
   Quinet on   125
   Rabaut on   10
   Rivarol on   18
   Schulz Friedrich on   24
October Revolution, *see* Russian Revolution
Olivetti, Angelo Oliviero   217
Onu, Aleksander   174
Opportunism   13, 27, 140, 159–60, 167, 194
Orano, Paolo   217
Ostrogorski, Moisei   154
Owen, Robert   70
Ozouf, Mona   247, 257–8

Paganel, Pierre   16
Pagano, Francesco Mario   29
Pagès de Vixouse, François-Xavier   11–2
Paine, Thomas   32–4, 36, 72
Palmer, Robert Roswell   254–5, 261, 263
   against American exceptionalism   248–52
   critic of Brinton   250, 252
   historian of democratic revolutions   219, 248–52
   historian of Year II   253
   re-evaluating Atlantic history   219, 248
Papi, Lazzaro   85–6, 282–3
Pareto, Vilfredo   210
Paris Commune, 1871   62, 110–11, 129, 132, 139–42, 157, 163–4, 175, 215, 224, 226, 246
   amnesty Communards   158
Pariset, Georges   187, 193
Parti Communiste Français (PCF) *see* French Communist Party (PCF)

Parti Ouvrier Français (POF) *see* French Workers' Party (POF)
Parti Socialiste Unifié (PSU) *see* Unified Socialist Party (PSU)
Pelloutier, Fernand-Léonce Émile   164
Perry, Sampson   34–5
Pétain, Philippe   197–8, 204, 220, 227
Peyrat, Alphonse   128–9
Pfeiffer, Laura Bell   177
Philip the Fair of France   17
Pierre, Victor   149, 154
Pigott, Charles   32
Pincus, Steven   264
Pitt, William   10, 34–5, 39
Pius IX, pope   115, 124
Pivert, Marceau   221
Playfair, William   35–6
Plenge, Johann   212
Pompidou, Georges   244
Poperen, Jean   243
Popkin, Jeremy   269
Poujoulat, Jean-Joseph François   147
Prairial 1, year III (1795), insurrection of   61, 225
Preuss, Hugo   213
Price, Richard   31–2
Priestley, Joseph   32
Proudhon, Pierre-Joseph   111, 132–3, 164, 170, 175–6, 197–8
Prudhomme, Louis-Marie   9, 12

Quinet, Edgar   93, 98, 125–9, 158
   anti-Napoleonism   121–3
   critic of Robespierrism   124
   critic of Thiers   121–2
   fighting Montagnards of 1848   77
   political engagement in 1848   121–2
   re-evaluating Directorial years   77

Rabaut de Saint-Étienne, Jean-Paul   10–11, 14–5, 53
Rambaud, Alfred   159, 161
Ranke, Leopold von   135–6
Raspail, François-Vincent   95
Raynal, Guillaume-Thomas   26
Rehberg, August Wilhelm   25, 27
Reinhard, Marcel   231, 253
Remusat, Charles-François-Marie, count of   65

Renan, Joseph Ernest   133–4, 198
revolutionary syndicalism   155, 164–5, 167, 169–70, 217, 221, 226
Revue blanche   152
Revue des questions historiques   147–50
Revue historique de la Révolution française et de l'Empire   190
Richelieu, Armand Jean du Plessis, cardinal and duke of   145
Richet, Denis   241–5
Ricotti, Ercole   174
Ritter, Gerhard   211–12
Rivarol, Antoine de   17–20, 200
Rives, William Cabell   13, 73
Roberts, John Morris   237–8
Robespierre, Maximilien   24, 36, 43, 67, 69, 71–3, 79–81, 83, 85–6, 90, 95, 101, 105, 107–11, 113, 127, 129, 132, 137, 158–9, 170–1, 173, 178, 182, 188–9, 191, 195, 200–1, 206–7, 215, 217–18, 220–5, 229, 236, 239, 262, 268
  accused of dictatorship   9, 23, 68, 124, 144
  Aulard on   160–2, 167–8
  Blanc on   105
  Buchez-Roux on   45
  Buchner on   85
  Buonarroti on   45, 65–6
  Cobb on   231
  a critic of factions   28, 86, 103
  Furet-Richet on   260
  Gallois on   75–6
  Lamartine on   79–81
  Laponneraye on   45
  Lefebvre on   195
  Marrast on   75
  Mathiez on   184–7
  Michelet on   103–4
  Quinet on   77, 124
  Soboul on   233
  Taine on   144
  Thiers on   60–1
Robinet, Jean-François   160
Robinson, James Harvey   177, 208–9
Roederer, Pierre-Louis   39
Romain, Georges   149
Rotteck, Karl von   135
Rous, George   32

Rousseau, Jean-Jacques   18, 26, 51, 107, 143, 144, 157, 165, 167, 201, 233, 265
Roux, Jacques   45, 66, 68–70, 90, 101, 104, 124, 169, 223, 230
Roux-Lavergne, Pierre-Célestin   45, 68–70, 101, 104, 124, 131
Rowan, Frederica   88
Rudé, George   219, 230–1, 234, 237
Rufer, Alfred   23
Russian historians of the French Revolution   169–74, 191–6, 214–16
Russian Revolution, 1905   169
Russian Revolution, 1917   181, 199, 205, 215, 232
  February Revolution, 1917   182–3
  and French Revolution   169
  Kornilov putsch   185
  October Revolution, 1917   5, 182–3, 215, 244, 259
  Western imagination of   185–6

Sagnac, Philippe   187, 189–91, 193–6, 228, 248
Saint-Domingue, French colony of   6, 35–7, 79, 167, 263, 269
Saint-Simonianism   68, 77, 85, 99
Saitta, Armando   230
Salvemini, Gaetano   139, 175–6, 218
Santerre, Antoine Joseph   126
Schama, Simon   238–40
Scheibe, Albert   172
Schelling, Friedrich Wilhelm Joseph   27
Schulz, Friedrich   24
Sciout, Ludovic   139, 149–54, 254
Scott, Walter   83, 88
Scott, William   240
Scrofani, Saverio   26–7
Section Française de l'International Ouvrière (SFIO) *see* French Section of the Workers' International (SFIO)
September massacres, 1792   33, 60, 79
  Aulard on   161
  and Barruel   22
  Blanc on   110
  Cabet on   70
  Carlyle on   90

G. Sorel on   171
  Lamartine on   80
  Quinet on   126
  and Staël   39
  Webster on   205
Serna, Pierre   1, 260, 263–4
Sesquicentennial of the French Revolution (1939)   193, 196, 231
Seven Years' War   251
Sforza, Carlo   191
Sieyès, Emmanuel-Joseph   29, 51, 246
Sister republics   2, 29, 150–1, 261, 263
Smyth, William   87
Soboul, Albert   219, 231–4, 237, 243–5, 248, 254, 258
  critic of Furet-Richet   244–5
  critic of Guerin   230
  historian of sans-culottes   230–1
  marxist interpretation of 1789   228, 232
Société bibliographique   148, 150
Société des droits de l'homme   66
Société des études robespierristes   1, 190–1, 195, 220–1, 227, 258
Sorbonne   1, 152, 156, 159, 163, 183, 189–91, 195–7, 199, 227, 233, 254
  Centre d'études de la Révolution française   195
  Institut d'histoire de la Révolution française   1, 195, 227, 231, 243, 253, 258, 260, 263
  Institut d'histoire moderne et contemporaine   1
  Institut international d'histoire de la Révolution française   196
Sorel, Albert   144–6, 167, 190
Sorel, Georges   165, 170–1, 176, 217, 222
Staël-Holstein, Anne-Louise-Germaine Necker, Baroness of   7, 38–44, 46, 48–51, 53, 56, 59, 64, 116, 121, 137, 149
  anti-Napoleonism of   44, 121
  critic of the First French Republic   43
  on Directory   42
  reception and legacy of   55, 83, 86, 119, 123, 179
  re-evaluating her father Necker   40–2
  re-reading of 1789   38–40
Stalin, Joseph   182, 211, 214–16, 233

Stavisky affair   203
Stephens, Henry Morse   176–8, 209
Stuart Restoration   57
Subrahmanyam, Sanjay   257, 263
Sutherland, Donald   238–9
Sybel, Heinrich Karl Ludolf von   93, 136–8, 140–1, 144–5, 157, 167, 172
Sydenham, Michael   237

Tackett, Timothy   240
Taine, Hyppolyte   141–5, 148, 152–3, 163, 165, 168, 171–2, 174–5, 194, 198, 201–3, 205, 236, 240
  anti-revolutionary interpretation   148, 152
  Aulard on   152–3
  critic of Carlyle   89
  on G. Sorel   165
  and Mortimer Ternaux   143
  psychological method   143
  reception and legacy of   152, 202, 205
  on Schama   240
  and Sybel   144
  and Tocqueville   141, 143–4
Talmon, Jacob   233, 236
Tarde, Gabriel   152
Tarle, Evgeny   214, 216
Tennis Court Oath, 1789   24
Terror, the   9–11, 14–5, 21–3, 25, 27, 34, 36–7, 39, 41–5, 50, 54–7, 61, 65–6, 68, 76, 80, 82, 88–93, 101, 103, 104, 108–11, 124–9, 131–2, 135, 143–51, 159, 169–73, 175, 178, 184, 186–7, 189, 191, 201, 202, 204–6, 209–10, 214, 226, 228–9, 232–3, 236–9, 242, 248–9, 252, 258–62, 268
  Aulard on   160–1
  Barante on   114
  Blanc on   105
  Dulaure on   64
  Esquiros on   72
  Ferrero on   217–18
  Furet-Richet on   246
  Gallois on   73–4
  Guérin on   226
  Lamartine on   95
  Lefebvre on   194
  Madelin on   146
  Mathiez on   189

Michelet on 104
Palmer 249
Quinet on 124
Thiers on 56
Thermidor 9 year II (1794), coup of 28, 34, 39, 60, 96, 102–3, 107, 109, 116, 129, 144, 146, 150–1, 158, 161, 162, 176, 182, 190, 194–5, 202, 215, 238–9, 242, 253
  Adolphus on 37
  Aulard on 161–2, 166
  Blanc on 107, 109, 129, 158
  Brinton on 210
  Buchez-Roux on 69
  Buonarroti on 65–6
  Dulaure on 64
  Émery on 226
  Esquiros on 72
  Fantin-Desodoards on 11, 14
  Fridland on 215
  Furet-Richet on 129
  Gallois on 77
  Gaxotte on 202
  Guérin on 225–6, 229
  Jaurès on 166
  Kautsky on 173
  Kropotkin on 169
  Lefebvre on 194
  Mathiez on 187–9
  Palmer on 253
  Prudhomme on 9
  Rambaud on 159
  Sagnac on 187
  Schama on 238–9
  Sciout on 151
  Sutherland on 238–9
  Taine on 144
  Thiers on 60
  Tocqueville on 116
Thibaudeau, Antoine Claire 117
Thierry, Jacques Nicolas Augustin 45, 52, 62–3, 82, 97, 113
  and 1789 51–2
  historian of the Third Estate 49–51
  and Staël 48–51
Thiers, Adolphe 45, 56, 58–9, 61, 63, 71, 75–6, 82, 85–6, 88, 90–1, 95, 97, 111, 113–14, 119, 120, 127, 129, 164
  his theory of circumstances 121–2

historian of the French Empire 62
  reception and legacy of 131, 137, 141, 143, 145, 150
  re-evaluating 1793 70
  re-evaluating Danton 60
  and Staël 55
Thiulen, Lorenzo Ignazio 26
Thomas, Albert 165, 184
Thompson, James Matthew 207–8, 220, 230, 236–7
Tiger, printer 223
Titone, Virgilio 3
Tivaroni, Carlo 174–5
Tocqueville, Alexis de 82, 97, 112, 114, 115, 127, 145–8, 179, 239, 245–6
  on American democracy 81, 97, 119
  on French administrative centralization 116–17
  on political myth of the French Revolution 118–20
  reception and legacy of 121–2, 129, 141–5, 175, 202, 239, 244
Tønnesson, Kåre 230–1
Toulongeon, François-Emmanueld'Emskerque, viscount of 7, 14
Treaty of Amiens, 1802 36–7, 158
Treaty of Lunéville, 1801 158
Treuttel et Würtz, publishers 14
Tridon, Gustave 111, 222
Trotsky, Leon 205, 221–3
Two-Thirds Decree, 1795 34, 243

Unified Socialist Party (PSU) 243

Vaillandet, Pierre 220
Vaillant, Édouard 164
Valmy, battle of 175, 196
Van Kley, Dale Kenneth 240
Varennes, flight to 26, 57, 59, 70, 96, 100, 126
  Cabet on 70
  and Condorcet 8
  Furet-Richet on 241–2
  Lamartine on 96
  Michelet on 96
  Mignet on 57
  Quinet on 126
  Rabaut on 10

Scrofani on   26
   and Staël   39
   Thiers on   59
Varlet, Jean-François   169, 223
Vendée war   8, 102, 167, 193, 257–9
Vendemiaire 13, year IV (1795),
   insurrection of   60
Venturi, Franco   230, 255
Versailles, march on, *see* October Days,
   1789
Vichy France   5, 181, 204, 207, 228
Viesseux, Giovan Pietro   83
Villèle, Jean-Baptiste Guillaume Joseph,
   count of   56
Viola, Paolo   4
Voltaire, François-Marie Arouet   25, 26,
   107
Vovelle, Michel   1, 244, 257–8

Wachsmuth, Wilhelm   135
Waitz, Georg   136
Waldeck-Rousseau, Pierre   157, 165, 167
Walton, Charles   3

Washington, George   35–6
Webster, Nesta H.   181, 204–9
Welcker, Karl Theodor   135
White, Andrew   177
Wieland, Christoph Martin   27
Wilson, Thomas Woodrow   183, 185
Wollstonecraft, Mary   31
World War I   90, 130, 169, 174, 178, 181,
   184, 187–8, 192, 201, 208, 211,
   213–14, 226, 236, 249
World War II   1, 146, 197–8, 204, 207,
   209, 218–19, 225, 227, 229, 230,
   245, 248, 254, 258, 263, 268

Year I constitution, *see* Constitution of
   1793
Year III constitution, *see* Constitution of
   1795
Year VIII constitution, *see* Constitution
   of 1799

Zach, Franz   172
Zay, Jean   1, 195